Trials and punishments

CAMBRIDGE STUDIES IN PHILOSOPHY

General Editor SYDNEY SHOEMAKER

Advisory editors J. E. J. ALTHAM, SIMON BLACKBURN,
GILBERT HARMAN, MARTIN HOLLIS, FRANK JACKSON,
JONATHAN LEAR, JOHN PERRY, T. J. SMILEY, BARRY STROUD

Trials and punishments

R. A. Duff

Department of Philosophy
University of Stirling

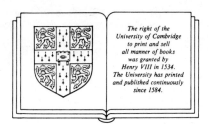

The right of the
University of Cambridge
to print and sell
all manner of books
was granted by
Henry VIII in 1534.
The University has printed
and published continuously
since 1584.

Cambridge University Press

Cambridge

London   New York   New Rochelle
Melbourne   Sydney

Published by the Press Syndicate of the University of Cambridge
The Pitt Building, Trumpington Street, Cambridge CB2 IRP
32 East 57th Street, New York, NY 10022, USA
10 Stamford Road, Oakleigh, Melbourne 3166, Australia

First published 1986

Printed in Great Britain by
Redwood Burn Limited
Trowbridge, Wiltshire

Library of Congress catalogue card number: 85–15128

British Library Cataloguing in Publication Data
Duff, R. A.
Trials and punishments.—
(Cambridge studies in philosophy)
1. Punishment
I. Title
364.6'01   HV8675

ISBN 0–521–30818–6

For my Parents

Contents

Preface

I have incurred many debts in writing this book. Those to the published works of others are, I hope, acknowledged in the text: but other, more personal debts should be duly and gratefully noted here.

Some of the ideas in the book have been tried out on audiences at the Association for Legal and Social Philosophy; at the Universities of Manchester, York, Lancaster and Glasgow; and on colleagues and students at Stirling: I am grateful to all of these for their comments, criticisms and suggestions. Chapter 3 is based on my article 'Legal Obligation and the Moral Nature of Law', (1980) *Juridicial Review* 61; I am grateful to the publishers (W. Green and Son Ltd.) for permission to reuse this material. I am grateful too for helpful comments from publisher's referees, from Tom Campbell, and from Joseph Raz: but I owe a special debt to Richard Francks, Murray MacBeath and Roger Shiner, whose detailed and constructive criticisms of earlier versions of the book have saved me from many errors and unclarities, and whose encouragement has helped me retain my belief that the book was worth writing. I have not tried to record particular debts to them in the text – there would be too many: but they must know how much they have contributed. I must also thank Jane Harrison of Cambridge University Press for her thorough and patient editorial work, which has saved me from numerous unclarities and infelicities. Above all, however, I must record – albeit inadequately – my gratitude to Sandra Marshall, with whom I have discussed every aspect of the book, and without whose support, assistance and encouragement it would never have been written. It would be a relief if I could also blame these friends and colleagues for the defects which remain: but, though they must accept their share of blame for encouraging me, I cannot in all honesty blame anyone but myself for the book's deficiencies.

R A D

Stirling, February 1985

Introduction

Philosophical discussions of the meaning and justification of criminal punishment tend to move along familiar and well-worn paths. It is agreed that a system of criminal punishment stands in need of some strenuous and persuasive justification: the briefest examination of our actual penal institutions confronts us forcibly with the question of how we can justifiably subject people to such treatment; and even a more abstract or idealised account of what punishment could or should be must recognise that any punitive practice will require powerful justification. But different moral perspectives generate different accounts of why it is that punishment needs justification – of what it is about punishment that makes it morally problematic: for some it is the fact that punishment inflicts, indeed is designed to inflict, pain or suffering that most forcibly raises the issue of justification; for others it is the coercive character of punishment – the fact that it is imposed on people against their express will, thus apparently infringing their freedom and autonomy – which is most disturbing. Such different perceptions of the problem of punishment are themselves related to quite different accounts of what does or could justify a system of criminal punishment.

Consequentialists, who have been for many years the predominant party in these discussions, insist that the point of a system of criminal punishment must lie in its beneficial effects (most obviously in the reduction of harmful modes of conduct by the deterrence, reform or incapacitation of those who do or might engage in them), and its justification in the extent to which these benefits outweigh the system's costs (the harm caused by punishment; the resources needed to identify and deal with those who are to be punished). Consequentialist accounts of punishment are as diverse as the ends which consequentialists may value and which punishment may serve: but I take it to be a common and defining feature of such accounts that they require punishment to be justified by reference to benefits to which it is *contingently* related as a means to a further end. Our initial specification of the ends which we are to pursue leaves open the question of the means by which they are to be pursued, since those ends do not of their nature require any particular method of attaining them: so we must go on to ask which methods are in fact likely to be most economically efficacious. To justify a system of punishment it is therefore not enough to show that it pursues ends which are worth pursuing, nor indeed that its benefits outweigh its costs: we must also show, by an empirical inquiry into the likely effects of actual or possible social institutions, that this way of dealing with disvalued conduct is more economically effective than other possible methods of achieving our desired ends – than, for instance, a system of 'social hygiene' which regards such conduct as symptomatic of a condition which needs curative treatment rather than as an instance of criminality requiring punishment.

This contingent relation between punishment and its justifying aims generates familiar objections to such consequentialist accounts. For the whole-hearted pursuit of such aims would surely sanction the imposition of manifestly unjust punishments: the punishment of innocent scapegoats; excessively harsh punishments for relatively trivial offences; a refusal to accept excusing-conditions which should in justice be accepted. It is at best a contingent truth that just punishments are consequentially efficient; and it may sometimes be true that unjust punishments are more efficient.

A consequentialist might respond to such objections by arguing that an adequately detailed consequentialist account, which attends to *all* the likely effects of particular kinds or systems of punishment, will not in fact have such disturbing implications; that it will come closer to an extensional equivalence with 'ordinary moral views' than its critics may suppose. She may also try to provide a role for, and an explanation of, the principles of justice which her critics regard as morally significant; by arguing, for instance, that we have good consequentialist reasons to obey strict rules which forbid the punishment of the innocent or the unduly harsh punishment of the guilty. But she will still face some familiar objections: that she is relying on large and unsubstantiated empirical claims about the likely effects of different kinds of practice; that her reductive and instrumental account of the principles of justice fails to capture the sense and significance of those principles, or the role which they properly play in our moral thought; and that she 'begs the institution' by assuming without adequate argument that a consequentialist concern to prevent harmful conduct will generate something like a system of criminal punishment, rather than some quite different system of social hygiene or behaviour-control.[1] Some more radical consequentialists have indeed taken this last route, and argued that a proper concern for the appropriate consequentialist ends should lead us to abandon punishment altogether.

An alternative response to these criticisms has been to insist that the positive justifying aims of punishment must indeed lie in its consequential benefits, but to allow that our pursuit of those aims is and should be limited by other considerations or side-constraints. Such limits may be set by our concern for ends other than, and conflicting with, those which provide the justifying aims of punishment; a concern to maximise the citizen's freedom in and control over his own life may set limits on who may be punished, and how, which are not dictated by the aim of preventing disvalued conduct: but they may also be set by an avowedly non-consequentialist concern for justice which forbids us to punish the innocent, and limits the kind or amount of punishment which may be attached to different offences. Punishment which efficiently serves its justifying aims may thus still be unjustified, if it fails to satisfy these further moral constraints – constraints which are independent of the consequential ends which punishment is to serve, and which focus on its intrinsic character.

It is here that retributivist ideas are allowed to play a part in an account of punishment. Traditional attempts to find the *positive* justification of punishment in its relation to a past offence are, their critics claim, unable to explain that justificatory relationship: insofar as they have any tolerably clear meaning they are seen to depend on an unargued and unarguable intuition that 'the guilty deserve to suffer' (itself perhaps reflecting a desire for revenge which hardly deserves our moral respect); or on a covertly consequentialist appeal to some particular, and arbitrarily selected, kind of beneficial effect. But we need not therefore eliminate all notions of retribution: we can deal with them (and defuse them) by allowing that they do, once properly understood, have a role in an adequate account of punishment – though not the dominant role which their traditional proponents claimed for them. Ideas of retribution and desert are now to play an aetiolated and negative role, setting constraints on our pursuit of the consequentialist goals which provide the positive justifying aim of

[1] On 'begging the institution' see M Mackenzie, *Plato on Punishment* 41 *et passim*. A brief word about my use of feminine and masculine pronouns: rather than favour one sex throughout (or have to use such clumsy locutions as 's/he' etc.), I have instead tried – within the constraints of grammar and context – to randomise the gender of my pronouns; I trust that this will neither inhibit comprehension nor reveal too many unconscious sexual biases of my own.

punishment: they express independent principles of justice; or logical principles involved in the meaning of 'punishment'; or subordinate principles within a Rule-Utilitarian system.

Retributivists, however, are unlikely to be satisfied with this subordinate role within a fundamentally consequentialist framework: and recent years have seen a revival of full-blooded retributivist attempts to locate the meaning of punishment, not in its contingent and instrumental contribution to some further end, but in its internal relationship to a past offence; and its justification in its intrinsic character as a response to that offence. This revival, involving both academic philosophers and more practically oriented legal theorists, has been motivated in part by the manifest failure of systems constructed or reformed along purportedly consequentialist lines to achieve their avowed ends, as well as by a more theoretical dissatisfaction with consequentialist accounts of punishment;[2] and it has led to new attempts to explicate and defend the idea that punishment is justified as merited retribution for a past offence.

We can usefully talk of the common features, and the common logical structure, of consequentialist accounts of punishment: but can we usefully talk of retributivist accounts in this way; or has the label 'retributivist' been applied to such a diversity of views and principles that it now lacks any unambiguous or unitary meaning?[3] We must indeed distinguish retributivist accounts of the justifying purpose of punishment from those which seek only to set limits on our pursuit of consequentialist aims; and amongst the former we find a notable diversity of explanations of how it is that punishment is an appropriate response to crime. Some talk of the payment of a debt incurred by crime, or of the restoration of a balance disturbed by crime; others of the expiation, atonement, or annulment of crime; others of the denunciation of crime: and we cannot suppose that these are simply different ways of expressing the same idea. But such accounts do share what can usefully be called a retributivist perspective on punishment: for they all find the sense and the justification of punishment in its relation to a past offence.

A retributivist must explain the meaning of this justificatory relationship, and the values on which it depends. She must defend herself against the accusation that her account amounts at best to a distortion of logical or moral principles which have their proper and

---

[2] See A von Hirsch, *Doing Justice: The Choice of Punishments*; N Morris, *The Future of Imprisonment*; M H Tonry and N Morris, 'Sentencing Reform in America'; Sir Leon Radzinowicz and R Hood, 'The American Volte-Face in Sentencing Thought and Practice'; D J Galligan, 'The Return to Retribution in Penal Theory'.

[3] See J G Cottingham, 'Varieties of Retribution'.

subordinate place within a consequentialist account of the justifying aims of punishment; and at worst to a piece of metaphysical mystery-mongering which conceals a desire for revenge or retaliation behind such opaque and unilluminating metaphors as 'restoring the balance' or 'annulling the crime'. She must meet the claim that a coercive institution like punishment can be justified only by showing that it does some significant consequential good; and she may do this by arguing that the justification of punishment has, and need have, nothing to do with its consequences, and everything to do with its intrinsic character as a response to crime: the imposition of punishment on criminals is right independently of its consequences – even, perhaps, whatever its consequences.

The range of familiar accounts of punishment thus offers us three models for its justification. A consequentialist model justifies punishment by reference to further ends to which it is contingently and instrumentally related as a means; an intrinsicalist or retributivist model justifies it by reference to its intrinsic character as distinct from, and rather than, its consequences; and a 'consequentialism with side-constraints' model seeks to combine these two modes of justification by insisting that a justified system of punishment must be an efficient method of pursuing the further ends which provide its justifying aims, whilst also satisfying the independent and intrinsicalist demands of justice.

These familiar kinds of account of what does or could justify a system of criminal punishment provide the context in which this book is set. Many of the issues noted here will be discussed in more detail later. I will offer some general objections to consequentialist (and 'consequentialism with side-constraints') accounts of punishment which I believe will have force against any attempt to justify punishment by reference to consequential ends to which it is only contingently related. I will discuss some currently popular retributivist accounts, in order to show that they cannot fulfil their proponents' hopes for them. But I do not have a complete theory of punishment – a coherent explanation and justification of all the significant features of an actual or ideal penal system – to offer in their place; and I suspect that none may be possible. It would clearly be absurd to try to explain any existing penal system, whose historical development reflects an unsystematic diversity of competing influences, in terms of some unitary set of coherent values and purposes: it may also be wrong to suppose that a more satisfactory system of punishment either could or should be justified in such coherent terms; for it may be that we face an irreducible conflict of values, which make irreconcilably conflicting demands on our attempts to envisage and develop more adequate legal institutions.

Whatever the merits of such scepticism about the possibility of finding *the* meaning, or *the* justification, of criminal punishment, my own aims are of a different character. My main aim is to explore the implications of the Kantian demand that we should respect other people as rational and autonomous moral agents – that we should treat them as ends, never merely as means – for an understanding of the meaning and justification of criminal punishment. I do not suppose that a plausible and practicable system of punishment can be founded solely on, or indeed be fully consistent with, this moral principle: but I do believe that we can find within it values which must be central to any tolerable system of punishment.

No general explanation or justification of this principle will be offered here: I will instead both exhibit its meaning and show its importance by examining its implications for our understanding of criminal punishment. By way of brief preliminary, however, to respect another person as a rational and autonomous moral agent is to treat him and respond to him as one who is able, and should be allowed, to conduct his own life and determine his own conduct in the light of his own understanding of the values and goals which command his allegiance. It involves a refusal to manipulate him, or to use him merely as an instrument for the attainment of social or individual goals; insofar as I may properly attempt to modify his conduct (or, more accurately, attempt to bring him to modify his own conduct), I should do so only by bringing him to understand and accept the relevant reasons which justify that attempt. I call this principle Kantian, since it is clearly related to Kant's notions of autonomy and respect; but I do not call it Kant's principle, since I do not aim to capture or express Kant's own views on these matters.[4]

It is punishment's coercive character which makes it most obviously problematic in the light of this Kantian principle: for how can we respect a person's autonomy whilst imposing punishment on her against her will? It will, not surprisingly, become clear that this principle both precludes any purely consequentialist account of punishment, and helps to explain the force of the objections to such accounts. But it will also preclude the kind of account which recognises non-consequentialist side-constraints on our pursuit of the consequential aims of punishment: for while such an account may

---

[4] For an interesting recent discussion of the notion of autonomy, see J Benson, 'Who is the Autonomous Man?'

allow the Kantian principle a negative role in setting some of those side-constraints, it still cannot show the imposition of punishment to be consistent with, let alone expressive of, that respect for the criminal which the principle demands.

Should we then look to the other familiar justificatory model; forswear any attempt to find a forward-looking, goal-directed justification for punishment; and portray it simply as merited retribution for past wrongdoing? I think not: for there is a further possibility which merits our attention.

We may portray punishment as essentially goal-directed, thus abandoning the traditional retributivist's insistence that it must be justified without reference to any further goals which it may serve: but we may also insist that it is *internally* related to its justifying goals, thus rejecting the consequentialist view that the relationship is purely contingent. Punishment is justified as an attempt to achieve certain goals (primarily the moral reform of the offender, although the notion of 'reform' will need careful explication): and its relation to those goals is contingent insofar as it may in fact fail to achieve them, and insofar as the extent to which it does achieve them will depend on contingent facts about the world. But what makes punishment an appropriate method of pursuing those goals is not, as it is for the consequentialist, the contingent fact of its ef-ficiency as an instrumental means; nor indeed that fact together with its satisfaction of moral demands independent of those goals: it is the character of the goals themselves, understood in the light of the Kantian demand that we should respect the criminal, which makes punishment appropriate. In this context 'means' and 'ends' are logi-cally, not merely contingently, related. Furthermore, the justifi-cation of punishment does not depend entirely on its actual or likely success in achieving its goals: we may justifiably punish someone, as an attempt to achieve the appropriate goals, even when we are practically certain that that attempt will fail.

I will explain the sense of these somewhat programmatic intro-ductory remarks, and the character of this fourth justificatory model, in the course of the book. Two themes will be particularly important. First, that there are illuminating connections and anal-ogies between the criminal process of trial and punishment and our informal and personal responses to the moral wrongdoings of others: we should understand criminal punishment, not merely in the impersonal terms of familiar types of political theory, but in terms of our personal dealings with each other as moral agents. Second, that though punishment may obviously be imposed against the criminal's express will, we should not simply see her as the passive victim of her punishment; we should rather see the criminal process of trial and punishment as one to which the defendant is meant to respond, and in which she is called to participate, as a rational moral agent.

To talk of a criminal participating in her own punishment may sound absurd. It is closely related to the ideas that a criminal has a *right* to be punished ('But what is this right which so few wish to claim?'); that she should *benefit* from her punishment ('But what is this benefit which most criminals seek so strenuously to avoid?'); and that she should *will* her own punishment ('But how can we say that she wills something which she so clearly resists?'). I will show what sense these ideas can make.

But this book is not wholly concerned with punishment: it will also discuss some of the other aspects of a system of criminal law on which criminal punishment depends. For a system of punishment depends on the existence of a set of substantive laws which define certain types of conduct as offences and attach penal sanctions to them; and of a set of procedural rules and principles which structure the criminal process of trial, verdict and sentence. We may of course talk of punishment in contexts which lack the formal apparatus and institutions of a modern system of municipal law; and I do not suppose that punishment must find its primary meaning within such a system of law, or that other kinds of punishment must be understood as derivative or aetiolated versions of criminal punishment: indeed, I will try to explicate the meaning of criminal punishment in part by examining the role which notions of punishment can play in our personal dealings with each other as moral agents. But my main concern is with the meaning and justification of punishment as part of a system of criminal law; and I believe that this can be illuminated by attending to aspects of the criminal process of trial and verdict which are too often ignored in discussions of punishment, and to fundamental questions about the nature of law to which adequate answers are too rarely given.

Though philosophers and jurisprudents have had much to say about the nature of law in general, and of the criminal law in particular, there has been a relative dearth of theoretical discussion (at least in the United Kingdom) of the criminal process of trial and verdict. But that process (and the values and purposes which should structure it) deserves more serious attention both for its own sake and for the light which it may throw on the meaning of criminal punishment. In particular, an examination of the proper nature of the criminal law and the criminal process will help to clarify the significance of the Kantian principle of respect for the individual; the relation between the criminal process and the activities of moral criticism and blame; and the idea that the defendant should participate in her own trial and punishment.

Amongst justifying accounts of the criminal law and the criminal process, as amongst accounts of punishment, we can identify two familiar models: purely consequentialist accounts which find the justification of these institutions in their contingent and instrumental contribution to certain further ends; and accounts which also recognise certain non-consequentialist side-constraints on our pursuit of those ends.

Thus a strict consequentialist may see a system of law essentially as a particular kind of technique for controlling behaviour. If asked why we should prefer this method of behaviour-control (why we should think it important for a society to be governed by 'the rule of law'), he would refer to the superior efficiency and economy of this method of achieving our ends; and in deciding on the proper structure and content of a system of law he would similarly need to assess the relative efficiency and economy of different kinds of legal system. He will then face the familiar charge that he cannot adequately explain the values which we think are, or should be, integral to a system of law.

A more qualified consequentialist might agree that the positive justifying aim of a legal system must lie in the consequential benefits which flow from this technique for controlling human conduct, but allow that our pursuit of those benefits is constrained by a non-consequentialist respect for certain individual rights and freedoms. It may be such values as these, and not merely considerations of economic efficiency, which lead us to prefer the rule of law to other possible methods of controlling behaviour, and which help to determine the proper structure and content of a system of law.

So too with accounts of the criminal process. The justifying aims of this process are often located in its consequential benefits: its purpose, it may be said, is to assist the aims of the legal system by identifying those who should be liable to punishment or other kinds of coercive treatment. A strict consequentialist will then give a purely instrumental account of the criminal process, and of the procedural rules and principles by which it should be governed. She must then face the charge that her account allows no adequate role to values which we think important and which require us, for instance, to protect the innocent against conviction and to give the defendant a fair hearing. She must also recognise the possibility that, just as she might not in the end be able to justify a system of *punishment*, so too she might not end up with anything identifiable as a system of *law* or of criminal *trials*.

A qualified consequentialist will accept some of these objections to a strictly consequentialist account, and build certain non-consequentialist constraints into his account of the proper structure of the criminal process. He may say, for instance, that individuals have a right to procedures which protect them against being wrongly convicted, even if such procedures will make the system less economically effective in securing the consequential benefits which provide its justifying aim – by making it more likely that some who are guilty will be acquitted; or by making the process of proof more costly. Or he may say that we must respect the individual's rights against certain kinds of coercion, and the defendant's right to be heard, even when a denial of these rights might assist the consequential aims of the criminal process.

In contrast to such primarily consequentialist models, I will offer an account of the proper nature of the criminal law and the criminal process which allows a more central role to certain non-instrumental values concerned with the respect which we owe each other as moral agents. This account may be called intrinsicalist, insofar as it finds the justifying purpose of a system of criminal law and criminal trials in values which are intrinsic to the proper nature of the criminal law and the criminal process: but it will also insist on the purposive character of these institutions; they are directed towards goals which lie beyond themselves and which they may, contingently, fail to achieve. However, whereas a consequentialist will posit a purely contingent relationship between such institutions and their justifying aims; and whereas a qualified consequentialist will deny any logical connection between those aims and the non-consequentialist values which constrain our pursuit of them; I will argue that the values which are intrinsic to these institutions are also intrinsic to the ends which they should properly serve. It is the character of those ends themselves, and not merely considerations of economic efficiency or the demands of independent moral values, which makes such institutions the appropriate means by which to pursue them; here too 'means' and 'ends' are logically, not merely contingently, related.

I will not, however, offer an exhaustive account of the proper character and structure of a system of criminal law and criminal trials. Nor indeed will I try to develop the kind of general political theory of the state on which any such account must depend, though my claims will have obvious implications for the content of such a theory.[5] My aim is rather to show that an adequately justificatory account of a system of criminal law, trials and punishments must be founded on the Kantian principle of respect for individual autonomy, and to explore the kind of account which that principle can generate. We may also have to recognise, however, that any plausibly practicable legal system will include significant elements which cannot be explained in terms of, and which may indeed be inconsistent with, that Kantian principle.

Three final points by way of introductory explanation. First, my discussion will begin with certain features of the English legal system, which are also to be found in many other legal systems. I will argue that they should be explained and justified in terms of certain non-consequentialist and Kantian values: but their role in my argument is meant to be illustrative and heuristic rather than probative. If we think that these are important and valuable features of a legal system (and if my account of their rationale is plausible) we should be led towards the kind of account of criminal law and punishment which I want to offer: but that account is not to be justified simply by the claim that it explains these features of our actual legal system. For, quite apart from the fact that there are other features of our legal system which are clearly at odds with the Kantian principle on which my account depends, and which I would want to criticise in the light of that principle, my aim is not simply to offer an explanatory analysis or justification of the *status quo*: it is rather to explicate the values and purposes – the ideals – which *should* be central to a system of criminal law and punishment, and in the light of which we can criticise existing legal institutions and practices which fall short of them. These ideals do, I believe, play some part in our actual legal system: but any reasonably informed reader must be struck by the radical disparity between the actual character of our legal institutions and my account of the proper nature of law, of the criminal trial and of punishment. This disparity marks, I will urge, the extent to which our existing institutions fall short of the ideals which they should embody, rather than the extent to which my account of those ideals is itself inadequate. But my claim that these are the ideals towards which the law should strive must therefore be

[5] See N Lacey, 'Punishment, Justice and Consequentialism'; T Honderich, *Punishment: The Supposed Justifications* 237–9.

II

shown to be plausible independently of the extent to which any existing legal system actually embodies them; and this I will aim to do.

Second, such a non-consequentialist account of the ideals which should inform a legal system, of what a system of law and punishment would need to be in order to be fully justified, must face a serious problem about the relation between the ideal and the actual or the practical. Any account of how a system of punishment is to be justified should be more than an attempt to justify the *status quo*: it should provide a standard or ideal against which our existing practices are to be judged, and towards which our reformative efforts are to be directed.[6] Now an adequately developed consequentialist account should be able to show us a direction in which we can realistically hope to improve our existing institutions; and to reassure us that, while those institutions will no doubt remain imperfect, they will at least do more good and less harm than any available alternative. It should, in other words, enable us to make the best of what may be a bad job; and a consequentialist need have no larger ambition than that. But one who holds that a system of punishment which is to be properly justified must satisfy certain categorical demands of justice, and must accord an unqualified respect to each citizen as a rational and autonomous moral agent, may have to recognise not only that our present penal practices are radically unjust and unjustified, but also that we cannot realistically hope so to reform them that they approximate at all closely to what they ideally ought to be; and perhaps too that no practicable human system of punishment could hope to approach that ideal. She may thus find that in providing an account of what punishment ought to be she has also shown why no actual penal system can be properly justified. A consequentialist, while he must be disturbed by imperfection, may still justify a penal system as being the least of the available evils: but how can someone who appeals to the categorical demands of justice and of respect for persons either tolerate or justify a penal system which fails to satisfy those demands? I will have more to say about this problem and its implications later.

Third, my claims will be in part conceptual: I will argue that the concepts of law, of a criminal trial, and of punishment themselves embody certain substantive and non-consequentialist values, and that this is why it will be difficult to characterise, let alone to accept, a strictly consequentialist account of law and punishment. I do not suppose, however, that such conceptual claims will by themselves

[6] See J G Murphy, 'Marxism and Retribution'.

either establish a unique and determinate set of values which must be embodied in anything which is to be recognisable as a system of law and punishment, or settle the substantive questions of value on which consequentialists and non-consequentialists disagree. They will serve rather to mark out the range of contestable value-concepts in terms of which systems of criminal law and punishment are to be understood, justified and criticised; and to show that the issue between consequentialists and non-consequentialists is in part the issue of whether and why our legal institutions should be structured by such concepts as these. To claim, as I will claim, that a strictly consequentialist perspective cannot generate any secure justification for a system of criminal law and punishment is not yet to claim that such a perspective is therefore untenable, since a consequentialist may simply reply, 'So much the worse for criminal law and punishment': but it will help to direct our attention towards the non-consequentialist values on which a system of criminal law and punishment must be founded; and my main concern is to explicate, and thus to defend, those values. I do not believe that knock-down arguments or rigorous demonstrations are available here: but I hope to develop a conception of criminal law and punishment, and of the values which should be intrinsic to them, which will show itself to be morally plausible, even persuasive.

1

On Being Fit to be Tried and Punished

> And it seems agreed at this day that if one who has committed
> a capital offence becomes non-compos before conviction, he
> shall not be arraigned, and if after conviction that he shall not
> be executed.
>
> Serjeant Hawkins, *Pleas of the Crown*, I.3, p. 2

My main topic is the meaning and justification of the criminal process of trial and punishment. But I will approach it by a somewhat circuitous route, which begins by considering some of the provisions for dealing with mentally disordered defendants within the criminal process – provisions which have been unduly neglected in theoretical discussions of the relevance of mental disorder to criminal liability.

Such discussions usually focus on the ways in which a defendant's disorder at the time of his offence may secure him either a special verdict at his trial or some mitigation of sentence. There are important questions here: about the concept of mental disorder; about whether and why an agent should not be held fully liable for acts committed while he was disordered; about the extent to which different theories of punishment can provide adequate accounts of mental disorder as an excusing-condition. But a defendant's *present* disorder, at the time of his trial or punishment, can also make a crucial difference to his fate within the criminal process: far more use is made of the legal provisions for such presently disordered defendants than is made of the formal insanity defences; and they are considerable theoretical interest for the light they may throw on the nature and purposes of the criminal process itself.

I will describe three such provisions for the disordered defendant; suggest that they cannot readily be explained either by a consequentialist account of the criminal process or by familiar kinds of retributivist account; and indicate the kind of explanation which I think they require. An account of the criminal process which cannot explain these provisions is not by that very fact shown to be inadequate, since the provisions themselves may lack any adequate justification: but I will try later to show why these provisions are important, in the light of a more adequate account of the criminal process. They may serve for the moment simply to provoke some reflection on why a legal system should include them.

I FIT TO BE HANGED

There are several other situations in which, for the furtherance of justice, or on other urgent considerations, the convict must have a temporary respite, or a change must be allowed of the day of execution. For what if a capital convict should fall into a state of furiosity after sentence? Is it to be imagined, that the Court must allow him to be executed in this unhappy condition, which disables him from attending to his spiritual concerns, and where his death would so ill serve any of the purposes, for which the spectacle of public punishment is appointed by the laws?

(Baron Hume, *Commentaries on the Laws of Scotland, respecting Crime*, vol. 2, p. 455)

My first example is now of largely historical interest: the provisions which in the days of capital punishment saved the insane from execution. As far back as the reign of Henry VIII it was held to be obviously cruel and inhuman to execute a person who had become insane since his commission of a capital offence.[1] More recently a 'statutory medical inquiry' was held on any condemned prisoner whose sanity was in doubt: if he was certifiably insane at the time set for his execution, he was not fit to be hanged.[2]

In theory and originally, as Baron Hume indicates, such insanity may only have secured a postponement of the execution until such time, if ever, as the prisoner was fit to be hanged; in practice and latterly it exempted him from execution altogether, and secured instead his indefinite detention in hospital, whence he could be released only on the decision of the Home Secretary. The specified criteria for such a remission of execution ('certifiable insanity') were admittedly vague: but to determine the criteria by which we should identify those who, being disordered, should receive special treat-

[1] See N Walker, *Crime and Insanity in England* vol. 1 (referred to hereafter as *Walker*), 196, and chs. 12–13 on the historical development of these provisions.
[2] *Criminal Lunatics Act* 1884, s.2(4); see *Report of the Royal Commission on Capital Punishment* (referred to hereafter as *RCCP*) paras. 359–71; *Report of the Committee on Insanity and Crime* (referred to hereafter as *Atkin*) 13–19; *Walker* ch. 13. The provisions for statutory inquiries were repealed in 1959, but reprieves were still granted in cases of insanity (*Walker* 215–16).

ment we must first ask why we should make any such special provision for them; why, in this context, a murderer who is now insane should not be hanged.

The statutory inquiry often saved from execution those who were insane at the time of their crime, but who had not sought or obtained an insanity verdict at their trial. Since the inquiry used criteria more generous than those imposed on the insanity defence by the M'Naghten Rules, it was often seen as a partial remedy for the restrictive provisions of the insanity defence: it was accordingly welcomed by some as a properly humanitarian measure, and criticised by others as an improper usurpation of the functions of the criminal courts.[3] This function lost much of its importance with the introduction of the partial defence of Diminished Responsibility into English law in 1957:[4] for a disordered killer who did not satisfy the requirements of the full insanity defence could then avoid execution by obtaining a conviction for manslaughter rather than murder. But this was anyway not the inquiry's sole function: for it concerned the prisoner's condition at the time of the inquiry itself, not at the time of his offence; it thus saved from execution those who had become insane *since* their offence. A murderer who was sane and responsible when he killed, and at his trial, was not to be hanged if he had become insane since then: but why not? Why, whatever our views on capital punishment, should his execution seem utterly improper?

It may be said that the answer to this question is obvious, and has nothing to do with the meaning of punishment. The execution of one who is now insane is, *qua* punishment, as justified as any execution: but we exempt her from execution for humanitarian reasons which are independent of the justification of punishment as punishment. We might then ask whether such humanitarian considerations do not apply equally to any execution, but I think that this suggestion anyway misses the point: it is precisely *as* punishment that the execution of the insane is improper; quite apart from humanitarian objections to killing the insane, there are objections to executing them which depend essentially on the meaning of execution as a punishment.

A consequentialist cannot easily explain why we should not execute such people. If the point of capital punishment is to prevent the killer killing again, and to save the resources which would otherwise be spent in keeping her in prison, we should hang the insane as

[3] See Lord Goddard's comments, reported in *RCCP* para. 365.
[4] *Homicide Act* 1957, s. 2; see *Walker* 215.

16

well as the sane murderer: for the insane are just as likely to kill again as the sane. If its point is to add a further and more effective deterrent to that provided by life imprisonment, we may still be required to execute the insane: for while a person who is insane when she kills might not be susceptible to such deterrence (though her execution may still deter others), this consideration does not apply to one who becomes insane after her offence; and the efficacy of capital punishment as a general deterrent may be impaired if we exempt such people from execution.

It has admittedly been claimed that the execution of one who is now insane cannot serve the aim of general deterrence.

By intendment of law the execution of the offender is, for example, *ut poena ad paucos, metus ad omnes perveniat*...; but so it is not when a mad man is executed, but should be a miserable spectacle, both against law, and of extreme inhumanity and cruelty, and can be no example to others.[5]

But why can his execution not still be an example to others? If death is a more effective deterrent than life imprisonment, it is also more effective than indefinite psychiatric detention; and if that efficacy justifies the execution of sane murderers, it must also justify the execution of those who are now insane: for the greater the chance of avoiding execution by suffering or faking insanity, the less its deterrent efficacy.

Or could a consequentialist claim that any preventive or deterrent benefits of executing the insane would be nullified by the disgust which such executions would arouse: that 'everyone would revolt from dragging a gibbering maniac to the gallows';[6] and that, while other executions might also satisfy the feelings of the public, or of the victim's friends and family, the execution of an insane murderer would disgust rather than satisfy them? But an insane prisoner is not herself likely to be more distressed by her execution than a sane prisoner: and we must ask *why* the public, or those involved in the execution, should be so revolted by it; *why* the desire for vengeance or satisfaction should not encompass the execution of one who is now insane. We cannot simply take such repugnance as a raw datum to be fed into our consequentialist calculus: we must ask whether it expresses, not merely a non-rational and perhaps modifiable response, but a rational moral judgment on such executions; and, if so, what the sense of that moral judgment might be.

---

[5] Sir Edward Coke, quoted in *3rd Report of the Criminal Law Revision Committee: Criminal Procedure (Insanity)* (referred to hereafter as *CLRC*) 16.
[6] *Atkin* 19.

Furthermore, even if a consequentialist could show by arguments such as these that he would not be committed to executing the insane, and thus secure an extensional equivalence between his views and those reflected in the law, I think he misses the point. What is wrong with executing the insane is not that it might in fact be inefficient or counter-productive (its wrongness is not contingent on its effects), but that it is *in itself* inappropriate as a punishment.

No better explanation of the impropriety of executing the insane is provided by those modified consequentialist accounts which allow independent considerations of justice or fairness to constrain our pursuit of consequentialist ends. To say, for instance, that we can justly punish a person only if she had a fair chance to conform her conduct to the law, since we otherwise deny her the opportunity to predict and control her own future,[7] may give us reason not to execute someone who was so disordered when she killed that her ability to conform her conduct to the law's demands was seriously impaired (though since she is still liable to indefinite psychiatric detention we must ask why *punishment*, as distinct from other kinds of coercive treatment, should so crucially depend on the person's past voluntary conduct). But it gives us no reason not to execute someone who has become insane since he killed, if his execution would assist the consequentialist aims of the penal system: for at the time of his offence he had as fair a chance to obey the law as anyone else.

For a consequentialist the execution of the insane could in principle serve the justifying aims of punishment: it is wrong, if at all, only because it does not as a matter of contingent fact serve those aims efficiently; or because it is inconsistent with some independent value which constrains those aims. My claim is that it is wrong because it is inconsistent with the aims and values which should inform the very idea of punishment: but how could this be so?

It was argued, by Hale, Hawles and Blackstone among others, that we should not execute an insane prisoner because he might, were he sane, be able to offer some reason why he should not be executed.[8] One might wonder what this reason could be which could not have been offered at his trial, or be offered by his counsel on his behalf. But, more crucially, this suggestion still fails to capture the idea that it is his insanity itself which makes his execution wrong: its

<hr />

[7] See H L A Hart, 'Legal Responsibility and Excuses' 44–9.
[8] See *Walker* 197.

wrongness is still contingent on the possible existence of some *further* reason why he should not be executed.

Could we instead argue that for reasons of logic, of utility or of justice the punishment for an offence must be imposed on the person who committed that offence; and that the necessary continuity of identity between the offender and the person who is now to be executed is broken if insanity intervenes between offence and execution?[9] But we normally suppose that identity *is* preserved even through serious insanity. Although Jane Smith is radically changed by her disorder it is still she, Jane Smith, who suffers that change: so why should we regard that identity as destroyed in this context? A consequentialist must anyway be unimpressed by this suggestion. For the preventive aims of punishment depend on what the person who is to be punished is likely to do in the future, not on her identity with a past offender. And while the deterrent efficacy of punishment depends on its effect on potential offenders, the belief that I might go mad before my execution is, I think, unlikely to reduce the deterrent efficacy of that threatened punishment by persuading me that it might not be *me* who was hanged. A retributivist will of course insist that the person who is punished must be the person who committed the offence: but why should she deny the ordinary view that identity is preserved even when insanity intervenes?

I will discuss an alternative interpretation of this suggestion below: but it may seem that traditional retributivist accounts of punishment must, if they justify capital punishment, justify the execution of the insane. For the murderer's action, if he was sane at the time, disturbed the balance which punishment must restore, or incurred the debt which punishment must repay: so why should his present insanity forbid us to exact that debt from him, or to restore that balance by his execution?

Could a retributivist appeal to the maxim that '*satis furore ipso punitur*'?[10] A murderer who becomes insane is sufficiently punished by her insanity itself, which thus pays her debt or restores the balance: for even if it does not cause her conscious suffering it is necessarily harmful to her. Courts may indeed on occasion mitigate an offender's punishment if she has already suffered some serious loss, especially if this was itself a result of her crime (though *this* need not be true of a disorder which intervenes between offence and punishment). But it is not clear that this can provide a sufficient retributivist justification for exempting the insane from execution:

---

[9] This was suggested to me by Vinit Haksar.
[10] This maxim originates in Roman law: see *Digest* I.18.14; *Walker* 27.

partly because it is not clear that a natural misfortune could in principle pay the criminal's debt, or restore the balance disturbed by her crime; partly because a statutory inquiry into whether the prisoner's disorder was severe enough to exempt her from execution was not an inquiry into whether that disorder was severe enough to serve as a *substitute* for execution (it would have been both bizarre and improper for an inquiry to conclude that, while the prisoner's disorder was severe enough to serve as a *partial* substitute for punishment, she should still receive some lesser punishment to make up the difference between what she deserved and what she had already suffered through her disorder).

A different suggestion, however, though at first sight strikingly odd, may lead us in a more fruitful direction.

The strongest reason for a penalty is that it inflicts suffering upon the punishable person: a reason which is clearly lacking in the case of the insane person.[11]

This claim may seem simply false: a disorder which renders a person unfit to be hanged need not render him unable to experience either the physical agony of being hanged or the psychological anguish of knowing that he is to be hanged. But if we ask more carefully just what kind of suffering punishment should aim to inflict we may find more sense in this suggestion, and more insight into what a retributivist notion of punishment could mean.

For suppose a murderer becomes so disordered that, while she realises *that* she is to be hanged, she cannot understand *why* she is to be hanged; she cannot grasp the connection between what is to be done to her now and what she did in the past which makes her hanging an execution (the claim that insanity breaks the continuity of personal identity which punishment requires might now be reinterpreted as the claim that the disordered offender cannot see the appropriate connection between her present punishment and her past offence). Her execution might cause her an injury which externally matches the harm caused by, or the wrong involved in, her crime: but it cannot now be a process through which *she* pays for that crime, or restores the balance which her crime disturbed, or expiates or atones for her crime; for she cannot understand, respond to, or participate in her execution as a punishment for what she has done.

The idea that a prisoner should be able to participate in his own execution may at first sound as odd as the idea that hanging cannot inflict suffering on a madman. But it suggests that the essential pur-

---

[11] Diego de Covarrubias, quoted in *Walker* 197.

pose of punishment may be not just to inflict suffering on an offender (whether to deter others or to balance his crime), but to induce suffering which the offender can understand, and to which he can respond, as a punishment for his offence; that what is wrong with hanging someone who is so disordered that he cannot understand his execution in these terms is that it cannot properly count as a *punishment*, since it cannot serve the purpose which is central to the meaning of punishment.

This suggestion may explain Lord Hewart's suggested criterion for determining whether a prisoner is so disordered that he should not be hanged:

> If this condemned man is now hanged, is there any reason to suppose from the state of his mind that he will not understand why he is being hanged?[12]

But why should such understanding be so important? We do not always think it wrong to do something to a person which he cannot understand, or the reasons for which he cannot grasp: a disordered killer who avoids execution is still liable to indefinite detention, which is not rendered inappropriate by the fact that he can no more understand the reasons for it than he could understand his execution; indeed it is partly because he is so disordered that he is detained. So what is so special about punishment, or capital punishment, that his ability to understand it should be thus crucial to its justification?

I will suggest an answer to this question later (though I will not try to justify capital punishment): my claim here is simply that it is one which is worth asking; and that neither a consequentialist nor a retributivist who attends only to the external aspect of punishment as something imposed *on* an offender can readily answer it. But we may note here one final suggestion about why we should not execute the insane which, though it might not appeal directly to a secular age, may yet be illuminating.

> It is inconsistent with religion, as being against Christian charity to send an offender quick, as it is stiled, into another world, when he is not of a capacity to fit himself for it.[13]

The thought here may be simply that we should not kill a person who is able to prepare himself to meet his Maker: the execution of an insane killer may be justified as a punishment, but it conflicts with our concern for the criminal's spiritual well-being. However,

[12] Quoted in *Walker* 213.
[13] Sir John Hawles, quoted in *Walker* 197; the same suggestion is found in the comments from Baron Hume quoted at the beginning of this section.

it might also involve the more ambitious claim that capital punishment is itself partly justified by the fact that it may lead the murderer to repentance: it is through his execution that he can make his peace with God, which he clearly cannot do if he cannot understand why he is being hanged. (I heard of a bishop who argued more recently for the retention of capital punishment on the similar grounds that the prospect of execution can induce genuine death-cell repentances.) I do not suggest that this is an adequate justification of capital punishment: but I will suggest that it expresses, albeit in a distorted form, an important truth about the nature of punishment.

2 FIT TO BE PUNISHED

(1) Where a person is convicted before the Crown Court of an offence punishable with imprisonment other than an offence the sentence for which is fixed by law, or is convicted by a magistrates' court of an offence punishable on summary conviction with imprisonment, and the conditions mentioned in subsection (2) below are satisfied, the court may by order authorise his admission to and detention in such hospital as may be specified in the order . . .
(2) The conditions referred to in subsection (1) above are that –
(a) the court is satisfied, on the written or oral evidence of two registered medical practitioners, that the offender is suffering from mental illness, psychopathic disorder, severe mental impairment or mental impairment and that . . . the mental disorder from which the offender is suffering is of a nature or degree which makes it appropriate for him to be detained in a hospital for medical treatment and, in the case of psychopathic disorder or mental impairment, that such treatment is likely to alleviate or prevent a deterioration of his condition; . . . and
(b) the court is of the opinion, having regard to all the circumstances including the nature of the offence and the character and antecedents of the offender, and to the other available methods of dealing with him, that the most suitable method of disposing of the case is by means of an order under this section.
(*Mental Health Act* 1983, s.37)

We need no longer worry in practice about executing the insane. But mentally disordered offenders may also be diverted from other kinds of punishment, most notably under the provisions of the Mental Health Act 1983. Subject to the conditions specified in section 37 of the Act, a court may make a Hospital Order on a convicted but disordered offender, thus committing him to hospital for treatment rather than to prison for punishment. The court may also subject him to a Restriction Order, of limited or of indefinite duration, on the grounds that, given 'the nature of the offence, the ante-cedents of the offender and the risk of his committing further offences if set at large', 'it is necessary for the protection of the public from serious harm to do so'. The main effect of a Restriction Order is to make his release from hospital depend, not on the decision of his doctors, but on the decision of the Home Secretary, or, in certain circumstances, the decision of a Mental Health Review Tribunal.[14] Instead of being subjected to a Hospital Order an offender may, under section 3 of the Powers of Criminal Courts Act 1973, be required to accept psychiatric treatment under the terms of a Probation Order.[15]

What is the rationale of a Hospital Order? It is supposedly an alternative to punishment, not a kind of punishment;[16] and it may clearly be used to save from punishment an offender who was disordered and non-responsible at the time of her offence.[17] But an Order can also be made on an offender who was not disordered at the time of her offence, or whose disorder had no connection with her offence:[18] why should *she* avoid punishment? If she is now disordered she should of course be offered psychiatric treatment *whilst* she is being punished; and if her disorder is serious her punishment should perhaps be remitted or mitigated on purely humanitarian grounds: but the Act goes further than this, to suggest that punishment may be inappropriate or unsuitable for such an offender; it is this suggestion which needs to be explained.

What might a consequentialist say about such special provisions for mentally disordered offenders? Some have hailed them as an im-

[14] For Restriction Orders, see ss. 41–4 and 73–5 of the Act. Apart from the provisions noted here, Part III of the Act also makes provision for a court to remand an accused person to hospital for a report on his mental condition or for treatment (ss. 35–36), or to make an Interim Hospital Order on a convicted offender (s. 38); for a magistrates' court to make a Hospital Order on a defendant suffering from mental illness or severe mental impairment without convicting him, 'if the court is satisfied that the accused did the act or made the omission charged' (s. 37(3)); and for the Home Secretary to order the transfer of a mentally disordered offender from prison to hospital (ss. 47–50). See T Whitehead, *Mental Illness and the Law* chs. 5–7.

[15] My main concern in this section is with Hospital Orders: but since the 1983 Act has not been long in force, my discussion will have to focus on their use under the provisions of the *Mental Health Act* 1959 (which the 1983 Act replaced and revised). On the 1959 Act, and other provisions for mentally disordered offenders, see D A Thomas, *Principles of Sentencing* (referred to hereafter as *Thomas*) ch. 7; N Walker and S McCabe, *Crime and Insanity in England* vol. 2 (referred to hereafter as *Walker and McCabe*) ch. 5; *Report of the Committee on Mentally Abnormal Offenders* (referred to hereafter as *Butler*) ch. 14.

[16] See *Mental Health Act* 1983, s. 37(8); *Walker and McCabe* 72–3.

[17] See *Cox* (1968) 1 All E.R.386.   [18] See *Hatt* (1962) Crim.L.R.647.

portant step towards a properly Utilitarian 'occasionalism', which will treat an offender's past offence simply as the occasion for his appearance before the court: courts will then ask of any offender (disordered or not), not what penalty he deserves, but which of the available methods of disposal will be most economically effective in dealing with him; efficacy being measured primarily by the effect of the disposal on his future conduct and on the future incidence of crime, and economy by the cost of the disposal in human suffering and in resources.[19] The 1983 Act admittedly sets strict limits on the Utilitarian discretion which it allows the courts: the offender must be suffering from one of the specified kinds of disorder; his offence must be one for which he could be imprisoned. Nor does it *require* courts to take a strictly Utilitarian view: they may still send a disordered offender to prison on the grounds that he *deserves* punishment.[20] An occasionalist must deprecate these limits, and these vestiges of retributivism: but she may still claim that these provisions for mentally disordered offenders, and the way in which the courts have in fact tended to use them, can best be understood within the framework of a consequentialist perspective on punishment.

For the criteria actually used by the courts in deciding whether to make a Hospital Order do not usually refer back to the defendant's past offence, except insofar as that may be a basis for predicting his future conduct, but look to the future. If he is likely to benefit from hospital treatment (and if he needs to be detained in hospital for the protection of the public, so that a psychiatric Probation Order would not be appropriate), a Hospital Order should be made. Even if he has only been convicted of a minor offence the court may properly make a Hospital Order together with an indefinite Restriction Order, if 'in the interests of both the appellant and the public it [is] necessary for him to receive treatment for a protracted period in a secure hospital': for in that case 'the fact that the offence itself was of a minor character is neither here nor there'.[21] If on the other hand he is unlikely to benefit from hospital treatment; or if he needs to be securely detained but no place is available for him in a sufficiently secure hospital: he will be sent to prison.[22] Indeed, if for some reason a Hospital Order cannot be made on him, but he is 'suffering from some disorder of personality or instability of character which

[19] See *Walker and McCabe*, especially 101–2.
[20] See *Morris* (1961) 2 Q.B.237; *Gunnell* (1966) 50 Cr.App.R.242; *McBride* (1972) Crim.L.R.322.
[21] *Allison*, cited in *Thomas* 299.   [22] See *Thomas* 296–8.

makes [him] likely to commit grave offences in the future if left at large or released from a fixed term of imprisonment', he may receive an indefinite sentence of life imprisonment.[23] What justifies this sentence is not that it is 'proportionate' to the offence for which he has been convicted, which may only have been a (relatively) minor offence of arson or of robbery;[24] nor need the future offences which it is feared he might commit be of the same kind as the offence for which he has been convicted:[25] the point of the sentence is purely and simply to prevent the commission of future offences.

A consequentialist may thus claim that a mentally disordered offender's fate within the criminal process should depend entirely (and does in fact, in the courts, depend primarily) on which disposal will most efficiently serve the consequential aims of the penal system. Whether she receives a psychiatric disposal which is labelled 'non-punitive'; or a term of imprisonment which is labelled 'punitive': should depend not on some mysterious notion of what she deserves, but on which disposal is likely to have the most beneficial effects.

Such a claim raises some fundamental questions about the character and possibility of a consequentialist account of punishment. Can a consequentialist provide an acceptable account of the significance and purpose of punishment as a distinctive response to crime, by saying, for instance, that punishment is a particular kind of technique for controlling behaviour, which is to be preferred to other possible techniques if and insofar as it is likely to be more economically effective in securing the desired results? Or should we insist that punishment has a retributive meaning which cannot be captured within a consequentialist perspective; and that it differs from, for instance, a psychiatric disposal not merely in its relative efficiency as a *technique* for controlling behaviour, but in the moral status which it accords to the offender, and in the kind of relationship with him which it presupposes or tries to create? Might a consequentialist not be committed in the end to abandoning the practice of punishment altogether: might she not favour, at least as an ideal towards which our reformative efforts should ultimately be

---

[23] *Thomas* 301.

[24] See *Thornton* (1975) Crim.L.R.51 (*Thomas* 306); *Ashdown* (1973) 58 Cr.App.R.399. It should be noted, however, that in other cases the Court of Appeal has insisted that the offence for which the defendant has been convicted must itself be grave enough to warrant a very long sentence: see *Hodgson* (1967) 52Cr.App.R.113, and other cases cited and discussed in Sir R Cross and A J Ashworth, *The English Sentencing System* 49–51.

[25] See *Hildersley* (1974) Crim.L.R.197 (*Thomas* 304).

directed, a system of tribunals and disposals which, while its aim would be the humane and efficient prevention of harmful kinds of conduct, would not involve the infliction of *punishment* on offenders for their offences?[26] This would not of course yet show the consequentialist's perspective to be untenable, since she might insist that punishment *should* be abandoned: but it would show that there cannot be a consequentialist account of *punishment*, and that we must look elsewhere for an adequate account of its meaning, its purpose, and its possible justification.

I will return to these questions in Chapter 6, to argue that a justificatory account of punishment must appeal to values which can find no place within a purely consequentialist perspective; and that it is these values which make punishment a more appropriate response to crime than other, possibly more effective, techniques of behaviour-control. My immediate concern, however, is with the fact that the courts' actual treatment of disordered offenders is by no means whole-heartedly consequentialist: for though they do often appeal to the kinds of consequentialist consideration noted above, they may also appeal to quite different considerations which suggest that what is wrong with punishing a disordered offender is not that it may be ineffective or inefficient, but that it is in itself quite inappropriate.

Courts have certainly appealed to the retributivist demand that the punishment imposed on an offender should be proportionate to the offence for which he has been convicted: the Appeal Court has sometimes upheld sentences of life imprisonment which were imposed to prevent the commission of future offences rather than because of the gravity of the offence for which the defendant was convicted; but it has also overturned prison sentences which were imposed for that kind of reason, declaring that:

[t]he Courts exist to punish according to the law those convicted of offences. Sentences should fit crimes.[27]

It may also be partly for this reason that courts have been unhappy about cases in which they feel that they have to impose a prison sentence on a disordered offender for whom a Hospital Order would be more appropriate, but whom no suitable hospital is able or willing to admit.

---

[26] As some have argued: see, for instance, B Wootton, *Crime and the Criminal Law*.
[27] *Clarke* (1975) 61 Cr.App.R.320; see also *Eaton* (1976) Crim.L.R.390.

Judges took a judicial oath to do justice to all men and when they had to send men to prison because no secure hospital beds were available their judicial consciences were strained almost to breaking point.[28]

There may of course be consequentialist grounds for concern in such cases: that the offender would benefit from treatment in hospital; that his behaviour in prison is disruptive and difficult for both staff and inmates.[29] But if the offender was already disordered, and thus perhaps less than fully responsible, at the time of his offence, what strains the judicial conscience may be the retributivist thought that he does not *deserve* punishment for what he did.[30]

Such a retributivist thought, however, cannot explain why a Hospital Order should be appropriate for an offender who has only become disordered *since* his commission of an offence for which he was fully responsible, or whose disorder has no connection with the offence for which he has been convicted: but a Hospital Order may still be appropriate in such cases as these; and a judge may still feel uneasy if, for good consequentialist reasons, she has to send such an offender to prison. Why should this be so, if his offence was one which merits imprisonment, and if this is also the most economically effective way of dealing with him?

I suggest, in line with my earlier comments on capital punishment, that what is crucial here (apart from considerations of past deserts or of future consequences) is the offender's capacity to understand and respond to her imprisonment *as a punishment*: if she is now so disordered that she lacks this capacity she is not fit to be punished, whether or not she has committed an offence which merited punishment, and whether or not imprisonment would be the most efficient way of protecting others against her. For punishment aims, and must aim, if it is to be properly justified, to *address* the offender as a rational and responsible agent: if she cannot understand what is being done to her, or why it is being done, or how it is related as a punishment to her past offence, her punishment becomes a travesty. In Chapter 9 I will offer an account of the proper meaning and purpose of punishment which will explain this suggestion; show why this capacity is so important and what it must involve;

---

[28] *Officer* (1976) Crim.L.R.698; see also *McFarlane* (1975) 60 Cr.App.R.320; *Cox* (1968) 1 All E.R.386: but contrast *Watson* (1976) Crim.L.R.698.

[29] See *Report of the Committee of Inquiry into the United Kingdom Prison Services* (The May Report) paras.3.34–3.44.

[30] It was clear, for instance, that Officer, Cox and McFarlane were all disordered at the time of their offences.

and thus show why we cannot justifiably punish an offender who lacks it.

To say that we should not punish such an offender is not to say that he must simply be released: if his disorder is such that he is a danger to himself or to others he may still need to be detained; and if there is no available psychiatric treatment which can help him his detention may be nothing more than a kind of preventive or protective custody. Such detention may be longer and more restrictive than any prison term he would have received for his offence; and it clearly needs to be justified. That justification is not my main concern here: but it is at least arguable that someone who is so disordered that he is not fit to be punished should pass out of the jurisdiction of the criminal courts altogether, and be subject only to the ordinary, non-criminal provisions for 'compulsory admission' to hospital.[31] For he is to be detained not because he *has* committed an offence, but because he *is* dangerous: so why should the criteria for detaining him, and for deciding on his release, differ from those which govern the detention of someone who has not committed an offence; why should we retain a special category of Hospital and Restriction Orders for those convicted of offences?[32] What is more important for my present purposes, however, is to insist that such detention is not a kind of *punishment*, though some have portrayed it as that;[33] and that an adequate account of punishment will enable us to see how punishment differs, in its meaning and its justification, from such psychiatric detention, and in particular how it differs in the moral status which is ascribes to the offender. For punishment is justified as a response to the wrong-doing of someone who was and is a rational and responsible agent: part of what justifies psychiatric detention, however, is the fact that the disordered patient is no longer a rational and responsible agent.

Such an account of punishment will also explain why a sane offender may claim a *right* to be punished rather than being subjected to psychiatric treatment or to some other, possibly more effective, method of behaviour-modification. The point is not that punishment might be less unpleasant or restrictive for her than psychiatric detention, since the right to be punished is not simply a right to a less unpleasant or restrictive disposal: it is rather that punishment, unlike psychiatric detention, respects and addresses the offender as a rational and responsible agent.

[31] Under Part II of the *Mental Health Act* 1983.
[32] But see H Fingarette, *The Meaning of Criminal Insanity* 128–42; and the discussion of Restriction Orders in *Gardiner* (1967) Crim.L.R.231.
[33] See, for instance, T Szasz, *Law, Liberty, and Psychiatry*.

> Nothing is more certain than that a person who falls mad after
> a crime is committed shall not be tried for it.
>
> (Sir John Hawles)[34]

I have talked so far about the fate of convicted offenders who are
now disordered. But a disordered person who is suspected of an
offence may not even be brought to trial;[35] and if he is brought to
trial he may be found 'unfit to plead' ('under disability in relation to
the trial'), and be committed to hospital without being either tried
or convicted.[36] The various provisions for exempting the disordered from trial all raise similar problems: I will concentrate here
on the formal procedures for finding a defendant unfit to plead.

The criteria for such a finding have traditionally concerned the
defendant's ability to understand her trial.

> The humanity of the law of England ... has prescribed that no man shall
> be called upon to make his defence at a time when his mind is in that situ-
> ation as not to appear capable of so doing. For however guilty he may be,
> the enquiring into his guilt must be postponed to that season when, by col-
> lecting together his intellects, and having them entire, he shall be able so to
> model his defence as to ward off the punishment of the law.[37]

The crucial question to be decided was whether the defendant was

> of sufficient intellect to comprehend the course of proceedings in the trial
> so as to make a proper defence – to know that he might challenge any of you
> to whom he may object, and to comprehend the details of the evidence.[38]

More recently it has been suggested that the criteria for fitness to
plead should concern the defendant's ability to plead with understanding to the indictment; to understand the course of the trial and
the evidence brought during it; and to instruct her legal advisers. A
finding of unfitness to plead historically and in theory justified only
a postponement until such time, if ever, as the defendant should re-
cover: in practice, however, one who is found unfit to plead is now

---

[34] Quoted in *CLRC* 16.

[35] See *Butler* ch. 9; Whitehead, *Mental Illness and the Law* 86–8.

[36] *Criminal Procedure (Insanity) Act* 1964, ss.4–5. See *Butler* ch.10; *Second Report of the Committee on Criminal Procedure in Scotland* (referred to hereafter as *Thomson*) ch. 52; C Hampton, *Criminal Procedure* 199–200; G H Gordon, *The Criminal Law of Scotland* ch.10, ss.42–5; A R Poole, 'Standing Mute and Fitness to Plead'; *Walker* ch. 14.

[37] Lord Kenyon, speaking in *Frith* (1790) 22 St.Tr.307; quoted in *Walker* 224.

[38] Baron Alderson, speaking in *Pritchard* (1836) 7 Carrington & Payne 303; quoted in *Walker* 225.

brought to trial only if he recovers very rapidly, or if his plea of unfitness is found to have been fraudulent.[39]

While both justice and humanity are thought to preclude the trial of someone who cannot understand his trial, it is also thought to be important that the defendant *should* be tried if this is at all possible. The criteria for unfitness to plead have accordingly been strictly delimited, so that they capture only those who are seriously incapacitated: a disordered defendant who may conduct his defence rashly or imprudently is still fit to plead, so long as he can understand the course of the trial and the matters relevant to it;[40] so too is a defendant who is suffering from amnesia covering the period of the alleged offence.[41] The reasons for this latter ruling may be partly pragmatic – to allow amnesia to constitute unfitness to plead might open the door to too many fraudulent pleas of unfitness; it was also claimed in *Podola*, however, that fitness to plead is a matter of the defendant's present capacity to understand his trial, which is not impaired by amnesia. But if we are to decide which kinds and degree of disorder should constitute unfitness to plead, we must first ask *why* we should not try a seriously disordered defendant; and why it should be so important to try him if this is at all possible.

A disordered defendant's unfitness to plead depends on her condition at the time of her trial, not at the time of her alleged offence; she is not exempted from trial merely on the grounds that she would anyway be eligible for an insanity verdict. The most obvious reason for refusing to try her is the danger of convicting the innocent: if we try someone who cannot understand her trial we may convict a person who, had she been in possession of her faculties, could have rebutted the charges against her; and neither justice nor, usually, utility are served by the conviction of the innocent. Correlatively, the most obvious reason for insisting on trying the defendant if this is possible is the need to secure the conviction of the guilty: if it was too easy to avoid trial too many guilty people would evade the law's grasp. These reasons portray the criminal trial in essentially instrumental terms, as a procedure whose justifying aim (an aim which may itself be set by the demands either of justice or of efficient crime-prevention) is to secure the conviction and punishment of the guilty and the acquittal of the innocent; they specify conditions for the efficient pursuit of that aim. Such considerations are clearly im-

---

[39] See *Butler* 143 (on the criteria) and 147 (on the possibility of later trial).
[40] See *Robertson* (1968) 3 All E.R. 557.
[41] *Podola* (1959) 3 All E.R. 418. For a defence of this rule see *Butler* ch. 10, paras. 4–11; for the opposing view see N Walker, 'Butler v. The CLRC and Others'.

portant: but they do not, I think, tell the whole story, for two reasons.

First, though a conviction would often be unsafe if the defendant was unfit to plead, in *some* cases his guilt could surely be conclusively established even though he could neither understand nor take part in his trial: but even then ('however guilty he may be') he is not to be tried. But why should we not try, and convict, a defendant who, though he cannot understand what is going on in court, can be proved beyond reasonable doubt to be guilty of the offence with which he is charged? Is it simply because a court can never be sufficiently certain that it is dealing with such a case; or is there, as I will suggest, something *inherently* inappropriate in trying and convicting someone who can understand neither the trial nor the verdict?

Second, a finding of unfitness to plead does not allow the defendant to evade the law's clutches altogether.

When fairness to the accused requires that the trial should not there and then proceed, the public interest equally requires that the accused should not there and then be virtually acquitted untried.[42]

What this now means is that someone found unfit to plead is automatically committed to indefinite detention in hospital: though she has not been convicted of any offence, she finds herself in the same position as someone who is convicted of the offence charged and then committed to hospital under a Hospital Order together with an indefinite Restriction Order.

The reasons for such automatic detention are obvious enough: to secure the detention of those who are likely to be a danger to others; to deter those who might otherwise hope to avoid trial by claiming or pretending to be unfit to plead. The objection to it is equally obvious: someone who might have committed no offence, and who might have been acquitted and released had he been tried, is treated as a disordered offender. Someone who is disordered enough to be unfit to plead is admittedly also likely to be eligible for the ordinary process of compulsory admission to hospital: but that process requires a judgment that his detention 'is necessary for the health or safety of the patient or for the protection of other persons';[43] and it results in a less restrictive detention than a finding of unfitness to plead. This objection is sometimes given a pragmatic slant – that those committed to hospital in this way may labour under a sense of grievance which hinders their treatment:[44] but its true basis is surely

---

[42] Lord Cooper, in *Russell v HM Advocate* (1946) J.C.37, at 47.
[43] *Mental Health Act* 1983, s.3(2)c.   [44] See *Butler* ch. 10, para. 14; *RCCP* para. 223.

a requirement of justice; that a person should not be treated as an offender unless he has been proved to be one.

The fact that a finding of unfitness to plead results in detention rather than freedom provides another reason for insisting that the defendant should, if possible, be tried: if we care for her rights and interests we must give her a fair chance to secure an acquittal and thus avoid such detention. But there is more to the story than this, as we will see if we examine some of the reforms which have been suggested to current procedures.

One suggestion is that the issue of fitness to plead might be postponed until after the substantive issue of guilt or innocence has been tried, so that an innocent defendant may be acquitted and freed:[45] but this is bizarre, since the question of whether the substantive issue *can* be properly tried must depend on the question of whether the defendant is fit to plead. A more coherent possibility is found in the rule that a judge may postpone the issue of fitness to plead until the end of the prosecution's case: she may then decide that a disordered defendant has no case to answer, and order his acquittal and release.[46] But this is only a partial solution to the problem: a defendant who has a case to answer might still, were he fit, be able to secure an acquittal; and it is unjust that he should be liable to such a restrictive detention merely because he is not in a fit condition to answer the case against him.

A more radical suggestion would be that a disordered defendant should be found unfit to plead at the start of the trial, and should then pass out of the jurisdiction of the criminal court, to be liable to detention only by the ordinary non-criminal process of compulsory admission. For why should someone who has been charged with an offence be for that reason liable to detention, in the absence of firm evidence that she is dangerous to herself or to others; and why, even if she is dangerous, should she be liable to a more restrictive detention than someone who may be equally disordered and dangerous, but who happens not to have been charged with an offence? Even if we accept the arguable view that dangerously disordered *offenders* should be dealt with by the criminal courts, and should be liable to a more restrictive kind of detention than non-offenders,[47] this cannot justify such automatic and restrictive detention for someone who has not been proved to be either an offender or dangerous to others:

---

[45] See *CLRC* ss. 18–24; *Thomson* ch. 52, paras. 07–10; and Lord Devlin's comments in *Roberts* (1954) 2 All E.R.340.

[46] *Criminal Procedure (Insanity) Act* 1946 s.4; J Smith and B Hogan, *Criminal Law* 167–8.

[47] See n.32 above, and text thereat.

but it may incline us towards a different suggestion which has recently received some support, and which will bring into sharper focus the issue which is my main concern here.

The suggestion is that the trial of an unfit defendant should be replaced by a judicial 'inquiry into the facts' which will determine his fate. This inquiry should as far as possible follow the normal rules of a criminal trial; and the defendant should, if possible, be present and allowed to contribute to it. The inquiry may acquit him of the offence charged, in which case he must be released (or detained only briefly to allow the normal process of compulsory admission to hospital to be initiated); it may find that he committed the offence but was at the time so disordered as not to be responsible for it, in which case he is to be treated in the same way as someone acquitted by reason of insanity (i.e. he is to be committed to hospital as if under an indefinite Restriction Order); or it may find that he committed the offence charged and was at that time sane and responsible. But in this last case the court may not *convict* him.

If it were not for the accused's present disability the verdict would be a conviction, but we do not think that in the circumstances it should carry either the name or the effect of a conviction; and we have chosen the formula that 'the defendant should be dealt with as a person under disability'.[48]

Such a finding precludes any punishment for the defendant: but he may be subjected to a Hospital Order or to other special restrictions.

This suggestion respects the belief that disordered offenders should be dealt with by the criminal courts, whilst remedying the most objectionable aspect of the present law – the fact that someone found unfit to plead is automatically treated as if she were guilty. Its most striking feature, however, is that the inquiry which a criminal court is to hold into the defendant's guilt or innocence is not to be called a *trial*, and may not lead to the verdict of 'Guilty' which a trial may produce. What, then, is the significant difference between such an inquiry and a criminal trial?

It is not merely that the unfit defendant should not be punished: for a conviction can also lead to a Hospital Order. Nor is it that a conviction would be unsafe, in view of the possibility that 'some explanation could have been given if the defendant had been able to defend himself': for if 'the normal rules of evidence and burden of proof' are to apply to the inquiry, the court must acquit the defendant if the charge against him is not proved beyond reasonable

---

[48] *Butler* ch. 10, para. 24; the ingredients for this suggestion are drawn from *Butler* ch. 10, paras. 24–26, and *Thomson* ch. 52, paras. 15–24.

doubt, and must attend to that possibility if it raises a reasonable doubt.[49] Nor is it simply that his trial 'could result in some harrowing and intolerable scenes in court':[50] for this is as true of a judicial inquiry as it is of a trial; and a distressed or disruptive defendant can be removed from a trial, as he can from the inquiry, to avoid such scenes. So why should we believe that

to go through the motions of trying a person unable to understand what was taking place would be absurd and might be cruel,[51]

but yet subject him to such an inquiry?

A purely instrumental view of the criminal trial, which supposes that its purpose is simply to identify, by a conviction, those offenders who should be liable to the coercive provisions of the criminal law, and to save the innocent from such coercive provisions by acquitting them, can discern no significant difference between a criminal trial and a judicial inquiry into the facts: for in both cases the court's task is to discover the facts about the defendant's past conduct and present condition which are relevant to determining her future disposal. Her present disorder may in either case be a contingent obstacle to the attempt to discover whether she broke the law, and whether she was at the time sane and responsible, if it makes her unable to understand or contribute to the inquiry: but if we suppose that her disposal should depend on such facts about her past conduct that attempt must be made; and it is not rendered *inevitably* futile by her disordered lack of understanding. That supposition, whether it is based on a retributivist or a consequentialist view of the purpose of the criminal process, clearly underpins the suggestion that disordered defendants should be subjected to a judicial inquiry into the facts; and my concern here is with the significance of the distinction which that suggestion draws between such an inquiry and a criminal trial.

The significance of that distinction, and of the related distinction between a trial and the kind of psychiatric inquiry which may be held into someone's past conduct and present condition in order to determine his future disposal, cannot, I think, be understood in instrumental terms: for it depends on purposes which are *internal* to the trial. Central to a trial, as distinct from such judicial or psychiatric inquiries, is the idea that the defendant should *participate* in his trial: he is called to answer the charges laid against him; even if he is represented by counsel, it is for him to plead to the indictment and

---

[49] The quotations are from *Butler* ch. 10, para. 25 and para. 24.
[50] *Thomas* ch. 52, para. 16.   [51] *CLRC* s.21.

to answer, or admit, the charges. His participation is important not merely because it gives the court a better chance of reaching an accurate verdict, but because of the very meaning of the trial and the status which it accords to the defendant: for whereas a judicial or psychiatric inquiry may be held *on* a person, a criminal trial is a process of argument and judgment which is meant to be conducted *with* the defendant; a process which respects and addresses him as a rational and responsible agent who can be called to answer for his actions. Similarly, the crucial difference between a criminal verdict of 'Guilty' and a judicial inquiry's finding that a disordered defendant committed the offence with which he was charged is that the verdict is passed not just *on* the defendant but *to* him: he is asked to understand and accept it as a proper judgment on his past conduct.

This suggestion, that the defendant's participation is central to the meaning of the criminal trial, will be more fully explained in Chapter 4. It will show why we should neither try nor convict a defendant who is so disordered that he cannot understand his trial: for if the aim of the trial is not just to make an accurate determination of the facts, as a basis for further decisions about the defendant's disposal, but to engage *with* the defendant in a rational process of argument and judgment, the trial and conviction of someone who cannot understand or take part in such a process becomes a travesty of the due process of law. It can have neither the meaning nor the purpose which are integral to that process. We will then also see more clearly how a criminal trial differs from the kind of judicial inquiry which may be appropriate for those who are unfit to plead; and why a sane defendant may insist on her *right* to be tried – and convicted.

I have discussed three ways in which a mentally disordered defendant may be exempted from the criminal process of trial and punishment. I have suggested that a consequentialist or instrumentalist view of that process cannot adequately explain these exemptions, which should rather be explained in terms of purposes and values which are *internal* to that process; by reference, in particular, to the idea that it is a process to which the defendant is meant to respond, and in which he is meant to participate, as a rational and responsible agent. My task now is to explain and defend this suggestion; to provide an account of the criminal process which will show what such participation must involve and why it should be thought important. But two further preliminary comments are needed before I embark on this task.

First, I have clearly begged some large questions about the concept of mental disorder and its relevance to these exemptions from the criminal process; questions which will remain begged in what follows. The mere fact that a defendant is in some way mentally disordered does not of course make her unfit for trial or punishment; and I have said a little about the kind of effect which her disorder must have if it is to make her unfit. But the notion of mental disorder is itself controversial. Some would say that we should see *all* crime as a product of mental disorder, which would make it pointless to try to distinguish sane from disordered offenders.[52] Others argue that the concept of mental disorder is itself illegitimate: we should either abandon it altogether or at least not suppose that it has any bearing on an agent's responsibility.[53] If my discussion of the treatment of mentally disordered defendants is to play any part in my argument, must I not therefore first explain and justify my use of the notion of mental disorder itself?

But any finite argument must presuppose something; and I cannot here provide a full discussion of the notion of mental disorder.[54] I believe, however, and will assume here, that there are genuine mental disorders which impair a person's capacity for rational thought and action, and which thus make it inappropriate to respond to him as we do to normal, rational and responsible agents. Insofar as a person is seriously disordered he is unable, or far less able than others, to think or deliberate rationally; to understand the nature and quality of his own beliefs, feelings and actions, or the actions and responses of other people; and to guide his actions in the light of rational policies and values. This is not to say that every mental disorder will destroy these capacities over the whole range of a person's life: disorders vary greatly in the range and severity of their effects. To see whether someone's disorder makes it inappropriate to maintain our normal attitudes and responses to him, we must ask what kinds of rational capacity are presupposed by those normal responses, and how far that presupposition is satisfied in the particular case.

Thus if we are to decide whether someone was responsible for a past offence, we must ask whether she had the relevant capacities for understanding her situation and acting rationally in it. If we are to

---

[52] See, for instance, K Menninger, *The Crime of Punishment*.
[53] See, for instance, T Szasz, *The Myth of Mental Illness; Law, Liberty, and Psychiatry*.
[54] But see H Fingarette, *The Meaning of Criminal Insanity*; H Fingarette and A F Hasse, *Mental Disabilities and Criminal Responsibility*; also R A Duff, 'Mental Disorder and Criminal Responsibility'.

decide whether she is now fit to be tried or punished, we must ask what her role is meant to be in her trial and punishment: she is unfit to be tried or punished if she lacks the capacities which that role requires; and it requires, I will argue, a capacity for certain kinds of moral thought and action.

My omission of a detailed account of the concept of mental disorder should be rendered less disturbing by the fact that my discussion of our treatment of disordered defendants serves a purely heuristic role in relation to the argument of this book. I do not aim to *justify* my account of the criminal process by claiming that it explains, as other accounts cannot, why we should exempt the disordered from that process: my hope is rather that by asking whether and why we should make such provisions for disordered defendants we may become aware of dimensions of the criminal process which are too often overlooked, but whose significance is ultimately independent of these provisions.

Second, we must remember the dual nature of the law's provisions for the disordered defendant: they do not just *exempt* him from liabilities (to trial and punishment) to which others are subject, but also *expose* him to kinds of coercion to which others are not liable. A sane defendant is liable to continued detention or coercion only if she is convicted; and her sentence will set strict limits on the duration and nature of that detention or coercion: but a disordered defendant may suffer continued detention without being either tried or convicted; and that detention may be indefinite in duration and more intrusive in character. The fate of someone found unfit to plead, or not guilty by reason of insanity, or unfit to be punished, may thus often seem worse than the fate of someone who is punished for an offence of which she has been convicted.

We may for this reason talk of a sane defendant's *right* to be tried or punished, rather than being detained as unfit for trial or punishment. Such talk may seem unproblematic in this context: for insofar as psychiatric detention may be more restrictive and intrusive than punishment an offender has an interest in claiming such a right in order to avoid such detention. But I think that this is too superficial a view of the right to trial and punishment: what is wrong with refusing to try or to punish a sane offender is not merely that it exposes him to more restrictive or intrusive kinds of treatment, but rather that it denies him the moral status which is his due, and which his trial and punishment would respect. An adequate account of the criminal process must show both why we should exempt the disordered from that process and why we should recognise the sane defendant's right to be tried or punished; and such an account will show that the right to trial and punishment is more than the right to trial and punishment *rather than* psychiatric detention.

2
Criticism, Blame and Moral Punishment

These acts have in fact been forbidden and subjected to punishment not only because they are dangerous to society, and so
ought to be prevented, but also for the sake of gratifying the
feeling of hatred – call it revenge, resentment, or what you will
– which the contemplation of such conduct excites in healthily
constituted minds.... It will follow that criminal law is in
the nature of a persecution of the grosser forms of vice, and an
emphatic assertion of the principle that the feeling of hatred
and the desire of vengeance above-mentioned are important
elements of human nature which ought in such cases to be
satisfied in a regular public and legal manner.

J F Stephen, *Liberty, Equality, Fraternity*, p. 152

Morality and law are alike rule systems for controlling behaviour, and what blame is to one, punishment is to the other.
Since they are closely analogous as techniques for controlling
undesirable conduct, by making its consequences in different
ways disagreeable, the principles for awarding them largely
coincide.

S I Benn, 'An Approach to the Problems of Punishment',

p. 340

I MORAL BLAME AND CRIMINAL PUNISHMENT

I want to portray the criminal process of trial and punishment as one
in which the defendant is meant to *participate* as an active subject, not
merely as a passive object. To this end I will relate the proper meaning of that formal criminal process to the informal activities of
moral criticism and blame. To criticise someone is to charge her
with a moral offence; to blame her is to hold her guilty of, and perhaps to punish her for, that offence. Correlatively, to indict someone for a criminal offence is to offer a particular criticism of his
conduct; to try him is to seek to determine the justice of that criticism; to convict him is to blame him publicly for that offence; and
the punishment which he may then receive must be understood, I
will claim, by reference to our responses to those whom we blame
for moral offences.

My concern in this chapter is with the proper meaning of moral criticism and blame; more specifically, it is with the activity of criticising and blaming a person *to her face* for a *past act* of moral wrongdoing. Blame need not involve this activity: it may simply involve forming a private *judgment* on someone's conduct; or having a certain *attitude* – of resentment, indignation, anger or contempt – towards her because of her wrong-doing; or criticising her to others in her absence. Blame may also be directed at past or present attitudes, habits and character-traits, or at present acts or omissions, as well as at past acts. But to see the connections between moral blame and the criminal process we must attend to the activity of blaming – criticising, rebuking, reproving, condemning – a person to her face for some past action.[1]

That activity need not take any one form, and need not involve saying 'I blame you'. What makes an utterance or action one of blaming someone is that it expresses to him my judgment that he acted wrongfully; a judgment both on his action, as being wrong, and on him as its agent, as having neither excuse nor justification for it. To express such a judgment to a person *is* to blame him: 'You acted wrongly (despicably, unjustly, dishonestly), and I don't blame you for it' is usually nonsensical. I might sometimes say 'You acted wrongly, but I don't blame you', where the 'but' indicates that I am withdrawing the normal implication of my judgment: but this will be because I accept that the agent did have some kind of excuse or partial justification for what he did; or because I can respect, though I cannot share, the moral beliefs which informed his action.

In blaming someone I may also express a certain attitude towards her and her conduct; resentment or indignation, anger or contempt, even pity. What unifies these attitudes is the judgment of wrong-doing which informs them. What differentiates them is the particular content or spirit of that judgment, or the kind of relationship which they presuppose with the person towards whom they are directed. I can resent only injuries to myself or to people connected to me, but I can be indignant at any wrong; only certain kinds of wrong-doing, such as petty acts of spite or cowardice, are possible objects of contempt; and the pity or compassion which may be felt for a wrong-doer involve a distinctive moral concern, and a distinctive conception of moral good and evil.[2]

---

[1] On the various kinds and aspects of blame, see E Beardsley, 'A Plea for Deserts' and 'Moral Disapproval and Moral Indignation'; R B Brandt, 'Blameworthiness and Obligation'; S Cohen, 'Distinctions among Blame Concepts'.
[2] See ch. 2 (7) below.

An account of moral blame must, therefore, discuss the kinds of judgment and attitude which it expresses, and the kinds of relationship which it may presuppose or seek to create with the person blamed. But what kind of connection may we find between moral blame and the criminal process?

Blame, like punishment, is intended to induce suffering in an alleged offender for an alleged offence. I will say more later about the nature of this suffering: but blame is clearly meant to be unpleasant. It must also purport to be of an offender for an offence: while I can blame someone whom I believe to be innocent, in blaming him I allege, albeit fraudulently, that he *has* done some wrong for which I am blaming him. This conceptual connection between blame and wrong-doing may be emphasised by a retributivist account of blame as a proper response to wrong-doing: but it can also figure in a consequentialist view of blame as a technique for achieving certain further ends, thus distinguishing blame, as a mechanism which operates through the purported condemnation of an offender, from other kinds of social mechanism.

This definitional point provides only a limited analogy between blame and the criminal process: my concern is with the more substantial claim that the aims and principles of the criminal law should be closely related to those of moral blame. This claim holds, at its strongest, that there should ideally be an identity of aims and principles between the legal and moral spheres, and that criminal convictions and punishments should have the same purpose as moral blame. The criminal law, therefore, should ideally prohibit all and only such actions as are seriously immoral, *because* they are immoral; and the criteria of criminal liability should accordingly match the criteria of moral responsibility.[3] In its weaker version it holds that, while criminal punishment may properly have purposes beyond those of moral blame, an essential part of its meaning and justification lies in its relation to moral blame; and that immorality should be at least a necessary, if not a sufficient, condition of criminal liability. I will defend the latter thesis, and explore the extent to which the stronger thesis can be maintained.

Both retributivists and consequentialists may find close connections in meaning and purpose between blame and punishment, since both may see the punishment which is imposed on a criminal as a

[3] The view that the criteria of criminal liability should ideally match those of moral responsibility may of course be maintained independently of such claims about the proper purposes of the criminal law; see H L A Hart, 'Legal Responsibility and Excuses' 44–9.

formal or dramatic version of the blame imposed on a moral wrong-doer. In Stephen's view criminal punishment serves to express and to satisfy the feelings of hatred and resentment which vice properly excites in 'healthily constituted minds', and which are expressed less drastically in moral blame: 'the sentence of the law is to the moral sentiment of the public what a seal is to hot wax'.[4] A consequentialist, on the other hand, might suggest that

Moral criticism is a mild form of punishment; its occurrence is a sanction, the operation of which can warn and teach just as do criminal codes and criminal proceedings. Moral criticism, like legal sanctions, is a device for social control that is justified – at any rate, among other things – by its good effects.[5]

My own account of the relations between moral blame and the criminal process will emerge later; my task now is to give an account of moral blame itself.

2 CONSEQUENTIALISM AND BLAME

I cannot hope in one chapter to do justice to the rich and complex variety of ways in which blame may figure in our relationships with each other; my aim is rather to sketch the features of moral blame which are relevant to the purposes of this book.

I will shortly offer an account of blame which may be called 're-tributivist', insofar as it finds the meaning and purpose of blame in its character as an appropriate response to moral wrong-doing, but I will begin by sketching and criticising a simple consequentialist account. A consequentialist might argue that our habit of blaming others is unproductive or harmful, and that we should find other ways of modifying their conduct; or she may believe that blame, and the attitudes and habits of thought which belong with it, can play a useful role in our social relationships. I will argue, however, that moral blame plays a central and ineliminable part in our re-lationships with each other as members of a moral community which cannot be explained in consequentialist terms. I will not deny that blame serves certain further purposes concerned with the modi-fication of attitudes and conduct, but its relation to those purposes is logical rather than contingent: what makes blame appropriate as a way of pursuing its proper aims is not its contingent efficiency as a

---

[4] J F Stephen, *A History of the Criminal Law of England* vol. 2, 81.
[5] R B Brandt, 'Determinism and the Justifiability of Moral Blame' 150; see also S I Benn, 'An Approach to the Problems of Punishment'; P H Nowell-Smith, *Ethics* 301–4.

means to them, but its accordance with the values which those aims themselves embody. There are more subtle consequentialist accounts of blame than those which I discuss here; accounts which posit different and more complex aims for blame: but the account I offer will show the inadequacy of any consequentialist account which posits, as such accounts must typically posit, a purely contingent or instrumental relationship between moral blame and its justifying aims or purposes.

To justify a habit of blaming moral wrong-doers, a consequentialist must show both that its benefits outweigh its costs and that those benefits cannot be more economically produced by other means. The most obvious benefit which blame may bring is the modification of the future conduct of the person blamed: by blaming him for moral defects of conduct or character we hope so to change his attitudes and motives that he will behave better in the future. But other benefits may also accrue: we may reinforce our own attitudes and habits, or those of others; we may give ourselves and others, particularly those injured by a wrongful act, the satisfaction of seeing its perpetrator condemned. The cost of blame consists primarily in the distress it may cause: but we must also attend to any harmful side-effects which a willingness to blame may have on our dispositions.

Blame may thus be seen as a social technique for securing certain desirable ends, and it may then be thought that the judgment that someone is blameworthy depends logically on the utility of blaming him; so too with praise:

> ... although, in the view of a Utilitarian, only the useful is praiseworthy, he is not bound to maintain that it is necessarily worthy of praise in proportion as it is useful. ... [We] must mean by calling a quality 'deserving of praise', that it is expedient to praise it, with a view to its future production: accordingly, in distributing our praise of human qualities, ... we have to consider primarily not the usefulness of the quality, but the usefulness of the praise.[6]

Such a consequentialist is open to the familiar objection that the pursuit of utility may sanction blame which is not *deserved*: the blaming of the innocent, and a refusal to accept excuses which should in justice be accepted.[7] These possibilities are most obvious when we

---

[6] H Sidgwick, *The Methods of Ethics* 428; see also J J C Smart, *An Outline of a System of Utilitarian Ethics* 49–56, and 'Free-will, Praise and Blame'; and the Utilitarian account of responsibility offered in M Schlick, 'When is a Man Responsible?'.

[7] See R L Franklin, *Freewill and Determinism* ch. 9; N Gallagher, 'Utilitarian Blame – Retrospect and Prospects'.

attend to the beneficial effects which blaming someone may have on or for *other* people; but they may arise even if we attend only (as a strict consequentialist cannot) to its effects on the person blamed: for it is not obvious that the conditions which render blame undeserved are equally, or only, those conditions which render it ineffective or unnecessary as a means of modifying the future conduct of the person blamed.

Our consequentialist may reply that any benefits secured by blaming the innocent will be outweighed by its costs, in pain, resentment and loss of trust; or that there are good reasons, connected with the utility of certain kinds of expectation and relationship, for maintaining a practice which limits blame to those who are morally at fault.[8] But even if she could sustain such a claim for the utility of blaming only the guilty, she is wrong to found judgments of blameworthiness on the utility of blame; for such judgments are logically prior to any acts of blaming. To blame someone is to express the judgment that he is blameworthy; that he *deserves* blame, independently of considerations of utility: we cannot explain that judgment, or its justification, in terms of the utility of blaming him. It is of course possible, and could be useful, to blame a person whom we believe to be innocent: but the sense of that blame still depends on the judgment of blameworthiness which it dishonestly expresses.

But we have yet to see the fundamental defect in any such consequentialist account of blame. To see this we may construct a modified account which, while insisting that the justifying aim of blame lies in its instrumental utility as a technique for producing certain desirable results (in particular the modification of the attitudes and conduct of the person blamed), allows that voluntary wrong-doing is a necessary, if non-consequentialist, condition of justified blame. Thus our use of this technique is to be constrained by the requirement that the person blamed must be blameworthy; and the claim that he is blameworthy must express a justified judgment on the moral character of his conduct which does not depend on the utility of blaming him for that conduct. Blaming someone, then, requires a two-stage justification: we must show first that he is blameworthy, and then that it would be useful to blame him.

Such an account may avoid the charge that it commits us to blaming the innocent: but it is still inadequate as an account of the justifying purpose of blaming the guilty.

The fundamental objection to any such consequentialist account of blame is that it portrays blame as a *manipulative technique* for the

[8] Compare J Rawls, 'Two Concepts of Rules'.

modification of attitudes and behaviour. Decisions about whether to blame someone to her face may often be determined in part by consequentialist considerations; and blaming a person necessarily involves an attempt to modify her attitudes and conduct (unless she has already made or undergone the relevant change for herself): but this consequentialist perspective distorts the nature of that attempt, and the role and significance of blame in our lives and relationships.

The relevant issues can best be clarified by focusing my discussion on a particular example – so long as we bear in mind that what is true of one example may not be true of other kinds or contexts of blame.

I find that a friend, Jasper, is exploiting his position at work to make sexual advances to his secretaries: he uses his expense account to wine, dine and seduce them, and his position of authority to pressure them into accepting his advances. My reaction to this discovery of course depends on my position as well as on my own moral views: I may be concerned about the harm he has done to his victims, to his wife, or to the proper functioning of our office; I may be indignant at his harassment of these women, and at his abuse of his position of trust and authority; I may be disgusted by his sexism and his dishonesty, and resentful if he has used me to assist these activities; I may pity him for what he has become, as well as feeling sympathy for his victims. Each of these reactions involves judging his conduct to be inconsistent with the moral demands which I take to be binding on him as they are on me; and each involves seeing in his actions a betrayal of the values on which our relationships with each other, and our existence as a moral community, depend.

Whether I criticise Jasper's conduct to his face, and the form which any such criticism should take, depends on various factors: have I the right or the duty to intervene; will my intervention do any good; how does he view his own conduct? I will return to these questions later: my present concern is with the consequentialist claim that the primary purpose of such criticism or blame is so to modify Jasper's motives that he will in future avoid such conduct; and with the question of *how* blaming him may secure this desirable change in him. We can distinguish three possibilities.

(a) By appealing to the values on which my judgment of his conduct is founded ('Don't you see how dishonest and corrupt that is?') I bring home to him the wrongness of his conduct: I remind him of values for which he already cares, or bring him to understand and to care for moral demands by which he was not previously moved.

My blame gives him reason to modify his conduct: it persuades him to judge his past actions, and thus to guide his future conduct, by those moral values which inform and justify the blame itself.

(b) He is unmoved by my moral appeals, but finds my criticism so unpleasant or inconvenient that he will try to avoid it in future by behaving, or seeming to behave, as he knows I think he should. My blame still gives him reason to behave differently; but the prudential considerations which now lead him to judge his past actions as 'wrong', and to modify his future conduct, are quite different from the moral considerations which justify my criticism of those actions.

(c) Blaming him operates non-rationally, to induce a change in his motives and attitudes which is not mediated by his understanding and acceptance of *reasons* for condemning his past actions or for modifying his future conduct. We can imagine here a kind of psychological pressure or manipulation akin, perhaps, to a process of conditioning or aversion therapy.

Blaming Jasper might have these three kinds of effect on his attitudes and his conduct (I will comment later on the oversimplified character of these distinctions between them). These are not three ways of producing the *same* effect: for their effects – moral reform, prudential change, non-rational conditioning – differ. But if my aim is to modify Jasper's future conduct; and if my specification of that aim makes no essential reference to his motives, being only that he stops harassing his secretaries: I may see these as three ways of securing *that* effect. And it is that kind of effect which is often central to consequentialist accounts of blame; according to which the primary purpose of blame is to produce more acceptable behaviour from the person blamed.[9] In deciding whether and how to blame Jasper such a consequentialist must therefore ask whether blame is likely to be effective in any of these ways, and which of them will most efficiently secure the desired end; but she must also attend, of course, to any relevant side-effects which these different ways of trying to achieve that end may have on Jasper or on others.

So long as the pain and any harmful side-effects caused by blame are likely to be outweighed by the benefits it secures, such a consequentialist may regard blame as justified if it is likely to secure the desired modification in behaviour by any of these three methods. But she may also see reason to prefer, in general, to use the method

---

[9] See n. 5 and 6 above.

of moral persuasion. For this method, if it works, is likely to be more lastingly effective: one who believes for himself that such actions are wrong is more likely to avoid them than one whose reason for avoiding them is merely the chance of being blamed if he is found out; one who understands why such actions are wrong is more likely to identify and avoid them than one who has only been subjected to non-rational psychological pressure; and people will be happier and more cooperative if they realise that they are being appealed to as rational moral agents, rather than being coerced by threats or conditioned by non-rational means.[10]

Such reasons for preferring the method of moral persuasion rest on some large empirical claims; and such a justification of blame would also need to show that it is more economically effective than other methods of preventing wrongful conduct which do not operate through the criticism and condemnation of such conduct. But we can identify the fundamental defect in such a consequentialist view of blame without pursuing these issues.

3 BLAME AS MORAL PERSUASION

Blame is portrayed, on this consequentialist view, as a technique; as something we do *to* someone in order to modify her conduct. Though it focuses, necessarily, on an alleged moral offence, the offence is the occasion rather than the primary justification for blame, warning us that its agent may, if unchecked, behave in similarly undesirable ways in the future, and that we may therefore need to modify her conduct by blaming her. As a technique, then, blame is contingently related to the ends which it serves: the specification of those ends makes no essential reference to blame as the means by which they are to be achieved, and the justification of blame depends on its contingent efficacy in achieving them.

I will claim, against this view, that blame is a kind of moral argument *with* another person. Blame is focused on and justified by the other's wrong-doing. It also aims, normally, to modify her attitudes and conduct: but the means by which that modification is to be achieved are as important as the end. Indeed, the means enter into the specification of the end itself: for the end is that of moral reform or persuasion; we cannot separate blame from that end as a means which is only contingently related to it.

---

[10] She might also attend to the suggestion that blame is more likely to have the desired effect if it is seen to be deserved – i.e. if it is seen to express a justified judgment on the agent's conduct: see Franklin, *Freewill and Determinism* 166; J Charvet, 'Criticism and Punishment'.

In blaming Jasper I claim that he acted wrongly: there were good moral reasons, which he could and should have seen for himself, why he should not have acted thus. In expressing this judgment on his conduct I attempt to engage him in a moral discussion of that conduct, and to persuade him to accept this judgment on it. I tell him that and why I think he acted immorally, and thus challenge him to respond to this moral charge: to admit it and accept my criticism, or to offer some defence of his conduct. If he already shares my view, and blames himself for what he has done, I will be expressing my agreement with his own self-criticism: but if he does not already agree with me my criticism is an attempt to persuade him to share my view of his conduct; to see and to accept the moral considerations which justify that view. I may try to show him that his conduct was at odds with moral values which he himself accepts; or to persuade him of the significance and relevance of values by which he was previously unmoved. If he comes to accept my judgment on his past conduct, he must also agree that he should act differently in future, if the occasion arises. Thus, in persuading him to accept my criticism of his past conduct I also persuade him to modify his future conduct. Such a modification may not in fact be at stake, or may not be central to my intentions in blaming him: but it is part of the normal purpose of blame.

It matters crucially, however, not just *that* I persuade him, but *how* I persuade him; *what* I persuade him of, and what kind of change I secure in his attitudes and future conduct. Suppose he comes to see his past actions as 'wrong', and thus to modify his future conduct, not because he grasps and accepts the moral reasons on which my criticism is founded, but because he thinks it imprudent to persist in conduct which attracts such inconvenient responses; or because the emotional pressure to which I subject him makes him so anxious that he avoids such conduct in future, despite seeing no moral substance to his anxiety. I have now succeeded in the pragmatic aim of so modifying his motives and attitudes that his future conduct accords, externally, with my beliefs about how he should behave: but my blame has failed in its *proper* aim, which was to persuade him (by a process of moral argument which seeks his understanding and acceptance of relevant moral reasons) to judge his past conduct and guide his future conduct by those moral standards which inform my criticism of him.

Suppose instead that I fail to change his beliefs, attitudes or conduct: he listens and responds to my criticism, but remains unpersuaded. He may claim that I have misinterpreted his actions; or that they were consistent with the values which he and I share, or with those to which he himself was and is committed. My criticism has now failed to achieve its proper aim of persuading him to accept it, as well as the pragmatic aim of modifying his conduct. But if he responds to it seriously it has not been a complete failure in relation to its proper end; it has indeed achieved significant success – in engaging him in a moral examination of his conduct. For though blame, like other kinds of rational argument, aims at persuasion, its initial purpose is to engage the other person in a serious moral discussion; and it fails in *that* purpose only if he refuses to listen at all, or refuses to respond with any kind of moral seriousness.

Blame, like other modes of argument which seek the voluntary participation and assent of the other person, is necessarily fallible; for Jasper may remain deaf to, or unpersuaded by, my criticism. It is essential too that *I* should be prepared to be persuaded by *him* to modify my original judgment on his conduct: to be shown that I had misinterpreted his actions, or that they were consistent with the values which we share; or even to be brought to modify my own moral beliefs in the light of the values to which he appeals in justifying his conduct. Perhaps there is no real possibility that Jasper will thus persuade me (a readiness to be persuaded should not be mistaken for a half-hearted commitment to the values in which I believe): but a proper awareness of my own fallibility, and of the complexity and difficulty of moral understanding, requires me to attend seriously to any response to my criticism and to be ready, if necessary, to modify my own judgments. For I can properly aim to persuade Jasper to accept my judgment on his conduct only insofar as I believe that judgment to express a just and accurate understanding of the moral character of that conduct. Indeed, the proper aim of my criticism is to persuade him to see and to accept, not *my* judgment, but the truth about the moral character of his conduct; to engage *with* him in a search for and an attempt to understand that truth, not simply to force my own fallible and imperfect judgment on him.

If I fail to persuade Jasper of the justice of my criticism, I might look for other ways to stop him harassing his secretaries. Perhaps I can make the consequences of such conduct so unpleasant for him that he will be prudentially deterred from it; or bully and pressurise him into behaving as I think he should. Such methods may effectively modify his conduct: but they are not, and logically cannot be, ways of achieving the ends proper to moral blame; for they are not ways of bringing him to understand and accept the moral considerations which justify my criticism of him.

But why should this, rather than the efficient modification of behaviour, be the proper aim of moral blame? Why should moral blame, as thus portrayed, be the appropriate response to the wrongdoings of others? Why should we try to modify their conduct only by means of such rational moral persuasion?

The answer lies, not in the consequential efficiency of this method of modifying conduct, but in the moral demand that we should respect others as rational and autonomous agents, which forbids us to manipulate those with whom we deal. I manipulate someone if I try to get her to think, feel or act in a certain way by any means other than offering her relevant and appropriate reasons to think, feel or act thus. I am then treating her merely as a means, not as an end in herself; and failing to accord her the respect which I owe to her as a rational and autonomous agent. For that respect requires me to allow, assist and encourage her to conduct her own life and determine her own actions in the light of her own understanding. It does not forbid me to try to persuade her to change her beliefs, attitudes and conduct: but it does impose strict requirements on the kind of change which I may try to bring about, and on the methods by which I may try to bring it about. For if she is to think and act as a rational and autonomous agent any change in her thoughts and actions must be mediated and structured by her own understanding of the reasons which justify or require that change. If I am to treat her as a rational and autonomous agent it is therefore that kind of change which I must try to bring about; and the methods which I use must be appropriate to securing that kind of change.

This means, firstly, that I may try to get her to behave, or think, or feel differently only by offering her reasons to do so – reasons which she must grasp and accept for herself. Thus I manipulate Jasper if I get him to stop harassing his secretaries only by a kind of emotional pressure which plays on his irrational fears and anxieties. I have secured a change in his behaviour by methods which do not involve bringing him to see good reason to behave differently, and do not appeal to him as a rational agent. It means, secondly, that I must offer her what I take to be good and appropriate reasons for behaving differently: for a rational and autonomous agent is one who acts in the light, not just of some reason or other, but of good and appropriate reasons; it is therefore such reasons that I must offer her if I am to treat her as a rational and autonomous agent. I breach this requirement if I lie to her. If I persuade Jasper to stop harassing his secretaries by telling him, untruthfully, that he will be sacked if he carries on like this, I have certainly persuaded him to modify his conduct by offering him reason to do so: but I have equally certainly failed to treat or respect him as a rational agent. I have instead manipulated him by lying to him – by offering him, as a good reason for action, what is not (since it is untrue) a reason at all. But I also breach this requirement if I offer her what I regard as bad or inappropriate reasons: for to persuade someone to act for bad or inappropriate reasons is not to persuade her to act as a rational and autonomous agent. (This could also be portrayed as a kind of dishonesty: to offer someone a reason for action is to purport to offer her a good and appropriate reason; in offering her what I actually take to be a bad or inappropriate reason I am thus guilty of a kind of dishonesty or pretence.)

What counts as a good or appropriate reason depends on the context. It must be appropriate to what I am trying to persuade her to do, to what justifies or motivates my attempt to persuade her, and to my relationship with her; and there will often be both disagreement and uncertainty about what kinds of reason are thus appropriate. I will not try here to discuss what kinds of reason might be appropriate in other cases and other contexts: my present concern is simply with the kinds of reason which I can properly offer Jasper in an attempt to persuade him to stop harassing his secretaries.

What is crucial here is that I am trying to bring Jasper to behave as he *ought* to behave: it is the belief that his present conduct is morally wrong that both motivates and justifies my attempt to get him to behave differently. In such a case the reasons which I offer him for behaving differently should properly be *identical* with the reasons which justify my belief that he ought to behave differently and my attempt to persuade him to behave differently. I should, that is, try to persuade him to see that and why his present conduct is wrong, and thus to see that and why he should behave differently; and this is the proper purpose of moral criticism and blame. For suppose that I instead try to bribe him to leave his secretaries alone, by holding out the prospect of some financial gain, or perhaps a promotion; or that I try simply to deter him from his conduct by making its consequences unpleasant for him. I now offer him, indeed create for him, reasons which are inappropriate and irrelevant to the action I am urging on him. It is not the desire for personal gain or the fear of unpleasant consequences which should lead him not to harass his secretaries, but his recognition of the wrong involved in harassing them.

In offering him that kind of reason I cease to treat him as a rational moral agent: for I no longer try to bring him to guide his conduct in the light of the appropriate kinds of moral consideration; I instead use his morally irrelevant desires and anxieties as a means of controlling his conduct.[11]

Blame, as I have portrayed it, is thus an appropriate response to Jasper's wrong-doing because it respects and addresses him as a rational and autonomous moral agent: it aims to persuade him to see and accept for himself the wrongfulness of his past conduct, and therefore to modify his future conduct. The demand that I should not manipulate him determines the ends which I may pursue in my dealings with him. So in trying to stop him harassing his secretaries my aim should not be simply to bring his conduct into external conformity with the appropriate moral standards, but to bring him to act morally and autonomously – to act rightly because he sees for himself that he should do so. It thus also determines the means which I may use to achieve my ends: for neither prudential deterrence nor non-rational pressure are possible ways of trying to secure such a moral improvement in his conduct. It should be noted too that in responding in this spirit to Jasper's wrong-doing I treat him as an equal; as someone whom I may try to persuade, but may not simply try to control or manipulate. I appeal to him as someone who can and should recognise and accept for himself the moral standards by which I judge his conduct, and my own; I am ready to listen to his arguments, and to be persuaded by him to modify my own judgments; and I am ready to respond to, and if necessary to accept, *his* criticisms of *my* conduct and attitudes; I see us *both* as fallible moral agents who are subject to the demands of morality, and who may fail to grasp or respond appropriately to those demands.

We can now see why the consequentialist account of blame which I sketched above is open to the charge that it makes blame manipu-

<hr />

[11] I might of course offer him other kinds of reason for action. Instead of *creating* new prudential reasons for him to behave as he should, I might remind him of prudential reasons which already exist; I warn him, truthfully, that if he carries on like this he is likely to be sacked, or be beaten up by irate secretaries or their husbands. Or I might show him that in terms of his own moral beliefs (which I regard as corrupt) he should not be behaving as he is. Do I now manipulate him, by offering him the wrong kind of reasons for action; or do I at least to some degree respect his autonomy, by drawing to his attention considerations which *he* would regard as good reasons for the kind of action I am urging on him? I will not pursue these questions here, but will content myself with the claim (which is all I need for my present purposes) that I certainly manipulate him if I create for him new and inappropriate reasons for action; and that I should ideally try to persuade him of the relevance and force of what I take to be the appropriate reasons. For a related line of thought, see T Nagel, 'War and Massacre'.

lative. For it takes blame's primary purpose to be the efficient modification of behaviour: both the ends which I pursue and the means by which I pursue them are determined by considerations of consequential efficiency. I may find it best to aim for rational moral persuasion: but this will be because this is the most efficient way of securing the most useful kind of modification, not because it is in itself the proper way to respond to another moral agent; and I must be ready, if necessary, to use blame in any other way in which it is likely to be effective, or to use any other available method of modifying her conduct. But I now fail to respect her as a rational moral agent: I am prepared to manipulate her, if this will have the desired effect; I regard her as someone *on* whom I must work in order to produce some desirable change, not as someone *with* whom I must argue as an equal, and whom I must persuade to change herself.

Nor will it do to say that, while the justifying purpose of blame lies in its consequential benefits, our pursuit of those benefits is constrained by the independent requirement that we should not manipulate others: for that requirement determines not only the means by which we may properly pursue our ends, but the very ends which we may properly pursue. What makes blame an appropriate response to Jasper's wrong-doing is neither its instrumental efficiency as a means to a further end to which it is only contingently related, nor its accordance with a moral requirement independent of that end, but its internal relationship to its proper end. The 'end' which a proper respect for Jasper enjoins on me – that of persuading him to reform his own conduct – itself specifies moral criticism and blame as the 'means' by which it is to be pursued.

Having said that moral criticism and blame should properly be modes of rational moral argument with another person, I should say a little more about what this may involve; this will also add some necessary refinements to the distinctions drawn in the previous section between the different kinds of effect which blame may have on the person blamed.

The distinction between non-rational manipulation and rational moral argument is not a distinction between those modes of persuasion which do and those which do not rely on an appeal to the emotions. In criticising Jasper I may try to bring home to him as forcefully as I can the true nature of his conduct, by trying so to arouse and engage his emotions that he will be moved by the feelings of those he has injured, and will look with disgust on his own behaviour. Moral persuasion appeals to the other person's moral understanding, and thus to the emotions which are involved in such understanding; what is crucial is that it should appeal only to those emotions which are appropriate to the particular context, and should seek to arouse them only by appealing to those aspects of the context which make them appropriate. It is to be contrasted, not with appeals to the emotions as such, but with modes of persuasion which do not appeal to the other person's moral understanding, or which attempt to arouse morally irrelevant emotions.[12]

'I only really understood what I had done when I saw how upset Celia was, and when her friend came in and began shouting at me and abusing me; that got to me, and brought home to me how despicably I had been behaving.' Such a realisation of wrong-doing involves Jasper's emotions; if he was not upset by Celia's distress, and disgusted by his own conduct, we might doubt whether he really saw how despicable it was: but it gives him a moral *understanding* of his conduct. It is also a process which may be stimulated by the hostile reactions of others. Jasper might initially see the responses of Celia and her friends merely as a disagreeable effect of his conduct towards her, and as providing at most a prudential deterrent against repeating it; but the force and spirit of those responses might lead him to reflect more thoughtfully on his conduct, to ask himself why they should react like that. He might then come to see his conduct as despicable, not merely imprudent; and to see their reactions as appropriate moral responses to his conduct, not merely as unpleasant effects of it. Whether this happens will of course depend on such factors as his relationships with these people, the character of their responses, and his own willingness to see his conduct in the appropriate moral light. But the fact that it can happen should remind us that the distinctions between moral persuasion, prudential deterrence and non-rational manipulation – though still crucial, I believe, to an adequate understanding of the proper meaning of moral criticism and blame – are neither as clear-cut nor as simple as my earlier comments might have implied.

4 BLAMING THE DISORDERED

Moral blame, as a response to past wrong-doing, looks back towards a person's past conduct, and judges and condemns it as the conduct of a responsible moral agent: its propriety thus depends on her condition at the time of that conduct; if she was not then a re-

---

[12] On the central role of the emotions in moral understanding, see M Midgley, 'The Objection to Systematic Humbug'; B Williams, 'Morality and the Emotions'.

sponsible agent it would be unjust to blame her for what she then did. But blame also addresses her as she now is, in attempting to persuade her of the truth and justice of the judgment which it expresses: we must therefore ask whether there may be features of her present condition which render blame unjustified or inappropriate.

Jasper may have already passed the same judgment on his conduct as that which my blame would express: he recognises his own guilt, condemns himself before I condemn him, and is already resolved to reform his attitudes and behaviour. I may then see no need to add my condemnation to his: though that condemnation would be just, it might be needlessly hurtful to express it to him. Or I may be sure in advance that he will be unmoved by and unresponsive to my criticism: nothing I can say will bring him to see his conduct as I think he should see it, or to behave any differently; he will simply laugh at me for a prude. I may then think it a waste of time and effort to express to him the condemnation which he deserves, or to try to persuade him of its justice.

Such concerns with the effects of blame may lead me not to criticise someone whom I think is blameworthy. Even in these cases, however, I may still feel that I should tell her what I think of her conduct, and blame her for it; not because this may still have some useful effect on her or on others, but because she deserves blame. An already repentant Jasper asks me what I think of his behaviour; my regard for him and for the values to which we are both committed requires me to tell him the truth – that he did indeed behave despicably. Or I might persist in criticising an unresponsive Jasper; not because I hope to persuade him, but because to remain silent in the face of what he has done would be to betray the values which he has flouted and the people whom he has injured. Though my blame still has the character of an attempt to persuade him, it is not an attempt in which I engage with any hope or expectation of success. Nor need it serve any *further* purpose, such as reinforcing my regard for the values to which I appeal, or assuring others of my concern for them.[13] It serves rather to *express* my regard for those values; my concern for his victims; and my regard for Jasper himself as a responsible moral agent to whose actions I should respond honestly and openly. For that I should still blame him in such cases is in part a matter of honesty; I should not lie to him about the moral character of his conduct; and a failure to speak the truth sometimes amounts, even when speaking it will do no practical good, to a betrayal of the

[13] Contrast Charvet, 'Criticism and Punishment'.

truth. (It should be clear that I am talking here, as throughout this chapter, of what moral blame *should* ideally be; the gap between this ideal and the actual character of our critical responses to the wrong-doings of others is discussed in section 8.)

This of course assumes that I have the *right* to blame Jasper – to form and to express this judgment on his conduct. I will have more to say later about this point, and about the difference which Jasper's own response to his past conduct should make to the character of my response to him.[14] What I want to emphasise here, however, is that what makes blame still appropriate in these cases is not just the fact that Jasper's past conduct merits blame, but also and crucially the fact that he is *now* able to understand and respond to my criticism. An already repentant Jasper understands and accepts my blame, and joins with me in condemning his past conduct; and even an unrepentant Jasper *can* understand, and *could* respond to, my criticism of him.

But someone who was sane and responsible at the time of her wrong-doing might now be so disordered that she cannot understand or respond to my criticisms. She can see that I am angry with her: but she cannot understand the moral values to which my criticism appeals, or appreciate the moral dimensions of her own actions, and so cannot join in a critical discussion of the moral character of those actions. Blame may still have some useful effect on her or on others, and her past conduct merits blame. But once we realise that moral blame is meant to be a process of rational communication and argument with the person blamed, we can see why blame is inappropriate in such a case. Robbed of its proper meaning or purpose, it becomes a travesty of itself.

We do admittedly blame children for their misdeeds before they are fully able to appreciate the moral values which inform and justify that blame. But if this is to be a proper moral response to their wrong-doing, and not simply an attempt to cow or frighten them into obedience to our wishes, it must be part of a process of moral education which aims to develop their grasp of those values, and their capacity to understand, to judge and to guide their own actions in the light of those values. Blaming them still aims, in the end, at the kind of moral communication and persuasion which I have emphasised, and must involve an attempt not simply to modify their attitudes or pass judgment on their conduct, but to bring them to understand and accept the justice of that judgment.[15]

[14] See ch. 2 (7)–(8) below.
[15] See H Fingarette, *On Responsibility* ch. 2; W Moberly, *Responsibility* ch. 3.

Moral blame aims to communicate to a wrong-doer a judgment on her conduct; it also aims to make her suffer. We can distinguish three kinds of pain which blame may cause: they differ primarily in the relationship which the person blamed sees between the pain which she now suffers and the conduct for which she is blamed. My claim will be that, while a consequentialist might see a useful role for any of these kinds of pain in helping to modify future behaviour, the kind of pain which blame should properly aim to induce is one which is essentially, not merely contingently, related to the agent's wrong-doing.

(a) Jasper may be pained by my forceful criticism just because he dislikes being shouted at, or (if my condemnation disrupts a useful or enjoyable relationship) dislikes losing the goodwill of someone with whom he wants to be on good terms. He does not accept the moral judgment on his conduct which my blame expresses, or even care that it expresses a moral judgment; what matters is that I am no longer as friendly or amenable as he would like me to be. He sees a purely contingent relation between his present suffering and his past conduct: that conduct happened to bring about this effect. He now has a prudential reason to modify or conceal his conduct in future: but that reason is unrelated to the moral character of his past conduct and of my criticism; it depends on the contingent fact that I respond to that conduct in a way which he finds painful or inconvenient.

(b) What pains him may alternatively be the fact that I *disapprove* of him; that someone whose opinion he respects condemns his conduct. This pains him not just because I am now inconveniently hostile, but because it matters to him that I should think well of him. There is now more than a merely contingent relation between his present pain and the conduct which I condemn; for what pains him is the judgment on that conduct which my blame expresses. But he does not fully make that judgment his own. He sees his conduct through my condemnation, as something of which I disapprove; he does not yet see it directly under the relevant moral categories of sexual exploitation or dishonesty. He now has more than a merely prudential reason to reform his conduct, and his concern for the good opinion of others may be such that he will not repeat the conduct which they condemn even when there is no chance of detection. But his reasons for this reform are not the same, and do not manifest the same moral concerns, as those which are expressed in the blame he receives.

(c) He may instead be pained by the moral character of his own conduct, which my criticism brings him to realise. His pain now expresses his recognition of guilt, and his remorseful concern for the wrong he has done and the people he has injured. Now he truly makes the blame, and the judgment on his conduct which it expresses, his own: he makes that judgment for himself; and his suffering, and his desire to reform his conduct, are motivated by the very reasons which justify my criticism of him. In the first two cases my condemnation was essential to his suffering; it was the primary object of his distress. But now it plays only a contingent role in inducing a kind of suffering which is *essentially* related to his past wrong-doing. He may only have come to realise his guilt when I condemned his conduct: but his attention is now focused on that conduct, not on my condemnation; and he could come to recognise that guilt, and suffer that pain, without my criticism. He is pained by my condemnation: but what really pains him is its justice, and the wrongness of his own conduct.[16]

In each case Jasper suffers a different kind of pain, reflecting a different understanding of the blame he receives, of its relation to the conduct which provoked it, and of the reasons he now has for reforming his conduct. If I have a consequentialist interest in 'controlling undesirable conduct, by making its consequences . . . disagreeable',[17] I must ask which kind of pain will be most efficient in modifying Jasper's conduct; and I may see good reason to try to induce the third kind of pain: for one who blames himself, and understands for himself the wrongness of his conduct, is more likely to act rightly in future without any need for intervention by others. But I may also use the other kinds of pain as inducements to good behaviour, in case my appeal to his conscience fails, or his own conscience is inadequate to the task. The pressure of social dis-

[16] See S Kierkegaard, *Purity of Heart* 78–81; P Winch, 'Ethical Reward and Punishment'.
[17] Benn, 'An Approach to the Problems of Punishment' 340.

approval may modify his conduct even if he is unmoved by its moral content.

But in doing this I manipulate him: the pain which I try to cause him is only contingently related to his past wrong-doing; and the reasons which it offers him for modifying his conduct do not match those which justify my claim that he should behave differently. I respect his autonomy, and use blame for its proper purpose, only when I aim to induce in him the pain of recognised and accepted guilt. Only then do the reasons which I give him for modifying his conduct match those which justify my condemnation of him; only then is the pain which I try to induce in him appropriately related to his wrong-doing.

In blaming Jasper I do not simply try to inflict pain on him, either for the sake of its deterrent effect on his future conduct or because 'he deserves to suffer for what he has done'. I try to persuade him to accept and to make for himself the judgment on his conduct which my blame expresses; to feel remorse for what he has done. The pain which I hope he will feel is the pain which is integral to a repentant recognition of guilt. Such pain must be mediated and aroused by his own understanding of and judgment on his conduct; I can try only to bring him to achieve that understanding and to make that judgment. Blame thus seeks the participation of the person blamed: for its aim is not a kind of suffering which I can impose on him, but one which he must impose on himself.[18]

The pain which I suffer merely from the hostile reactions of others may, however, assist my recognition of my own guilt. My distress at the anger or contempt which they exhibit towards me may lead me to ask *why* they should react in this way; to see their reactions as a moral response to my conduct; to accept the justice of the judgment which that response expresses, and thus to suffer the pain of guilt and remorse. Their condemnation at first causes me a pain which is only contingently related to my wrong-doing, but it may be transformed into the kind of pain which is the proper end of moral blame.[19]

It may be said that I have exaggerated the importance of the

[18] See H Morris, 'Guilt and Suffering'. It may seem unduly dramatic to talk of *suffering* for relatively minor moral wrongs: but a sincere recognition that I have done wrong must involve repentance for that wrong; and that repentance must of its nature be painful – though the extent and nature of the pain will depend on the nature of the wrong.

[19] For some illuminating examples of the roles which the judgments of others may play in a person's understanding of their own conduct, contrast Rosamund Vincy in George Eliot's *Middlemarch* with Gwendolen Harleth in Eliot's *Daniel Deronda*; and both of them with Septimus Harding in Anthony Trollope's *The Warden*.

demand that we respect the autonomy of others: is it not more important to stop Jasper harassing his secretaries, which infringes *their* autonomy, by the admittedly coercive pressure of social disapproval, than to respect his autonomy?[20] But I have not claimed that this demand must always override every other consideration; only that it expresses a moral demand which is central to the proper meaning of moral blame. An unrepentant Jasper may indeed present me with a moral conflict between my concern for his secretaries and my respect for his autonomy: but even if I am then prepared to use (to *misuse*) moral blame as a prudential deterrent, I can still pay some regard to its proper meaning. I must recognise the moral cost of what I am doing; and I can try to ensure that my condemnation of his conduct is such as may also encourage and assist his repentant recognition of his own wrong-doing – that it *can* still serve its proper purpose.[21]

6 BLAME AND MORAL PUNISHMENT

Moral blame should be understood as a response to another's wrong-doing which aims to persuade her to accept the moral judgment on that wrong-doing which it expresses, and thus to bring her to impose on herself the pain which belongs with guilt and remorse. In blaming Jasper I am thus, we might say, trying to punish him, or to bring him to punish himself. But this 'punishment' is not something separate from blame: I cannot first blame him and then decide whether to try to make him suffer thus, since to blame him *is* to try to induce such suffering; he cannot accept my blame and hope to avoid such suffering, since to accept blame *is* to suffer thus.

However, I have talked so far only of what is involved in the explicit criticism of someone's conduct – which is likely to be just one aspect of my response to a serious moral wrong. An examination of further aspects of this response will reveal further kinds of moral 'punishment' which a wrong-doer might suffer, and will lead to a more careful consideration of the spirit in which, and the concerns with which, I should respond to her.

As well as suffering the condemnation of others, Jasper may find that he has lost the trust or respect which he once enjoyed from them; that his once amicable and intimate relationships with colleagues, friends and family have been damaged or destroyed. Such responses to his wrong-doing may be to some degree involuntary: I

[20] Compare J R Lucas, 'Or Else' 228.
[21] I have more to say about this kind of dilemma later: see ch. 7 (1), ch. 10 (3) below.

do not *decide* to withdraw my trust or friendship, but find that I *cannot* now trust or respect him as I did before. But they may also be deliberate, or to some degree within our control; and we must ask whether they can be appropriate, or whether they mark some moral failing in ourselves.

These further responses might be seen as a kind of punishment, since they involve the (possibly deliberate) infliction of suffering or harm on a wrong-doer because she has done wrong. But they should not be seen in simple consequentialist terms, as further ways of controlling undesirable conduct by making its consequences unpleasant; for that would portray them as manipulative. Nor is it clear that they should be seen in simple retributivist terms as penalties which we have a right or duty to impose on a wrong-doer: for what gives us this right or duty; what makes such 'penalties' appropriate?[22]

Can we say that Jasper ought to suffer for what he has done? Certainly he should not himself be able to carry on just as before, untouched and unmoved by what he has done: he should at least feel remorse for his actions, and perhaps make some apology or reparation to those he has injured; and in blaming him we try to persuade him of this. But why should he suffer, and why should we make him suffer, more than this? Because we might feel that his wrongdoing cannot but alter our relationships with him; that to behave as if he had done nothing wrong would be to deny the true implications of his actions. He has by those actions injured his relationships with his colleagues, his friends, his family, and other members of the community: for he has denied the values, and the bonds of mutual trust and concern, on which that community and those relationships depend.[23]

To talk in such terms is to see the wrong-doer as a fellow member

---

[22] A word about my use of the first persons singular and plural. I do not want to talk only of 'my' response to Jasper's wrong-doing, since this is not meant to be merely an account of my own moral attitudes. Nor, however, should I talk without qualification of 'our' responses: though I hope to show that these further responses to another's wrong-doing can be both intelligible and appropriate, I do not want to claim that any adequate response to serious wrong-doing *must* take some such form. When I talk in what follows of how 'we' might or should respond, I am talking about those who share the moral attitudes which I am trying to explicate – and, by explicating, defend. (On the problem of how far one can talk in moral philosophy of 'we', and how far only of 'I', or of 'all of us who, like myself' share a certain view or feeling, see L Wittgenstein, 'A Lecture on Ethics'; and Wittgenstein's comment that 'at the end of my lecture on ethics, I spoke in the first person. I believe this is quite essential': quoted in F Waissmann, 'Notes on Talks with Wittgenstein' 16.)

[23] See Morris, 'Guilt and Suffering'.

of a community from which his wrong-doing threatens to exclude him − a community made up of a complex web of social and personal relationships which structure our understanding of and our responses to each other's wrong-doing. But it is also to see that community and those relationships in moral terms; as dependent for their existence and their identity on a shared concern for each other as members of the community, and for the values which inform that concern.

The claim that Jasper's actions injure his relationships with others concerns not simply the contingent effects of those actions, but their essential implications. His wife may in fact leave him, his friends or colleagues shun him; and *he* may see *this* as the damage which his actions have caused: it is because others react like this that his relationships with them are damaged. But those others might insist that it is his actions themselves which have damaged those relationships, by breaking the moral bonds on which they depend. Jasper might say to his departing wife, 'Why break up our marriage over this?', and she might with justice reply, '*You* broke up our marriage by your adultery; you denied and thus destroyed the bonds of mutual fidelity on which our marriage depended'. She leaves him because he has already destroyed their marriage. So too his colleagues may shun him because his actions manifested a complete lack of concern for the values which should inform their work together, for its proper ends, and for the kinds of relationship which are appropriate to it; his actions showed, they might say, that he was not truly their colleague.

Of course his wife and colleagues might not see his actions, though wrong, as being thus injurious to their relationships with him. This could reflect an accurate understanding of the character of those relationships: not every marriage, friendship or common activity is founded on the kinds of concern and value of which actions like Jasper's are destructive. I might then comment on the moral character of a relationship which is not injured by such actions ('what kind of marriage is it if it does not involve a commitment to fidelity?'); or simply accept that these relationships are not such that Jasper's actions injure them; or suggest that a better understanding of his actions and of those relationships would show that they are indeed mutually inconsistent. (Though it may not be easy to distinguish such claims about the real character of a relationship from claims about the kind of character which it *should* have.) Much would depend here on the fine detail of particular examples; and there is wide scope for both disagreements and differences in our understanding of the implications of a person's actions for our relationships with him. But any recognisably human life must (and this 'must' is as much conceptual as moral) be lived within a community whose relationships are founded on some shared values and concerns; and different kinds of wrong-doing will be in different ways injurious to such relationships.[24] My concern here is with the character of our responses to wrong-doings which we see to be thus injurious to our relationships with the wrong-doer.

So should we now say that Jasper is *punished* for his actions by the break-up of his marriage or the loss of his friends? Even if he himself is neither moved nor pained by these results of his wrong-doing, we must suppose that they are harmful to him, as involving the loss of relationships which are constitutive of human well-being. Insofar as such responses are within our control, in withdrawing our friendship from him we thus intentionally inflict harm or suffering on him because of his wrong-doing. These are not, however, penalties which we decide to *attach* to his wrong-doing: rather they express our understanding of the implications of his conduct, and of the difference which it makes to our relationships with him. They are in that sense internally related to his wrong-doing. We could perhaps try to preserve our friendship with him and carry on as if nothing had happened (though that would involve a pretence), or *refuse* to let his actions destroy our friendship. I will say more about this latter possibility shortly: my point here is that we *recognise*, rather than *decide*, that Jasper's actions are injurious to our friendship with him; and in abandoning that friendship we express our recognition that the injury is, or our willingness that it should be, fatal.

Two other, more institutional, examples may clarify this point. A student who persistently fails to do the work required of her may be expelled from her college; and she may see this as a punishment. But it is not simply a penalty which the college decides to impose on her, like a fine which might be imposed to encourage hard work: rather it expresses an understanding of the implications of her conduct. To be a student is to engage in a process of learning of which the work required of her is an integral part. In failing to do that work she is thus failing to be a student; she brings about her own expulsion by excluding herself from participation in the life and work of the college.

A church may excommunicate a member for a grave sin; this too may be seen as a punishment. The church has to determine which kinds of sin merit expulsion, and whether that expulsion should be

[24] See Morris, 'Guilt and Suffering'; P Winch, 'Nature and Convention'.

temporary or permanent: but in doing so its concern must be with the nature and implications of the sin itself. I am excommunicated because I have by my sin separated myself from God and from the church; I can be readmitted to the church only if my sin and my response to it are such that my relationships with God and with the church can be restored. My excommunication is not a penalty which the church decides to attach to my sin: it is rather the outward expression of the harm and exclusion I have brought upon myself by my sin.[25]

Such responses to wrong-doing have the character of exclusions: the wrong-doer is excluded from the relationships he once enjoyed. They may be called punishments, which the wrong-doer has himself willed by his own wrong-doing; for they involve the infliction of a kind of suffering which is purportedly justified as an appropriate response to that wrong-doing. We could also say that his true punishment is the damage which he has done to his relationships with others, however they in fact respond to him; for this kind of punishment is inseparable from his wrong-doing,[26] and the responses of others simply express their understanding of its nature. Now I will argue later that punishment can have a richer meaning than this, involving not just the damage which the wrong-doer does to and suffers in his relationships with others, but an attempt to repair that damage and restore those relationships. But an understanding of punishment in both moral and, I will argue, legal contexts must begin, even if it does not end, with such results of a wrong-doer's actions: they are forms, though not the only forms, of punishment which he may suffer; and they will play an important role in my account of criminal punishment.

7 MORAL PUNISHMENT AND PENANCE

I have so far painted a bleak picture of one kind of response to another's wrong-doing; I condemn Jasper's conduct, withdraw from him, and exclude him (claiming that he has excluded himself) from the friendship he once enjoyed with me. But is this really the

[25] See K Rahner, *Theological Investigations* vol. 2, 135–74, vol. 10, 125–49. Suppose that Jasper is sacked for his conduct: should we see this as, for instance, a deterrent penalty which is attached to such behaviour; or could we see it as a punishment which is internally related to his wrong-doing (he has excluded himself from that community of work by denying the values and the bonds on which it depends and by which it is structured)?

[26] Compare Winch, 'Ethical Reward and Punishment', on Wittgenstein's claim (*Tractatus Logico-Philosophicus* 6.422) that 'ethical reward and ethical punishment . . . must reside in the action itself'.

spirit in which I should respond to his wrong-doing: is it consistent with the love which I should have for him as my friend; or with the charity which a proper concern for a wrong-doer, and a proper awareness of my own imperfections, requires of me? We are told to forgive those who trespass against us; and though it is not for me to *forgive* wrongs which are done to others, should not my response to them be informed by the same spirit?

What then is required of me? Surely not that I *ignore* the serious wrong that Jasper has done, or try to think, feel and act as if he has done nothing wrong; for that would be to deny that a concern for the people he has injured, for the values he has flouted, or for his own moral good has any place in my relationship with him. Should I then, though my initial response is still to withdraw from community with him, be prepared to restore that community if he repents, and seeks forgiveness for, what he has done?

To ask to be forgiven is in part to acknowledge that the attitude displayed in our actions was such as might properly be resented and in part to repudiate that attitude for the future (or at least for the immediate future); and to forgive is to accept the repudiation and forswear the resentment.[27]

The indignant withdrawal of my friendship would be an appropriate response to Jasper's conduct; his wife would be justified in resenting that conduct and in leaving him: but then we are willing, if he expresses a suitable remorse, to forswear those reactions and to restore or maintain our relationships with him, though we leave it to him to seek such a restoration by seeking our forgiveness.

Such talk of the restoration of relationships is too vague: what can be restored may not be the same as what was lost; my friendship with Jasper, and his marriage, may be altered by his wrong-doing and by our mutual responses to it. But, though it is his wrong-doing which threatens his marriage and our friendship, should we place the onus of restoring or saving those relationships so firmly on his shoulders: is it enough that we simply wait for him to make the first move by expressing his repentance and seeking forgiveness?

This may sometimes be all that we can do, and we may sometimes feel that a friendship or a marriage is beyond saving. But we can sometimes express a more active concern for the wrong-doer, which *seeks* to bring her to repentance, and *refuses* to let her wrong-doing destroy our love or friendship for her (and the fact that we cannot or will not always respond thus may say as much about our

---

[27] P F Strawson, 'Freedom and Resentment' 6. See also R S Downie, 'Forgiveness'; H J N Horsburgh, 'Forgiveness'; W R Neblett, 'Forgiveness and Ideals'; P Twambley, 'Mercy and Forgiveness'.

own inadequacies as about the implications of her wrong-doing). We may do this not just for the sake of ourselves or others, but for the sake of the wrong-doer herself: *she* is harmed by the loss of these relationships; and if we care for her we should try to save her (to help her save herself) from the harm to which her wrong-doing would otherwise condemn her. Her wrong-doing injures her as well as others: we might say too that it harms her most seriously by separating her not just from other people, but from God or the Good; and that the worst harm that a person can suffer is to fall into sin and not be saved from it. We can talk now of a concern for her soul; and whether we see her wrong-doing as injurious primarily to her relationships with other people, or to her relationship with God or the Good, we now understand her well-being in moral terms, as depending essentially on her participation in relationships which are defined and structured by moral concerns and moral values.[28]

If I am to respond to Jasper in this spirit, what form can my response take? I want to repair the harm which flows from his wrong-doing, but it can only be repaired through *his* recognition and repentance of that wrong-doing. What will restore his relationships with other people or with God is not some change in him which *I* can try to effect by whatever techniques are available, but a kind of moral reform (of *self*-reform) which he must undergo for himself, and which I can only persuade him to undertake and help him to carry through.

I may do this by criticising his conduct; and moral blame, as an attempt to communicate *with* the wrong-doer, fits more happily with a concern to maintain our relationships with him than with a willingness to exclude him from those relationships. I do not try to play down the extent and nature of his wrong-doing, or to save him from suffering: he should be distressed by the harm he has done to others and to himself; and my response aims to induce such distress in him, and to bring him to impose it on himself. That distress, however, is not simply something he should suffer for what he has done; it is also a benefit to him, since it is an essential part of the process of moral reform.

So wonderful a power is remorse, so sincere is its friendship that to escape it entirely is the most terrible thing of all. A man can wish to slink away from many things in life, and he may even succeed, so that life's favoured one can say in the last moment, 'I slipped away from all the cares which other men suffered'. But if such a person wishes to bluster out of, to defy,

---

[28] See Plato, *Gorgias*; Kierkegaard, *Purity of Heart*; I Dilman, *Morality and the Inner Life* ch. 5; P Winch, 'Can a Good Man be Harmed?'; H Morris, 'A Paternalistic Theory of Punishment'.

to slink away from remorse, alas, which is indeed the most terrible to say of him, that he failed, or that he succeeded?[29]

Such a painful process of remorse and repentance may be seen as a kind of self-imposed punishment. But can punishment play any larger part than this in a response which aims to benefit the wrong-doer by persuading her to repent and to reform herself; or is such a concern for her moral and spiritual well-being incompatible with any kind of *punitive* response to her wrong-doing?

We can, I have suggested, see the loss of his friends or of his wife as punishments which Jasper suffers. But such responses may serve a communicative and reformative purpose: their aim may be not simply to exclude him from relationships he has damaged or de-stroyed, but to communicate to him our understanding of the nature and implications of his wrong-doing; to help him attain such an understanding for himself; and thus to help him see the need for and the way towards a restoration of those relationships through remorse and repentance. So too a church may excommunicate a sinner in an attempt, not to cast her out for ever, but to bring her to understand the true nature of her sin; and in the hope that she will restore herself to the church by repenting that sin.

If instead I refuse to let Jasper's wrong-doing destroy our friend-ship, I may still try to focus his attention on its nature and its impli-cations; by insisting on telling him what I think of his conduct, by refusing to be distracted onto other topics, or to continue our ordi-nary intercourse as if nothing had happened. So too a sinner may be kept within the community of the church, but be subjected to the critical attentions of her priest or her fellows, who urge her to confess and repent her sin, either publicly before the congregation or privately with her priest. Jasper (or the sinner) might also see this kind of response as a punishment which others inflict on him, though they would not portray it as such: he would prefer me to ignore what he has done, and regards my insistence on trying to make him confront his own wrong-doing simply as a punitive attempt to make him suffer.

An unrepentant Jasper may not share my view of his conduct, or see it as necessarily injurious to him and to his relationships with others. For he does not share my moral view of the nature of that conduct, of his well-being, or of those relationships; any injury which *he* sees himself as suffering (the hostility of others; the loss of friends or of his wife) he sees as the effect of our prudish reactions to his behaviour. He may say that he is being punished for his conduct;

[29] Kierkegaard, *Purity of Heart* 35.

but he sees that punishment as a contingent effect of that conduct, as something we decide to impose on him by way of retaliation or revenge. What of a repentant Jasper, however? He suffers the pain of guilt and remorse; he sees that he has harmed both others and himself, and that he has separated himself from the Good, and injured his relationships with others. Even if he does not find himself excluded by others from those relationships, he sees that he has damaged them, and that the damage must be repaired by their good-will and by his own repentance; if he does lose his friends or his wife he may see this as a punishment which is *internal* to (a necessary implication of) his wrong-doing.[30]

A repentant wrong-doer might also punish himself. He might, in an extreme case, be so horrified by what he has done, and by what he has become in doing it, that he withdraws into a penitential exile or solitude. He feels that he can no longer live with his family or his friends and fellows; for he has denied the values, the structures of mutual concern and respect, on which his relationships with them depend. The duration and character of such an exile would depend on his understanding of the nature of his own wrong-doing and of the possibility of any restoration of the relationships which he has destroyed; he might even feel that his crime was so terrible, so destructive of the values which are essential to human life, that he should kill himself.

We may think that some such self-exiles or suicides manifest an irrationally exaggerated or distorted apprehension of the implications of their wrong-doing, or an intelligible but illegitimate despair at the possibility of continuing to live with those one has wronged. We might see others, not as genuinely penitential responses to wrong-doing, but as attempts to escape from it and to avoid confronting its implications.[31] But they can also be genuine moral responses to one's own wrong-doing – punishments which the wrong-doer imposes on herself; only by exiling herself, she feels, to a solitary life of penitential contemplation can she express her remorseful understanding of what she has done and what she has become. Even the most apparently destructive self-punishments can have this expressive character. They may thus serve, paradoxically, to reconcile the wrong-doer to those from whom she has sundered herself; by thus expressing the depth of her concern for the values she has flouted she may be reunited, if only in death, with her

---

[30] Compare Winch, 'Ethical Reward and Punishment' and 'Trying'.
[31] For illuminating discussions of such suicides, see R F Holland, 'Suicide'; and Graham Greene, *The Heart of the Matter*.

community or with God. But other, less extreme penances provide a more obvious way in which a penitent may seek to repair the harm she has done.

A penance may be formal and institutional, as when, having confessed my sins, I undertake the penance which my confessor assigns as being appropriate; or informal and individual, when I deprive myself of some pleasure, or impose some arduous task on myself, as a penance for the wrongs I have done. It may be public, if I need to express my penitence to others, or private, if I see my wrong-doing as a matter between me and God or my conscience; it may take a symbolic form, or involve an imposition which is itself arduous or painful. It may involve an attempt to repair the material harm I have done; or some public act of confession and apology which exposes me to the criticism and condemnation of others; or some task which has no such obvious relation to my wrong-doing. I undertake and undergo a penance as a punishment for my wrong-doing; not simply because I deserve to suffer for it, but to assist and express my repentant understanding of what I have done. It enables me to express, for myself and to others, my remorse for my wrong-doing; my concern for the values I have betrayed and for the people I wronged; and my desire to restore myself to the community from which my wrong-doing threatens to exclude me. For penance looks to the future as well as to the past; back to the wrong I have done, and forwards to the possibility of reforming myself and healing the breach in my relationships with others or with God.[32]

I do not suggest that anyone who sincerely repents his wrong-doing *must* express this through a penance: he may feel that it is enough to make a private apology to those he has wronged; to criticise and condemn himself; and to try to reform himself. My claim is only that he may intelligibly feel the need for a penance which will assist his penitential contemplation of his wrong-doing, and provide a more forceful expression for that penitence. We should not find it puzzling that people may need to give such overt expression to their deep moral concerns; nor that a penance must be painful or burdensome, since what it expresses is the wrong-doer's painful awareness of his guilt and of the wrong he has done to others. A penance must, however, be *self*-imposed if it is to express, as it should, my repentant recognition of my wrong-doing. Others may

---

[32] On penance see Rahner, *Theological Investigations* vol. 2, 135–74, vol. 10, 125–49; E L Long, *A Survey of Christian Ethics* 91–4; J Pelikan, *The Christian Tradition* vol. 3; J T McNeill, *A History of the Cure of Souls*; and ch. 9 (5) below.

suggest a penance to me, or require one of me: but it loses its meaning if I see it merely as a penalty which they impose on me; I must accept and undertake it for myself.

8 OBJECTIONS AND CONCLUSIONS

I have described moral blame as an attempt to communicate to the wrong-doer a moral understanding of his wrong-doing; to bring him to recognise his guilt and repent what he has done. I have also described the kinds of punishment which he may suffer or impose on himself: punishments which exclude him from the relationships which he has injured, or which seek to restore those relationships through his repentance. Both blame and punishment express our concern for the values he has betrayed, and for the people he has wronged; they can also express our concern for the wrong-doer himself. We respond to him, and care for him, as a fellow member of a moral community within which both his obligations and his well-being are to be found – we do not try to ignore or conceal the nature and implications of his wrong-doing. We accord him the respect which is his due as a responsible moral agent – we do not simply try to manipulate or coerce him into conformity. He may therefore claim a *right* to be blamed, or even punished, for his wrong-doing; a right to be treated, respected and cared for as a moral agent.

Moral blame and punishment are retributive insofar as they focus on, and seek to induce suffering for, past wrong-doing; and I have tried to show what it can mean to say that a wrong-doer deserves to suffer thus for what she has done. But they are not purely backward-looking; for the suffering which they aim to induce is also a path towards reform and rehabilitation. It would however be wrong to say, in consequentialist tones, that their justifying aim lies in the reform of the wrong-doer; for they are internally, not merely instrumentally, related to their proper end. Their justification lies, not in their contingent efficiency as means to some further and separate end, but in their character as appropriate modes of communication with, and response to, another moral agent. Their proper reformative end can *only* be achieved by such means – by bringing the wrong-doer to recognise and suffer for her wrong-doing; and they may still be justified, as appropriate responses to that wrong-doing, even when there is in fact no hope of securing that reformative end.

To object that blame is an inefficient or uneconomical way of modifying attitudes and conduct; or that it aims to induce an unhealthy and unproductive, because purely backward-looking, kind of guilt and suffering; is thus to miss the point.[33] Moral blame and punishment can be productive of future good – though they are not simply instrumental means towards that good; and though both blame and guilt can be self-indulgent, melodramatic and inauthentic modes of response to wrong-doing, they can also, even when they are purely backward-looking, express a proper moral concern. If I love another person I will be grieved by their death; and it would be crassly insensitive to tell me that I should try to stop grieving, and turn my attention to other things, simply on the grounds that my grief looks to the past rather than the future. My grief is a natural and proper expression of my love for the person who has died. So too, in blaming myself or another for past wrong-doing, I express my commitment to the values which have been betrayed, and my concern for those who were wronged.

There is, however, a different objection to our willingness to blame and punish the wrong-doings of others. 'He that is without sin among you, let him first cast a stone':[34] by what right do we take it upon ourselves to castigate others for their wrong-doings? I have portrayed, it may be said, a society of moral vigilantes, ever concerned to judge and improve their fellows by criticism and punishment. But such people exhibit an arrogant assumption of moral superiority and insight; and their claim to care for the moral values to which they appeal, or for the moral well-being of those whom they condemn, will too often be merely a self-deceptive cover for a prurient quest after vice and a false relationship to the values which they preach.

The supposed wrong-doings of others certainly provide fertile ground for some of the less attractive forms of hypocrisy and self-righteousness. Furthermore, we often do not know enough about another's actions and their context to form, let alone express, a firm judgment on them. To try to engage him in a critical discussion of their moral character, or to try to save him from the moral evil into which we think he has fallen, will often be to interfere with cack-handed insensitivity in something which we would do better to leave alone. We should more often turn our eyes away from the sins of others towards the moral character of our own actions and attitudes, and of our motives for criticising and condemning others.

---

[33] Compare William James on 'sick' and 'healthy' souls (*The Varieties of Religious Experience*, Lectures 4–7); and see Morris, 'Guilt and Suffering'.
[34] St John's Gospel viii.7.

But my concern here is with the ideal rather than the actual: my aim is not to justify our actual responses to wrong-doing, but to explicate the ideals by which those responses are purportedly informed. To say that moral blame is *essentially* an attempt to engage with another in the search for a true understanding of the moral character of her actions, or that moral punishment is essentially an attempt to bring a wrong-doer to repentance and reform, is not to say that this is in fact the intention with which, or the spirit in which, we respond to the wrong-doings of others: rather that this is what our responses *should* involve – that these are the ideals which are appropriate to them.

It is by reference to such ideals that we must understand and assess our own responses to moral wrong-doing; for they show us the values and purposes by which those responses should be structured, and in the light of which those responses can be seen to be variously imperfect, distorted or inadequate. The distance between the ideal and the actual is a measure both of our own inadequacies and of the arduous demands which these ideals make of us. Our critical response to another's wrong-doing must be informed by a humble and selfless concern for the values by which we judge her conduct, and must also judge our own; by a regard for her, and a concern for her well-being, as a moral agent; by an awareness of the imperfections of our own understanding and of our own moral characters; by a readiness to be persuaded that our own judgment is wrong; and by a willingness to criticise and condemn ourselves, and to be criticised and condemned by others, as vigorously as we criticise and condemn them. It is not surprising that our actual responses should all too often fall far short of these ideals; and our recognition of this should impart at least a certain caution and reluctance to those responses.

Perhaps for this reason the more drastic kinds of moral punishment should play little or no part in our moral relationships with others: I will not discuss this issue further here, since my aim so far has only been to show the meaning which such punishments could *ideally* have.[35] But this does not mean that we should never be prepared to criticise and blame the conduct of others; nor that our responses to wrong-doing should not exhibit our understanding of the kinds of punishment which are internal to wrong-doing and to an agent's own repentant recognition of his wrong-doing. If we admit that people do act in ways which are despicable, cruel, unjust and dishonest; and if we regard them as moral agents who are re-

[35] But see ch. 10 (3) below.

sponsible for their actions: then we must either allow that criticism and blame are sometimes appropriate, or argue that we should always conceal our understanding of, and our attitudes towards, the conduct of others. But such a concealment would be a betrayal of the values to which we claim to be committed. Our regard for those values, our concern for those who are injured by wrong-doing, and our respect for the wrong-doer himself, require us to be prepared to criticise and blame others for their wrong-doing, as we are prepared to criticise and blame ourselves. To show that it is hard or even impossible to attain the ideal is not to show that that ideal has no claim on our attention, or should play no part in our actions.

3

The Law's Demands

Law is nought else than an ordinance of reason for the common good made by the authority who has care of the community.

St Thomas Aquinas, *Summa Theologiae* 1a2ae90.4

The existence of law is one thing; its merit or demerit is another. Whether it be or be not is one enquiry; whether it be or be not conformable to an assumed standard, is a different enquiry. A law, which actually exists, is a law, though we happen to dislike it, or though it vary from the text, by which we regulate our approbation and disapprobation. This truth, when formally announced as an abstract proposition, is so simple and glaring that it seems idle to insist upon it. But simple and glaring as it is, when enunciated in abstract expressions, the enumeration of the instances in which it has been forgotten would fill a volume.

John Austin, *The Province of Jurisprudence Determined*, p. 184

I THE MORAL DIMENSION OF LAW

Moral blame should be understood, I have claimed, as an attempt to bring a person to recognise and repent his wrong-doing. It addresses, and respects, him as a responsible moral agent: hence his right to be blamed, and the impropriety of blaming someone who is now so disordered that he cannot understand or respond to the judgment on his conduct which our criticism expresses and explicates. Such an understanding of moral blame and moral punishments will help us to understand the meaning and purpose of the criminal process: the reasons why we should not try or punish a disordered defendant; and the sense of the claim that an offender has a right to be tried and punished. But an account of the criminal process requires a preliminary discussion of the criminal law.

Moral blame presupposes a set of moral standards by which we judge the conduct of another (as we judge our own); which we believe she should recognise for herself as the proper determinants of her actions; and which justify our criticisms of her when she flouts or ignores them. We understand moral blame in part by understanding the kind of demand which these standards make of the moral agent, and her status in relation to those demands: we blame her for flouting standards which make an unconditional demand on her allegiance and obedience as a responsible agent and as a member of a moral community.

A criminal trial presupposes a set of substantive criminal laws which prohibit certain types of conduct, and for alleged breaches of which citizens may be tried and convicted. To understand the meaning and purpose of a criminal trial, and the defendant's role in his trial, we must first understand the kind of demand which the criminal law makes on the citizen, and the status which it must accord to those who are subject to its requirements. I will argue that the law must make a moral demand on the allegiance and obedience of the citizen as a rational agent; that a criminal trial must therefore accord the defendant the status of a rational moral agent who is called to answer a charge of wrong-doing; and that we can usefully see the criminal trial and its verdict as a formal or institutional analogue of a moral process of criticism and blame.

To say that the law must make a moral claim on the citizen may seem to commit me to a traditional Natural Lawyer's view that we can find in the essence of law, and of human nature, moral criteria which define what it is to *be* law; that we can recognise a system or rule as (valid) law only if it accords with these substantive moral criteria. But such views are surely inconsistent with our willingness to count as (valid) law rules and systems which breach the most fundamental moral requirements: they ignore the distinction established by the 19th century Legal Positivists between law as it is and law as it ought to be (between analytical and censorial jurisprudence). We must distinguish the descriptive concepts of law and legal validity from the moral notions by reference to which we criticise the law; the factual question of what legal obligations I have from the moral question of whether I ought to obey the laws which impose those legal obligations.[1]

Legal systems and valid laws may indeed be morally corrupt; legal obligations may have no tenable moral claim to our obedience. But despite this; despite the demise of the metaphysical notions which informed traditional Natural Law theories; and despite Posi-

---

[1] See J Bentham, *Of Laws in General*; J Austin, *The Province of Jurisprudence Determined*; H L A Hart, 'Positivism and the Separation of Law and Morals': but compare J Finnis, *Natural Law and Natural Rights* (referred to hereafter as *Finnis*) ch. 2 on the proper meaning of traditional Natural Law theories.

tivist attempts to provide suitably sterilised translations of the more tempting aspects of Natural Law theories:[2] there is more to an adequate account of the concept of law, and of the concept of legal obligation in particular, than can be provided by a Positivist who insists on a rigorous separation between legal and moral concepts. Hart argued that a Benthamite or Austinian account cannot distinguish legal obligation from coercion:[3] but his own account, which remains one of the more plausible Positivist analyses of the concept of law, is open to the same objection.

There is, I will argue, an essential and ineliminable moral dimension to the concept of law: to see a system or a rule as law is necessarily to see it as requiring a certain kind of moral justification, and as subject to certain moral demands. An analytical jurisprudence cannot indeed generate determinate moral criteria which positive law must satisfy if it is to count as law: there may be irresoluble disagreement about the meaning of the moral concepts which are relevant to the law; and those concepts provide standards for assessing law as good or bad, rather than criteria for identifying it as law. But positive laws and legal systems must be justified and criticised by reference to moral notions which are internal to the concept of law itself; these moral notions are essentially, not contingently, related to the existence of law as law.[4]

2 LEGAL OBLIGATION; A POSITIVIST VIEW

It is a fair criticism of some jurisprudents that they distort the concept of law by concentrating unduly on the criminal law.[5] But my concern is with, and my discussion will therefore focus on, the criminal law – though I trust that my comments will be consistent with other aspects of a developed legal system.

A system of criminal law seeks to guide and control the conduct

[2] See, for instance, H L A Hart, *The Concept of Law* (referred to hereafter as *CL*) ch. 9.

[3] *CL* 79–83; see also P M S Hacker, 'Sanction Theories of Duty'.

[4] This chapter is based on my article 'Legal Obligation and the Moral Nature of Law', where some of the issues are discussed more fully. My criticisms of Legal Positivism focus on Hart (who still maintains the basic tenets of *CL* – see the Introduction to his *Essays in Jurisprudence and Philosophy*), and largely ignore the revisions and refinements to a Hartian Positivism developed by writers like J Raz (see especially *The Authority of Law*) and D N MacCormick (see especially *Legal Reasoning and Legal Theory*, and 'Law, Morality and Positivism'): a thorough discussion of the possibilities of Positivism would need to attend to their more subtle accounts of the relations between law and morality (on Raz, see R Shiner, Review of *The Authority of Law*).

[5] See Hart's comments on Austin, *CL* ch. 3.

of those who are subject to it by prohibiting certain types of conduct, and by attaching sanctions to proven failures to obey those requirements. Two familiar questions now present themselves. First, what, if anything, distinguishes a system of law from an arbitrary tyranny which seeks obedience to its dictates by whatever means may be effective; or from other modes of social control which seek the most efficient way of modifying behaviour into desired patterns and towards desired ends? Second, why should we value 'the rule of law': is it because this is the most efficient way of achieving our favoured ends; or because we recognise certain independent moral constraints on our pursuit of those ends, which preclude other, possibly more effective, modes of social control; or because the justifying aims of a system of law are themselves such that they cannot properly be pursued by other means?

An initial answer to the first question is that law, unlike other methods of social control, consists of rules which individual citizens are to grasp, apply and obey for themselves: Legal Positivists and Natural Lawyers can agree that law is an 'enterprise of subjecting human conduct to the governance of rules'.[6] But this is only the beginning of an answer; for what is it to subject conduct to the governance of rules, and what distinguishes law from other kinds of social rule? A tyrant may issue general orders, backed by the threat of sanctions, which his victims are meant to grasp and apply for themselves: is he subjecting their conduct to the governance of rules? If so, what, if anything, distinguishes his rules from a system of law? If not, what is missing?

Perhaps his orders lack, and a system of law must include, a set of 'secondary rules' of recognition, change and adjudication which validate the primary rules of the system and authorise the activities of those who create, declare and administer those primary rules.[7] But the tyrant could issue 'secondary orders', specifying criteria by which his victims may identify the primary orders which they are to obey: for instance, 'Obey all orders issued by me and by the following specified people unless/until they are cancelled or modified by further orders from one of these sources . . .' Would a complete set

[6] L Fuller, *The Morality of Law* 122.
[7] *CL* chs. 5–6. I leave aside here detailed questions about the consistency and adequacy of Hart's distinctions between primary and secondary rules, and about the primacy he claims for them in the analysis of a legal system (see L J Cohen, Review of *CL*; R Dworkin, *Taking Rights Seriously* chs. 2–3; D N MacCormick, 'Law as Institutional Fact'; J Raz, 'The Identity of Legal Systems'; R Sartorius, 'Hart's Concept of Law'), and assume that a legal system must at least include 'secondary' rules which define and authorise the activities of officials in making and administering the law, and 'primary' rules which prescribe conduct to the citizens.

of such secondary orders be enough to transform a tyrant's reign of terror into a (no doubt reprehensible) system of law?

I think not: there are crucial differences between such a tyrannical system of orders backed by threats and anything which could count as a system of law. One difference is that between the impersonal character of law and the personal character of the tyrant's orders: a prescriptive law says, 'This ought to be done'; but the tyrant says, 'I want this to be done'.[8] A system of law may have a determinate sovereign who makes and issues laws: but we will see that neither her laws nor her status as legislator can be validated merely by an appeal to her own will. The tyrant I have described, however, can found his demands only on his own will and his ability to coerce others into obedience to it.

But this simply reflects a more fundamental difference between a system of law and a mere tyranny; that the law involves claims of *obligation* and *authority*. When a legal official says to a citizen, 'You ought to do this because the law requires it', she claims that the citizen has an obligation to obey that law; that the law has, and gives her as its officer, authority over the citizen. Now the tyrant may say that we 'ought' to obey his orders: but if his tyranny is open and unashamed he must admit that he has no authority to require our obedience, only the power to enforce it by threats; that he may oblige us to obey, but is neither imposing obligations on us nor reminding us of obligations which we already have; that his 'ought' merely expresses his own will and his power to make obedience to it the most prudent course of action for us.

So we face another familiar question. What distinguishes the claim that someone has an obligation to obey a rule from the claim that she will be forced by threats to obey it; or the claim that I, or that rule, have the authority to require her obedience from the claim that I have the power to coerce her?

A criminal trial involves various claims of obligation and authority: the defendant has, supposedly, an obligation to obey the law which she is charged with breaking, to accept the authority of the court, and to obey the procedural rules of the trial; the judge is authorised and obligated to conduct the trial in accordance with the relevant rules and principles; and counsel, juries and witnesses all have their rights and duties. I will concentrate on the obligation-claims which are made on the defendant, and thus on the authority-claims which are correlative to them.

An indictment charges a defendant with a breach of legal obli-

[8] Compare Aristotle, *Politics* 3.10, 1286a9.

gation. Jones is charged with failing to wear a crash-helmet while riding her motor-cycle, contrary to section 32 of the Road Traffic Act 1972; the charge presupposes that she has a legal obligation to obey that Act, and thus to wear a helmet. Such obligation-claims figure in her trial prescriptively, not merely descriptively: they do not just report the existence of a certain rule, but prescribe obedience to it; and the indictment presupposes that they make a justified claim on her obedience. To understand the meaning of the criminal trial we must therefore understand the kinds of prescriptive obligation-claim on which it depends.

Statements of legal obligation need not be prescriptive. A detached observer, describing this legal system, may note that it imposes on Jones a legal obligation to wear a crash-helmet without committing himself to any prescriptive view about how Jones ought to behave: but what he notes is that this is a system of law within which a prescriptive claim that Jones has that obligation is or could be made. Jones herself, who is a participant in this legal system in the sense that its rules are held to bind her, may recognise that she in fact has a legal obligation to wear a helmet without accepting that obligation. Thus she may, fearing punishment, obey the law, but it figures in her practical reasoning as just one of the facts relevant to determining the likely consequences of her actions, not as a normative guide to conduct; she is 'externally' rather than 'internally' related to this law or to this system of law. But in noting that she has this obligation she is noting that, within this legal system, certain prescriptive obligation-claims are or may be made on her.[9]

Such obligation-descriptions are parasitic on the prescriptive claims which they describe. To see what it is for Jones to have a legal obligation we must see what is meant by the prescriptive claim that she has such an obligation. Similarly, I may use a moral language normatively, as one who accepts the values which it embodies; or descriptively, to describe a particular moral view: to explain the meaning of such a language we must explain the meaning of the normative claims which it is paradigmatically used to make.

'You have a legal obligation to wear a helmet on your motor-cycle', says the judge to Jones. From Hart's account of the con-

---

[9] On these distinctions between observers and participants, and between external and internal relations to rules, see *CL* 54–7, 86–8; A Gewirth, 'Obligation: Political, Legal, Moral'; F A Siegler, 'Hart on Rules of Obligation'. See also J Raz, 'Legal Validity' 153–9, on 'detached normative statements' of law – statements made from the point of view of a detached observer who may be a member of the legal system he describes but does not speak prescriptively as one who accepts its rules.

ditions given which we can say, *as observers*, that Jones has such a legal obligation, we can infer the Hartian conditions given which the judge can make such a *prescriptive* claim.

(a) There must be a primary rule, validated by the secondary rules of the system of which it is part, requiring the wearing of helmets.
(b) That system of rules must be generally obeyed by the citizens and must, on the whole, be stringently enforced.
(c) The system's secondary rules must be accepted as normative at least by the officials whose legislative and administrative activities they define and authorise.[10]

Condition (a) is necessary but not sufficient. To show that Jones has this obligation we must show that the rule which purports to impose it is validated by the system's Rule of Recognition: but we must also show, and the judge must presuppose,[11] that this system *exists* as the legal system of Jones' community, in that its rules are generally obeyed by the citizens and enforced against those who disobey them. The citizens need not *accept* these rules, since a legal system can exist and impose obligations on citizens who are for the most part externally related to its rules. But it can exist as a system of law only if its defining rules are accepted at least by those who administer it. We can describe Jones' legal obligations only if we can see that the system's officials accept the secondary rules which generate those obligations and authorise their own official activities; for in making his prescriptive claim the judge implies that he, and his fellow-officials, accept the rules which validate the Road Traffic Act 1972, and which define and authorise his own judicial activity. In accepting these rules as normative guides for his official conduct, however, the judge need not see them as *morally* justified or binding: his acceptance could be found on habit, tradition, imitation, or pure self-interest.[12]

Suppose now that the judge justifies his prescriptive claim to Jones in the most minimal Hartian terms. 'This law is part of a system of primary and secondary rules which is effectively enforced and obeyed; it is validated by the system's secondary rules; I and other members of the official elite accept these secondary rules and

---

[10] See *CL*, especially chs. 5–6; also P M S Hacker, 'Hart's Philosophy of Law'.
[11] See *CL* 101.
[12] *CL* 198; see also *CL* 113 – not even the officials need accept those primary rules which apply to them 'in their merely personal capacity'.

guide our conduct by them. We have of course structured the system and its rules purely with a view to our own interests (the Minister of Transport's husband, for instance, has the sole concession for the manufacture of crash-helmets, and we all have shares in his firm); and we recognise that, while we have self-interested reason to accept and enforce these rules, the citizens do not accept them: but this does not rebut the claim that you have a legal obligation to obey this rule.'

Hart would no doubt insist that this is a *morally* inadequate justification; that Jones has good *moral* reason to withhold her allegiance from such a system of law; and that a system which ignores its citizens' interests, and fails to gain their consent, will not long survive.[13] But, he must also insist, such comments belong to censorial jurisprudence: there is nothing *logically* amiss in the judge's prescriptive account of Jones' legal obligations; as observers we must agree that Jones has a legal obligation to wear a helmet. My claim, however, is that while the judge has shown how Jones may be *obliged*, by the threat of sanctions, to wear a helmet, he has not offered an intelligible justification for the claim that she has a legal *obligation* to do so; nor does an observer yet have reason to say that Jones has such an obligation.

The Oligarch family seized power in Doulia twenty years ago: they have consolidated their power over the unwilling but terrified populace with the help of the well-paid thugs who make up the 'army' and the 'police'; and they now enforce a system of primary and secondary rules whose sole aim is, they openly admit, to further their own interests. Having read *The Concept of Law*, they now claim that this is Doulia's legal system; and that the Doulians are legally obligated to obey these rules. Now a legal system may be morally corrupt; and people may have legal obligations which make no tenable moral claim to their allegiance. But we cannot see the Doulians as having even legal obligations under the Oligarchs' rules: for we cannot see those rules as constituting a system of law.

I do not suppose that we will often find a system like the Oligarchs'. They would be more familiar if they claimed, as tyrants usually claim, to have some right (other than the 'right' of might) to rule over Doulia, and to have some concern for the Doulians'

---

[13] See *CL* 189–96. Hart almost seems to accept here (*CL* 196) that authority, as distinct from mere power, must as a matter of *logic* be accepted voluntarily by a sufficient number of those over whom it is asserted: but this claim (which is anyway arguable) is hardly consistent with the general tenor of his account.

interests; and we will see shortly why such claims are important.[14] Hart himself would claim that any system of law must by 'natural necessity' include 'the minimum content of Natural Law', and must thus offer the populace certain minimal protections and benefits.[15] But if this is simply the pragmatic claim that even a purely self-interested ruler should in prudence offer her subjects such protections and benefits, it will not meet my claim that such prudential considerations provide a *logically* inappropriate basis for a system of law (and thus that if the Oligarchs include that minimum content in their system for purely prudential reasons, this is not enough to transform that system – or even those parts of the system which incorporate that content – into a system of law).[16] If it is simply the moral claim that any system of law *ought* to include this content, it will not meet my claim that there is something *logically* amiss with a purported system of law which lacks this content, or which includes it for the wrong kind of reason. And if it is meant to amount to something more than such pragmatic or moral claims, it is inconsistent with the Positivist aims of Hart's account.[17] But my claim so far is only that a Hartian Positivist must count the Oligarchs' imaginary system as a system of law; by seeing why it cannot count as a system of law we will see more clearly what is lacking in such a Positivist understanding of the concept of law.

3 OBLIGATIONS, RULES AND VALUES

What is wrong with the Oligarchs' claim that their rules impose legal obligations on the Doulians; or with the judge's attempt to justify his prescriptive claims about Jones' legal obligations?

Obligation-claims, both legal and non-legal, are addressed to rational agents, and seek their assent as well as their obedience: this is part of the logic of such claims. They must be justified *to* the person whose obedience they claim, by reference to *reasons* which he allegedly can grasp and should accept for himself as good reasons for doing what the claim requires.

[14] This has to do, no doubt, with the considerations adduced in *CL* ch. 9: but also, as my later arguments should show, with the concept of law itself; and with the very notion of a human society (on which see P Winch, 'Nature and Convention'). Perhaps what I have sketched here cannot even be recognised as a possible human society: but all I need claim for my present purposes is that it cannot count as a system of law.

[15] *CL* ch. 9.

[16] Compare R Dworkin, 'Philosophy, Morality, and Law'.

[17] See R Shiner, 'Hart and Hobbes' 218–25; 'Towards a Descriptive Theory of Legal Obligation'.

To justify a particular legal obligation-claim to its addressee, we may first show that the primary rule which purports to impose that obligation is validated by the system's secondary rules; but that is not enough. For she may ask why she should obey rules which are thus validated; and we must then show that she has an obligation to obey that *system* of rules. We may maintain a prescriptive claim of legal obligation against one who refuses to accept it: but what we must then maintain is that she *ought* to accept it; that she ought to recognise the good reasons which require her to accept and obey both the primary rules which impose particular obligations on her, and the secondary rules which give those primary rules their legal standing.

Now the Oligarchs can give the Doulians reason to obey their rules; the sanctions which they threaten provide prudential reasons for obedience. But this cannot justify the claim that those rules impose obligations: if the only reason you can give me for obeying a rule is the sanction I will suffer if I disobey, you cannot claim that I have an obligation to obey it. A threatened sanction may give me prudential reason to perform my obligations, but it cannot *create* those obligations; rather it gives me further reason to perform obligations which I *already* have. Obligation-claims must be justified to those on whom they are allegedly binding, by reference to reasons which are independent of any sanctions which may be threatened in order to give them further incentives to do what they ought to do.[18]

There should indeed be an *identity* between the reasons which I claim to have for making and trying to enforce an obligation-claim against you and the reasons which I offer you for accepting and obeying that claim (the logic of obligation-claims thus incorporates the moral demand that we should treat and address others as rational and autonomous agents);[19] and this identity is lacking if the only reason I give you for obedience is the sanction which I attach to my claim. Now the reasons which the Oligarchs, secure in the knowledge of their own power, avow for creating and enforcing their system of rules refer only to their own interests: but they cannot claim that these are reasons which the *Doulians* should accept for obeying these rules. For rules which thus serve the interests of a particular group cannot embody a general requirement of altruism; nor is any reason offered for giving the interests of this group a special claim on the Doulians' concern, apart from the fact, irrelevant in this context, that this group has a monopoly of effective power. A

---

[18] Compare *CL* 79–88.   [19] See ch. 2(3) above.

ruler who is to claim that the law which he administers has authority over, and imposes obligations on, the citizens must be able to justify that law to those citizens; and neither the fact that the law serves his own interests nor the fact that he has the power to enforce obedience to it can provide such a justification.

We must also look more carefully at the idea of accepting a rule. Hart insists that a legal system's officials, who must accept its secondary rules as normative guides for their conduct, may accept these rules for purely self-interested reasons. Now the Oligarchs accept their own secondary rules as rules of prudence: but they cannot give the Doulians reason to accept, nor can they themselves be said to accept, those rules as the rules of a system of law.

Hart offers a formal and general account of what it is to accept (to be internally related to) *any* kind of rule: I must obey the rule because I take it seriously as a normative standard of conduct.[20] But we cannot understand what *this* involves without attending more carefully both to my reasons for obeying the rule and to the meaning of the rule itself. For a rule does not simply prescribe a certain pattern of conduct: it prescribes it in the light of values and purposes which are themselves integral to its meaning and its identity as a particular kind of rule; and it is these values and purposes which must motivate a genuine acceptance of the rule.

Moral rules provide the obvious example here. Someone may 'make it a rule' to act justly because she sees that this will in the long run serve her interests; her conduct will then conform, externally, to the requirements of justice; in a Hartian sense she 'accepts' those requirements. But she is not a just person; she is externally rather than internally related to those requirements as moral requirements of justice, since she accepts them merely as principles of prudence. The point is not merely that she, unlike a just person, will abandon those requirements if and when they no longer serve her interests: rather that what justice requires of me is a concern for justice itself, whether or not it serves my interests. A just person and a self-interested person may superficially follow 'the same rule'; they may agree that one 'ought' to pay one's debts, guide their own conduct by that demand, and respond critically to any failure to obey it. But they do not truly accept the same rule; for one who is just understands and accepts her rule as a moral requirement of justice, but one who is self-interested sees her rule as a rule of prudence, which coincides to this extent with the demands of morality. To understand a rule as a moral rule is to see it as embodying certain moral values;

[20] *CL* 54–7; see Hacker, 'Hart's Philosophy of Law' 14–16.

to accept it as a moral rule is to accept it because I care for those values.[21]

One whose relationship to the requirements of morality is structured by self-interest is only externally related to them; she does not obey them for the kind of reason which is appropriate to them. Now not all rules are moral rules; and it is not true of all rules that they must be accepted for moral reasons: there are indeed rules of prudence which are properly accepted for reasons of self-interest. But what *is* true is that any rule exists as part of a social practice which is structured by certain values and purposes. To understand and accept a rule is to understand it as embodying, and to accept it *because* it embodies, the values and purposes which thus give it its meaning and its identity; and insofar as those values and purposes are independent of self-interest, self-interest is irrelevant and inappropriate as a reason for accepting that rule. A thorough justification of this general claim would require a detailed examination of different kinds of rule, to show what kinds of motive may be involved in or compatible with a genuine acceptance of different practices and their rules, and what part self-interest may properly play in an internal relationship to some kinds of rule. But one further example must suffice here.

The rules of etiquette define and structure a range of social activities and relationships; they specify what counts as 'correct' behaviour in various social contexts. To understand these rules we must ask not just which particular patterns of conduct they prescribe, but *why* they prescribe them; we must understand the values, and the conception of social life, which the rules embody. A person might follow these rules purely for the sake of the further social profit which this will bring her: but her relationship to them is then merely external; they cannot be understood as rules of self-interest. To suggest revising the rules in order to make it easier or more profitable to follow them would be to suggest, not a revision within the terms of etiquette, but an abandonment of etiquette; for though the rules of etiquette can and do change, the values internal to the social practice set logical constraints on the kinds of reason which can justify a deliberate change, and exclude considerations of self-interest as irrelevant and inappropriate. But if convenience and profit are, from the point of view of etiquette, improper reasons for changing its rules, they must also be inappropriate as reasons for

---

[21] This paragraph asserts, without adequate argument, a particular view of the relationship (or lack of it) between morality and self-interest: but see D Z Phillips and H O Mounce, *Moral Practices* chs. 3–4, as against P R Foot, 'Moral Beliefs'.

accepting its rules; a concern for etiquette is not a concern for ease or profit.[22]

Of course different communities will have different conceptions of social life and different systems of etiquette; and we may find different and conflicting views within one community about the values which the rules of etiquette should embody, and thus about those rules themselves. No analytical inquiry can show that a system of etiquette *must* be structured by one particular and determinate set of values; but it can explicate the range of value-concepts in terms of which such systems must be understood – a range which will not include self-interested considerations of profit or convenience. Many who follow the rules of etiquette might indeed do so for reasons of self-interest, or from mere habit; and the day might come when no one followed those rules out of any real concern for the values they embody or for the kinds of relationship they define. The rules would still have a kind of existence, so long as they were followed, and used in the justification and criticism of actions; but we would have to say, not just that they would then be unlikely to last, but that, though its skeleton survived, etiquette was dead. For the existence of etiquette as a live social practice is logically dependent on, and the possibility of following its rules from self-interest or mere habit is parasitic on, there being (or having been) some at least who follow its rules out of a genuine concern for the values which those rules embody; and a self-interested or merely habitual relationship to the rules is necessarily defective by the standards internal to the rules themselves. We might talk in such a case of those who follow the letter, but not the spirit, of the rules: my point is that an *acceptance* of the rules must involve a recognition and acceptance of their spirit; and that the letter is parasitic on the spirit.

In giving an account of what it is to accept the rules of such a social practice we may note, as Hart does, the possibility of following those rules from self-interest or habit. But we must also note, as Hart does not, that such a relationship to the rules is defective by the standards of the practice itself; and to do this we must give an account of the kinds of value which are internal to the practice. If we fail to do this, we will take the defective cases to be standard cases of accepting the practice and its rules; and we will then fail to understand what the practice *is*. This is not to say that we must condemn

---

[22] Compare Dworkin, 'Philosophy, Morality, and Law' 679–82. On etiquette, see D Z Phillips, 'In Search of the Moral "Must": Mrs Foot's Fugitive Thought'. The rules of games would provide further useful examples here; compare R Dworkin, 'Hard Cases' 101–5.

the person who is thus externally related to the rules of a practice; for we may regard the practice as worthless, and believe that no one *should* accept it. But to understand the practice we must understand the values which are internal to it, and give a richer account than Hart's of what it is to accept its rules.

What is true of other social practices is also true of the law. The concept of law is not just that of an abstract structure of rules whose content or purpose is logically quite indeterminate: it is that of a social practice which, like other social practices, is structured by particular kinds of value and purpose. A system of law can exist in a community only if some at least of its members, and in particular its officers, profess to accept its rules as binding on their own and others' conduct, and use those rules to generate prescriptive claims about how they and others should behave: some of these claims will concern the citizens' obligations, and must thus include the claim that the citizens themselves ought to accept those obligations and the rules which generate them. But to understand what it means to accept a system of rules as a system of law, and thus what it means to make prescriptive claims about people's obligations under such a system, and thus what it is for a system of law to exist, we must identify the kinds of value and purpose which are internal to the law.

But how can we do this? An analytical jurisprudence might show that any system of law will be structured by *some* notion of value: but we must surely recognise that different systems will embody irreducibly diverse values; and that any attempt to show that law *must* serve certain values, by showing them to be internal to the concept of law itself, simply confuses censorial with analytical jurisprudence by importing into an analysis of the concept of law moral ideas which, though they might figure in a censorial conception of what law ought to be, have no necessary connection with the concept of law.

The argument of this section should at least have shown that a system of law cannot properly be founded on the self-interest of a particular group. The Oligarchs avowedly follow and enforce their rules for the sake of their own interests: but they cannot then claim to be operating a system of law. For they cannot claim that these rules impose, as law must purport to impose, obligations on the Doulians, since they cannot intelligibly claim that 'serving the Oligarchs' interests' gives the Doulians good reason to obey these rules. Nor can they claim that they themselves accept these rules as a system of law: for if the mere fact that a system of rules serves the interests of a particular group cannot serve to justify that system, as a system of law, to those on whom it is imposed, it equally cannot provide a relevant reason for accepting that system as a system of law.[23] The Oligarchs' claim that theirs is a system of law, and the judge's attempt to justify his prescriptive claim to Jones, are not merely morally unimpressive, or unlikely to persuade their addressees: they are logically incoherent. But can we now say anything more positive about the kinds of value or purpose which must be cited in the justification of, and which must motivate a genuine acceptance of, a system of law?

4 LAW AND THE COMMON GOOD

We might begin by recalling a familiar Natural Lawyers' theme, which emphasises the essentially rational nature of law as a system of obligations.

Law is nought else than an ordinance of reason for the common good made by the authority who has care of the community.[24]

Law's rational nature was traditionally taken to lie primarily in its derivation, direct or indirect, from the objective law of nature; thus positive law is appropriately justified insofar as it accords with Natural Law.[25] But law, as a *rational* enterprise, must also be justified *to* those whom it purports to bind: rulers, legislators and officials are engaged in a rational, rather than a purely manipulative or coercive, relationship with the citizens; law aims, not merely to control the citizens' conduct, but to guide it by rules which impose obligations on them, and can be justified to them, as rational and responsible agents. This is the proper force of Fuller's contrast between law and 'managerial control': law differs from other modes of social control in the moral status it accords to the citizen; only within such an understanding of law can we find logical space for the ideas of legal authority and obligation, as distinct from those of mere power and coercion.[26]

---

[23] Compare Hart's own recognition of the problematic character of his claim that 'it is both intelligible and important to distinguish the general acceptance of the legally ultimate rule of a system of law which specifies the criteria of legal validity from whatever moral principles or rules individuals act upon in deciding whether and to what extent they are morally bound to obey the law' (in his Review of Fuller, *The Morality of Law* 1294).

[24] Aquinas, *Summa Theologiae* 1a2ae90.4.

[25] See *Finnis* ch. 10.7.

[26] Fuller, *The Morality of Law* 207–13; see my article cited above (n.4) for the difference between my claims and Fuller's.

The requirement that the law should address the citizen as a rational agent is thus integral to its character as an attempt to subject human conduct to the governance of obligation-imposing rules. It generates further constraints on the purposes which law can properly serve, and on the means by which it may serve them: for those purposes and means must be consistent with the respect which is owed to the individual citizen, and must be justified to her by reasons which she can be expected to grasp and accept for herself. I will not discuss these constraints here (their implications for the criminal process will be discussed in future chapters): but they would, I think, help to show why the law must allow to the individual citizen certain fundamental rights appropriate to her status as a rational agent under the law; why justice must thus be a crucial legal concept; and why a system of law which is to claim the allegiance of its citizens must at least offer them the kinds of minimal protection and benefit which are contained in Hart's 'minimum content of Natural Law'. All I want to argue here, however, is that the law, as a rational enterprise, must address and respect the citizen as a rational and responsible agent; and that its claim on her obedience must be a *moral* claim which is justified to her in moral terms. This latter point can best be clarified by considering the second element in Aquinas' definition of law; the idea that a system of law must serve 'the common good'.

If we ask what kinds of reason could appropriately justify a legal system and its laws, it is tempting to reply that they must refer to the common good of the community: law must be justified to those whose obedience it claims by being shown to serve their common good; its officials must profess to direct their legislative and administrative activities towards that common good; and their activities, and the laws which they create and administer, must be critically assessed by reference to that common good. For the law claims authority over a whole community, and imposes sometimes arduous obligations on its members: only by reference to the community's common good can the law's claims be justified to all its members. But this suggestion needs at least two qualifications.

First, the idea of 'the common good' sets no very tight constraints on the particular ends or values which the law must claim to serve; it need not, for example, be understood in Utilitarian or egalitarian terms as the harmonious satisfaction of the interests of all members of the community.[27] For conceptions of the common good – of

---

[27] See J Smith, *Legal Obligation* chs. 3–5, who wrongly gives such a consequentialist bias to the notion of obligation; on the common good, see *Finnis* ch. 6.

what is good for, or the good of, a community – may be informed by a whole range of different and irreducibly diverse values. Different systems of law, and different normative theories of law, will embody different conceptions of the common good; and though an analytical inquiry might show that certain specific moral concepts must figure in any intelligible conception of a community's good, it cannot show that one particular conception of that good, or of the precise meaning and significance of those moral concepts, is *the* right one. Such concepts as these are essentially controversial; and it is not for conceptual analysis to judge between competing interpretations of them.[28]

Second, a law may be justified by reference to the good, not of the particular community whose law it is, but of others outside that community: it might require members of the community to contribute to the relief of suffering in other countries; or it might require the performance of other obligations which this community and its members are thought to have to other communities.[29] We cannot plausibly argue that such a law must either be justified in terms of the good of *this* community (by reference to further profits which it may then gain, or to a moral conception of its good), or be condemned as unjustified: we must rather allow that not all laws need to be justified by reference to the common good of the particular community whose laws they are.

Despite these qualifications, the claim that it is the essential or proper purpose of a system of law to serve the common good of the community whose law it is contributes significantly to an adequate understanding of the concept of law. For it emphasises that the law's demands on the citizen must be justified to her in moral terms; and that a conception of the community whose law this is must play a central role in that justification. Given the extent and the nature of the authority which the law claims over a citizen's life and conduct, and of the obligations which it imposes on her; and given the respect which it must accord to the citizen as a rational agent (and must thus also require her to accord to her fellow-citizens): its claim on her allegiance and obedience can be justified only by an appeal to moral considerations which require that allegiance and obedience of her. But the law is binding on individuals as members, whether permanent or temporary, of the particular community whose law it is: its

---

[28] But see *Finnis* for an ambitious attempt to establish a set of basic human goods which law must serve: I think the attempt fails (see D N MacCormick, 'Natural Law Reconsidered'); but my argument anyway requires only the more modest claims which I make here.

[29] I am grateful to Stanley Kleinberg for making me see the importance of this point.

claims on them must therefore be justified by reference to moral considerations which apply to them as members of that community; to the duties which they owe to that community and its members; and to the values which identify that community's good and determine its duties to the outside world.

Bearing these qualifications in mind, we can therefore say that it is the essential and proper purpose of law to serve the common good. If we are, as participants, to justify a system of law to one who is subject to its requirements, we must show that it serves the common good of the community of which she is a member – a good which she herself ought to recognise and care for. If we are, as observers, to identify a system as a system of law, we must show that those who enforce and profess to accept its requirements are prepared to justify those requirements in these terms. The Oligarchs must, if they are to claim legal authority over the Doulians, be able to claim that their rules are designed to serve not just their own good but the common good – perhaps by claiming that the moral values which determine that common good justify giving such special weight to the interests of this particular group within the community.

So too a judge who is to justify the prescriptive claim that Jones has a legal obligation to wear a crash-helmet must claim that the rules which impose that obligation are designed and administered to serve the common good of the community of which Jones is a member. In a system which separates legislative from judicial functions he may not need to claim that this particular law serves some aspect of the common good: though a legislator must justify the laws which she makes in these terms, a judge may argue that citizens are obligated to obey, and courts to apply, even laws which they think are bad laws, and that it is not for individual courts or citizens to decide which laws they should apply or obey. But this argument must itself depend on the claim that this system of law does as a whole serve the common good; and that the secondary rules which require courts to apply, and citizens to obey, even laws which they think are bad laws are themselves justified in terms of the common good.[30]

An analysis of the concept of law thus finds certain notions of value and purpose, concerned with the common good and with the moral

---

[30] See ch. 4(9) below; and compare the discussion of 'protected' and 'exclusionary' reasons as characteristic of the law in J Raz, *Practical Reason and Norms* 35–48, 141–6; and in 'Legitimate Authority' 16–33.

status of the citizen, within the concept of law. These provide an *ideal* model of what a system of law *ought* to be. It should be structured by an adequate conception of the common good: for that is the proper concern of the law. Its officers should guide, justify and criticise their legislative and administrative activities in the light of this conception of the common good, and be motivated by a concern for that good: for a legal system's officers should accept the rules which define and authorise their activities; and to accept those rules as law is to accept them because they serve the common good. Its citizens should voluntarily accept the authority of the law and the obligations which it imposes on them: for a system of law seeks the assent, as well as the obedience, of all those who are bound by its rules.[31] The ideal of law is that of a community of rational agents co-operating in the pursuit of the common good.

Actual legal systems fall well short of this ideal: law as it is is rarely law as it ought to be. I may think that a particular legal system is not founded on an adequate conception of the common good; that its laws are ill-suited to serve that good; and that the ideological structure of values in terms of which it is justified by and to its members is nothing more than a spurious or self-deceptive rationalisation which conceals its truly oppressive nature. Despite their claims, the system's officers may not be motivated by a concern for the common good, but by a desire to further their own interests, or to keep power in the hands of a particular group; and many of its citizens may not accept its authority voluntarily, but obey it, if at all, only unwillingly through fear, or unthinkingly in blind submission to an 'authority' whose legitimacy they do not understand.[32] Systems such as these are still legal systems, so long as the appropriate kinds of prescriptive claim are made, and the appropriate kinds of justification are offered, within them; but they are *necessarily* defective as systems of law, by the standards which are internal to the concept of law itself.

To say that law must serve the common good is not to say that we can count a system as one of law only if we can agree that it does serve that good: but we can recognise it as a legal system only if those who accept it justify it in terms of some conception of the common good; we must see it as a defective system of law insofar as we think that justification to be spurious or inadequate; and we can

---

[31] See J R Lucas, 'The Phenomenon of Law' 85 on the ideal of an internal relationship to the law on the part of all the citizens. It follows from this, paradoxically, that insofar as law may also be defined by reference to its use of coercive sanctions the ideal of law is also the death of law as a coercive system.

[32] See *CL* III.

accept it as a system of law which is binding on us only if we can agree that it serves the common good. To say that the law's officers must be motivated by a concern for the common good is not to say that they count as officers of the law only if they are thus motivated: but they must claim to be thus motivated if they are to claim to be operating a system of law as distinct from a merely self-interested tyranny; and they are necessarily failing in their legal duty insofar as that claim is hypocritical or unfounded. To say that the law requires the voluntary allegiance of all its citizens is not to say that a system which fails to secure such unanimous assent is not a legal system, or that a citizen only has such legal obligations as she herself accepts; the law can claim to bind both those who accept and those who reject its demands: but a system of law is necessarily imperfect to the extent that its authority is not voluntarily accepted by all its citizens (though whether we should ascribe that imperfection to the citizens' failure to accept the law's justified demands, or to the impropriety of the law's demands on them, is another matter).

Legal obligation is thus a species of moral obligation: the obligations which the laws of my community impose on me are aspects of my moral obligation to care for the good of that community. To claim, prescriptively, that someone has a legal obligation is to claim that a law is morally binding on her; to accept a legal obligation is to accept it as morally binding; and to recognise that I do in fact have certain legal obligations, without accepting those obligations or the system which generates them, is to recognise that certain moral demands are made on me by others, without accepting that those demands are justified.[33]

This is not to assert an identity between legal and moral obligation: for my moral obligation to obey the laws of my community, because they serve the common good, can conflict with other moral obligations which I recognise; and some of these may also concern the common good (this is often a feature of civil disobedience). Nor is every aspect or precondition of the common good the law's proper concern: the fact that an activity is injurious, or conducive, to some aspect of the common good does not by itself justify proscribing, or prescribing, that activity by law; and I have not here tried to determine the proper scope of the criminal law. But a certain kind of immorality should be a necessary, though not a sufficient, condition of criminality: if we are to justify prohibiting a certain type of conduct as criminal we must at least be able to show

[33] Compare Gewirth, 'Obligation: Political, Legal, Moral'; C D Johnson, 'Moral and Legal Obligation'.

that it is injurious to some aspect of the common good – either as a *malum in se*, which is injurious in itself, or as a *malum prohibitum*, which is properly prohibited by a law which serves the common good; and such a justification must presuppose that the citizen has a moral obligation towards the common good of her community.

5 POSITIVISM AND NATURAL LAW

I can best summarise my argument in this chapter by relating it briefly to some of the dominant themes of the Positivist and Natural Law traditions.[34]

My argument fits within the Natural Law tradition insofar as it posits a necessary connection between law and certain moral concepts, and between legal and moral obligation. But I have not claimed that an analytical jurisprudence will reveal determinate moral criteria which positive law must satisfy if it is to count as law at all: it rather reveals a range of moral concepts in terms of which positive law must be justified and criticised, but which are themselves susceptible to different and conflicting moral interpretations. We can recognise as law systems and rules which are unjust, cruel and oppressive, so long as the appropriate kind of justification is *offered* for them: but to see them as law is to see them as needing such a justification; and we must condemn them as bad law insofar as we find that justification inadequate or hypocritical. Unjust law may still be law: but it is necessarily defective or perverted *as* law.[35]

My argument thus accepts the central Positivist contention that

in the absence of an expressed constitutional or legal provision, it could not follow from the mere fact that a rule violated standards of morality that it was not a rule of law; and, conversely, it could not follow from the mere fact that a rule was morally desirable that it was a rule of law.[36]

But Positivists too often suppose that that contention suffices to es-

[34] I am, however, aware of the dangers of trying to talk of *the* theories of Natural Law or of Legal Positivism: see Hart, 'Positivism and the Separation of Law and Morals'; *Finnis* ch. 2; MacCormick, *Legal Reasoning and Legal Theory* chs. 8–10.

[35] Compare Aquinas, *Summa Theologiae* 1a2ae90–97: law which fails to accord with the ideal standards which are part of its 'ratio' (95.4) is not so much not law at all as a *perversion* of law (92.1), an *abuse* of law (93.3), or a *spoilt* law (95.2). A perspective of this kind generates a richer idea of 'the pathology of a legal system' (compare *CL* ch. 6.3) – of the ways in which a system of law may be defective by the standards which are, as a matter of logic, appropriate to it; and a more detailed examination of that pathology would need to attend to the way in which we might deny the title of 'law' to a system which is, we think, *utterly* unjustified, or whose 'rulers' offer a justification which we can see to be utterly hypocritical.

[36] Hart, 'Positivism and the Separation of Law and Morals' 55.

tablish a complete logical separation between the concept of law and any moral notions by reference to which we may justify or criticise positive law; that the criteria by which we can recognise the existence of legal systems, the validity of laws, and the existence of legal obligations, must make *no* essential reference to any moral notions. I have argued, however, against such a complete separation of law and morals, that the concepts of law and legal obligation are *internally* related to moral concepts which provide criteria for the justification and criticism of positive law. My claim is not merely that those who administer or enforce a system of law must profess to regard its demands as morally justified;[37] but that law of its nature requires a particular kind of moral justification. In prescribing, administering or enforcing the demands of what purports to be a system of law we thus commit ourselves to offering the relevant kind of justification for those demands, and subject both ourselves and those demands to the relevant kinds of moral criticism; in identifying or describing a system as one of law we must see it as a system to which such justifications and criticisms are appropriate; and in analysing the concept of law we must recognise the logical relationship between that concept and such justificatory criteria.

We can and should still distinguish law as it is from law as it ought to be, and analytical from censorial jurisprudence. Thus we distinguish the actuality of existing systems of law from the ideal standards in whose light we criticise those systems; the analytical task of explicating the concept of law, and the moral concepts which are related to it, from the censorial task of arguing for a particular interpretation of those concepts or for a particular conception of what law ought to be; and an observer's descriptive analysis of a legal system and the prescriptive claims which are made within it, from a participant's prescriptive assertion of its demands, or a critic's normative assessment of the system and its rules as good or bad law in the light of her own conception of what law ought to be. But our descriptive analyses of law as it is are *logically* related to the moral concepts which structure our conceptions of law as it ought to be.

A Positivist might still claim that what I have offered is not an analysis of the concept of law, but a particular moral conception of what law ought to be: that a properly conceptual analysis must be freed from such moral accretions, and limited to a more austere and value-free model of the kind which Hart provides. In defence of my

[37] Compare Hart, 'Legal Duty and Obligation' 153–61 (though I am not sure whether the views which he there ascribes to Raz are views which Raz actually offers).

claim that these notions of value are internally related to the concept of law, and not just part of a realm of moral discourse which – while no doubt shared by all right-thinking people – has no necessary connection with the concept of law, I would emphasise three aspects of my argument.

First, Hart showed that an account of the concept of law must move beyond the austere simplicities of an Austinian model of habitual obedience to a sovereign's commands, and talk of systems of rules which are accepted as normative by at least some of those within the system. I have argued that one who moves that far beyond an Austinian model must move yet further, to give an account of what it is to *accept* a rule or system as law; and this requires an account of the kinds of value or purpose which are internal to this, as to any, kind of rule.

Second, I have argued that the law's moral dimension is crucial to an adequate understanding of the notions of legal obligation and authority. Hart must allow it to be intelligible, though no doubt both immoral and imprudent, for a tyrant to claim that he is operating a legal system, whose rules authorise his actions and obligate his subjects; but also that, since he has the power to enforce them, these rules need no further justification than that they serve his interests – which is why he follows and enforces them. I have argued that, although he can claim the power to enforce his will, he cannot intelligibly claim legal authority for his actions, or obligation-imposing force for his edicts: for he cannot justify those edicts to his subjects as rules which they ought to accept.

Third, our censorial discussions of law may reveal deep disagreements about what law ought to be, and about the ideals to which it should aspire: but such discussions and disagreements are possible only if we *agree* on the range of concepts which are relevant to them. We may disagree about the justice of particular laws or legal systems; about what justice itself amounts to; or about what the common good is or requires: but we agree that considerations of justice and the common good are relevant to any critical assessment of law; and we agree in our recognition of logical constraints on the interpretation of these concepts. We agree, that is, on the logical grammar of the concept of law; and without that agreement our critical discussions and disagreements would not be possible.

6 THE RULE OF LAW

We can now offer more adequate answers to the two questions posed at the beginning of section 2 of this chapter.

The law makes a moral demand on the citizen's allegiance: not merely that she obey its coercive orders, but that she accept its requirements as morally binding on her. Law differs from mere tyranny in just this: that the basis of its appeal and its justification is not a coercive threat, but a moral demand which the citizen is to understand and accept for herself. The law may also enforce its demands on those who will not obey voluntarily, and threaten sanctions against those who disobey; and future chapters will discuss the extent to which, and the way in which, this coercive dimension to the law can be justified. But the law's right to impose such sanctions depends on the claim that it imposes obligations which are binding both on those who accept them voluntarily and on those who do not, and which give good reasons for action, in advance and independently of any sanctions which are attached to them.

Law, then, differs from other modes of social control which simply seek the most efficient way of controlling conduct, in the moral status which it accords to the citizen who is bound by its requirements: it addresses her as a rational and responsible agent. It aims to guide her conduct, not by whatever means may be effective, but by imposing obligations on her; it seeks her voluntary acceptance of and obedience to requirements which can themselves be justified to her.

We can now see why we should prefer the rule of law to other modes of social control. It is not just because law aims at the common good: for other modes of social organisation may have that aim. Nor is it just because a system of law is in fact the most efficient way of achieving our social goals:[38] for the importance of the rule of law is not thus contingent on its efficacy as a means to further and independently identifiable ends, but depends crucially on the values (concerned with the moral status of the citizen) which are internal to the concept of law itself. Particular decisions about how best to pursue some aspect of the common good will be guided in part by consequentialist considerations of efficiency: but what makes law an appropriate method of social control is not that it is more efficient than other more manipulative or coercive methods, but that it embodies a proper respect for the citizen as a rational agent.

Should we then value the rule of law because it is consistent, as other modes of social control are not, with certain independent side-constraints on our pursuit of the common good? That good provides the consequentialist justifying aim of a system of law: but our

[38] Compare *CL* 38, 125.

pursuit of that aim is constrained by the independent requirement that we must treat and respect the individual citizen as a rational and responsible agent – a requirement which the rule of law (unlike other possibly more effective, but also more manipulative or coercive, methods of pursuing that aim) respects. But this implies that an account of the common good of a community need make no essential reference to the moral status of the beings who compose that community; that the citizen's claim to our respect is something quite separate from the common good which provides the justifying aim of a system of law. We should rather say that the common good is the good of a community of rational agents; and as a matter of logic, rather than of contingent fact or independent moral side-constraints, we can pursue *that* good only through social institutions which themselves respect the citizen's status as a rational moral agent. The values which are internal to the concept of law are also internal to the ends which law should serve; the rule of law is internally related to, and intrinsically appropriate to, its proper ends.

I have not offered a complete account either of the concept of law or of the values which are internal to it. My aim in this chapter has been to explicate and defend my claim that the law must address the citizen as a rational moral agent, making a moral claim on her allegiance and obedience; and my task now is to show what part this essential feature of the law should play in our understanding of the criminal process of trial and punishment. I have yet to discuss the *coercive* dimension to the law, though it is this which generates the most serious doubts about whether a system of law can be fully consistent with a proper respect for the citizens as rational and autonomous agents: but future chapters will take up this problem.

4

Trial and Verdict

For less the sturdy criminal false witnesses should bring
His witnesses were not allowed to swear to anything,
And lest the wily advocate the Court should overreach
His advocate was not allowed the privilege of speech.
Yet, such was the humanity and wisdom of the law
That if in the indictment there appeared to be a flaw,
The Court assigned him Counsellors to argue on the doubt,
Provided he himself had first contrived to point it out.
Yet lest their mildness should by some be craftily abused,
To show him the indictment they most steadfastly refused,
But still that he might understand the nature of the charge,
The same was, in the Latin tongue, read out to him at large!

Unattributed, quoted in G Williams,
The Proof of Guilt, pp. 9–10

No proposition can be more clearly established than that a man cannot incur the loss of liberty or property for an offence by a judicial proceeding until he has had a fair opportunity of answering the charge against him, unless the legislature has expressly or impliedly given an authority to act without that necessary preliminary.

Bonaker v Evans (1851) 16 Q.B. 162, at p. 171, *per* Parke B

I THE DEFENDANT ON TRIAL

The law makes a moral claim on the citizen's allegiance: it does not merely demand that she obey its coercive orders, but claims to impose on her obligations which can be justified to her in terms of the common good of her community; it addresses her as a rational and responsible agent who can understand and accept that justification. If she is suspected of breaking the criminal law, she may be brought to trial on a criminal charge; if she is then convicted she may suffer punishment or some other kind of coercive imposition. This chapter concerns the proper purposes of a criminal trial, and the values which do or should structure its procedures.

Any thorough discussion of the criminal trial would need to attend to a whole range of procedural rules and principles, including the rules governing the admissibility and presentation of evidence;

the evidentiary and probative burdens to be borne by prosecution and defence; the contrast between, and the respective merits of, adversarial and inquisitorial systems of criminal justice. Many of these matters, however, will receive little attention in this chapter: for my aim is not to offer a complete account of the criminal trial, but to examine more specifically the status and role which the trial allows, or should allow, to the defendant. Such an inquiry will reveal some important points about the proper purpose and meaning of a criminal trial – points which will also assist our understanding of the proper character of criminal punishment.[1]

The first of the quotations which head this chapter offers a critical view of the ordinary defendant's position three centuries ago – a position which effectively denied him the opportunity to defend himself. Its present relevance lies not in its historical accuracy, but in its implicit claim that a defendant must in justice be given a fair chance to answer the charges laid against him. This claim appeals to one of the two fundamental principles of Natural Justice, *Audi alteram partem*; and it is this right to be heard which the second quotation asserts. The context of that quotation is administrative rather than criminal law; and most English discussions of the scope and meaning of this principle concern its relevance, not to criminal trials, but to different kinds of administrative hearing, in which the right to be heard is anything but absolute, as the quotation makes clear. But such discussions presuppose the relevance and importance of this right in a criminal trial; the question of how far it should be binding on various kinds of administrative tribunal is often expressed as the question of how far their procedures should resemble those of a court of law.[2]

The defendant's right to be heard brings with it other rights: to be given due notice of his trial, of the charges against him, and of the

---

[1] On the structure and evolution of the criminal process in England, see P Devlin, *The Criminal Prosecution in England*; G Williams, *The Proof of Guilt*; C Hampton, *Criminal Procedure* (referred to hereafter as *Hampton*); Royal Commission on Criminal Procedure (referred to hereafter, after its chairman, as *Philips*), *Report*, and *Law and Procedure*.

[2] On *Audi alteram partem* and the other requirements of Natural Justice, see especially J F Garner, *Administrative Law* ch. 6; P Jackson, *Natural Justice*; S A de Smith, *Judicial Review of Administrative Action*; H W R Wade, *Administrative Law* Part 5; D H Clark, 'Natural Justice: Substance and Shadow'. On the comparable right to 'due process' enshrined in American law by the 5th and 14th amendments to the Constitution, see J R Pennock and J W Chapman (eds), *Due Process*. I am indebted to Dr Joseph Jaconelli for making me aware of the relevance of these issues to the argument of this book.

evidence relevant to his case; to have the assistance of counsel.[3] It is a right, not a duty: he may remain silent both before and during his trial, and refuse either to give evidence himself or to offer evidence on his behalf; it is for the prosecution to prove his guilt beyond reasonable doubt, not for him to prove his innocence. However, if the prosecution show that he has a case to answer, he risks conviction if he offers no defence; and apart from cases, such as an insanity defence, in which the burden of proof is explicitly laid on the defendant, the various presumptions of fact and of law with which courts operate serve in fact to shift some of the evidentiary or probative burden onto the defence.[4] But he has a *duty* to appear for his trial and to be present during it; to plead from his own mouth, not merely through his counsel, 'Guilty' or 'Not Guilty' to the indictment; and to be present to hear the verdict and, if convicted, the sentence of the court.[5] Indeed, a defendant who refused to plead to the indictment, and was found to be 'mute of malice' rather than 'by the visitation of God', was formerly subjected to the *'peine forte et dure'* (being slowly crushed under a large weight) to persuade him to enter a plea. Now, however, a plea of 'Not Guilty' is simply entered on behalf of an unresponsive defendant who is fit to plead.[6]

It is the rationale of provisions such as these which will mainly concern me in this chapter: why should we only convict and punish a criminal if she has had a fair hearing at a properly conducted trial; why should the defendant's presence at, and participation in, her trial be so important? To answer these questions we must inquire into the purposes and values which should structure criminal trials; and into the nature and significance of the difference between a criminal trial and the kind of judicial 'inquiry into the facts' which may be thought appropriate for a defendant who is unfit to plead.[7]

Three kinds of account may be offered of the trial and its rationale. The first portrays the trial in purely instrumental terms as a means to certain further ends; its procedures should be those which will enable it to serve those ends most efficiently. The second also takes a consequentialist or instrumentalist view of the justifying aims of a system of criminal trials, but allows that our pursuit of

---

[3] See Devlin, *The Criminal Prosecution in England* 93–6; Williams, *The Proof of Guilt* 6–14.

[4] On these burdens see R Cross, *Evidence* (referred to hereafter as *Cross*) ch. 4; G Williams, *Textbook of Criminal Law* ch. 2

[5] See *Hampton* 178–9, 184, 338–40, 347–8, for these requirements and the qualifications to them (especially in the case of summary trials).

[6] See Williams, *The Proof of Guilt* 12–13, ch. 3.

[7] See ch. 1(3) above.

those aims is constrained by certain independent values: some of the trial's provisions are to be explained and justified by reference to those non-consequentialist side-constraints. The third, however, gives the trial a more thoroughly non-consequentialist rationale – a purpose to which it is internally rather than merely contingently related: the defendant's role in his trial – his participation; his right to be heard – is explained neither in instrumental terms as an efficient means towards some further end, nor by reference to independent side-constraints on our pursuit of that end, but as being integral to the proper purpose of the trial.[8]

I will offer an account of the third kind, which relates the purposes of the criminal trial both to the character of the law's demands on the citizen and to the purposes of moral criticism and blame: but I will begin by discussing the two kinds of instrumentalist account. I will claim that my account provides the best justification for central features of our own system of criminal trials: but my main concern is with various *ideal* models of what a trial *ought* to be; and, here as elsewhere, we will need to attend to the gap which exists between the ideal and the actual.

2 TRIALS AND DIAGNOSTIC TRIBUNALS

It may seem obvious that we must understand the criminal trial in primarily instrumentalist or consequentialist terms; surely its justifying aim must be something like this: 'that the guilty should be detected, convicted and duly sentenced'?[9] The criminal law aims to prevent injurious kinds of conduct by prohibiting them, and by imposing sanctions or other coercive measures on those who engage in them; the primary purpose of a criminal trial is to assist the aims of the law by identifying those who should be subject to such coercive measures.

There are difficulties in trying to characterise a *purely* consequentialist account of the criminal trial. A criminal trial belongs with a

---

[8] Apart from works cited elsewhere in this chapter, useful discussions of these issues are found in J R Lucas, *On Justice* ch. 4; G Maher, 'Human Rights and the Criminal Process'; H L Packer, *The Limits of the Criminal Sanction* Part 2; T M Scanlon, 'Due Process'; M Kadish, 'Methodology and Criteria in Due Process Adjudication: A Survey and Criticism'; R S Summers, 'Evaluating and Improving Legal Processes; A Plea for "Process Values"'. I have also learned much from an as yet unpublished paper by Gerry Maher – 'Towards a Theory of Criminal Process'.

[9] A J Ashworth, 'Concepts of Criminal Justice' 412; see also his 'Prosecution and Procedure in Criminal Justice'. Ashworth insists that our pursuit of these consequentialist ends must be constrained by non-consequentialist concerns with fairness and with the rights and moral status of the citizen.

system of criminal law and punishment; and a pragmatic consequentialist, who asks how we can best use our existing institutions, will no doubt find significant consequential benefits in such a system, even if it is not in fact structured by purely consequentialist considerations, and will see a useful role for criminal trials as part of such a system. But we cannot assume in advance that a more speculative consequentialist, who asks what kinds of institution would be appropriate for a society structured by strictly consequentialist principles, would find any use for a recognisable system of criminal law and punishment. I have indeed already argued that certain non-consequentialist values are integral to the very idea of the rule of law; and I will argue later that similar values are integral to the proper meaning of criminal punishment.

Let us suppose, however, that such a consequentialist would find a use for something like a system of law, as one kind of technique for encouraging desirable kinds of conduct. For amongst the techniques available to us, an important part can be played by explicit rules and principles which prescribe or proscribe particular types of conduct; and while some of these will simply constitute the community's social morality, others can usefully be given a more formal and authoritative status by means of secondary rules of recognition and change. Furthermore, while obedience to these rules may be encouraged by the citizens' own consciences, and by informal kinds of social pressure, it will also be useful to have some more organised way of dealing with actual or potential disobedience. Thus potential offenders might be deterred by the threat of formal sanctions; the conduct of actual offenders might be more efficiently modified by some organised kind of treatment; and perhaps those who are especially likely to offend could be identified and subjected to pre-emptive treatment. We would then need a system of tribunals to identify and determine the disposal of those who should be subjected to such special measures.[10]

But how far would such tribunals resemble criminal courts? The question of whether they would, like criminal courts, have the particular task of identifying and sentencing those who are liable to *punishment* will be discussed later; but we may already doubt whether they would, like criminal courts, have the particular task of identifying those who should be liable to special treatment because they have offended against the system's rules. For if the purpose of such treatment is to prevent prohibited or injurious kinds of conduct, it might need to be imposed on some who have not yet broken

[10] See H L A Hart, *The Concept of Law* 89–95.

a rule; perhaps on those who are shown to be especially likely to offend, or to be in other ways a danger to themselves or to others. Why then should we have special tribunals to deal with those whose need for such treatment is evidenced by the fact that they have broken a rule; why not have, for instance, a system like the Scottish Childrens' Hearings, whose tribunals would deal with *anyone* alleged to be in need of such special treatment, whatever the grounds for that allegation?[11]

This is certainly the natural implication of consequentialist suggestions that our courts should move towards a more properly Utilitarian 'occasionalism' which treats the offenders' past offence simply as the occasion for his appearance in court, and as evidence that he may need remedial treatment; or that notions of responsibility should be eliminated from the criminal law – that courts should 'convict' any 'defendant' whose conduct satisfied the definition of the *actus reus* of an offence, ignoring questions of *mens rea*, and then leave to an expert panel the task of deciding what treatment, if any, should be imposed on him.[12] For his past criminal conduct would now figure simply as evidence that some special treatment may be necessary in order to prevent future anti-social conduct; but since it is not the only kind of evidence which may suggest this, why should we have tribunals whose particular task it is to deal with such cases?

I will return to these issues in Chapter 6: but let us for the moment suppose that such a consequentialist would still favour a special system of tribunals for those who have broken the law. Their role would be essentially diagnostic: to identify and determine the disposal of those who should, because they have broken the law, be liable to special coercive measures; and the question which concerns me now is whether we should understand the purpose of a system of criminal trials in similarly instrumental and diagnostic terms.

Such tribunals should clearly try to reach an accurate determination of the relevant facts about the past conduct of those who appear before them; for they will be ineffective insofar as they fail to identify those who have broken the law, and uneconomic insofar as they mistakenly identify as offenders those who have not broken the law. But their efficiency will not depend simply on their accuracy. For accuracy, if attainable at all, is expensive in time and resources.

---

[11] See F M Martin and K Murray, *Children's Hearings*; T D Campbell, 'Discretion and Rights within the Children's Hearing System'.

[12] See N Walker and S McCabe, *Crime and Insanity in England* vol. 2, 101–2; B Wootton, *Crime and the Criminal Law* (on which see H L A Hart, *Punishment and Responsibility* papers 7–8).

We must therefore decide what resources to devote to these tribunals, and weigh the costs of inaccuracy against the benefits of faster and cheaper procedures; and we must ask in which direction the tribunals should err, if err they must. Should we try to capture as many offenders as possible, at the cost of subjecting some 'innocents' to unnecessary treatment; or to ensure that the 'innocent' are freed, at the cost of allowing some offenders to escape the treatment which they should receive?[13] If we are sufficiently disturbed by the cost and likelihood of mistaken 'convictions', we will then have reason to create a 'presumption of innocence' to dissuade the tribunals from being too ready to 'convict'.

I will not try to determine here whether such tribunals would operate with a presumption of 'innocence' or of 'guilt', or with no such presumption either way: that would depend on our assessment of the relative costs and probability of either kind of mistaken judgment; and my concern here is with the nature of those costs. The obvious cost of mistaken 'acquittals' is that a failure to identify actual offenders as such frustrates the preventive aims of the law. A mistaken 'conviction', on the other hand, may inflict unnecessary and unpleasant treatment on someone who is in fact harmless; deprive her, needlessly, of the ability to predict and control her own life; and injure her reputation and her prospects, if it leads others to believe mistakenly that she is a law-breaker.

What of a 'defendant's' role before such tribunals? Her presence, her evidence and the opportunity to question her will be instrumentally valuable in determining the relevant facts about her past conduct, her present condition and her future prospects; and she herself will be more likely to accept, and less likely to resent, the tribunal's decision if she is allowed to put her side of the case. So we may require the tribunals to ensure her presence at, and her ability to participate in, their hearings; and we may require her to give evidence and submit herself to questioning. If we think that tribunals might otherwise be unduly inattentive to her contributions, we might even make it a *strict* rule that she should be heard, and should be given notice of the evidence which will be put to the tribunal; we might declare that a tribunal's decision will be null and void if these

---

[13] Compare the difficulties involved in trying to predict dangerousness as a basis for preventive sentencing, on which see A von Hirsch, *Doing Justice: The Choice of Punishments* 1.3; J Floud and W Young, *Dangerousness and Criminal Justice*. The quotation marks in this and succeeding paragraphs are meant to remind us that notions of 'innocence', 'guilt' and 'conviction' may not carry the same meaning for such tribunals as they do for a criminal trial (especially if, as Wootton suggests, such diagnostic tribunals would ignore questions of *mens rea*).

conditions are not met, even if they would probably have made no difference to the outcome of the particular case. For while such a provision will sometimes secure the release of an offender who should be detained, it will give tribunals a strong incentive to follow procedures which are most likely to produce well-founded and acceptable decisions.[14]

Once again, my concern is not to determine whether such tribunals would actually be bound by such rules, but to identify the considerations which might justify such procedural requirements. We must recognise, however, that we will not always be able to secure the 'defendant's' participation in the hearing. If she refuses to take part, or behaves so disruptively that she has to be removed, the tribunal will have to proceed without her participation or in her absence; but what if she is so disordered that she cannot from the beginning understand or contribute usefully to the inquiry? If she is likely to recover quickly we can simply postpone the hearing: but if there is no prospect of a rapid recovery we must hold some kind of inquiry to determine her disposal; and since her disposal will depend in part on whether she has actually committed an offence, the tribunal might as well proceed with its hearing. For her participation is of purely instrumental importance to the inquiry: it may help the tribunal reach an accurate judgment, but is no more essential to its diagnostic purposes than other kinds of evidence which may or may not be available; the inquiry can, if necessary, be carried through without it.

I have sketched the bare bones of a simple system of diagnostic tribunals whose task would be to identify those who should, because they have broken the law, be liable to special coercive measures; and I have indicated the kinds of reason which might lead such tribunals to adopt something like a 'presumption of innocence', and to recognise something like a 'right to be heard'. I do not claim that a consequentialist must favour a system of this kind, though it is the natural implication of one kind of consequentialist view: my aim is rather to ask whether this provides an adequate model for understanding the purpose of a criminal trial; and whether we should understand the presumption of innocence and the right to be heard in such instrumental terms.

3 THE PRESUMPTION OF INNOCENCE

We may begin with the presumption of innocence. No practicable

[14] Compare R M Hare, *Moral Thinking* 161–4.

system of criminal trials could ensure that it *never* mistakenly convicts an innocent; it must strike a balance between protecting the innocent and capturing the guilty, and must run the risk of convicting some who are in fact innocent.[15] My concern here is not with just where that balance should be struck, but with the costs which must now be balanced, as compared with those involved in a system of diagnostic tribunals.

A tribunal which mistakenly 'acquits' an offender is guilty, at worst, of inefficiency; it fails to capture for treatment someone who may need it. Should we not say, however, that a mistaken acquittal at a criminal trial is also a matter of *injustice*; that even though a verdict of 'Not Guilty' means 'Not proved guilty' rather than 'Innocent', the guilty deserve to be convicted, and their acquittal is therefore unjust? Nor is this simply to say that they deserve to be punished: we might agree that a particular offender should not be punished, but still insist that she ought in justice to be convicted.

We can see the sense of this by considering the harm involved in the conviction of an innocent. It has been argued that, quite apart from the consequential harm which such a conviction may cause, it inflicts a *moral* harm which is *intrinsic* to its character as unjust treatment. Whatever the consequences of a mistaken conviction, and whether or not that mistake is deliberate, an innocent suffers an injustice, and is by that very fact harmed, if she is convicted.[16] Now this is true of a criminal trial; and we may accuse a purely Utilitarian account of the criminal trial of failing to recognise the moral harm inflicted by a mistaken conviction. But it is not true of a diagnostic tribunal, and we cannot accuse such a tribunal of that failure; for its mistaken judgments inflict no such moral harm. An 'innocent' who is 'convicted' and subjected to coercive treatment by a tribunal is a victim of administrative error, not of injustice; and she should be able to console herself with the thought that her suffering is a necessary cost of a system which is justified by its cost-efficient role in preventing crime. Her case is like that of someone who is detained because she is supposedly carrying a contagious disease when she is not in fact a carrier: she is unlucky, and has cause for complaint if she is the victim of inefficient procedures; but if the procedures used were the safest which it was reasonable to adopt, she has suffered no

[15] See R Dworkin, 'Principle, Policy, Procedure'; R Nozick, *Anarchy, State, and Utopia* 96–108; and ch.6 (2) below for the difficulty which this point may pose for some objections to a consequentialist account of punishment. The idea of a balance in the criminal process is emphasised in *Philips, Report* 1.11; see also G Maher, 'Balancing Rights and Interests in the Criminal Process'.
[16] See Dworkin, *op. cit.*

injustice. For a diagnostic tribunal's 'conviction' simply expresses the diagnostic judgment that this person should probably be subjected to special treatment because she has probably broken the law; thus one who is mistakenly 'convicted' is the unlucky victim of a mistaken but, one hopes, well-founded diagnosis.

But someone who is mistakenly convicted of a crime may admit that the court acted reasonably in convicting her, yet still insist that she has suffered an (unintentional) injustice: she may fight to prove her innocence even if she is given an absolute discharge; and she may refuse the parole which would release her from prison, on the grounds that to accept it would be to admit that she was guilty, whereas she wants an official admission of her innocence. Now one who is mistakenly 'convicted' by a diagnostic tribunal, but is released at once as needing no further treatment, may still want to clear her name; she objects to being wrongly labelled as an offender: but unless she is accusing the tribunal of acting improperly she is not trying, unlike the victim of a mistaken conviction, to remedy an *injustice* which she has suffered.

To understand the moral harm – the injustice – involved in the conviction of an innocent, we must recognise the difference between the verdict of a criminal court and the judgment of a diagnostic tribunal. A criminal conviction *condemns* the defendant, by declaring that she is *guilty* of an *offence*, not merely that she has acted in a way which suggests that she might need preventive or remedial treatment. That is why one who is mistakenly convicted may fight to prove her innocence: she wants to show the injustice of the condemnation she has suffered, not simply to correct a mistaken description or diagnosis of her conduct which may have unpleasant consequences for her. That too is why we may see the acquittal of the guilty as unjust; for they deserve the condemnation which a conviction expresses. This dimension of the trial fits naturally with the account of law offered in Chapter 3: the law imposes obligations on the citizen; the trial's initial task is to determine the justice of an accusation that she has flouted her legal obligations. This also provides an initial connection between criminal trials and moral criticism: both aim to determine the justice of a charge of wrong-doing; and both may lead to a condemnation of the wrong-doer.

Can we explain, and justify, this feature of the criminal trial in consequentialist terms? A criminal process of this kind might be more useful than a system of purely diagnostic tribunals: for besides serving, as the tribunals do, to identify law-breakers who should be liable to the further coercive measures which the law provides, it serves the further purpose of denouncing, and thus discouraging, criminal conduct, and may also serve to free the innocent from unjustified suspicions which they might otherwise suffer.

Such a purely consequentialist account invites the familiar objection that it would sanction the deliberate conviction of the innocent if this would serve the preventive aims of the law: to which it might be replied that such convictions would not in fact serve those aims; or that even if they might on rare occasions be useful, it would be so dangerous to allow courts even to contemplate acting in that way that we should make it a *strict* rule to aim to convict only the guilty. Such arguments will be discussed later:[17] I will for the moment simply assert that the conviction of an innocent should be understood as an *intrinsic* wrong; that it is a requirement of justice, not merely of direct or indirect utility, that courts should aim to convict and condemn only the guilty. But even if such a purely consequentialist account of the criminal trial is for this reason as inadequate as a purely consequentialist account of moral blame, we might hope to remedy its defects by recognising certain non-consequentialist side-constraints on the criminal process; and it is the structure and adequacy of such a modified consequentialist account which interests me now.

The general justifying aim of that process still lies, we may now say, in its instrumental contribution to the aim of preventing criminal conduct, by denouncing such conduct, and by identifying those who should be subject to the law's coercive provisions. It is however a requirement of justice, not merely of utility, that a criminal conviction should express an accurate judgment on a defendant's past conduct: justice requires that we subject to the coercive sanctions of the criminal law only those who have voluntarily broken it; and that we aim to convict and condemn all and only those who deserve such condemnation by reason of their guilt. We cannot always achieve this aim; and since the unintentional conviction of the innocent is a greater evil than the unintentional acquittal of the guilty (and since it would be an intolerable imposition on the individual citizen if he was required to defend himself against any accusation, however ill-founded, which was brought against him), we should therefore adopt a presumption of innocence which requires a conviction to be justified by conclusive proof of guilt, and which thus lays the burden of proof on the prosecution.[18]

Such an account provides a firmer basis for the presumption of

[17] See below ch. 6(2).
[18] Compare Ashworth, 'Concepts of Criminal Justice'.

innocence, and recognises that requirements of justice are intrinsic to the criminal process. I will return later to the question of whether we should understand the justifying purpose of that process in the consequentialist or instrumentalist terms which this account still favours; but I want first to turn from the right of the innocent not to be convicted to the right of any defendant to be given a fair hearing at her trial. For this account still portrays the trial itself in instrumental terms, though it now serves the aims of justice as well as those of utility: the purpose of trying alleged offenders is to ensure, as far as we reasonably can, that the innocent are acquitted and released, and the guilty convicted and condemned; and the point of the *Audi alteram partem* rule, and of the other requirements of Natural Justice, is to specify reliable procedures which protect the innocent against unreasonably mistaken conviction. I will argue, however, that we should not understand these requirements in such instrumental terms, since they express non-instrumental values which are themselves integral to the proper purposes of a criminal trial.

4 PROCEDURAL JUSTICE AND THE RIGHT TO BE HEARD

We are asked to see the criminal trial as an instance of what Rawls has called '*imperfect* procedural justice'. We can specify the correct or just outcome of a trial independently of its procedures – that 'the defendant should be declared guilty if and only if he has committed the offence with which he is charged': it is thus not an instance of '*pure* procedural justice', when we have no criterion for the justice or correctness of the outcome other than that it is the outcome of fair or just procedures. The proper procedures for a trial will be those which 'are best calculated to advance this purpose consistent with the other ends of the law'. But we cannot design procedures which will *guarantee* the right outcome in every case: trials are not instances of '*perfect* procedural justice', and will sometimes produce the wrong result; the best we can do is design procedures which will be reasonably, though not ideally, efficient.[19]

Many of the trial's procedural rules can be explained in this way. The primary purpose of many of the rules governing the acquisition, admissibility and presentation of evidence, for instance, is to ensure that courts are likely to reach an accurate verdict on whether or not the defendant committed the offence charged; that the evidence presented in the case is both relevant and reliable. Even here

[19] J Rawls, *A Theory of Justice* 85–6, 235; see D Resnick, 'Due Process and Procedural Justice'.

there are complications. Sometimes, for instance, evidence is excluded not because it is epistemologically irrelevant, providing no rational support for the prosecution's claims, but because 'its probative value is greatly outweighed by the prejudice likely to be caused to the accused in the minds of a lay jury'.[20] Or evidence may be excluded not (or not only) because it is unreliable, but because it was improperly obtained, in a way which infringed the rights or liberties of the citizen.[21] We might say that it would not be 'consistent with the other ends of the law' to admit such evidence: to admit it would be to condone such improper investigative procedures, while to exclude it is to give the police and the prosecuting authorities a strong incentive to act properly.

What, however, of the right to be heard, and the other rights which go with it: to the assistance of counsel; to fair notice of the trial, of the charges, and of the evidence on which the prosecution will rely; and to disclosure of relevant material which the prosecution do not intend to use?[22] Do these provisions too serve the instrumental purposes of making an accurate verdict more likely, and of protecting the defendant against the danger of a mistaken (and thus unjust) conviction by ensuring, as far as possible, an appropriate equality of resources and opportunity as between defence and prosecution?

Smith is tried and convicted for an offence of which she is indeed guilty, and receives a sentence which is appropriate to her offence. But her trial involved a substantial breach of the requirements of Natural Justice: she was not given an opportunity to put her side of the case, or given due notice of the charges she would face or of the evidence to be used against her. If we understand the trial and its procedures in these instrumental terms, we must agree that 'the right result' has been achieved; for the trial has produced a just and accurate verdict, and Smith has received the condemnation and the punishment which she deserves. Why then should we object to the means by which this right result was achieved? Two maxims are often quoted in this context. Firstly –

> Qui statuit aliquid parte inaudita altera
> Aequum licet statuerit, haud aequus fuerit.[23]

---

[20] *Hampton* 220; see *Cross* ch. 1.5
[21] See *Cross* ch. 12.3; *Hampton* 32–7; *Philips, Report* 4.123–34; *Sang* (1979) 2 All E.R.1222, on the English provisions (such as they are) for excluding such evidence: American law is much stricter in this respect; see T C Grey, 'Procedural Fairness and Substantive Rights'.
[22] See the Attorney General's Guidelines (1982) 74 Cr.App.R.302.
[23] Seneca, *Medea* 199–200.

One who decides a case without having heard the other side may have reached a just decision, but he has not himself been just. Secondly –

It is again absolutely basic to our system that justice must not only be done but must manifestly be seen to be done. If justice was so clearly not seen to be done . . . it seems to me that it is no answer to the applicant to say: 'Well, even if the case had been properly conducted the result would have been the same'. That is mixing up doing justice with seeing that justice is done.[24]

If justice is to be seen to be done, the decision of a tribunal which fails to observe the requirements of Natural Justice must be overturned, even if a properly conducted hearing would have produced just the same decision.

A court acts wrongly if it convicts a defendant without giving him a fair hearing, even if he is in fact guilty as charged: but what kind of wrong does it commit? If the right to be heard is an instrumental right – a means of achieving accurate verdicts – we can still criticise a court which reaches an accurate verdict despite denying the defendant that right: for it has reached the right result by luck rather than by good judgment; and while its verdict is objectively right, it acted improperly in reaching that verdict by a dangerously unreliable procedure. Observed obedience to the requirements of Natural Justice will also reassure the defendant and others that the courts are trying to reach accurate verdicts. When justice is thus both done and seen to be done the courts' decisions should be accepted and respected; but too frequent an appearance of injustice will, even if it is only an appearance, breed mistrust and discontent. Such considerations, and the desire to give courts a powerful incentive to follow reliable and acceptable procedures, might lead us to criticise, and invalidate, the decision of any court which denies the defendant a fair hearing.[25]

On this account, however, we cannot yet say that a *guilty* defendant is injured by a court's failure to give her a hearing. An innocent defendant is injured; for if he is convicted he suffers an unjust verdict, and even if he is acquitted he is exposed to an unreasonable risk of an unjust conviction. But one who is in fact guilty as charged is in no danger of suffering an unjust conviction: if the verdict is in fact correct she suffers neither injustice nor injury. The court acts

---

[24] *R v Thames Magistrates' Court, ex parte Polemis* (1974) 1 W.L.R.1371, at 1375, *per* Lord Widgery CJ; on the controversy about the proper effect of a breach of Natural Justice, see Clark, 'Natural Justice: Substance and Shadow'.

[25] See Jackson, *Natural Justice* ch.4.

wrongly, in following an unreliable procedure, but does not wrong *her*; if her conviction is quashed on appeal, because she was denied a hearing, she is the lucky beneficiary of a rule whose proper purpose is the protection of the innocent. But surely she *has* suffered an injustice in being denied a hearing: every defendant, innocent or guilty, has a right to be heard in her own defence; Seneca's judge is guilty of an injustice *to* the person whom he refuses to hear.

How could we argue this? If justice requires that we convict only the guilty, every citizen has the right to be convicted only if she is guilty. But we cannot know in advance who is guilty, and we therefore owe it to every citizen to convict her only if we have made reasonably sure that she is guilty; only if we have proved her guilt by reliable procedures which protect the innocent against mistaken conviction. Any citizen who is accused of an offence thus has the right to be tried in accordance with the requirements of Natural Justice, which specify such reliable procedures, and to be convicted only if her trial has observed these requirements.[26]

The right of the innocent not to be convicted, and the consequent right of every citizen to be convicted only if he has been tried in accordance with the procedural requirements of Natural Justice, thus set further constraints on our pursuit of the consequential aim of preventing crime; and one whose trial flouts the requirements of Natural Justice suffers an injustice even if he receives the conviction, condemnation and punishment which he deserves. The right to a fair hearing, however, is still an instrumental right, derived from (as a means to protecting) the right not to be convicted unless one is guilty; and a guilty defendant's right to be heard is itself parasitic on the right of the innocent not to be convicted. I will argue that the right to be heard should be given a more substantial and autonomous status than this account allows.

We should note too that we do not yet have a fully adequate account of why it is wrong to try someone who is unfit to plead. We have identified one significant difference between a criminal trial and a judicial inquiry into the facts: that a criminal conviction, unlike an inquiry's finding that the unfit defendant committed the offence charged, is condemnatory – not merely descriptive or diagnostic. We can see too that a court which tries a defendant who can neither understand nor respond to the indictment hardly gives *her* a fair hearing. But why is the right to be heard so crucial to the justice

---

[26] See Dworkin, 'Principle, Policy, Procedure'; Nozick, *Anarchy, State and Utopia* 96–108.

of a criminal trial that one who *cannot* exercise that right must not be tried? If she is in fact guilty, and her guilt can be proved beyond reasonable doubt despite her incapacity, a conviction which condemns her would still on this view be just; and her disposal after a judicial inquiry might be the same as it would have been after a criminal conviction. The accuracy of a criminal conviction does matter more than that of an inquiry's finding; the victim of a mistaken conviction suffers a moral harm which is not suffered by the victim of an inquiry's mistaken judgment. Is this, and the danger of allowing courts too wide a discretion in deciding whom they can safely try, why we should make it a strict rule not to try a defendant who is unfit to plead? But then an unfit defendant who is in fact guilty as charged is again simply the lucky beneficiary of a rule designed to protect the innocent; she herself would suffer no injustice if she was tried and convicted. I want to insist, however, that her trial would be unjust and improper even if it produced an accurate verdict.

We can throw light on these matters, and on the inadequacy of even this qualifiedly instrumentalist view of the criminal trial, by examining more critically the distinction between ends and means in the criminal process. If we see that process and its procedures in instrumental terms, as a means of accurately identifying those who should be condemned and punished because they have broken the law, we allow that a criminal could, albeit improperly, receive a just conviction and punishment without being given a fair hearing at her trial: her trial could produce the right result by improper means. Seneca thought that a judge *might* still reach a 'just decision' without hearing both sides; courts distinguish 'doing justice' from 'seeing that justice is done', and aim to reach 'just ends by just means'.[27] To distinguish 'just ends' from 'just means' in this way is to allow that a court could reach a just verdict by means of unjust procedures; that a trial which lacks even *im*perfect procedural justice could still, if only by chance, produce a 'just outcome'. I will argue, however, that we cannot thus distinguish just ends from just means in the context of a criminal trial.

5 A NON-INSTRUMENTAL VIEW OF THE TRIAL

We can sometimes distinguish the justice of an end-state from the justice of the process by which it is achieved. It may be just that benefits and burdens are distributed according to a certain pattern; and there may be just or unjust methods of securing that just distri-

[27] *Local Government Board v Arlidge* (1915) A.C. 120, at 138, *per* Lord Shaw.

bution.[28] But can we thus distinguish the ends of the criminal process from the procedures through which we pursue them?

Take an extreme example. We agree that a fine of £100 is an appropriate penalty for an offence which you have committed: knowing that you will not be brought to trial for that offence, I take it upon myself to extract £100 from you, and send it to the appropriate authority. Have I now achieved a just end – imposing on you a just punishment for your offence – albeit by unjust means? Surely not: you can suffer your just and proper punishment only at the hands of a court which has duly and properly convicted you. Similarly, a criminal who is convicted of an offence of which he is indeed guilty, but after a trial whose proceedings were unjust and improper (he was denied a fair hearing; or the police, convinced of his guilt but despairing of their ability to prove it, falsified the evidence), is *unjustly* convicted; for we cannot separate the justice of a conviction from the justice of the procedures through which it is achieved.

What is at issue here is the character of the trial as a supposedly *rational* enterprise. This means in part that it must aim to reach a well-founded and justified verdict; that the quality of the verdict itself is impaired by any unreliability in the procedures by which it is reached. We can see the verdict as a claim to knowledge: in convicting the defendant the court claims to know that he is guilty. But if my claim to know that Carter is guilty is to be tenable, it is not enough that she in fact be guilty. I must also have good grounds for my claim, my belief, that she is guilty; and my claim to knowledge will be rejected, even if she is in fact guilty, if it turns out that I lacked such grounds. So too, a court's verdict may in fact be accurate; but it is unjustified, and untenable, if it is founded on inadequate evidence or reached by unreliable procedures.[29]

But there is more than this to the trial's rational character, and to the injustice suffered by even a guilty defendant whose conviction is secured by improper or unjust procedures. For just as the law itself must be justified *to* those on whom it is binding, so too a criminal verdict must be justified *to* the defendant on whom it is passed. The aim of a criminal trial is not merely to reach an accurate judgment *on* the defendant's past conduct: it is to communicate and justify that judgment – to demonstrate its justice – *to* him and to others. In this context at least, if justice is not both seen and shown to be done, it is not and cannot be done at all.

This is the further connection between criminal trials and moral criticism, and the further difference between criminal trials and ju-

---

[28] See Nozick, *Anarchy, State, and Utopia* 153–5.
[29] For this argument, see Resnick, 'Due Process and Procedural Justice'.

dicial inquiries into the facts. A trial, like moral criticism but unlike such an inquiry, is a rational process of proof and argument which seeks to persuade the person whose conduct is under scrutiny of the truth and justice of its conclusions. The law addresses and respects the citizen as a rational agent; it seeks her acceptance of obligations which can be justified to her. A criminal trial, as part of a system of law, must also address and respect the defendant as a rational agent; it must seek her participation, and her assent to its verdict.

A criminal indictment charges a citizen with a breach of her legal obligations; with doing what she could and should have known that she ought not to do: it is an institutional analogue of a moral accusation.[30] The indictment does not just make an accusation *about* the defendant, but is addressed *to* her as a charge which she must answer. In responding to the indictment she recognises the authority of the court; its right to try her case and to determine her guilt or innocence: she accepts that she is bound by the laws of her community and must answer to the community, through its courts, if she breaks those laws. That is why it matters that the defendant should herself plead to the indictment: not merely as a precaution against misunderstandings which might ensue if her counsel pleads on her behalf, but because she thus acknowledges the charge against her and submits herself to the judgment of the court. That too is why one who rejects the authority of the court, or of the laws which it administers, may refuse to plead, thus refusing to play her prescribed part in an illegitimate procedure.[31]

The indictment summons the defendant to answer for her actions: she is to be a participant in her trial, not merely its object. If she pleads 'Guilty', she accepts the justice of the charge; she avows, and purports to repent, her wrongdoing.[32] If she pleads 'Not guilty', and the prosecution show that she has a case to answer, it is then for her to answer that case, by herself or through her counsel; and it is to her, as well as to the court, that the prosecution must

---

[30] It thus presupposes that she knew or ought to have known the law – a presupposition which is hardly plausible for some of the more esoteric *mala prohibita*: but I will not inquire into the justice of *ignorantia juris non excusat* here.

[31] On pleading, and the conditions under which the accused need not plead in person, see *Hampton* 184, 347–8. Compare M Foucault, *Discipline and Punish: The Birth of the Prison* 38–9 on the importance historically attached to confession as 'the act by which the accused accepted the charge and recognised its truth; it transformed an investigation carried on without him into a voluntary affirmation': the accused 'was called upon – if necessary by the most violent persuasion [compare the *peine forte et dure*] – to play the role of voluntary partner in the procedure'. See also J Baldwin and M McConville, *Negotiated Justice* 40.

[32] But see ch. 4(10) below on the actual character of guilty pleas.

prove its case. That is why it matters that she should be present during the trial; so that she may hear and respond to the evidence against her.

A court may sometimes continue the trial in her absence: if she behaves so violently or disruptively that the trial cannot proceed in her presence; if she is summoned to trial but absconds; and 'if [s]he is seriously ill [s]he need not be disturbed'.[33] We may say of the first two cases that she has been offered, but has refused, the opportunity to take part in her trial; that it is she who has wilfully made her participation in the trial impossible; but that we cannot allow her to escape trial simply by absconding, or by disrupting the proceedings; and that even if the court cannot communicate and justify its verdict directly to her, it can still communicate and justify it to the community as a whole.[34] Even in these cases something important is lost from the trial; and the third case should certainly disturb us: for how can we properly try in her absence someone who is willing but *unable* to attend the trial? If she is so ill that she cannot reasonably be expected to attend her trial, she is in effect unfit to plead; and justice then surely requires that her trial be postponed. Perhaps, however, considerations both of efficiency and of humanity – to spare her the anxiety of waiting for her trial – could allow us to proceed with her trial for a relatively minor offence if, but only if, she herself requests it and intends to plead guilty.[35]

We can now see the true significance of the right to be heard. The point is not simply that a court which refuses to hear the defendant may reach an inaccurate verdict, but that it is refusing to recognise his status as a participant in the trial; it commits the same kind of injustice as one who criticises another for an alleged moral offence but refuses to listen to his response to that criticism. Both guilty and innocent defendants have a right to be heard which is independent of the right to be acquitted if innocent. A guilty defendant's right to be heard is not the right to secure a different verdict, since his testimony might make his conviction *more* likely; it is the right to play his proper part in his trial. That is why a conviction should be quashed if the defendant did not receive a fair hearing: not merely because his conviction is then unsafe, or to give courts an incentive to follow reliable procedures, but because his trial was intrinsically unjust; it failed to accord him the status which was his due.

---

[33] *Hampton* 178–9; I am grateful to Martin Wasik for drawing my attention to this.
[34] See ch. 4(7) below.
[35] On fitness to plead see ch. 4(6) below; and note that the defendant who is ill can still be expected to understand the verdict she receives.

The right to be heard in a criminal trial is thus more than a side-constraint on a primarily instrumental criminal process. Compare the suggestion that –

Both the right to be heard from, and the right to be told why, are analytically distinct from the right to secure a different outcome; these rights to interchange express the elementary idea that to be a *person*, rather than a *thing*, is at least to be consulted about what is done with one. . . . At stake here is not just the much-acclaimed *appearance* of justice but, from a perspective that treats process as intrinsically significant, the very *essence* of justice.[36]

This view finds an intrinsic, not merely an instrumental, significance in the right to be heard, but not one which is peculiar or intrinsic to the criminal trial; for it interprets that right as an entirely general right which

grants to the individuals or groups against whom government decisions operate the chance to participate in the processes by which those decisions are made, an opportunity that expresses their dignity as persons.[37]

I do not deny that citizens should have such a right, which constrains the ways in which governments may pursue their aims. But a defendant's right to be heard at her trial is more than the right to have a say in a decision which will have a serious impact *on* her: it is the right to respond to charges which are laid *against* her; and this right is internal to the idea of a criminal trial as a process which calls a defendant to answer for her actions. A court which refuses to hear the defendant is guilty of both injustice and inconsistency; it refuses to allow her the status of a *defendant* in a criminal trial.

That status is also shown in the verdict. A verdict of 'Guilty' does not simply express a judgment on the defendant's past conduct: it communicates that judgment to him and to the community; and it expresses a condemnation of his conduct which he should accept as being justified by the trial which preceded it. What makes that verdict just is not simply the fact that he did commit the offence charged, but that the charge has been proved against, and to, him by a rational process of argument in which he was invited to participate. Like moral blame, a criminal conviction must justify to the accused the condemnation which it expresses. An acquittal, on the

---

[36] L H Tribe, *American Constitutional Law* 503; see also Lucas, *On Justice* ch.4; Ashworth, 'Prosecution and Procedure in Criminal Justice'; F I Michelman, 'Formal and Associational Aims in Procedural Due Process'.

[37] Tribe, *op. cit.* 502.

other hand, declares to the defendant and the community, if not her proven innocence, at least her release from the accusation which was made against her, and from any authorised imputation of guilt. She stood accused before the court; it is to her, as well as to the community, that the court must now declare her release.[38]

To convict a guilty defendant without giving her a hearing is not to produce a just verdict by unjust means; for the justice of a verdict is internally related to the justice of the procedures which produce it. The verdict may express a true judgment on her conduct: but it no longer expresses, as a just verdict must express, the conclusion of a process of rational argument *with* her; she has not been shown that she ought to accept this verdict, since she has not been allowed to participate in her trial. To say that the trial aims to reach an accurate judgment on her conduct, either as a justification for condemning her or as a precondition for punishing her, is therefore at best inadequate and at worst misleading; for it ignores her essential role in her trial as one who is to receive the verdict and participate in the argument which justifies it. The right to be heard is neither simply an instrumental means to some further end, nor simply a side-constraint on our pursuit of consequentialist goals, but a right which is integral to the meaning and purpose of the criminal trial.

6 FITNESS TO PLEAD

What can we now say about unfitness to plead; about the kind of judicial or psychiatric inquiry to which a disordered defendant may be subjected instead of a trial; and about a fit defendant's *right* to be tried?[39]

A defendant is unfit to plead if he cannot plead, with understanding, to the indictment, or understand the course of the trial. The reason why such a person should not be tried is not merely that this might lead to an inaccurate verdict, or to distressing scenes in court (for judicial or psychiatric inquiries involve similar risks), but that his 'trial' would be a travesty: we would be attempting or pretending to treat as a rational agent, answerable for his actions, someone who *cannot* answer for them. The indictment challenges him to admit or deny his guilt; if he cannot understand that challenge it makes no sense to indict him. The trial attempts a rational dis-

---

[38] The requirement of justification belongs with the idea that Natural Justice requires tribunals and courts to give reasons for their decisions: see G Marshall, 'Due Process in England'; E L Pincoffs, 'Due Process, Fraternity, and a Kantian Injunction'; R Cross and A J Ashworth, *The English Sentencing System* 105–6.

[39] See ch. 1(3) above on the issues discussed in this section.

cussion of the evidence for and against his guilt; if he cannot understand or engage in such a discussion it makes no sense to try him. A
conviction seeks to communicate to him, and to persuade him to
accept, a judgment on his past conduct; if he can understand neither
that judgment nor its justification it makes no sense to convict him.

One who can understand, and could respond to, the indictment
may refuse to do so, or to play any part in his trial. He can still be
tried, just as I can still blame someone who refuses to respond to my
criticism. His trial can still make its proper sense as an attempt to
bring him to answer for his actions, respond to the charges laid
against him, and accept the verdict of the court; and the failure of
that attempt does not vitiate the trial or its verdict. We cannot claim
to be engaged in such an attempt, however, if the defendant is
clearly *incapable* of understanding or responding to the indictment,
the trial or the verdict.

A defendant who is to be fit to plead must be able to understand
the 'nature and quality' of his own past actions and of his present
trial.[40] He must be able to understand the factual claims and evidence which are relevant to his case, and thus to take part in the discussion of whether he in fact performed certain actions: but he must
also be able to understand the moral dimensions of the law and of his
own actions. The charge against him is that he acted, not simply in a
way which satisfied certain descriptive criteria, but in breach of his
obligations; and though his trial may include no explicit discussion
of those obligations, it must presuppose that he can understand
them as obligations – as claims which are supported by a particular
kind of moral justification. For if he cannot thus understand his obligations he can understand neither the charge which he faces nor the
conviction which he may receive. If, for instance, he *cannot* see the
law as (if he cannot understand how it could be or be thought to be)
anything more than a set of orders backed by threats which give him
prudential reasons for obedience, he is not fit to be tried: for he
cannot understand the trial for what it purports to be. We must,
however, distinguish him from a defendant who understands the
claims which the law makes on him, but refuses to accept those
claims or to ascribe any legitimate authority to the law.[41]

We can see now why we should be uncertain about the fitness of a

---

[40] See the criteria of criminal responsibility laid down in *M'Naghten* (1843) 10 CL & F
200, at 209; and the controversy over the meaning of 'nature and quality', on
which see N Walker, *Crime and Insanity in England* vol 1, chs. 5–6.

[41] Contrast A J Kenny, *Freewill and Responsibility* 42–4.

defendant who is suffering from a partial amnesia covering the time of her alleged offence. She can still understand the indictment, the trial and the verdict. Nor need the fact that a defendant has forgotten some relevant matter (even whether she committed the offence – though *this* will not always be an intelligible possibility) render her trial improper or her conviction unsafe: it is simply further evidence which the court must consider – has she really forgotten; can any inference be drawn from this; is the rest of the evidence strong enough to convict her? But an amnesiac has not just *forgotten* what she did; the gap in her memory is not just a missing piece of evidence: she is *cut off* from that part of her past. The testimony of others may convince her that she committed the offence, but she cannot avow it as her own act: her amnesia breaks that continuity between past and present which is essential to her sense of herself as the agent of her past actions. Thus she can come to believe that she is guilty, but she cannot truly accept that guilt or make it her own. Her amnesia does not just make it harder for the court to reach an accurate verdict: it inhibits the trial's proper purpose, of bringing her to answer for her own actions. But her trial would not be an utter travesty; for she can still understand it as a trial, and can understand and see to be justified the condemnation which a conviction would express.[42]

An unfit defendant should not be tried. How then can we properly subject him to a judicial inquiry into the facts, or to a psychiatric inquiry into his past conduct and present condition in order to determine his future disposal? Such inquiries may attend to the same features of his past conduct as a criminal trial: if past wrongdoing is good evidence of future danger, a psychiatric inquiry will want to discover whether and how he has broken the law; if voluntary offenders should, even if they are now disordered, be liable to special restrictions imposed by a criminal court, a judicial inquiry will need to establish whether he committed the offence with which he was charged. But their purposes are not those of a criminal trial.

A psychiatric inquiry serves a purely instrumental and diagnostic purpose in identifying those who should, because they are dangerously disordered, be liable to compulsory detention or treatment. The subject of the inquiry should, if and as far as possible, be allowed and encouraged to take part in the discussion, both because

---

[42] On amnesia see C W Whitty and O L Zangwill (eds.), *Amnesia*; T Ribot, *Diseases of Memory*: and see ch. 9(6) below on punishing the amnesiac.

this will help the tribunal to understand his past conduct and his present condition, and because he has a right to take part in an inquiry which so vitally concerns him; and the inquiry's purpose and its findings should be explained to him if he can understand them. But the inquiry *can* achieve its proper aims without his participation or his understanding: it does so improperly if it refuses him a hearing or an explanation when he could understand and participate in its proceedings; but it will have to do so if he is incapable of such understanding and participation. For its essential purpose is to reach a finding on or about a person and to decide what should happen to him, not to engage in a process of argument and communication with him. It is a side-constraint on the pursuit of that purpose, as well as a means to it, that he should participate in the proceedings if he is capable of doing so; but it is not essential to that purpose in the way that it is essential to the purpose of a criminal trial.

A judicial inquiry into the facts serves a similar instrumental purpose – to decide what should be done with the disordered defendant. And if the only reason for establishing whether she committed the offence charged is to decide whether she should be liable to certain special restrictions, its purpose is purely instrumental, though her past offence now serves not merely the evidential role of a predictor of future danger, but the justificatory role of a precondition for those special restrictions. But a judicial inquiry can also serve to declare the defendant's guilt or innocence to the community, and to express the community's regard for the law; and these are *non*-instrumental purposes which it may share with a criminal trial. They are non-instrumental in that they do not refer to ends beyond the inquiry and its finding, to which the inquiry is related as a contingent means; declaring and expressing are what the tribunal does *in* making its inquiries and issuing its finding, not further consequences which it tries to bring about.[43] But one essential purpose which it does not and cannot share with a trial is that of engaging *with* the defendant in a communicative process of argument and justification; and that is why its finding that the defendant was guilty of the offence charged should not 'carry either the name or the effect of a conviction'.[44]

Why then should a fit defendant have or claim a *right* to be tried? The basis of the answer to this question, and to the related question

[43] See ch.4(7) below.
[44] *Report of the Committee on Mentally Abnormal Offenders* (*Butler*) ch.10, para.24.

of why we should have a system of criminal trials at all, should be evident already: that a criminal trial addresses and respects the defendant as a rational and responsible agent; and that citizens have a fundamental right to be thus addressed and respected. An adequate account of the scope and significance of the right to be tried, however, requires a more extensive discussion of that related question.

7 THE RIGHT TO BE TRIED

Why should we have a system of criminal trials? Why indeed have any formal method of dealing with actual or alleged breaches of the law, rather than a purely declarative system of law which announces the law's demands, and then leaves it to the citizens' own consciences, and the informal kinds of social pressure which they can apply to each other, to ensure that the law is obeyed?

The answer to this question may seem too obvious to need any extensive explanation. A purely declarative system of law would be so ineffective in securing its proper aims that it could hardly count as an attempt to *subject* human conduct to the governance of rules, and would certainly not long survive. If we make no formal attempt to enforce the law's demands, those who are unimpressed by its moral justification will see no good reason to obey it; those who are initially willing to obey it will soon cease to do so if others can break it with impunity, if only because their obedience would make them even more vulnerable than they would otherwise be to the depredations of the lawless; and the informal kinds of self-defence and retaliation which people would then organise for themselves would soon destroy any semblance of peace, security or the rule of law.

We need some organised means of preventing breaches of the law before they occur; but since such preventive efforts will not be entirely successful, and could be made more successful only at the cost of unacceptable intrusions into individual liberties, we also need some organised means of dealing with actual or alleged breaches of the law. Why then not simply establish a system of diagnostic tribunals, to administer the range of preventive, reformative and deterrent measures which are to be imposed on actual or potential offenders? Even if our primary concern is to ensure that the law is obeyed, and the common good thus served, we may see good reason to institute something like a system of criminal trials which, besides determining the defendant's eligibility for such further measures as the law may provide, addresses and respects her as a rational agent, provides a formal and authoritative declaration of her guilt or innocence, and condemns her conduct if she is convicted.

Such a system will have consequential benefits beyond those of a system of diagnostic tribunals: by its formal declarations and condemnations it will, we may hope, reinforce the public's respect for the law; reassure the law-abiding, and assure potential offenders, that the law's demands are taken seriously; settle doubts about whether or by whom an offence has been committed; and provide convicted and potential offenders with a further incentive to obey the law in the desire to avoid conviction and condemnation at a criminal trial. It will also, unlike a system of purely diagnostic tribunals, be consistent with certain non-consequentialist side-constraints: for it respects, as a diagnostic system might not respect, the citizen's status as a rational agent; and also, if it aims to convict only those who have voluntarily broken the law, the requirement that sane and responsible citizens should be subjected to the law's remedial or deterrent measures only if they have voluntarily disobeyed its demands.

This line of thought captures part of the significance of a system of criminal trials as an appropriate way of dealing with alleged breaches of the law, and recognises that a respect for the defendant as a rational agent is integral to the character of a criminal trial. But that character is distorted if it is explained within such a fundamentally consequentialist framework, in terms either of the trial's efficiency in serving certain further and independently identifiable goals, or of its consistency with independent side-constraints on our pursuit of those goals. For a trial's proper purposes are internally, not contingently, related to its essential character: what makes a system of criminal trials an appropriate method of pursuing the proper ends of a system of law is that the trial expresses the values which those ends themselves embody.

Three kinds of consequential purpose for a system of trials were suggested: diagnostic (identifying those who should be liable to further coercive measures); persuasive (persuading the convicted offender, and others, to obey the law); and expressive (declaring the law's demands and the defendant's guilt or innocence). The first of these will be discussed in later chapters, when I discuss the character and justification of the further coercive measures on which it depends. It might seem to be a purpose which a criminal trial shares with a diagnostic inquiry, and which has no essential connection with the communicative character of a trial; but we will see later that a trial which is to justify punishing an offender must justify that punishment *to* him. This diagnostic purpose, however, is not essential to the meaning of a criminal trial: a system of criminal trials from which no further formal consequences followed – in which acquittal or conviction completed the formal criminal process – would still serve intelligible purposes, unlike a system of diagnostic inquiries from which nothing followed.[45] My present concern is with these other, non-diagnostic purposes.

One such purpose is indeed persuasive; a criminal conviction may, quite apart from any further punishment to which it might lead, dissuade both the convicted offender and others from engaging in the kind of conduct which it condemns: but this is not to say simply that it may be an effective instrument for the modification of behaviour. A conviction could modify the offender's conduct, or that of others, in two obvious ways. It could induce or reinforce a more active understanding of the wrongness of the conduct which it condemns; or it could provide a prudential deterrent against such conduct: for quite apart from the further consequences which may flow from a conviction, even someone who is indifferent to his legal obligations may find the process of trial and conviction unpleasant. The proper persuasive purpose of a conviction, however, is not to make criminal conduct imprudent, but to bring home to the offender and to others the wrongness of his conduct, by condemning it; like moral blame, a conviction should appeal to the offender's moral understanding, not merely to his self-interest.

Recall, first, the proper purpose of a system of law; that citizens should not merely obey its demands, but should accept, as justified, the obligations which it imposes on them. If a criminal conviction is to assist the law's proper purpose it must therefore not merely give citizens a prudential incentive to obey the law, but must remind or persuade them of the justice of the law's demands – of the obligations which they ought to recognise and accept. Recall, second, the relation between this feature of the law and the respect which is owed to a rational moral agent: an attempt to persuade someone to do what she ought to do should aim, not to create new and irrelevant prudential reasons for her to act as she should, but to bring her to understand and accept the moral reasons which justify the claim that she ought to act thus; a criminal conviction which is to persuade a citizen to obey the law should therefore aim to do so by bringing her to recognise the wrongfulness of the conduct which it condemns.

The trial also has a declarative purpose apart from any attempt to

[45] See ch. 5 below.

modify conduct; it expresses our respect for the law. In trying alleged offenders we show that we take seriously the question of whether they have broken the law; in convicting and condemning proven offenders we show that we care for the law's demands as being both justified and important, and are not prepared to let breaches of those demands go unnoticed and uncondemned. We do this not simply in order to induce or reinforce a proper regard for and obedience to the law in ourselves or others; but because our concern for the law and its purposes itself requires us to take notice of illegality, just as our regard for the demands of morality requires us to take notice of immorality. In providing authoritative determinations of guilt and innocence – authoritative condemnations of the guilty and acquittals of the innocent – a system of criminal trials gives formal expression to our regard for the law.

Why have a system of criminal trials? Not only as a prelude or precondition for the imposition of punishment or other coercive measures on offenders; nor only because a system of law which took no formal notice of breaches of its requirements would be ineffective: but also, and essentially, because such a system expresses and serves the values which are internal to the law. It addresses, as the law must address, the citizen as a rational moral agent; it seeks, as the law must seek, to persuade her to accept and obey the obligations which the law imposes on her; and it expresses that concern for the law's demands which the law itself expresses and enjoins on us.

This is not to say that a system of law *logically* requires a formal system of criminal trials. We might imagine a community, perhaps smaller than our own and sharing a deeper regard for the common good, which maintains a system of declarative law, to provide an authoritative declaration of the rules which should be obeyed, but has no formal system of trials and verdicts. Notice would still be taken of actual and suspected breaches of the law, but that notice would be informal: suspected or known offenders would be subject only to the informally critical or condemnatory attentions of their fellows. Or we could imagine a semi-formal practice of public criticism: members of the community are summoned to answer to their fellows for their alleged offences; to face their accusers; to confess or deny the wrong-doing alleged against them; and to accept the judgment and the criticism of their fellows. Such practices would have their drawbacks, both practical and moral: they might be notably inefficient; they could easily become vehicles for coercive attempts to induce conformity. We might deny that such a community would, insofar as it lacked formal institutions of adjudication, have a fully-fledged system of *law*, and insist that a community like our own needs some more formal system of adjudication – just as it needs a formal system of law rather than simply a shared social morality.[46] What I want to emphasise here, however, is that such informal or semi-formal practices would embody values and purposes which are continuous with those involved in moral criticism and blame; and that any more formal system of adjudication must, if it is to be appropriate to a system of law which respects its citizens as rational agents, be informed by those same values and purposes.

A system of criminal trials need not be exactly like our own; and I have ignored here many of the structural and procedural questions which would need to be addressed by any complete account of the criminal process. All I have tried to show is that a system of criminal trials must have the central and essential purpose of engaging an alleged offender in a critical examination of his conduct, and of expressing and justifying, to him and to others, an appropriate judgment on that conduct. The structure and procedures of a trial must therefore be such as will assist and be consistent with this communicative and justificatory purpose. It should by now be clear, however, why we should have something like a system of a criminal trials rather than a system of purely diagnostic tribunals; for a criminal trial is informed, as a purely diagnostic inquiry is not, by the purposes and values which are entailed by a proper respect for the citizen.

A suspected offender therefore has, if she is sane, a *right* to be tried for her alleged offence, rather than being subjected to a diagnostic or psychiatric inquiry: not because the further consequences of a trial may be less unwelcome, but because the trial will respect her status as a rational agent who is answerable for her own actions. A diagnostic inquiry treats her as someone about whom we must make a decision (is she a danger to herself or others?), and on whom we might have to impose treatment which aims to modify her behaviour; she is the object of its investigations and its decision. But a trial addresses her as a subject: as a rational agent who must answer for her own actions; whose actions we judge under the categories of right and wrong, not simply those of harmless and dangerous; with whom we must engage in the process of inquiry and judgment; to whom we must justify our judgments and criticisms; and whom we must persuade to modify her own conduct by offering her relevant reasons to do so. She has a right to be tried because a suspected

[46] See Hart, *The Concept of Law* ch. 5.

offender has a right to the respect which the law should accord to every citizen.[47]

Is the right to be tried anything more than the right to be tried *rather than* being subjected to some other kind of treatment or inquiry which does not thus respect my status as a rational agent? If I am suspected of an offence, by the police or by other members of the community, can I claim a right to be tried for that offence; or should the decision whether to prosecute me be determined solely by considerations of public policy and of justice to others?[48]

It would be absurd to suggest that *anyone* who is suspected of an offence has a right to be tried for it. Investigation might show the suspicion to be unfounded; and the suspect could not then be entitled to anything more than a public announcement of his innocence. Suppose, however, that the announced reason for not bringing him to trial is that there is *insufficient* evidence to justify proceeding with charges against him. Others may then still suspect that he is guilty, though not provably so: might not the suspect, if innocent, then claim the right to be tried, in order to clear his name and avert the harm involved in or consequent on being thus mistakenly suspected; and might he not, whether innocent or guilty, claim the right to have those suspicions publicly aired and tested at a trial? Such claims do have force; just as someone who is suspected of a moral offence might properly insist that her accusers should either withdraw their suspicions or put them to the test and give her a chance to answer them, so too one who is officially suspected of a criminal offence may claim the right to respond to those suspicions, and to have them publicly aired and tested, at a criminal trial. There are practical objections to allowing such an extensive right to be tried; the cost in time and resources, and the risk of acquitting a suspect against whom more conclusive evidence might later be found: but it should at least carry significant weight in the decision whether to prosecute.

Suppose instead that the prosecuting authority, though persuaded both of my guilt and that it can be proved, decides not to proceed with the case against me. Once again, there may be persuasive reasons of policy against prosecuting *everyone* who could be proved to be guilty. Once again, however, an innocent suspect may claim the right to try to clear his name in a court of law; and a guilty suspect may claim the right to have this official belief in his guilt

---

[47] Compare H Morris, 'Persons and Punishment'.
[48] On the criteria for prosecution see *Philips, Report* 8.6–11; *Law and Procedure* Appendix 25.

tried and tested in a court of law. The rules for the use of the formal police caution, instead of prosecution, seem to recognise this: a caution, it is said,

is only appropriate where the offender admits his guilt, if the police are satisfied that they have a provable case and provided any complainant does not insist on prosecution.[49]

A citizen should be presumed to be innocent unless and until he is proved to be guilty; he should be treated, as a caution treats him, as being guilty only if he is either proved to be guilty at a properly conducted trial, or prepared to admit his own guilt and thus in effect waive his right to be tried.

Only a citizen who is sane and responsible, however, can have a right to be tried. One who is unfit to plead – incapable of playing her part in the rational and communicative process of the trial – cannot have a right to be tried, since she cannot exercise that right or receive that to which it would entitle her. This is not to say that she has no rights; but I am not concerned here with the rights of, or the appropriate treatment for, the mentally disordered. We need some kind of tribunal to deal with them; perhaps a general system of diagnostic tribunals to deal with any disordered person; or perhaps a special system of judicial inquiries to deal with disordered defendants or offenders. But a criminal trial is not appropriate for or owed to someone who is so disordered that she can neither understand nor take part in her trial.

8 THE RIGHT OF SILENCE

I have argued that a criminal trial has as its central and essential purpose a process of argument and communication *with* the defendant: to engage with her in a rational inquiry into her guilt or innocence; to communicate and to justify to her the verdict which it reaches. A criminal trial is thus closely related, in its purpose and meaning, to moral criticism and blame: both express a proper respect for the accused as a rational and responsible agent, as well as for the obligations or values which she is accused of flouting; both seek to bring her to answer for her actions, and to accept a justified judgment on them; both may also aim to persuade her to modify her conduct, by persuading her of the wrongfulness of what she has done; both may also communicate to others a proper regard for the law or for the requirements of morality.

[49] *Hampton* 23; see *Philips, Report* 6.40, *Law and Procedure* paras. 150–4.

I do not claim that this provides a fully accurate description of the actual character of criminal trials in our own or other legal systems. It describes, rather, the *ideals* by which such systems should be, and often purport to be, informed; ideals which are revealed in some of their central provisions, and by reference to which the actual is to be judged, and criticised. Nor do I claim that these are the *only* values and purposes which either do or should inform a system of criminal trials: such systems may in fact, and may rightly, also serve other purposes and values; my claim is only that a system which is to accord to the citizen the respect which is his due must take this communicative endeavour to be its central and essential purpose. It would be wrong, however, to leave the matter there; to pay no attention to significant features of actual systems of criminal trials which are apparently at odds with my account of the trial's proper purpose. Some such features may simply – though crucially – reflect the distance between the ideal and the actual; the extent to which our actual practices fall short of the ideals towards which they are or should be striving. Others, however, may reflect the influence of different and conflicting values or purposes; and we must then ask whether such values and purposes have a proper place in a system of criminal trials. Without any pretensions to completeness, I will attend to some of these features in this and the following section.

Take first the right of silence. For surely, it may be said, the purpose which I have ascribed to the criminal trial would preclude allowing any such right to the accused: if his trial summons him to answer to a charge of wrong-doing, he should be *required* to answer to it – to give evidence himself and to submit himself to questioning (just as he should, by parity of reasoning, be required to answer questions put to him by the police before he is brought to trial). Under English law, however, the defendant was not even *allowed* to give sworn evidence on his own behalf before 1898; and even now he has the right to refuse to give evidence, and thus refuse to submit himself to cross-examination by the prosecution (just as a suspect has the right to refuse to answer questions put to him by the police).[50] Does not the existence of this well-entrenched right of silence show that the trial does not have the purpose I have ascribed to it?

Both the actual and the proper extent of this right of silence are controversial: how far should suspects or defendants have the right to remain silent; how far may judges or counsel properly comment on, and invite juries to draw inferences from, a defendant's silence

[50] See *Cross* chs.8, 11.1; *Philips, Report* 1.24–31, 4.33–67.

before or during the trial (a formal right of silence loses its substance if juries are to be invited or allowed to take such silence as evidence of guilt)? I will not discuss the right of silence before trial here, nor all the details of the right of silence at trial; but some attention must be paid to the character and justification of that latter right.

Some limited right of silence is consistent with, if not required by, the account I have offered. I should not, for instance, be expected or required to respond to any and every accusation made against me, however ill-founded it may be; this is an implication of the presumption of innocence, and of the probative burden laid on the prosecution. I should normally be allowed to remain silent about, and thus not be questioned about, my general character and my previous convictions: for such evidence may unduly prejudice the jury against me; and it is unfair to the defendant, as a denial of his autonomy, to take past and different kinds of wrong-doing as good evidence of his present guilt.[51] But such considerations do not justify a *general* right of silence: they justify at most a defendant's right to remain silent unless and until the prosecution has shown that he has a case to answer, and his right not to be questioned about certain matters; they do not justify a right to remain silent about matters properly relevant to the trial, even after the prosecution has shown that he has a case to answer.

What could justify such a general right of silence? We do not, I think, recognise such a right in the context of moral criticism: if I think that I am justified in criticising another's conduct, I also think that she ought to respond to my criticism. Of course I cannot (and should not, even if I could) *force* her to respond, just as a court cannot force a defendant to speak; but I can, and would, criticise her for refusing to respond. So why should not a court convict a defendant who refuses to speak of a further offence of contempt? The person I criticise might of course claim that the matter is nothing to do with me, and for that reason refuse to make any response; and in insisting that she ought to respond I must assume, and be able to argue, that it *is* my business. So too a defendant who thinks that her conduct is not, in this instance or in general, any concern of the law's may for that reason refuse to make any response to the charges against her; and any claim that she ought to respond must involve the claim that the law, and thus this court, does have a legitimate interest in her conduct. But suppose that interest is conceded (as it is by those who nonetheless insist on the defendant's right of silence);

---

[51] See *Cross* chs. 14–15: for a closely related issue in the law of rape see *Sexual Offences (Amendment) Act* 1976, s.2; R A Duff 'Recklessness and Rape'.

131

why should we not lay on the defendant a legal duty to answer the charges, to give evidence, and to submit herself to relevant questioning?

Two questions must be distinguished here: first, should we say that a defendant has a *moral* duty to give evidence and submit to cross-examination; second, if she does have such a moral duty, is it one which the law should properly try to enforce by making it a *legal* obligation, the breach of which would make her liable to conviction and perhaps punishment? My account requires a positive answer to the first question: if the law's demands on me are appropriately justified, and if its adjudicative procedures are just and fair (and these qualifications are, as always, crucial) I have at least a moral duty, as a citizen, to respond to any well-founded charges which are laid against me; to submit myself to the judgment of the court; and to assist the court in reaching a just and accurate verdict on my conduct (from which it follows, we may note, that I have a moral duty to plead guilty if I know that I am guilty). For every citizen has a moral duty to assist the law in achieving its proper purposes, as an aspect of his duty to be concerned for the common good of his community; and those purposes include the maintenance and efficient working of a system of criminal trials which aim to bring wrong-doers to answer for their actions.

A positive answer to that first question gives some reason for a positive answer to the second question, and for transforming that moral duty into a legal obligation. But not every moral duty need or should become a legal obligation; and some arguments in favour of the right of silence can be interpreted as offering a negative answer to the second, rather than to the first, question.[52]

Some such arguments appeal to the need to protect the innocent against unjust conviction and undue suffering. Given the pressures and anxieties to which defendants, especially innocent defendants who are not used to appearing in court, are subject, an innocent, frightened and confused defendant might be made to appear guilty if she was required to expose herself to the wiles and the bullying of prosecution counsel; while such a requirement might sometimes assist in securing the conviction of the guilty, it would also expose too many of the innocent to the risk of unjust conviction. To the extent that such an argument has force, it marks and seeks to remedy a serious defect in the actual structure of our criminal trials: a more properly ordered system of criminal justice would not

---

[52] Compare *Philips, Report* 3.90, 4.47 on the 'social or moral duty to assist the police' which is not, and should not be, 'legally enforceable'.

expose the defendant who is required to give evidence to such pressures and risks. Other arguments, however, appeal to a principle which does not depend on such contingent features of the trial – the principle that no citizen should be required to incriminate herself. A defendant who gives evidence swears to tell the truth; if her truthful evidence would incriminate her she can avoid incriminating herself only by committing perjury or by not giving evidence: since the law should neither encourage perjury nor require the defendant to incriminate herself, it should not require her to give evidence.[53]

But why should a guilty defendant not have a duty to incriminate herself: to confess her guilt; to answer truthfully the questions put to her, even if those answers would reveal her guilt? Even if we agree that she should ideally – in a just legal system – have such a moral duty, we might deny that that moral duty should in practice be transformed into a legal obligation: partly because such an obligation would weigh more heavily on the innocent, who are likely to take it seriously, than on the guilty, who are less likely to do so; partly because, given the imperfections of human nature, the existence of such a legal obligation might encourage police, prosecuting counsel and courts to put undue and improper kinds of pressure on suspects or defendants to confess their supposed guilt; and partly because there are limits to how far the law should *require* a citizen to expose herself to danger, even when that danger is of conviction and punishment for an offence of which she is guilty. I will not discuss these arguments here:[54] I want simply to note that if the right of silence is founded on such considerations as these I can still maintain my claims about the proper purposes of the criminal trial. For that right now operates as a side-constraint on the criminal process: that process still aims to engage with the defendant in a communicative enterprise of argument and justification; but we recognise that we should, in practice if not ideally, allow her to refuse to take part in it.

The right of silence might, however, suggest a quite different model of the criminal process, within which the defendant would not even have a moral duty to give evidence, let alone to incriminate himself. For suppose we portray the trial, not as a communicative enterprise in which the defendant is expected to participate, but as a *contest* between defence and prosecution. The purpose of each side (or at least of the defence) is then not so much to get at the truth as to

---

[53] See *Cross* ch. 11.1, and 185–7 on the defendant's right to make an *unsworn* statement.

[54] The third argument (which seems pretty weak in this context) is related to arguments about duress as a defence; see Lord Kilbrandon and A J Kenny on 'Duress *per Minas* as a Defence to Crime'.

win; and though there are limits set on the means by which victory may be achieved, the defendant should not be required to help the other side to victory by giving possibly self-incriminating evidence. Of course if he chooses to give evidence he is, within limits, fair game; and he must at least enter a plea in response to the indictment: but he should not be required to give evidence; and his plea of 'Not guilty' is not so much a (possibly dishonest) denial of guilt, as a challenge to the prosecution to prove his guilt – without his help.[55]

This is certainly how many of those involved in the criminal process actually see it: but it is, *or should be*, an inadequate view of that process, just as the bad man's view of the law as a system of coercive requirements backed by threats is, or should be, an inadequate view of the law. The latter view fails to recognise the moral character of the law's demands; the former view fails to recognise that the criminal trial, as part of a system of law, has the proper moral purpose of bringing wrong-doers to answer for their actions. If I owe it to my fellow-citizens to obey the requirements of a system of law which serves our common good, I ought also to be prepared to admit my guilt, and to accept their condemnation, if I break the law (so too, if I ought to obey the requirements of morality, I ought also to be prepared to admit my guilt, and to accept the criticism of others, for my moral wrong-doing). The qualification 'or should be' is, however, crucial. If the law's demands on me lack any adequate moral justification, the bad man's view of the law may be the view which I should myself take; if the trial to which I am subjected is not so ordered that it serves the proper aims of a justified system of law, it may be more appropriate for me to see it as a contest between me and the prosecution, rather than as the kind of communicative and justificatory enterprise which it purports to be.

Now if we are certain of the justice of our own legal system (certain that it makes a justified claim on the allegiance and obedience of each citizen, as a member of the community whose common good it serves), we can reject this view of the criminal trial, and this justification for a right of silence: we can expect and require the defendant to play her full part in her trial, as one who is called to answer for her actions. But if we recognise, as we should, that our actual system of law is more or less seriously imperfect; that its claims on the citizen's allegiance as a member of the community will not always be adequately justified: we may then feel that she should be allowed to hold back from a whole-hearted acceptance of the law's claims. The law still demands her obedience (we hope justifiably): but it should

[55] I owe this suggestion to Neil MacCormick.

not demand, though it still seeks, her *acceptance* of its claims; it leaves her the option – the right – of being externally related to it, so long as she obeys it. So too the trial should seek, but should not *require*, the defendant's participation in and acceptance of its proceedings: it should leave her the option of seeing it (externally) as a contest between herself and the prosecution; and one way to do this is to allow her a right of silence.[56]

We can therefore recognise the defendant's right of silence, whilst still insisting that the trial's proper and essential purpose is as I have described it: our pursuit of that purpose is constrained by the recognition that we should not transform the defendant's supposed moral duty to play her full part in assisting that pursuit into a legal obligation – that we should leave her *some* freedom to dissent from the demands which the law and the trial make on her.

9 CRIMINAL TRIALS AND MORAL CRITICISM

There are, I have claimed, close connections between the criminal process of trial and verdict and the moral process of criticism and blame; and a recognition of the defendant's right of silence at her trial does not, I think, seriously undermine this claim. There are, of course, other significant differences between the two processes. Many of these simply reflect the difference between an informal, personal relationship and a formal and institutional procedure; others are differences of emphasis rather than of fundamental substance. In a criminal trial, for instance, the emphasis is more likely to be on factual questions about who did what than on questions about the legality of what the defendant admittedly did, while moral criticism is more likely to be concerned with the morality of what was admittedly done. But a criminal prosecution always involves, and may have to prove, a claim about the illegality of what the defendant did (was his conduct, for instance, negligent or reckless; was it dishonest; was it justified); and moral criticism must always involve, and may have to prove, a claim about what was actually done (if you deny my account of what you did, I must then prove to you that you did act thus – i.e. that I know (have adequate grounds for claiming) that you acted thus). This difference of emphasis is, however, related to a difference which may be more substantial.

[56] Compare the idea that the law, unlike morality, demands only external obedience, and is not concerned about the citizen's motive or reason for obeying it. For an interesting recent discussion of the right of silence, see A Donagan, 'The Right not to Incriminate Oneself'.

If I criticise your conduct you may respond by arguing that, while your conduct was indeed wrong by *my* moral standards, those standards are misguided. A doctor agrees that she deliberately killed a patient, to save him from further suffering, and that my moral beliefs condemn such an action: but she claims that such killings *are* justified, and tries to persuade me to modify my own moral beliefs – to approve rather than condemn her action. Neither of us may in fact persuade the other: I continue to condemn her conduct; she continues to reject my criticism. But I must listen, and respond, to her arguments about the morality of such killings: though my belief that they are wrong may be unshaken by her arguments, I cannot exempt that belief from critical discussion.

But if the doctor is charged with murder, and admits in court that she deliberately killed her patient, the court must ignore such moral arguments. Once it is established that neither the patient's condition nor his consent can provide a legal defence against a charge of murder, there is nothing more to be said. She might argue, and persuade the judge and jury, that this should not be the law; that such killings *are* morally justified, and *should be* legally sanctioned: but unless she can show that the law *does* sanction such killings, or recognises such moral claims as possible *legal* justifications, her moral arguments are irrelevant to the court's verdict. They might in fact affect the verdict; juries are quite capable of acquitting a defendant whom they believe to be guilty in law if they regard her actions as morally justified: but such juries are failing in their legal duty to convict those who are guilty in law.[57]

The only limits on the arguments which moral criticism may involve are those of logic and relevance. Any claim which is relevant to, as part of the justification of, my criticism of another is involved in my argument with him; and if he challenges it I must be prepared to attend and respond to his challenge. But the law sets narrower limits on the issues which can be raised at a trial; limits of law rather than of logic. The defendant may challenge the facts alleged by the prosecution; their interpretation of the law; and the validity (in terms of the system's own criteria) of the law under which she is charged, or of the court's claim to have jurisdiction over her. Such challenges must be heard and met, if not by the court which first tries her, then by an appeal court. But she will not be

---

[57] Of course moral considerations sometimes enter into the question of whether the defendant's action fell within the definition of the offence; my point here is simply that the law also contains clear rulings on matters which are morally controversial.

heard to argue that, though she has broken a valid law, that law (or the system of which it is part) has no moral claim on her obedience.

Does this difference simply reflect the fact that criminal trials and moral criticism operate, quite properly, with different criteria of wrongness and thus of relevance? A court asks whether a defendant has acted illegally; considerations of morality are thus irrelevant to its task, unless the law itself makes them relevant. A moral critic asks whether a person has acted immorally; considerations of legality are thus irrelevant to *his* task, unless morality itself makes them relevant. But moral considerations *are* relevant to a criminal trial. The accusation that someone has broken the law, and her conviction and condemnation for breaking it, presuppose that the law has a *moral* claim to her obedience: if she could persuade us that the law which she has broken, or the system of which it is part, is so unjust and immoral that she has no moral obligation to accept or obey it, she would have persuaded us that she ought not to be convicted (and thus condemned) for breaking the law.

In refusing to consider questions about the moral legitimacy of the law under which the defendant is charged, the court is thus refusing to consider matters which are relevant to its proceedings. Now the demand that I should be ready to enter into argument about any matter which is relevant to my criticism of another person reflects the requirement that I should treat him non-coercively, as a rational and autonomous agent. I seek his assent to the judgment which my criticism expresses; I do not simply try to impose that judgment on him, but try to justify it to him. So must we not admit that a criminal court, in thus refusing to consider or respond to moral claims which are relevant to its proceedings, no longer addresses or respects the defendant as a rational agent; that it coerces her, by imposing the law on her rather than justifying it to her?

The point is not that the law does not allow a general defence of conscientious objection, and acquit any defendant who shows that she has a sincere moral objection to the particular law which she broke or to the whole legal system. I may sometimes respect, without sharing, another's moral beliefs, and therefore refuse to condemn him when he acts in accordance with them; and the law should perhaps recognise such a defence for some kinds of offence. But to suggest that the law must allow such a defence to *any* criminal charge if it is to accord the citizen the respect which is her due, so that citizens would be legally obligated to obey only those laws of which they approve, would be as absurd as to suggest that we should criticise only those whose actions are at odds with their own moral beliefs. I can still properly criticise someone who sees no wrong in what he did; and the law can still properly condemn someone who rejects its demands. The point is rather that the law does not even allow a defendant to secure an acquittal by persuading the court that the law is, not just that she believes it to be, morally unjustified; and that the court may not even listen to such arguments, though they are crucially relevant to its proceedings.

On closer inspection, however, this point is less disturbing than it might at first appear: for it simply reflects the fact that most legal systems involve a separation of powers which is not found in non-legal moral contexts. A court may tell a defendant who challenges the law's moral legitimacy that this is not the proper forum for such questions. The court's job is to apply the law as it is: questions of what the law ought to be are for the legislature and the community's political institutions; and every citizen has an obligation (legal and moral) to obey the law until she can get it changed through the appropriate legal and constitutional procedures. (I assume here that, whatever we may say about judges as lawmakers, and about the extent to which moral and political considerations enter into judicial decisions in hard cases, we can draw some such distinction between judiciary and legislature.)[58]

Such a separation of powers is not an essential feature of a legal system: we could imagine a system whose courts combined the functions of legislature and judiciary, in which a defendant could secure an acquittal by persuading the court to change the law. But the crucial point here is that a criminal trial in a system like our own must presuppose, not merely the fact of such a separation of powers, but the availability of an adequate moral justification for the secondary rules which thus limit the court's responsibilities and require the citizen to obey the law until it is duly changed; the existence of a forum in which this justification can be offered and criticised; and the availability of procedures through which the citizen can try to change the law. Only then can the claim, on which the trial itself depends, be maintained that the defendant has an obligation to obey the law, and to accept the authority of the court.

This difference between moral criticism and a criminal trial is thus not that between a process in which the standards by which actions are judged are justified and one in which they are merely asserted, but a difference between a unitary process of justification and argument and a more complex process in which different

[58] See, notoriously, R Dworkin, *Taking Rights Seriously*.

aspects of the justificatory argument belong in different contexts. We should note too that, while a court will still convict a defendant who challenges the moral legitimacy of the law, it cannot force her to accept the condemnation which that conviction expresses. The court seeks her assent to that condemnation, just as I seek the assent of one whose moral wrong-doing I criticise; but it must seek that assent by giving her reasons for accepting its judgment.

10 THE IDEAL AND THE ACTUAL

I have discussed one suggestion that the criminal trial has a coercive character which is inconsistent with the respect owed to the defendant as a rational agent, but there are other more obviously coercive aspects of the criminal process. The coercive *consequences* of a trial – the punishment to which a conviction may lead – will be discussed later, but two other aspects, which remind us of the distance between the ideal and the actual, deserve attention here.

Firstly, I have said that a trial summons an accused person to answer for his actions: but many defendants are not left free to obey, or disobey, that summons for themselves; they are brought to trial, willy-nilly, from pre-trial custody. More generally, those who are suspected or accused of an offence are subject to various kinds of restriction at the hands of the police and the courts before they have been either tried or convicted (and when they may indeed be innocent): they may be detained for lengthy periods before (or without) being brought to trial; they may be released from custody only if they can put up bail, and may indeed be refused bail; and even if they are released they may find their movements and activities restricted. The extent and nature of, and the justifying conditions for, such pre-trial restrictions on suspects and defendants are of course the subject of continuing controversy:[59] but those involved in such controversies usually take it for granted that *some* such restrictive and coercive provisions are justified for at least *some* suspects and defendants. Surely, however, such provisions are utterly inconsistent with a proper respect for the citizen as a rational and autonomous agent – and with the presumption that he is innocent until proven guilty.

The usual, and only possible, justification for such provisions is consequentialist: a person is detained, or subjected to special restric-

---

[59] See *Philips, Report*; and the controversy surrounding the Police and Criminal Evidence Act 1984. I will be concerned here only with the provisions for those who have been charged with an offence.

tions, in order to ensure that he appears for trial; that he is available for whatever punishment the court may impose if he is convicted; and that he does not interfere with the preparation of the case against him.[60] He is in effect coerced not because of what he *has* done or *is* doing, but because of what he *might* do if he is left free: but such coercion is inconsistent with a respect for his autonomy. The law may properly require him to attend to his trial, and forbid him to interfere with witnesses or to try to pervert the course of justice; and he may be convicted of a further offence if he disobeys these requirements. It may also be proper to use force to prevent him carrying through a criminal activity in which he is already engaged – to stop him harassing a witness or absconding from his trial.[61] Neither of these considerations, however, could justify coercing him on the grounds of what he might otherwise do. If we are to treat him as a rational and autonomous agent, who is innocent until proved guilty, we can coerce him only in reponse to what he has chosen to do, not in order to pre-empt the choices which we think he might otherwise make; we must leave him the freedom to decide for himself whether or not he will obey the law, in the light of what he sees, and of what we offer him, as good reasons for action.

The obvious answer to this argument is that, while accused persons are at present no doubt subjected to entirely unjustifiable kinds and degrees of coercion, a legal system which forswore *all* such coercive measures would be utterly ineffective in securing its proper goals: defendants would simply fail to appear for trial; witnesses would be interfered with; convictions would be difficult or impossible to obtain; and the law would be even more widely disobeyed. If we care for the common good which the law is meant to serve (if indeed we care about preserving the freedom and autonomy of all members of the community – for a central part of the law's purpose must be to prohibit and prevent actions which infringe the freedom and autonomy of others) we must to some extent be prepared to infringe the freedom and autonomy of some suspected offenders in order to secure that good. There is, I am sure, considerable force to this reply: it shows us that some coercive aspects of the criminal process are not simply moral wrongs which should be criticised, and eliminated, as being inconsistent with the ideals by which that process ought to be informed, but part of the moral cost which must be paid if we are to have a reasonably effective system of law. I will have more to say later about the kind of dilemma which a recognition of this fact must create for anyone who takes seriously the

[60] See *Hampton* 89–106.   [61] See ch.8(3) below.

non-consequentialist demand that the law should respect *every* citizen as a rational and autonomous agent.[62]

The coercive provisions discussed above are officially sanctioned by the law, and may be justified as an essential element in an effective system of law: but my second example is neither thus sanctioned nor so readily justified. The vast majority of criminal cases in England are decided by a guilty plea.[63] Now this fact might at first glance suggest that most of those who are charged are indeed guilty, and that they properly, and voluntarily, confess their guilt by pleading guilty; and if that were the case we would have no cause for concern. But there is strong evidence that this is not the case: that many defendants who plead guilty do so under the pressure of threats or inducements offered by the police, or because they are persuaded or pressured by their counsel into accepting an explicit or implicit bargain which offers them a lesser charge or a lighter sentence in return for a guilty plea; and that some such defendants are actually innocent, in whole or in part, of the charges to which they plead guilty.[64] Such explicit or implicit plea-bargaining is officially no part of the English criminal process:[65] but its existence, if not its extent, seems clear.

Such methods of obtaining guilty pleas are obviously inconsistent with the purpose which I have ascribed to the criminal trial, and with the respect which is owed to the defendant – and would remain so even if all those who pleaded guilty were indeed guilty as charged. For a guilty plea should properly express the defendant's recognition, and voluntary admission, of her guilt; it is *that* kind of admission which the court or the police may properly seek from the defendant, or urge on her by citing the relevant reasons which justify the claim that she ought to plead guilty if she is guilty. But if we obtain a guilty plea by offering her irrelevant and improper inducements or threats, which are meant to provide her with a purely prudential motive for pleading guilty, that plea loses its meaning and its value; and we no longer address or respect her as a rational agent. Such induced guilty pleas are no doubt useful; we would have to devote far more resources to the criminal process if more defendants contested the charges against them: but they should have no place in a just and rational criminal process; for they are destructive of its proper ends and values.

[62] See ch.7(1), ch.10(3) below.
[63] See A J Ashworth, *Sentencing and Penal Policy* 108.
[64] See J Baldwin and M McConville, *Negotiated Justice*, and *Courts, Prosecution and Conviction*; Cross and Ashworth, *The English Sentencing System* 115–19.
[65] See *Hampton* 184–6; *Turner* (1970) 2 Q.B.321; *Philips, Report* 8.36.

This is one obvious respect in which the actual character of our criminal process is at odds with the purpose and meaning which I have ascribed to it: there are many others. The reality of a criminal trial is, it may be urged, far removed from the kind of participatory attempt to establish and communicate a justified judgment on the defendant's conduct which I have described. The prosecution try to find a charge on which they can hope to get a conviction; the defendant aims to avoid conviction as best he can or, if conviction is unavoidable, to secure the lightest possible punishment; the institutions of the law and the workings of the trial are often so alien to the defendant that it is absurd to suggest that he could either participate in his trial or understand and accept his conviction as a justified condemnation of his conduct. What is happening in a trial, it might further be urged, is not a disinterested attempt to engage the defendant in a critical examination of his conduct, but an attempt to coerce the recalcitrant or the unfortunate into conformity with the beliefs and wishes of those whose sectional interests the law actually serves, through a procedure in which they cannot be, and are not, seriously expected to participate.[66]

I need not deny such claims: for they do not threaten my argument. They may indeed support it, insofar as they condemn, and do not merely describe, the actual character of our criminal trials: for they then condemn our actual institutions for failing to live up to the ideals and values by which they ought to be, and purport to be, informed; and my aim has been to explicate those values and ideals. The distance between my account of those ideals and an accurate description of what actually happens marks, I would claim, not the inadequacy of those ideals or of my account of them, but the radical imperfection of our existing institutions and practices; the extent to which our actual criminal trials fail to serve, or pay only lip-service to, the purposes and values which are appropriate to them – which are indeed involved in the very idea of a criminal trial. Insofar as a trial does not aim to establish and communicate a justified judgment on the defendant's conduct, in the light of laws which have a justified claim on her allegiance; insofar as she finds her trial, and the laws on which it depends, unintelligible or alien, and not because of any deficiency in her own attitudes or concerns; insofar as she is not enabled to understand and participate in her trial: her trial becomes a travesty. That is why the first quotation which heads this chapter is so forceful: not merely because a person is subjected to a process

---

[66] Compare Baldwin and McConville, *Negotiated Justice* ch. 5 on defendants' feelings of non-involvement in, and exclusion from, the criminal process.

which will have a serious impact on his well-being, and is not enabled or allowed to take part in it; but because what purports to be a
process which summons him to answer the charges against him is in
fact so structured that he *cannot* answer them.

I have claimed that a trial is properly (i.e. should be, in terms of
the values and purposes which are internal to the idea of a criminal
trial) a communicative process of argument and justification which
seeks the participation and the assent of the defendant, and which
addresses him as a rational and responsible agent. I have not claimed
that our actual criminal trials do in fact have this character; the
extent to which they lack it shows the extent to which our existing
legal practices are radically imperfect.

5

Trial and Punishment

All punishment is mischief, all punishment in itself is evil.
J Bentham, *Principles of Morals and Legislation*, ch. 13.2

... while punishment, which God in his wisdom has connected with every transgression, is a Good, there is no denying
that it is such a Good only when it is gratefully received, not
when it is simply feared as an evil.
S Kierkegaard, *Purity of Heart*, pp. 81–82

My discussion of the criminal law and the criminal trial has not so
far referred to punishment as an essential part of their meaning or
purpose. This may seem absurd to anyone who believes that the, or
an, essential purpose of the criminal law is to attach punishments to
certain types of conduct; or that the essential purpose of a criminal
trial is to identify those who are to be punished. I have argued, however, that the primary purpose of the law is rather to promulgate
and to justify to the citizen rules which she can and should see that
she ought to obey, independently of any sanctions which are
attached to them; and that the primary purpose of a trial is to bring
the defendant to answer the charges against her, to engage with her
in a rational inquiry into her guilt or innocence, and to reach a verdict on her conduct which can be justified to her as one which she
ought to accept. The law and the trial address the citizen as a rational
and responsible agent: they seek her assent as well as her obedience,
and offer her reasons to accept their demands.

The respect which a system of law should accord to all its citizens
is integral both to its character as law and to the purposes which it
should properly serve: it aims not simply to prevent certain kinds of
conduct which are injurious to the common good, by whatever
means may be effective, or by whatever means are also consistent
with moral side-constraints which are themselves independent of
that consequential purpose; but to dissuade citizens from such conduct by declaring and showing it to be wrong. That respect is also
integral to the character of the trial and to its proper purpose: it aims
not merely to reach an accurate verdict on the defendant's conduct,

but to justify that verdict to her by a process of proof and argument in which she is to participate. These purposes embody, while the purposes of merely preventing harmful conduct or of reaching an accurate verdict do not embody, an appropriate respect for the citizen as a rational and responsible agent; what makes a system of criminal law and criminal trials a proper method of pursuing these purposes is that it itself embodies and expresses that same respect.

But the criminal law does not merely exhort the citizens to obey its rules; it attaches punishments to breaches of those rules. A criminal trial does not merely condemn the offender; it may impose a punishment on him. Whether or not such penal provisions are *definitive* of a system of criminal law, any account of such a system must have something to say about their meaning and justification. But are they not utterly at odds with the kind of account which I have offered so far? I have noted one respect in which our actual criminal process relies on coercion, rather than on an appeal to reason; a defendant may be detained or restricted *before* his trial. Such measures can be justified, if at all, only consequentially: to secure the results which justice or utility require we are prepared to coerce the citizen if we cannot safely rely on his voluntary co-operation. Is not punishment, however, equally coercive, and equally incompatible with a proper respect for the citizen's freedom and autonomy? Must I not, therefore, either admit that my account of the criminal law and the criminal process is inadequate, since it cannot justify the penal provisions which are central to actual systems of criminal law; or hold that such provisions can never be justified?

It is of course no part of my task to justify our actual penal practices; they are likely to be at best imperfect and at worst radically unjust. But it must be part of my task to ask whether and how a system of criminal punishment *could* be justified in terms of the values and purposes to which I have so far appealed; and it is this question which I must now address.

We can approach this question in various ways. We might note that the idea of law which I have sketched contains an ideal model of the proper relationship between the citizen and the law: ideally, every citizen would voluntarily accept, and obey, the law's justified requirements. Ideally, therefore, there would be neither trials nor punishments. There would be no offenders to be condemned or punished; if an innocent person were suspected of an offence the mutual trust which would obtain in such a community would allow others simply to accept her denial of guilt; such a community would need, at most, a system of advisory tribunals to decide, in cases of uncertainty, which kinds of conduct were wrong.

That would be a society of angels: a human system of law must make provisions for actual and suspected breaches of the law. But a properly ordered, and non-coercive, system of criminal trials, whilst it would mark our failure to attain the law's ideal, could still serve the values internal to that ideal: for it would aim to bring the offender to recognise her guilt, and to accept and obey the law's justified requirements; it would address her as a rational agent, and seek her voluntary assent. What of punishment, however? Could a system of punishment still serve that ideal, and express those values – could it be required by, or at least consistent with, a proper respect for the criminal's autonomy? Or must we admit that punishment, which is imposed on the criminal against her will, is inconsistent with such respect; that its justification must appeal to values which conflict with, and override, such a Kantian concern; and that our use of punishment manifests our recognition that we must abandon or compromise that ideal of a society fully structured by a respect for its citizens' rational autonomy, and find some more effective way of preventing criminal conduct than an appeal to actual and potential offenders to recognise its wrongfulness?

We might ask why the criminal process should include punishment: why should it not end with the formal verdict which condemns or acquits the defendant? A system of law which made no provision for punishment to follow conviction would not lack an intelligible purpose. The law would promulgate obligatory standards of conduct for the citizens to accept and obey. The trial would express our concern for the law's demands, by bringing the citizen to answer for her allegedly wrongful conduct, and by condemning her if she is proved guilty; it could modify the offender's future conduct – not, if it is to respect her autonomy, simply by deterring her from future crimes, but by persuading her of the wrongfulness of the conduct which the law and her conviction condemn. So why should we subject offenders to anything more than a formal conviction which condemns their crime?

We might say, of course, that a criminal conviction (like moral blame) is itself a kind of punishment: it is imposed on an offender for an offence, and aims to cause him the pain of confronting his own guilt and of being condemned for it (the extent to which his conviction pains the criminal, however, depends as much on his own moral attitudes as on the gravity of his offence: one who repents his crime, or is shamed by the condemnation of others, will be pained by his conviction; but an unregenerate criminal who cares neither for the law nor for the opinions of those who condemn him will be unmoved).

Furthermore, even if a conviction is not followed by formal punishment it will, if publicised, affect the offender's relationships with others. It might gain him their admiration or sympathy, if they have a sufficiently low regard for the law which he broke or for the system which convicted him: but the stigma of a criminal conviction, at least for a serious offence, will more usually injure his material prospects and his social relationships. He may find it harder to obtain employment or credit, and his relationships with others may suffer in the ways which I discussed in connection with moral blame. Nor are such consequences merely the contingent by-products of a public conviction: for internal to a system of law is the claim that the citizens should accept and respect the law as a source of obligations; and therefore that they should be prepared to condemn the conduct of those who break the law. It would be absurd to say that the law has a moral claim on our allegiance, and that its requirements are essential to the common good of the community, but that our attitudes and responses to a fellow-citizen should be unaffected by a public finding that he has flouted those requirements. A criminal conviction condemns the offender's conduct: those who accept and respect the law which he broke, and the criminal process which convicted him, must share in that condemnation. They will blame him for what he has done; he may therefore suffer the social and personal implications of being blamed.

These social effects of a public conviction might be seen as a punishment which the offender suffers; in which case we have not yet imagined a system of trials without punishments. Though such social punishments are not formally assigned or officially imposed, they are an implication of the social condemnation of the offender which his conviction sanctions and justifies, and an implication, not merely a by-product, of its character as a public conviction.

Such social responses to wrong-doing could, I have argued, have the character of moral punishments which respect the wrong-doer's autonomy: though they can – by design or in fact – operate coercively as prudential deterrents, they can and should instead express our understanding of the moral implications of wrong-doing, and our concern that the wrong-doer should herself come to recognise and repent that wrong-doing. We could of course inhibit such social consequences of a conviction by holding all trials *in camera*, and forbidding publication of their results: but there are obvious reasons for having a system of *public* trials and verdicts. The community should be able to see that the law is being properly applied and administered; the innocent should be freed from suspicion; public convictions may more effectively dissuade actual and potential offenders from crime. Furthermore, and perhaps more crucially, if the law is the proper concern of the whole community, and crime an offence against the whole community, it is appropriate that trials and verdicts should be observed and shared in by the community on whose behalf and in whose name they are carried out. Defendants should answer to and before the community for their actions; the guilty should ideally confess their guilt publicly, and should be publicly condemned; and the innocent should be publicly acquitted.

Why then should some such system of trials and verdicts without formal punishments not be a proper and adequate response to crime? Or, if formal punishments are to be imposed, why should those punishments not be purely symbolic, of a kind which cause pain to the criminal only through what they mean? Offenders could, for instance, be required to wear a special badge on their clothing: there is nothing inherently painful in this; it pains them only because of what it expresses to them and to others – only because it reminds them that they have been condemned, and tells others of their guilt. Such symbolic punishments would provide a formal and more striking expression for the condemnation which a conviction involves, and a public and more lasting reminder of the offender's guilt. Why then should the offender suffer anything more than this, or be subjected to the kinds of hard treatment which our actual penal practices typically involve?

There are two familiar kinds of answer to these questions. One is consequentialist: that a legal system which made no formal provision for punishments or other kinds of coercive measure to be imposed on offenders, or which provided only symbolic punishments, would be disastrously ineffective in securing its practical aims. If offenders stood to suffer nothing more than formal conviction and condemnation, or nothing more than a purely symbolic punishment, the law would be so widely disobeyed that it would cease to be an effective method of preventing harmful kinds of conduct. If the law did not itself impose some kind of coercive measures on offenders, others would not obey the law; offenders themselves might suffer, more severely than they would at the hands of the law, at the hands of private vigilantes and revenge-seekers; and the whole legal system would rapidly break down. Punishment, like other kinds of coercive imposition on the individual, is itself an evil: but it is a necessary evil if we are to maintain an effective system of law which serves the common good.

The second answer is retributivist: that justice requires that the criminal should suffer a punishment proportional in its severity to the gravity of his offence; and a legal system which imposed only formal convictions or purely symbolic punishments on offenders would not satisfy this requirement. Neither convictions by themselves, nor purely symbolic punishments, will ensure that offenders suffer as, and to the degree that, they should. Indeed, since it is the most hardened and unrepentant criminals who will be least moved or pained by such convictions and punishments, they will inflict least suffering just where severe suffering is most deserved. Nor can we rely on the informal social responses of others to impose the punishments which offenders deserve: for such responses are unorganised and to a degree arbitrary; they will not distribute punishments equitably, or ensure that offenders receive the kind and degree of punishment which they deserve. Punishment is, once a crime has occurred, a good; and it is a good which the law must secure.

The character, and the adequacy, of these two familiar kinds of justifying account of punishment will be the subject of the following chapters. The question which most concerns me is this: can either kind of account show punishment to be consistent with the values and purposes which are, I have argued, integral to the criminal law and the criminal trial? Can punishment be consistent with, or even an expression of, a proper respect for the criminal's autonomy?

One question for a strict consequentialist will be whether she can justify a system of *punishment* at all. But the fundamental moral objection to any consequentialist account – even one which allows that our pursuit of the consequentialist aims of a system of law and punishment should be constrained by certain non-consequentialist values – will be that it fails to accord to the citizen, and to the criminal, the respect which is their due.

If we take this charge seriously (as we should) we will be led to consider some of the recently revived versions of retributivism, which claim to show that punishment is consistent with a proper respect for the criminal. I will argue that the best known of these versions, which portrays punishment as the restoration of a fair balance of benefits and burdens among members of the community, is open to serious objections. I will then, however, discuss a different account of punishment, which may count as retributivist insofar as it makes the relation between past crime and present punishment central to the meaning and purpose of punishment; but which also ascribes to punishment a further, reformative purpose to which it is internally, not merely contingently, related. By bringing together the ideas of punishment as having an essentially expressive purpose, and of punishment as a kind of penance, such an account may hope to show how punishment can be continuous in its meaning and purpose with the criminal law and the criminal trial as I have portrayed them, and with our moral responses to the wrong-doings of others; how it can express a proper concern and respect for the criminal; and how it can be a good to the criminal himself.

However, even if such an account can show us what punishment should ideally be, if it is to be just and justified, it will at the same time show us how radically, and perhaps irremediably, imperfect and unjust our existing penal practices are. This drastic gap between the ideal of just punishment and the actuality of human punishment is, I think, a necessary implication of any adequate account of punishment; and it poses a grave problem for anyone who takes the demands of penal and political justice seriously. A consequentialist may do the best that he can in an imperfect world with imperfect institutions. But someone who believes that punishment can be justified only if it is just, and that punishments cannot be just within our existing political and penal system, must ask herself whether she can honestly say '*Fiat justitia et ruant coeli*'. Must we avoid punitive injustice, *whatever* the consequential cost; or must our concern for such ideals of justice, and of a true respect for the criminal's autonomy, be compromised by a more pragmatic concern for the prevention of crime, and thus of further kinds of injustice?

6

Consequentialist Punishments

As to the *end*, or final cause of human punishments. This is not by way of atonement or expiation for the crime committed; for that must be left to the just determination of the supreme being: but as a precaution against future offences of the same kind. This is effected three ways: either by the amendment of the offender himself; for which purpose all corporal punishments, fines, and temporary exile or imprisonment are inflicted: or, by deterring others by the dread of his example from offending in the like way, 'ut poenas (as Tully expresses it) ad paucos, metus ad omnes perveniat'; which gives rise to all ignominious punishments, and to such executions of justice as are open and public: or, lastly, by depriving the party injuring of the power to do future mischief; which is effected by either putting him to death, or condemning him to perpetual confinement, slavery, or exile.

Sir William Blackstone, Commentaries on the
Laws of England, IV.1

I DEFINITION AND JUSTIFICATION

This chapter concerns the possibility and adequacy of a consequentialist account of punishment: but I begin with some definitional remarks. For questions about the meaning of 'punishment' are not merely terminological: they concern the justificatory criteria internal to the concept of punishment, which enable us to criticise, as well as to identify, punishments and systems of punishment; and an account of punishment must explain and justify these criteria.

Punishment, it may be said, must logically be imposed on an offender, for an offence, by a duly constituted authority, and must inflict suffering on him.[1] What is imposed as punishment may not in fact satisfy these strict criteria: I may 'punish' someone in the mistaken belief that he is guilty of an offence, or that I have the authority to punish him; or in the knowledge that he is innocent, or that

---

[1] On these criteria (and the qualifications necessary to them) see H L A Hart, 'Prolegomenon to the Principles of Punishment'; K Baier, 'Is Punishment Retributive?'; S I Benn, 'An Approach to the Problems of Punishment'; A Flew, 'The Justification of Punishment'; G Fletcher, *Rethinking Criminal Law* 408–14.

I lack the authority to punish him. Such impositions may count as punishments, so long as I *claim* (honestly or fraudulently) that these criteria are satisfied – or at least that appropriate steps have been taken to ensure that they are satisfied (that, for instance, he has been duly convicted of an offence): as criteria for identifying instances of punishment these criteria concern what must be claimed rather than what must be the case. But such impositions must also be judged as *improper* punishments – as perversions of punishment – by the justificatory criteria which are internal to the concept of punishment.[2] To realise or admit that these strict criteria are not satisfied – that he is not in fact guilty of an offence, for instance – is to realise or admit that his punishment is improper *as* a punishment.

The definition of punishment shows us both what an action must purport to be if it is to count as punishment, and what it must actually be if it is to be justified as punishment. Punishment must, for instance, be justified by reference to the guilt of the person punished; and if that person is not in fact guilty he may insist that he is, by mistake or by design, being victimised, *not* punished:

> even if the world gathered all its strength, there is one thing it is not able to do, it can no more punish an innocent one than it can put a dead person to death.[3]

The punishment of the innocent is inconsistent with the justificatory criteria of punishment: to deny that the innocent victim is punished is to insist on the impropriety of what is done to him under the guise of punishment.

Punishment must not only be *of* an offender; it must also be *for* her offence: but what does this mean? A Utilitarian occasionalism would subject a person to coercive treatment only if she has committed an offence: but that treatment will depend on her present condition, not on her past offence; a minor offender might be found to have dangerous propensities which, though unrelated to the offence for which she has been convicted, now require lengthy reformative treatment.[4] Such treatment is not punishment; not merely because it is not intended to inflict suffering (it still involves the subjection of her will),[5] but because it is not appropriately related to her past offence. The offender is liable to coercive treatment

---

[2] Compare ch. 3(5) above on unjust law as a perversion of law.
[3] S Kierkegaard, *Purity of Heart* 85; on which see P Winch, 'Can a Good Man be Harmed?'
[4] See ch. 4.(2) above; N Walker and S McCabe, *Crime and Insanity in England* vol. 2, 101–2.
[5] See H Fingarette, 'Punishment and Suffering'.

because she has committed an offence; but she is not subjected to this particular treatment because of the particular offence which she committed. If punishment is to be *for* an offence, its nature and extent must be justified by reference to that offence. The claim that an offender's punishment should be 'proportionate' to her offence is thus rooted in the concept of punishment itself: an unusually harsh punishment which is imposed for the sake of general deterrence, not because the offence was unusually grave, is improper *as* a punishment.

But what counts as an offence? A government may discourage an activity by taxing it. The tax is imposed by an authority on those who engage in the taxable activity, because they engage in it, and is meant to be unpleasant; but it is not a punishment (like a fine), since the activity is not prohibited as an offence.[6] A criminal offence is something which the law prohibits and condemns as a wrong. I have argued that it must be prohibited as a moral wrong; it has also been argued that any non-circular definition of the concepts of crime and punishment must refer to the alleged immorality of the acts which are prohibited and punished as crimes.[7] Punishment must therefore, as punishment, be justified by reference to a moral wrong which the person punished has allegedly committed.

This is not to say that all moral wrongs should be crimes: some may be no concern of the law; others may be dealt with as torts rather than as crimes. Nor need conduct be immoral *before* it can properly be prohibited as criminal: *mala prohibita* are moral wrongs not in themselves, but as breaches of laws which serve the common good; regulatory offences, for example, are moral wrongs insofar as they involve the wilful or negligent breach of a law which properly seeks to control a dangerous activity. Nor is this to say that the law never in fact defines as criminal, conduct which is morally legitimate: but it is to say that the law is necessarily defective as law if it defines as criminal conduct which cannot be claimed or shown to be morally at fault.[8]

If a system of criminal punishment is to be justified in the terms which are appropriate to it, it must aim to punish only those who

---

[6] See Hart, 'Prolegomenon to the Principles of Punishment' 6–7; 'Legal Responsibility and Excuses' 44; also J Feinberg, 'The Expressive Function of Punishment' 105–10 on the use of purportedly administrative provisions as covert punishments.

[7] See ch. 3 above; and R Wasserstrom, 'Some Problems in the Definition and Justification of Punishment'.

[8] I will not discuss the proper scope of the criminal law here: but an account of the purpose and justification of criminal punishment, as a central feature of the criminal law, will clearly be relevant to that issue.

have committed a moral wrong by disobeying the law's justified requirements; it must relate their punishments to the offences which they have committed; and it must allow that excuses which exempt an agent from any imputation of moral fault should also exempt him from conviction and punishment. If these justificatory criteria are not satisfied by a particular system or in a particular case we may still recognise it as a system or instance of punishment: but we must also recognise it as an improper or defective system or instance of punishment.

A system of punishment is most obviously defective if it involves the deliberate punishment of the innocent; and we can now see more clearly what that may involve and why it is objectionable. Three kinds of case may be noted.

- An official procures the conviction and punishment of someone she knows to be innocent, in order to preserve the law's deterrent efficacy, or to put pressure on someone else. (For example, a dissident's husband is framed and punished in order to dissuade her from her activities.) In such a case the victim is punished unlawfully and deceitfully, under the pretence that he is guilty of an offence.
- The law prohibits and punishes what cannot properly be seen as an offence. Thus a shopkeeper who takes all the care which could reasonably be demanded of her finds herself guilty of the strict liability offence of selling adulterated milk;[9] a regime discourages dissidents by making it an offence to be married to a person who criticises the state. Here too the innocent are punished, for the reasons for punishing such conduct concern not its alleged wrongfulness, but the effect which punishing it will have on others. The shopkeeper is not deemed guilty of an offence because *she* has wilfully or negligently committed a wrong, but because a law this strict may deter *other* potential offenders; a dissident's wife is not deemed guilty of an offence because she should have prevented his activities (we should have different objections to such a law as that), but because this is a useful way of putting pressure on dissidents.
- Someone who is rightly convicted of an offence receives an unduly severe punishment for the sake of general deterrence, or as

[9] Compare the *Sale of Food and Drugs Act* 1875, s.6 (see *Parker v Alder* (1899) 1 Q.B. 20) with the *Food and Drugs Act* 1955, ss.32, 94(4), 113. See G Williams, *Criminal Law: the General Part* s.77; J C Smith and B Hogan, *Criminal Law* 93–110; G Williams, *Textbook of Criminal Law* 954–60.

preventive detention. He is not innocent, but he is not *that* guilty; he is not punished *for* the offence which he committed.[10] His punishment may accord with the system's principles of sentencing; or it may involve the deceitful pretence that his offence is one which merits such a severe punishment.

Such punishments of the innocent are not objectionable merely because they do not give their victims a fair chance to avoid them, but because they are a perversion of law and punishment:[11] their victims are not punished *for* something which can count as an *offence*; the criminal law is diverted from its proper purposes. Such punishments may not manifest the direct dishonesty involved in the framing of an innocent scapegoat, or inflict on their victims the particular injustice of being falsely convicted of a genuine offence:[12] yet they all involve the injustice of pretending to punish an offender for an offence, whilst in fact (whether openly or covertly) perverting the law to a quite different and improper purpose.

Imagine a Mental Illness Act which makes it an offence to be suffering from a severe mental illness, and prescribes detention in hospital as the 'punishment' for this 'offence'. We might object, as we should to any Act which prescribed detention for all such people, that we should detain the mentally ill only if there is a clear danger that they will otherwise harm themselves or others. But we should have a further objection to defining a person's illness as an offence, and his detention as a punishment for that offence: not because this necessarily makes a difference to his final disposal, but because it is grotesque to regard his illness as an *offence* of which he is *guilty*.[13]

To object, rather than simply note, that the punishment of the innocent is a perversion of the proper purpose of punishment is to assume that the values which determine that purpose deserve our respect; and I have yet to show what these values are or what claim they have on us. I have claimed so far only that a justificatory account of punishment must justify a system whose defining purpose is to impose suffering on offenders for their offences; and I

[10] See A H Goldman, 'The Paradox of Punishment'; H Gross, 'Culpability and Desert'.
[11] See Hart, 'Prolegomenon to the Principle of Punishment', and 'Legal Responsibility and Excuses'; J R Lucas, *On Justice* 137; W Moberly, *The Ethics of Punishment* 80.
[12] See R Dworkin, 'Principle, Policy, Procedure'; and ch. 4(3) above.
[13] Though one who regards mental illness as 'a myth' might object that in detaining the 'mentally ill' we are in fact and covertly punishing them; see T Szasz, *Law, Liberty, and Psychiatry*.

want now to ask whether a consequentialist can provide such an account – either in purely consequentialist terms; or in terms of certain consequentialist benefits which provide the justifying aim of a system of punishment, but whose pursuit is constrained by certain non-consequentialist values. The definitional criteria of punishment show that its internal logic is retributive; it must, as punishment, be justified and determined by a past offence by the person punished. However, it may still be argued that a practice of this kind can and must be justified by its consequential benefits.

My concern here is not only with accounts of punishment based on a specifically Utilitarian consequentialism which posits some one final good as the proper end of all human action, and defines that good in terms of pleasure, happiness, or the satisfaction of desires: it is with accounts of punishment which share two essential features.

First, they find the justifying purpose of a system of punishment in its future benefits, not in its relation to past offences. Its most obvious benefits are reductive: it assists the aims of the criminal law by reducing the incidence of criminal conduct. The threat of punishment may deter potential offenders, and its imposition makes that threat more credible; it may incapacitate offenders temporarily (e.g. by imprisonment) or permanently (e.g. by execution); it may reform or rehabilitate offenders so that they will in future obey the law voluntarily; it may remind actual and potential offenders of the wrongness of the conduct which is punished. Punishment may also bring benefits which are not specifically reductive; it may satisfy the vengeful desires of those whom the criminal has injured or offended, and reassure an anxious public that the law is being enforced. But the main justificatory burden is usually borne by the reductive benefits of punishment: we should attach sanctions to the law's prohibitions if and because such sanctions provide the most efficient means of making those prohibitions effective.

Second, the connections between crime, punishment and the justifying purpose of punishment are therefore purely contingent: the justifying aims of a penal system make no essential reference to the past offences which are punished, but refer only to its future effects; and it is not a necessary truth that we can achieve those aims only by punishing offenders. Since punishment is just one possible technique for achieving our consequentialist ends, a system of punishment must be justified by showing both that its benefits are likely to outweigh its costs, and that it is likely to be at least as economically effective as any other available technique for achieving those ends.

The contingent connection between punishment and its justifying aims raises the question of whether a consequentialist would favour a system of punishment at all: might other ways of achieving those aims not be more efficient? The contingent connection between past offences and the justifying aims of punishment raises the question of whether a consequentialist would not abuse a system of punishment: might not the pursuit of those aims require the occasional or systematic punishment of the innocent? Any consequentialist justification of punishment must confront these two questions.

The first question gains force from the fact that both consequentialists and their critics often take for granted the existence of a system of criminal law and punishment; posit some consequential ends which such a system could serve; and ask how a consequentialist would operate with or within such a system. But why should we suppose that a consequentialist would accept such a system? One reply to this is that consequentialists are practical beings, and must work – as private citizens, as officials, or as members of a government – with the social materials available to them. Our existing institutions may embody non-consequentialist values, rather than the consequentialist wisdom of the ages: but they can still serve a useful purpose; and their very existence in a reasonably stable society gives them some consequential value. For the dangers and uncertainties of a radical restructuring of existing institutions are such that a consequentialist may do better to try to use them towards her favoured ends, and try to reform them, if at all, only gradually and modestly. It is still true, however, that she might hope to reform them; even, in the end, to reform them radically. We must therefore examine the likely direction of such reforms; the ideals which will inform them; and the kinds of institution which would appear in a more perfectly consequentialist society than our own. Would a consequentialist find a place for punishment in a properly structured society; or must she see it as an institution which embodies fundamentally alien values – though one which may, meanwhile and *faute de mieux*, serve some useful purpose?

To show that a system of punishment must embody non-consequentialist values – and thus that a purely consequentialist justification of punishment is impossible – will not yet show that a consequentialist account of how we should deal with criminal or undesirable conduct is untenable; perhaps punishment is itself un-justified, and should be replaced by some consequentialist alterna-tive. But it will lead us to ask what values a system of punishment does express; whether they have any substantial claim on our regard; and whether they can be incorporated, as non-consequentialist side-constraints, in an account which still posits a consequentialist justifying aim for punishment.

I will begin, however, with the second question: would a conse-quentialist be committed to abusing a system of punishment within which he operates? To show that he must be so committed will not show that he would not favour a system of punishment; he may have reason to maintain institutions which he also has reason to abuse: but it will show that a consequentialist cannot adequately explain the values which are internal to the concept of punishment.

2 PUNISHING THE INNOCENT

I have noted three kinds of deliberate punishment of the innocent. Such punishments might be consistent with the positive rules of the legal systems within which they are perpetrated: but they are incon-sistent with the defining purpose of punishment. We can, however, imagine contexts in which they would probably bring some conse-quential benefit: so must a consequentialist not be prepared to abuse a system of punishment, by punishing the innocent in such ways as these?

A consequentialist might agree that she would be willing to punish the innocent; and argue that those who object to this have simply failed to accept the consequentialist principles which should properly guide our actions:[14] but this reply simply concedes the claim that she cannot justify the requirement that only the guilty should be punished. More usually, however, consequentialists argue that they need not be committed to the more disturbing kinds of punishment of the innocent, and offer a consequentialist justifi-cation for that requirement. Such arguments are, as we will see, doomed to failure: but we must first attend briefly to a different kind of response.

'You cannot object to a consequentialist account of punishment merely on the grounds that it would sanction the punishment of the innocent. No practicable system of punishment can hope to punish only the guilty; in ensuring that we punish a reasonable proportion

---

[14] See T Honderich, *Punishment: The Supposed Justifications* 66–76; and ch. 6(4) below.

of the guilty, we will inevitably punish some who are in fact innocent. We *could* avoid punishing the innocent, by refusing to punish anyone: in maintaining a system which we know will sometimes punish the innocent we therefore cannot claim that we punish the innocent unintentionally; we must admit that we too are abusing it as a system of punishment.'[15]

But we are not yet committed to the kind of perversion of punishment which a consequentialist must allegedly sanction, so long as we do not *aim* to procure the punishment of the innocent. There is, for a non-consequentialist, a crucial difference between the demand that we should take every possible precaution against the risk of punishing those who are in fact innocent, and the demand that we must never aim to procure the punishment of those whom we believe to be innocent. A practicable system of punishment cannot satisfy the former demand; it can take all 'reasonable', but not all possible, precautions against that risk. In maintaining such a system we thus consent to the expected punishment of some who are in fact innocent; but their punishment is, in terms of our and the system's aims, mistaken – it occurs *despite* our intention and our efforts to avoid it. But a system of punishment can, and properly should, satisfy the latter demand; and it is that demand which a consequentialist is allegedly willing to flout, by *intending* to procure the punishment of those whom she believes to be innocent.[16]

We must remember, however, that there are more ways of deliberately punishing the innocent than illegally framing a scapegoat. If we are to avoid such perversions of punishment our general principles of liability, and our definitions of particular offences, must be such that only those who are indeed *guilty* of the relevant kind of *offence* are liable to punishment. If for the sake of general deterrence we make liability for an offence so strict that one who conducts a legitimate activity with all reasonable care may still be guilty in law of an offence; or presume irrebuttably that agents foresee the natural and probable consequences of their acts (not because those who lack such foresight are truly guilty, but to guard against fraudulent defences by those who are truly guilty);[17] we do not simply consent

[15] See G Schedler, 'Can Retributivists Support Legal Punishment?'
[16] This moral distinction clearly needs further explication: see J G Murphy, 'The Killing of the Innocent'; T Nagel, 'War and Massacre'; A Wertheimer, 'Punishing the Innocent – Unintentionally'; A J Kenny, *Will, Freedom, and Power* 58; R A Duff, 'Intention, Responsibility and Double Effect', and 'Intention, Recklessness, and Probable Consequences'.
[17] See p. 154 above; *DPP v Smith* (1961) A. C. 290; R A Duff, 'Recklessness and Rape' 51–2.

to the mistaken punishment of some who are actually innocent: we intend to convict and punish some whom we believe to be properly innocent, in order to encourage others or to ensure the punishment of the guilty.

A consequentialist must allegedly approve the deliberate punishment of the innocent. But, she may now argue, this is not in fact true: for the likely effects of such punishments, or of a system which allowed them, would be harmful rather than beneficial. This reply, however (even if it is empirically well-founded), misses the point. The crucial charge is not that a consequentialist will in fact punish the innocent, but that she is ready to contemplate it as an open moral possibility. The impropriety of punishing the innocent is for her *contingent* on its likely effects: but her critic claims that its impropriety is *intrinsic* to its character as punishment of the innocent; that the consequentialist therefore cannot see *what* is wrong with punishing the innocent. The critic might even agree that the innocent must sometimes be convicted and punished as if they were guilty, in order to secure some significant social benefit; perhaps that pragmatic considerations require us to define the *mens rea* of certain offences in a way which is inconsistent with the strict demands of justice. But, he would insist, such situations create a moral conflict between the demands of justice and utility which a consequentialist cannot recognise for what it is: we must realise, as the consequentialist cannot realise, that we are now *sacrificing* justice to utility, and compromising the values which are internal to the law.[18]

'But a refusal to regard the punishment of the innocent as an open moral possibility can and must itself be justified consequentially. It might in fact, in rare cases, be useful to punish an innocent: but the dangers of allowing ourselves to regard this as a normally available option are such that we should cultivate in ourselves dispositions which make the very thought of it repugnant to us. When engaged in the kind of "intuitive" thinking which rightly structures most of our moral activity, we should think and act *as if* "Do not punish the innocent" is an absolute rule; but in our more "critical" or reflective moments we must recognise that it is a rule which must be justified consequentially, and which might have to be broken in an extreme and unusual situation. It is more than a mere rule of thumb: but we should accept and obey it only if and because giving it this role in

---

[18] See H L A Hart, 'Murder and the Principles of Punishment' 81; Nagel, 'War and Massacre'.

our lives will in the long run produce the best consequences, not because what it forbids is *intrinsically* wrong.'[19]

This sophisticated consequentialism aims to undermine the critic by showing both why he should, usually, think and feel as he does and why he is wrong to claim that his account of the matter is complete. If he insists that the punishment of the innocent is in itself so wicked that anyone who is prepared even to contemplate it shows a corrupt mind,[20] he exhibits a well-trained intuitive disposition: but he is failing to recognise or to engage in that level of critical thinking which alone can explain and justify his intuitive principles. For critical thinking must be consequentialist; and anyone who progresses beyond the stage of merely intuitive thinking must realise that it is wrong to punish the innocent only if and because the consequences of such actions, including the consequences of being prepared to contemplate them, are harmful.

This argument denies the sense of fundamentally non-consequentialist modes of moral thought. But a critic who insists that the punishment of the innocent is in itself unjust is not relying on an arbitrary and inexplicable moral intuition. He is appealing to a moral demand whose sense is to be found in a non-consequentialist account of the law, and in the moral conception of the individual as an autonomous agent which such an account involves; in explicating such an account I will thus also be rebutting this claim that the logic of moral thought must be consequentialist.[21] The critic will still object that a consequentialist who is engaged in 'critical' thinking must contemplate the punishment of the innocent as an open moral possibility; and that to regard the wrongness of such punishments as being ultimately contingent on their effects (even if we include the effects of being disposed or willing to punish the innocent) is to misunderstand their true moral character as abuses or perversions of punishment.

But the consequentialist's bolt is not yet shot. She might now argue that she cannot, as a matter of logic, be committed to contemplating the punishment of the innocent – not merely that she will not in fact be so committed. In its crudest form the argument runs thus: since punishment is by definition of the guilty, we cannot be committed to punishing the innocent; for no one can be committed to

---

[19] See R M Hare, *Moral Thinking*, especially ch. 3 and ch. 9.7.
[20] See G E M Anscombe, 'Modern Moral Philosophy' 17.
[21] For more direct rebuttals, see especially R W Beardsmore, *Moral Reasoning*; D Z Phillips and H O Mounce, *Moral Practices*; R F Holland, 'Good and Evil in Action'; Nagel, 'War and Massacre'.

what is logically impossible.[22] But there is a more plausible version.

'We must distinguish questions about the justification of actions within a practice from questions about the justification of the practice itself. The rule limiting punishment to the guilty is *definitive* of the practice of punishment; and we have good consequentialist reason to prefer a practice of punishment, which imposes penalties only on those who have been duly convicted of offences, to one of "telishment" which allows its officials to "telish" some whom they know to be innocent. Thus we should, as consequentialists, adopt a practice of punishment; and we cannot, within this practice, coherently contemplate punishing the innocent on consequentialist grounds.'[23]

Rawls himself discusses only the 'punishment' of scapegoats who are known to be innocent in law; but his argument might be extended to cover other kinds of case. It depends, of course, on large empirical claims about the likely effects of different practices; and an examination of those effects might show that practices whose defining rules allowed for some kinds of 'punishment' of the innocent would be consequentially justifiable.[24] We need not, however, embark on this examination here: for one who opts, on consequentialist grounds, for a practice whose defining rules limit punishment to the guilty may still be committed to procuring the punishment of an innocent scapegoat.

To see the basis of Rawls' argument, imagine a magistrate who thinks that she has good consequentialist reason to 'punish' someone whom she knows to be innocent in law. If she says to the defendant, in open court, 'I know you are innocent, but I am going to convict and punish you', she will no doubt fail to secure the consequential benefits at which she aims: for those benefits usually depend on others believing the defendant to be guilty. But she will also contradict herself: for to say, as a magistrate who is trying the case, 'I know you are innocent' is in effect to acquit the defendant and declare him to be ineligible for punishment. In announcing what she is doing the magistrate takes back with her second breath what she has declared with her first breath, thus reducing her

---

[22] See A Quinton, 'Punishment'; Benn, 'An Approach to the Problems of Punishment': for criticism of this simple 'definitional stop' see Hart, 'Prolegomenon to the Principles of Punishment' 5–6; Honderich, *Punishment: The Supposed Justifications* 62–4.

[23] J Rawls, 'Two Concepts of Rules': on which see H J McCloskey, '"Two Concepts of Rules": a Note'; D Lyons, *Forms and Limits of Utilitarianism* 182–7; J Feinberg, 'The Forms and Limits of Utilitarianism' 377–81.

[24] See McCloskey, *op. cit.*

utterance to nonsense; and that is why she allegedly cannot, even as a consequentialist, be committed to doing it.

The same argument, however, would seem to show that it can never be right to lie. When I lie to you I tell you that p, whilst knowing or believing that not-p. If I now spell out what I am doing, I talk the same kind of nonsense as the magistrate: I must say 'p, though I know that not-p', which renders my attempted deception futile, and my utterance nonsensical.[25] It is a defining rule of the practice of communication that we should not assert as true what we know to be false: it is because of this rule that a lie which is spelt out becomes nonsense; but it is also because of this rule that a lie which is not announced as such can be effective. Now I do not suppose that a Rawlsian consequentialist would agree that it can never be right to lie: but this argument does not in fact show that it is never right to lie. What it actually, and unsurprisingly, shows is that a lie must be deceitful; in lying I pretend to obey the defining rules of the practice of communication, whilst in fact breaking them. This may be reprehensible, but it is not logically incoherent.

The magistrate's case is the same. If she is to achieve her consequentialist ends, and avoid talking nonsense, she must *pretend* to be convicting and sentencing a guilty person; she must be publicly committed to a practice whose defining rules reserve punishment for the guilty, whilst secretly breaking those rules. This is dishonest and unjust, but not logically incoherent; nor should we be surprised that a consequentialist may have to do her good by stealth. For she may have to preserve, and declare her public allegiance to, practices whose defining purposes and rules she will secretly pervert or break if it is useful to do so. Whether we say that the magistrate punishes, or pretends to punish, her victim, it is an injustice to which she may, as a consequentialist, be committed.

The merit of Rawls' argument is that it sees the impropriety of punishing the innocent to be a feature of the concept of punishment itself; its failure shows that we cannot explain the values which that concept embodies in purely consequentialist terms. A strict consequentialist must be willing to contemplate the punishment of the innocent as an open moral option; she cannot give an adequate account of the values which condemn any such action as an abuse of punishment. She might justify a public commitment to a system of punishment – a commitment which she must in fact abandon if it conflicts with the demands of utility: but she cannot justify a genu-

---

[25] Compare G E Moore, 'A Reply to my Critics' 542–3; discussed by M Black, 'Saying and Disbelieving'.

ine commitment to a system of punishment which accepts its defining rules as being definitive of the just and proper use of punishment.

I have yet to explicate the non-consequentialist values which are embodied in the concept of punishment, and which forbid the punishment of the innocent. One might talk of the injustice or dishonesty of treating the innocent as if they were guilty; of using the innocent as a means to our further ends: but to clarify the significance of these notions I will return to the question of whether a consequentialist should anyway regard punishment as an appropriate method for dealing with socially undesirable conduct. This will reinforce the claim that a purely consequentialist account of punishment is impossible; and it will help us to see whether a modified consequentialism, which accepts these non-consequentialist values as side-constraints on the pursuit of our consequentialist ends, can generate a more adequate account of punishment.

3 PUNISHMENT AND DETERRENCE

I have argued that we cannot explain either the criminal law, as a system of rules which define and prohibit certain types of conduct as wrong, or the criminal trial, as a process in which a citizen is called to answer for his allegedly wrongful conduct, in consequentialist terms. They embody a regard for the citizen as a rational agent which makes it intrinsically proper, and not merely useful, to guide and respond to his actions in this way. We might accordingly doubt whether a more thoroughly consequentialist society than our own would operate with a system of criminal law – or, therefore, with a system of criminal punishment; and suppose that a system of criminal punishment, as an appropriate response to criminal conduct, must itself be structured by the non-consequentialist values and purposes which inform the criminal law and the criminal trial. It would be possible to argue, however, that our treatment of those who have been duly convicted of an offence may, unlike our treatment of those who have not been convicted, properly be guided by purely consequentialist concerns; and my account of the criminal law and the criminal trial may gain support from a discussion of punishment which does not simply presuppose that account. So I will assume here that a consequentialist would see good reason to operate with something like a system of criminal law, whose primary purpose is to prevent undesirable types of conduct.[26] She will then need some

[26] See ch. 4(2) above.

set of techniques for dealing with actual and potential breaches of the law – to ensure, as far as is economically possible, that the law is obeyed and its purposes achieved; but will punishment be a useful or appropriate member of that set?

The reductive aim of preventing crime does not by itself require a system of punishment. I have noted the possibility of a system of 'Adults' Panels' whose task would be to identify and deal with those who need some special (perhaps coercive) treatment in order to prevent some social harm;[27] and even if we limit their task to the prevention of criminal conduct, this would not be a system of punishment. Though past criminal conduct might bring a person to the Panels' attention, they need not impose their coercive measures only on those who have broken the law; though they may impose those measures on someone against his will, they need not intend to inflict suffering; and even if someone is subjected to coercive treatment in part because he has committed an offence, his treatment will not be *for* that offence. For the obvious methods which such Panels might use to prevent criminal conduct match the more specific purposes which usually provide the consequentialist aims of a system of punishment; to incapacitate, to reform, or to deter actual and potential offenders: but these purposes do not of their nature require a system of punishment.

If our aim is to incapacitate potential offenders, this does not require us to subject either *all* or *only* actual offenders to coercive treatment. The fact that someone has broken the law may be evidence that we need to incapacitate her from future offences: but it is neither conclusive evidence that we need to do this nor the only kind of relevant evidence; adequate predictive techniques might enable us to say that a past offender is now safe, or that someone who has not yet committed an offence is so likely to do so that we should now incapacitate her. Our treatment will be imposed against the person's will, but will not be intended to inflict suffering; nor is it *for* a past offence, since its imposition and nature depend on our expectations of future danger rather than on our understanding of a past offence.

The same is true if our aim is so to reform or rehabilitate the offender (so to modify his attitudes, dispositions and capacities) that he will in future, as he would not now, obey the law voluntarily. We need not limit such reformative treatment to those who *have* broken the law; nor need such treatment be focused on a past offence. I will discuss later the suggestion that there is a kind of

[27] See ch. 4(2) above; compare B Wootton, *Crime and the Criminal Law*.

criminal reform which must involve the infliction of punishment for an offence (like the kind of moral reform which is achieved by blaming someone for her wrong-doing); and that punishment, unlike the treatment which such Panels would impose, serves the expressive purpose of denouncing crime, thus persuading actual and potential offenders of the wrongness of the kind of conduct which is punished. Such purposes cannot, I think, figure prominently in a consequentialist account, since purely persuasive (as distinct from deterrent) punishments are not likely to be economically effective: one who takes these to be the proper purposes of punishment must appeal to certain *non*-consequentialist values.[28]

Deterrence is the consequentialist purpose which is most clearly connected to the idea of punishment: it is more obviously focused on offenders and their offences, and requires the intended infliction of suffering. But the aim of deterring potential offenders does not by itself require a system which inflicts suffering only *on* offenders *for* their offences. We might deter potential offenders by punishing an innocent scapegoat under the pretence that he is guilty; by threatening other people (by prescribing the execution of a spouse as the 'punishment' for a particular offence; or by making it an 'offence' to be related to someone who commits that offence); or by defining an offence so broadly that a person who is guilty of no wrong-doing is liable to conviction and punishment.

A system of Adults' Panels might use all these methods of preventing criminal conduct. Should a thorough-going consequentialist then favour such a system as a suitable way of preventing crime? The answer to such a question about the likely character of strictly consequentialist social institutions depends on the answers to some large empirical questions about the likely effects of different possible institutions; and I do not know what these answers would be. But we can ask what kinds of consideration *might* lead a consequentialist to prefer something more like a system of punishment as a better way to pursue her reductivist aims; and what kinds of consideration *should* lead us to object to a system of Adults' Panels, and to prefer a system of punishment. Why should we prefer a system which aims to impose its coercive measures only on offenders, and which determines the nature of those measures by reference to the character and gravity of the offender's past offence? Is it, for instance, because this is the most efficient way of pursuing the appropriate consequentialist ends; or because such a system accords,

---

[28] See ch. 9 below.

as a system of Adults' Panels would not, with certain non-consequentialist constraints on our pursuit of those ends?

The most obviously disturbing aspect of an Adults' Panel is that it may impose its coercive measures on those who have not yet broken the law, on the grounds that they are likely to do so (not, however, that it might punish the innocent, since it is not engaged in punishment); but why should this disturb us?

One consequentialist reply might appeal to the unreliability of the predictions on which such measures depend. If we subject someone to coercive treatment on the grounds, for instance, that she is dangerous and that this will be an economically effective way of preventing the serious offences she might otherwise commit, we subject her to a certain evil for the sake of a very uncertain good: given the unreliability of our existing predictive and psychological or penological techniques, we cannot be at all confident either that she is indeed dangerous or that any reformative, as opposed to merely preventive, treatment to which we subject her will be effective.[29]

One who wants to use this argument, but also wants to justify coercing some actual offenders (or detaining or forcibly treating someone who is mentally ill on the grounds that he is a danger to himself or to others), must of course be able to show that a past offence (or a present mental illness) can provide a more reliable basis for predictions of future danger than the grounds on which a Panel might detain someone who is neither an offender nor mentally ill; and it is not clear whether or how he could do this. We could, however, both meet this worry and strengthen the argument, which so far makes the wrongness of coercing *sane non-offenders* disturbingly contingent on the unreliability of our existing predictive techniques, by appealing to other values than the prevention of crime – values which could still figure within a consequentialist framework.

We might appeal, for instance, to the importance of individual freedom, as an essential aspect of human good. The state should allow its citizens the greatest possible freedom to control their own lives; and that freedom depends on the extent to which they can predict their own futures, and control those futures by their own choices and voluntary actions. The state may, for the sake of the common good, *require* certain kinds of conduct from the citizen, through laws which she must decide for herself to obey or disobey; and since such laws are likely to be ineffective if they are backed by nothing more than exhortations to obedience, the state may also

[29] See N Lacey, 'Dangerousness and Criminal Justice' 40–1.

have to resort to coercive measures, imposed on the citizen against her will, to secure obedience to the law. Now a citizen's freedom is seriously impaired if she may be liable to such coercive measures merely on the grounds that she is dangerous: but if she is only liable to them when she has voluntarily broken the law, she retains the power to predict and determine her own future.[30]

We should note that this line of argument could justify not only limiting the imposition of such coercive measures to those who have actually broken the law, but also setting limits on the nature and extent of the coercion to which they should be liable. An Adults' Panel, or a court concerned solely with the rehabilitation of offenders, might be allowed an almost unlimited discretion to impose whatever measures seemed necessary or desirable. One objection to allowing such a wide discretion to our tribunals would be that neither our predictive nor our penological techniques are reliable enough to ensure that it is used wisely and to good effect. Tribunals would be likely, out of an over-zealous concern to prevent crime and an over-confident belief in the efficiency of their techniques, to abuse their discretion and subject people to unnecessary or excessive kinds of coercion.[31] Another, more forceful objection is is that a citizen who is to have control over his own life, and whose future is to depend on his own choices and actions, must be able to know in advance not only when he will be liable to coercive treatment but also what kind of coercion he will be liable to. The extent and nature of the coercion to which he is liable, as well as the fact of coercion itself, must depend on what he has done rather than on our predictions about what kind of treatment will be useful; the law must tell him, through its specifications of offences and sentences and its public principles of sentencing, both what conduct is required of him and what will happen to him if he disobeys its requirements.

This line of argument offers us grounds for preferring a system which appears to resemble punishment in two crucial respects: it imposes its coercive measures only on offenders; and those measures are imposed *for* offences in the sense that their nature and extent is determined by reference to what the offender has done. There are, however, two reasons for doubting whether it can take us very far

---

[30] See Hart, 'Prolegomenon to the Principles of Punishment', 'Legal Responsibility and Excuses'; and see ch. 6(4) below on detaining the mentally disordered.

[31] Compare the American reaction against excessive discretion in sentencing, discussed in A von Hirsch, *Doing Justice: The Choice of Punishments* Part I; L Radzinowicz and R Hood, 'The American Volte-Face in Sentencing Thought and Practice'; M H Tonry and N Morris, 'Sentencing Reform in America'.

away from a system of Adults' Panels or towards a system of punishment. First, it does not in fact yet require us to impose such coercive measures only on those who are properly classed as *offenders* – who have done something *wrong*. The argument does require that the citizen be given fair warning that certain kinds of conduct will make her liable to certain kinds of coercion; but not that we attach such coercive consequences only to conduct which is properly condemned as wrong.

Second, if the argument expresses a consequentialist concern for freedom as a good, it ascribes to the state a duty to *maximise* (as far as is consistent with its other proper aims) the freedom of its citizens. If we suppose, however, as the argument allows us to suppose, that something more like a system of Adults' Panels might be a more efficient method of reducing crime, we must ask whether we might not be justified in reducing or infringing the citizens' freedom for the sake of the greater security which such a system would then bring; and indeed whether this might not be a more efficient method of actually maximising individual freedom. For though a citizen might be more likely to suffer a Panel's coercive attentions without having voluntarily brought this on herself, she would be less likely to have her freedom impaired by becoming the victim of a crime.[32]

Suppose, however, that we regard the freedom of the individual not merely as a consequential end, but as a *right* which sets constraints on the means by which we may pursue our consequentialist ends: the citizen has a right to be left free to conduct her own life, so long as she obeys the law's justified requirements; and the state has a duty to respect, not merely to maximise, her freedom. A citizen who voluntarily commits an offence, however (thus infringing the rights of others), gives up this right to freedom by her own voluntary and wrongful action; and the state can properly coerce her if this will serve the aim of reducing crime. Now it could of course be claimed that a citizen who breaks the law thereby surrenders *all* her rights against the state; that her disposal can properly be determined purely by considerations of consequential efficiency and humanity. But we might instead, and more plausibly, argue that only certain rights are thus given up: that citizens should be given fair warning of what they will suffer if they break the law; that there are constraints of justice on what the state may do even to offenders; and that the offender should not be subjected to a greater degree of coercion than is warranted by the seriousness of her offence.

The outlines of a familiar kind of account, which moves us well

[32] Compare J Harris, 'The Survival Lottery'.

away from a system of Adults' Panels and towards something much more like a system of punishment, are beginning to emerge. We retain as our primary justifying aim the consequentialist aim of reducing crime: but moral constraints other than those of economic efficiency help to determine the means by which we pursue that aim. We object to a system of Adults' Panels on the grounds that it would not respect the citizen's rights; for it could subject her to coercive treatment which is not warranted or justified by anything she has voluntarily done: but we can instead justify a coercive system which limits its coercive measures to offenders, and which determines the nature and extent of the coercion to which they are liable by reference to the nature and severity of their offences. The primary purpose of such a system, and the primary method by which it hopes to reduce crime, is now likely to be deterrence. Given the constraints on its operations, this may not be a very efficient way of reforming offenders, and will be able to incapacitate most of them only temporarily; but it can hope to deter many potential offenders by announcing in advance that those who break the law will be liable to specified kinds of coercion, and by imposing such coercive measures on those who do break the law. We can thus recognise it as a system of punishment which inflicts suffering – for that is how its measures will deter – on offenders for their offences.[33]

We can strengthen and enrich the claim that we should prefer a system of punishment to one of Adults' Panels, and that the primary purpose of punishment should be deterrence rather than incapacitation or reform, by referring again to the Kantian demand that we should respect the citizen – even when he breaks the law – as a rational and autonomous agent. If we are to respect his right to conduct his own life and determine his own actions, we must try to bring him to obey the law only by offering him reason to do so; and we must leave him free to decide whether he will obey the law or not. Now the law initially accords him this respect: it requires, but does not force, him to accept and obey obligations which can be justified to him. A system of Adults' Panels, however, denies him this respect: it is improperly coercive (it may subject him to coercive measures which are not warranted by what he has voluntarily done), and improperly manipulative (it seeks to modify the actual or potential offender's conduct by whatever means may be effective). It might subject him to indefinite preventive detention on the

---

[33] See, for example, H L A Hart, *Punishment and Responsibility*; von Hirsch, *Doing Justice: The Choice of Punishments*; H L Packer, *The Limits of the Criminal Sanction*; Goldman, 'The Paradox of Punishment'.

grounds that he might otherwise commit serious offences in the future: but while we may legitimately defend ourselves or others, by force if necessary, against an attack on which someone has chosen to embark, we cannot legitimately coerce him in order to prevent him doing what he has not yet chosen to do; we should not thus pre-empt his future choices, but must allow him to make those choices for himself.[34] A Panel might also subject a person to psychological techniques which aim to modify his attitudes and dispositions other than by giving him reason to modify them, or by bringing him to see that and why he ought to modify them; and this too is inconsistent with the respect due to him as a rational agent.[35]

A system of deterrent punishments, however, might claim to respect the citizen's autonomy. We add the threat of punishment to the law's demands in order to give those who are not sufficiently impressed by the law's moral claims on them prudential reason to obey the law; we impose the threatened punishment on someone only when and because he has broken the law – the coercion to which he is then subjected is justified by his own voluntary conduct; and (unless execution or a sentence of genuinely life imprisonment is warranted by the nature of his past offence) he is released at the end of the sentence which the law prescribes for his offence. His punishment leaves him free to decide for himself whether he will obey the law in future, subject only to the threat that he will suffer further punishment if he disobeys again. Our aim in threatening punishment against offenders, and in deciding what punishments to threaten, is primarily consequentialist; we see this as a useful way of securing a wider obedience to the law, and hope that these penalties will have the desired effect. However, we choose this method of pursuing that aim not because it is likely to be the most economically effective method (it may not be), but because it is consistent, as other methods are not, with the respect which is due to the citizen.

The consequentialist aim of preventing criminal conduct does not by itself justify a system of punishment which inflicts suffering on offenders for their offences; nor does the more specific aim of deterring people from criminal conduct: such aims may be more efficiently served by a non-penal system of Adults' Panels or by a system of 'telishment'. That consequentialist aim, however, does provide the essential justifying aim of this system of punishment: if

---

[34] On preventive detention, see ch. 6(4) below.
[35] On manipulation, see ch. 2 (3) above; also C S Lewis, 'The Humanitarian Theory of Punishment'; J R Lucas, 'Or Else'; H Morris, 'Persons and Punishment'.

we believed that punishment could not be a cost-effective method of reducing crime we would have to abandon punishment. For the demand that we respect the citizen's autonomy cannot by itself, as it has figured in the argument so far, justify a system of punishment which coerces offenders: it stands rather as a side-constraint on our pursuit of our consequentialist ends, and shows why we should pursue those ends through a system of deterrent punishments rather than by other, possibly more effective, methods. It shows too why the internal logic and the justificatory criteria of punishment should be retributivist; and why we should not abuse a system of punishment by punishing the innocent. What justifies having a system of punishment at all is that it will, consistently with a proper respect for the citizen, effectively reduce crime; but what justifies imposing *this* punishment on *this* person is that she has committed an offence for which this is the prescribed or permitted punishment. Having threatened to impose punishments on offenders, we are then committed to punishing actual offenders not only by the need to make that threat believable, but also because we have in effect promised to do so: but we are entitled to punish only those who have voluntarily broken the law, and to impose on them only the punishments prescribed for the offences they have committed. To punish an innocent is to deny him the respect which is his due; because instead of responding, as we have legitimately threatened to respond, to his own voluntary actions we simply use him as a means to our further social ends.[36]

4 PREVENTIVE DETENTION, QUARANTINE AND TAXATION

I have sketched a type of account which explains and justifies a system of punishment in terms of a consequentialist justifying aim whose pursuit is subject to certain independent moral side-constraints; and which thus allows – as a purely consequentialist account cannot allow – a role in the justification of punishment to those Kantian values which are, I have argued, central to the criminal law and the criminal trial. Such an account faces attack from two sides. It may be criticised by more rigorous consequentialists on the grounds that it attaches undue weight to alleged moral demands which cannot plausibly (or even intelligibly) be allowed such importance; and by those who take the Kantian requirement of respect seriously on the grounds that it does not, as it claims, accord the citizen the respect which is her due. My main concern will be with

[36] See Lucas, 'Or Else'; on using someone as a means, see ch. 6(5) below.

the second kind of criticism: but I should attend briefly to the first.

A consequentialist might simply claim that the non-consequentialist values to which such an account appeals lack any intelligible substance;[37] to which the only possible response is the kind of explication of the sense and significance of those values to which this book is meant to be a contribution. But he may instead offer a more specific critique, which points to various practices which do not supposedly respect the citizen's autonomy but which we do supposedly regard as justified; and which then asks why that respect should be thought so important in the context of punishment.

For instance, firstly, we think it legitimate to detain the mentally disordered, and subject them to forcible treatment, on the grounds that they are dangerous to themselves or to others; or to subject someone to quarantine if he is carrying a dangerously contagious or infectious disease. Such detentions are justified, not by any offence which the person detained has committed, but purely by the need to prevent him causing harm to others: so why should we be so reluctant to detain and try to reform potentially dangerous offenders in order to prevent them committing crimes in the future?[38]

For instance, secondly, we think it right to require a citizen to pay taxes, and to force her to pay them if she will not pay them voluntarily. What justifies this financial imposition is not any offence which she has committed, but the claim that she can reasonably be required to make this contribution to the common good. Now we may of course say that we initially *require* the citizen to pay her taxes, and only *coerce* her if she refuses to obey that justified requirement (as we might require a person to submit himself to quarantine or to psychiatric detention, and only *impose* that detention on him if he disobeys). Could we not, however, with equal justification *require* a potential offender to submit herself to preventive or reformative detention, as a sacrifice which she must make for the sake of the common good; and then impose that detention on her if she refuses to obey this justified requirement?[39]

For instance, thirdly, our actual system of criminal law contains provisions which pay at most only lip-service to the Kantian demands of respect for freedom and autonomy. For the sake of efficient law-enforcement and the prevention of crime we may make

[37] See, for instance, T Honderich, 'Culpability and Mystery'.
[38] For these and other examples see N Walker, *Punishment, Danger and Stigma* ch. 5; on quarantine see J Floud and W Young, *Dangerousness and Criminal Justice* ch. 3.
[39] Compare Walker, *op. cit.* 80–2.

liability for an offence to some degree strict (either by explicit statutory provision or, for instance, by the use of legal presumptions which allow us to disregard the defendant's actual state of mind), thus rendering liable to conviction and punishment those who are innocent of any *voluntary wrong*-doing; and even though English law at present makes no explicit provision for 'preventive detention', courts are nonetheless allowed to impose 'extended sentences' which in fact serve a similar role. These sentences are justified not by the offender's past offence, but by the need to protect the public against further offences which he is thought likely to commit.[40]

If a proper respect for the citizen's freedom and autonomy requires us to reject a system of Adults' Panels, and to condemn any abuse of a system of punishment, as being improperly manipulative or coercive, does it not equally require us to condemn all these practices? If on the other hand I admit that at least some of these practices are justified, must I not admit that a system of Adults' Panels, or the consequentialist abuse of a system of punishment, could also be justified; that a respect for the freedom and autonomy of the individual citizen cannot play the dominant role in our political practices which I have ascribed to it; and perhaps too that my account of the defining features of punishment is misguided – in particular that the requirement that punishment must be *for* an *offence* cannot carry the weight which I have placed on it? Now it is no part of my aim to justify all these current practices: it can be shown, however, that at least in the first two instances they are crucially disanalogous to the kinds of practice which I have been criticising.

Thus, firstly, as to quarantine and the detention of the mentally disordered. If we are to justify detaining and forcibly treating someone who is mentally disordered we must be able to show, not only that he is dangerous to himself or to others, but also and crucially that he is rationally incapacitated: that he is, because of his disorder, incapable of recognising that he is dangerous, or of controlling his conduct so that he is not dangerous; that he is incapable of exercising a rational autonomy, or of conducting his own life in the light of his own autonomous choices.[41] Now the demand that we respect the citizen as a rational agent, and leave him free to determine his own

[40] Compare Honderich, *Punishment: The Supposed Justifications* 66–76. On preventive detention and extended sentences, see the *Powers of Criminal Courts Act* 1973 s.28; R Cross and A J Ashworth, *The English Sentencing System* 34–5, 51–5; D A Thomas, *Principles of Sentencing* ch. 8; Floud and Young, *Dangerousness and Criminal Justice* (especially ch. 5); von Hirsch, *Doing Justice: The Choice of Punishments* ch. 3; N Walker, *Sentencing in a Rational Society* ch. 10.
[41] See p. 36 above.

actions, cannot require us to allow that freedom to someone who is *incapable* of exercising it; nor, accordingly, does the detention of the mentally disordered provide any warrant for detaining the *non*-disordered on the grounds that they are dangerous.

In quarantining the carrier of an infectious disease we do not claim that she is rationally incapacitated: but we do require her to stay in quarantine, and are prepared to stop her if she tries to leave, on the grounds that if she goes out into the world she will thereby expose others to a serious risk of serious harm. Now a potentially dangerous offender who is subjected to preventive detention is also forbidden to go, and prevented from going, out into the world on the grounds that he would endanger others: but there is a crucial difference between the two cases. If the carrier goes out into the world she is acting in a way which is itself, independently of her further choices or voluntary actions, dangerous to others; the harm which she will cause to others will occur independently of her will; in choosing to go out she is thus already choosing to endanger others. So in requiring her to stay in quarantine, and stopping her from leaving if she tries to, we are forbidding her to engage in, and frustrating her if she tries to engage in, an inherently dangerous activity. The potential offender, however, will injure others once he is out in the world only if he chooses to do so; the harm which he might cause will flow from the further choices which he makes, and from the further actions which he voluntarily undertakes. So in detaining him we are not frustrating his attempt to engage in an activity – going out in the world – which is dangerous independently of his will; we are instead pre-empting his future choices, and improperly coercing him because of what he *might* choose to do in the future.

If we suppose (as we must suppose if we are to be able to treat him as an autonomous agent) that the potential offender is and will be in control of his own actions, a proper respect for his autonomy requires us to leave him the freedom to determine what those actions will be. We may, consistently with that respect, prohibit him from engaging in, and prevent him from carrying through if he does engage in, a course of action which is itself dangerous to others; but we cannot, consistently with that respect, intervene coercively before he has embarked on such a course of action in order to prevent him embarking on it. Of course, if that supposition is untenable in a particular case, some measure of preventive detention or restriction may be permissible. If, for instance, we can properly say that a sex offender is *unable* to control his criminal and harmful behaviour; that once he finds himself in a particular kind of situation, such as the company of young children, he will be unable to prevent himself from attacking them: then his case becomes more like that of the carrier of a dangerous disease.[42] It may be that for him – unlike the potential offender who is in control of himself and his conduct – going out into the world would itself be dangerous activity, if he cannot hope to avoid those situations which would induce his criminal conduct; or that entering certain situations, such as becoming a baby-sitter or a teacher, would be inherently dangerous. Once he goes out in the world, or enters such a situation, he will not be able to determine (any more than the carrier can determine) whether he will cause harm or not. Depending on the severity of the danger which he presents to others, and on the severity of the restrictions which would be necessary to guard against that danger, we might then be justified in detaining him or in some other way requiring him to restrict his activities: but what would justify us in doing this is not simply the fact that it will avert a danger which would otherwise threaten, but that it aims to prevent dangerous or harmful conduct which he cannot himself control.

To say that the preventive detention of a potential offender is incompatible with a proper respect for his autonomy, since the harm which he may cause will depend on his further voluntary actions, is not to condemn all 'precursor offences' – all laws prohibiting conduct which is likely to cause harm but which has not yet got to the point of causing harm, and which might cause harm only in virtue of the agent's further voluntary actions.[43] A person can be guilty of attempt or conspiracy in English law even though she has not yet done all that is up to her to do to complete the relevant substantive offence;[44] and English law also contains offences such as carrying offensive weapons, or possessing articles for use in the course of 'any burglary, theft or cheat'.[45] Such laws can be justified, as being consistent with a proper respect for the citizen's autonomy, if, but only if, they prohibit conduct which is preparatory to, or part of, the commission of a substantive offence – which is *intended* to culminate

---

[42] The reality and character of such cases – of agents who are in some yet to be adequately explained sense 'unable' to control their conduct – is of course controversial: all I need say here, however, is that *if* there are such cases a respect for the agent's autonomy does not require us to leave him free to determine his own actions insofar as those actions are not within his rational control.

[43] On the notion of a 'precursor offence', see C M V Clarkson and H M Keating, *Criminal Law: Text and Materials* ch. 5 (especially 5.5).

[44] *Criminal Attempts Act* 1981 s.1(1); see Smith and Hogan, *Criminal Law* 259–63.

[45] *Prevention of Crime Act* 1953 s.1 (on this and similar offences see Smith and Hogan, *op. cit.* 391–402); *Theft Act* 1968 s.25 (see Smith and Hogan, *op. cit.* 570–3).

in the commission of such an offence: for its agent is then voluntarily engaged in a wrongful enterprise, albeit in the early stages of that enterprise. But it would be absurd to say that merely going out in the world is in that sense part of or preparatory to the commission of a substantive offence.[46]

Secondly, as to taxation. In requiring a citizen to pay taxes we are not requiring her to surrender her autonomy: she will lose the opportunity to use that money for other purposes; but she will not be giving up her ability to determine her own actions. In extracting the money from her against her will if she refuses to pay, we are exacting from her a debt which she owes, and preventing her from carrying through a wrongful course of action on which she has embarked. In requiring a person to submit to preventive or manipulatively reformative treatment, however, we require him to surrender his autonomy and hand over to others the power to determine his actions. To require this of him, or to impose it on him, is to deny him the respect which we owe him, and which he owes himself, as an autonomous agent.[47]

Thirdly, as to the existing criminal law. I will have more to say later about principles of sentencing: all I need say now is that legal definitions and doctrines which provide for the punishment of those who are properly innocent, or for the purely preventive punishment of the guilty, are objectionable – and are indeed objected to – as being inconsistent with the values which should inform a system of law and punishment. Laws or doctrines which impose criminal liability in the absence of voluntary fault, or which sanction purely preventive sentencing, are not generally accepted as being obviously and incontrovertibly justified by the demands of efficient crime-prevention. They are rejected by some as being manifestly

---

[46] Compare the objections raised when, during the 1984/5 miners' strike, the police stopped pickets from getting anywhere near the place where they intended to picket, on the grounds that they feared a breach of the peace. What was objectionable about this – given that picketing does not in itself constitute a breach of the peace – was that the police were presuming in advance that the pickets would create or provoke a breach of the peace; and what was objectionable about acting on that presumption was not so much that it was empirically ill-founded as that it did not allow the pickets to determine for themselves whether they would obey the law or not.

[47] I am not suggesting here that compulsory taxation is itself uncontroversially just (and the PAYE system which, rather than requiring citizens to pay their own taxes, extracts tax from their wages in advance and without their consent, is clearly not compatible with a proper respect for their autonomy): my point is only that preventive or manipulatively reformative detention is clearly incompatible with a respect for autonomy in a way that compulsory taxation need not be. On surrendering or losing one's autonomy, see further ch. 8(3) below.

unjust; and accepted only reluctantly by others who, recognising that they involve sacrificing the demands of justice to those of utility, think that this sacrifice must be made.[48] The account which I have offered shows why we should find such practices objectionable: it does not claim to resolve the dilemmas which we may face between the demands of justice and of utility – only that we must recognise these as genuine dilemmas.

I will not discuss these dilemmas here:[49] I want instead to turn to the second kind of criticism of this account of punishment – that, even ignoring such possible dilemmas, it does not render punishment consistent with the Kantian demand that we should respect the citizen as an autonomous agent.

5 DETERRENCE AND AUTONOMY

A system of deterrent punishments of the kind I have sketched punishes an offender because he has voluntarily broken the law, and imposes on him a punishment which the law has prescribed and threatened for his offence. But it may still be objected that it does not, properly speaking, either punish offenders *for* their offences or respect them as autonomous agents: for punishment is still justified in the end by its consequential benefits, not by its propriety as a response to a past offence; in punishing offenders we thus use them as *means* to some social benefit, and fail to treat or respect them as *ends*. Now the Kantian claim that we should treat people as ends, never merely as means, is notoriously obscure;[50] but it generates a crucial objection to this account of punishment.

The Kantian objection to treating someone merely as a means applies most obviously to the punishment of the innocent: if we frame an innocent scapegoat, or deem someone to be guilty of an offence just because this will deter others, we do not punish her for what *she* has done, but for the useful effect which this may have on others. It also applies to a system which, while it coerces only offen-

---

[48] Hence the agonised discussion in (and the controversy aroused by) the Floud Report (Floud and Young, *Dangerousness and Criminal Justice*): on which see Lacey, 'Dangerousness and Criminal Justice'; A E Bottoms and R Brownsword, 'The Dangerousness Debate after the Floud Report'; T Honderich, 'On Justifying Protective Punishment'. For another example, see the controversy aroused by *Caldwell* (1982) A.C.341 (see G Williams, 'Recklessness Redefined').

[49] On dilemmas of this kind, see Nagel, 'War and Massacre'; and see further ch. 7(1), ch. 10(3) below.

[50] I Kant, *Groundwork of the Metaphysic of Morals* 90–3, and *The Metaphysical Elements of Justice* 99–100: see J G Murphy, 'Kant's Theory of Criminal Punishment'; Honderich, *Punishment: The Supposed Justifications* 60–1.

ders, aims simply to modify their conduct by whatever means may be economically effective: for an offender's fate then depends, not on what he has done, but on the useful effects of what we do to him; nor is his conduct modified only by the provision of reasons. If we are to treat someone as an end, not merely as a means, we must at least be able to justify any coercion to which we subject her by reference to what she has done, not merely to its utility; and we must try to modify her conduct only by giving her reasons to modify it herself.

But the system I have sketched satisfies these requirements: it offers the citizen reason to obey the law; and offenders are punished only if and because they have broken the law. The system aims to secure certain social benefits: but if the citizen is given fair warning that, and how, he will be punished if he breaks the law, he is not being used *merely* as a means.[51] We can, however, find further force in this Kantian objection if we attend, not merely to the treatment of those who are punished within such a system, but to the treatment of all those whose obedience the law tries to secure by the *threat* of punishment.

A gunman invades a bank: he orders the staff to keep quiet, and the manager to open the safe; to add persuasive force to his demands he threatens to shoot anyone who disobeys, and shoots a cashier who tries to raise the alarm. Now it is clear that the gunman does not respect his victims' autonomy; he uses them merely as means for his own ends. How does he differ from a government which uses the threat of punishment to persuade its citizens to obey the law?

It is not enough to say that the government's demands are allegedly justified, whereas the gunman's are not: for we are concerned here not with the worth of the ends which are being pursued, but with the legitimacy of the methods by which they are pursued; if you extort money from me by the threat of violence you cannot justify your methods merely by claiming – justifiably – that I owe you the money. Now both gunman and government seek to modify the conduct of those whom they threaten by offering them reasons – by saying, in effect, 'Obey or else'; both to that extent treat them as rational agents: but should we not say that both offer their victims or citizens the *wrong kind* of reason for action?

A properly non-manipulative attempt to modify a person's con-

---

[51] Compare Benn, 'An Approach to the Problems of Punishment'; Walker, *Punishment, Danger and Stigma* 80–5: this provides part of an answer to J G Murphy's objections to deterrent punishment in 'Marxism and Retribution' 94–5.

duct must offer her not just reasons, but *relevant* reasons for action; reasons which are appropriate to the action in question.[52] Both gunman and government fail to satisfy this more stringent requirement: they do not try to secure obedience from their victims or citizens by offering them only relevant reasons for obedience. The gunman realises that he can offer the bank staff no relevant reason to give him the money: so he creates for them, and imposes on them, an irrelevant and coercive prudential reason for obeying his demands by threatening them with death if they disobey. The government realises that too few of its citizens will be sufficiently moved by the relevant moral reasons which justify the law's claim on their obedience; that too many will disobey the law if those are the only reasons they are offered for obeying it: so it creates for them, and imposes on them, an irrelevant and coercive prudential reason for obedience by threatening them with punishment if they disobey. Gunmen and governments do not only use those whom they actually shoot or punish as means: they manipulate, and thus use as means, *all* those whose obedience they try to secure by threats of death or of punishment.

Feuerbach bases his theory of punishment on threat and thinks that if anyone commits a crime despite the threat, punishment must follow because the criminal was aware of it beforehand. But what about the justification of the threat? A threat presupposes that a man is not free, and its aim is to coerce him by the idea of an evil. But right and justice must have their seat in freedom and the will, not in the lack of freedom on which a threat turns. To base a justification of punishment on threats is to liken it to the act of a man who lifts his stick to a dog. It is to treat a man like a dog instead of with the freedom and respect due to him as a man.[53]

The objection to a system of deterrent punishments is that, even when it respects the non-consequentialist constraints discussed in section 3, it is still improperly coercive and manipulative; it still fails to treat the citizen as a rational and autonomous agent. We can clarify the force of this objection, and the possibility of an answer to it, by looking at the likely fate of the mentally disordered within such a system of punishment.

A citizen is liable to punishment if and because she wilfully breaks

---

[52] See ch. 2(3) above.
[53] G W F Hegel, *Philosophy of Right* (Addition 62) 246; see also A C Ewing, *The Morality of Punishment* 60. This shows the flaw in C S Nino's attempt (in 'A Consensual Theory of Punishment') to justify punishment by claiming that the criminal, in breaking the law, consents to the 'legal normative consequences' of his crime: for Nino does not show how the *threat* of punishment is consistent with a proper respect for the potential criminal.

the law, despite the reasons which the law offers her for obedience. Thus she will presumably not be held criminally responsible for her actions if she was at the time of those actions so disordered that she was not susceptible to such rational persuasion – if she could not understand or be moved by the reasons for obedience which the law provides. Such a criterion of rational persuadability will exempt from criminal responsibility many of those who should be thus exempted because they are mentally disordered: but some cases should still worry us.

A 'partial psychopath' has some grasp of, and some concern for, his own interests; he can be moved by some kinds of prudential reason for action. But he has no comprehension of moral reasons for action; he cannot see how the interests of others, or an appeal to values independent of his own desires, can provide him with reasons for action: thus he cannot grasp or be moved by the moral considerations which allegedly justify the law's demands. He can however see that (though he cannot understand *why*) the law prohibits certain types of conduct; and he can grasp and be moved by the prudential reasons for obedience which the threat of punishment provides. Must we not therefore say, on this account of punishment, that he is legally responsible for his actions – that he should be convicted and punished for his offences; and is not this clearly unjust?[54]

The conviction and punishment of the partial psychopath is unjust because he cannot see the law as anything more than a system of coercive orders backed by threats – as a gunman writ large; and the Kantian objection to a system of deterrent punishments is that this is just how it presents the law. A system of law should present itself to the citizen as making a moral claim on his obedience; as imposing on him obligations which he should accept and obey. It cannot present itself in these terms to a partial psychopath, since he cannot understand such moral claims; and if its sanctions are meant to operate merely as deterrents it no longer presents itself in these terms to the ordinary citizen.

This objection might be met by insisting that the law is not *simply* a set of coercive orders backed by threats; its requirements must be justified to those on whom they are binding, by reference to the appropriate kinds of reason. The law initially seeks the citizens' allegiance and obedience by appealing to the relevant moral reasons

---

[54] On the partial psychopath see H Cleckley, *The Mask of Sanity* 195–234; on responsibility as deterrability see A J Kenny, *Freewill and Responsibility* 42–4; W Kneale, 'The Responsibility of Criminals'.

which justify its requirements; and many will obey the law because they see its requirements to be thus justified. But others will not be sufficiently persuaded by such a moral appeal; and it is to them that the threat of punishment is addressed. That threat, however, can be properly addressed only to those who can understand, but refuse to be moved by, the law's moral justification. For the threat is itself part of the law: it must therefore be justified to those who are subject to it – by the claim that it aims to persuade them to obey requirements which they *ought* to obey. Furthermore, I am liable to punishment only if I have broken a law which I had an obligation to obey: but I can have such an obligation only if I can understand the reasons in virtue of which that obligation is binding on me.[55]

This is the crucial difference between laws and gunmen. The gunman cannot justify to his victims his attempt to exact their obedience; he can offer them only coercive reasons for obedience. The law, on the other hand, must justify its threat and its use of deterrent punishments to the citizen; and that justification must appeal to the moral grounds on which both its requirements and its punishments depend. The gunman simply says, 'Obey or else': but the law says, 'Obey, because you ought to, or else'; it offers the citizen *both* relevant moral reasons and coercive prudential reasons for obedience. Since a partial psychopath cannot understand the moral considerations which justify the law, he cannot have an obligation to obey it, or be justifiably punished for failing to obey it.

But what now of someone who becomes seriously disordered after she has committed an offence? The law promised that she would be punished if she disobeyed its requirements: so why should that promise not now be kept, despite her presently disordered condition? Perhaps a system of deterrent punishments would prescribe Hospital Orders for such people if psychiatric detention and treatment would be a more humane and efficient way of dealing with them. So a sane offender should be subjected to punishment rather than to psychiatric treatment because punishment will respect his status as a rational agent; but our treatment of those whose rational capacities are so seriously impaired that they can no longer be seen as rational or responsible agents is not subject to this constraint. Such disordered offenders are, however, in principle eligible for punishment within such a system; for they have wilfully broken a law to which punishment is attached as a sanction: the question of whether they should be punished depends on the contingent question of whether the consequential ends of the system will best

[55] See ch. 3 above; Lucas, 'Or Else'.

be served by punishing them. We may object, however, that such people should not, even in principle, be eligible for punishment; that an offender's punishment is inappropriate *as* punishment if she cannot understand it for what it is – as suffering which is inflicted on her because she has broken a law which she had an obligation to obey.[56]

One response to this objection might be to set further constraints on our pursuit of the consequentialist aims of this system of punishment; to insist that punishment must be justified *to* the offender on whom it is imposed. The law must justify its demands and its threats to the citizen; and the court must justify its verdict and its sentence to the defendant: it must be able to say to an offender, 'Because you have broken a law which you had an obligation to obey, and because that law threatened this sanction against those who break it, you are to be punished'. If the offender is now so disordered that she cannot understand this justification, she is not fit to be punished; her inability to understand why, and thus to understand that, she is being punished renders her punishment unjustified.[57]

Is this response adequate? If we are dealing with a rational agent who can understand the moral considerations which justify the law's requirements and its punishments, we certainly owe it to her to justify her punishment to her in these terms. But why should the fact that an offender, whose criminal conduct satisfied the justifying pre-conditions of punishment, is now so disordered that she cannot understand this justification make it improper to punish her, if her punishment would serve a useful purpose? If we are prepared to commit her to hospital for psychiatric detention and treatment, we clearly do not suppose that we can properly subject her to coercive treatment only if she can understand the nature of and the justification for that treatment; and there is on this account nothing in the nature of punishment itself which makes it necessarily inappropriate for such a person. To punish someone is simply to impose on her the penalty which was threatened against her if she broke the law; and she was able to understand the nature of and the justification for that threat at the time when she broke the law and thus rendered herself liable to punishment. On this modified deterrent account, in other words, the punishment of an offender who is now disordered is still not intrinsically inappropriate. My claim, how-

---

[56] See ch. 1(2) above.

[57] See A Kassman, 'On Punishing' – though he does nothing to justify the claim that the offender must be able to understand the justification for her punishment.

ever, is that the punishment of someone who is so disordered that she cannot understand the nature of or the justification for her punishment is as intrinsically improper as the conviction of someone who cannot understand her trial or conviction; and that the character and significance of this impropriety cannot be captured by an account which portrays punishment in these deterrent terms.[58]

More generally, and quite apart from the problem of the disordered offender, such a system of deterrent punishments is still inconsistent with the strict Kantian demand that we should respect the citizen's autonomy – and thus with the values which are expressed in the criminal law and the criminal trial, and with those which should structure our moral dealings with each other. A system of law must seek the consent and the allegiance of the citizen as a rational moral agent: it must justify its demands to him and offer him relevant moral reasons for obedience. A criminal trial must address the defendant as a rational moral agent who is called to answer a charge of wrong-doing: it must justify its verdict to him by reference to the relevant reasons which justify the judgment expressed in that verdict. Moral criticism and blame, as legitimate responses to another's wrong-doing, must offer her only relevant reasons for modifying her conduct: our aim must be to bring her to see and to accept the moral considerations which justify the judgment expressed in our criticism. If we now use punishment and the threat of punishment as deterrents, we impose on potential offenders additional, irrelevant and coercive reasons for obedience to the law; we seriously compromise our allegiance to the values which should inform the law; and we manipulate those whose obedience we try to secure by these means, just as we do if we use moral blame as a prudential deterrent.[59]

To say, in answer to this objection, that the law must offer the citizen relevant reasons for obedience before it threatens her with punishment, and that it must justify the use and the implementation of that threat to her, is to offer only a partial answer: it does not fully rebut the charge that a system of deterrent punishments manipulates those whose obedience it secures by the use of threats; that it uses them as means towards our consequentialist ends.

This criticism could also be expressed by saying that deterrent punishment no longer serves the aims which are appropriate to a system of criminal law; that its purposes are discontinuous – where-

---

[58] See ch. 4(6) above.   [59] See ch. 2(3) above.

as those of the criminal law and the criminal trial are continuous –
with the purpose of moral blame. The purpose of moral blame is
not merely to modify a person's external conduct; it is to bring her
to see that she has good moral reason to modify her conduct, and to
act rightly for the right reasons. Similarly, the proper aim of a
system of law which addresses its citizens as rational agents is to
bring them not merely to obey its requirements, but to accept those
requirements as being appropriately justified; and the proper aim of
a criminal conviction is to communicate and to justify to the defendant an appropriate judgment on his past conduct, and thus to bring
him to recognise and accept his duty to obey the law. In using
punishment as a deterrent, however, we abandon the attempt to
secure *these* appropriate ends, and try instead merely to secure the
citizen's obedience.

This objection will remain so long as we retain a consequentialist
justifying aim for the practice of punishment. The point is not
simply that the efficient pursuit of that aim is always likely to conflict with the non-consequentialist values which constrain its pursuit: it is rather that we cannot do justice to those values by
portraying them only as side-constraints on our pursuit of some
consequentialist end.[60] In discussing moral blame, the concept of
law and the criminal trial, I argued that a respect for autonomy of
the individual does not simply constrain our pursuit of certain consequentialist aims, but helps to determine the proper aims and purposes of these enterprises. The same must be true of punishment. If
a system of punishment is to exhibit a proper respect for the citizen
as a rational and autonomous agent, its aims as well as the means by
which it pursues them must be structured by that respect; it cannot
be adequately justified by reference to a consequentialist end to
which it is contingently related as an instrumental means.

An account of punishment which treats the demand that we
should respect the citizen's rational autonomy as a side-constraint
on our pursuit of our consequentialist ends has significant merits. It
can claim to justify a system of *punishment* which, in order to deter
crime, inflicts suffering on offenders for their offences: not by
showing that it is a more efficient technique than others for preventing crime, but by showing that it accords with certain distinctively
non-consequentialist values. It shows that punishment, unlike other
more obviously manipulative techniques for preventing crime, can
to some extent treat the citizen as a rational agent: punishment offers

[60] Compare J Finnis, 'The Restoration of Retribution'; J Teichman, 'Punishment and
Remorse'.

him reasons for obeying the law, and is imposed on him only if and because he wilfully breaks the law. It thus also shows why a sane offender may claim a *right* to be punished rather than be subjected to some other, possibly more effective kind of manipulative or preventive treatment: to punish her is to treat her still as a rational agent.

Such a justification of punishment depends on the empirical claim – which I have not tried to justify here – that deterrent punishments can be economically effective; and on the moral claim that the laws which the citizen is required to obey under the threat of punishment are themselves justified (for punishment is unjust if the person punished has not committed a genuine wrong). What concerns me here, however, is that such an account is still open to the objection that it does not show punishment to be consistent with a proper respect for the citizen as a rational and autonomous agent; that it still portrays punishment as an improperly manipulative attempt to coerce the citizen into obedience to the law.

But if we cannot justify punishment as a rational deterrent, how else can we hope to justify it? Two possibilities suggest themselves. One is to justify punishment in traditional retributivist terms, as an appropriate response to past wrong-doing which has, and needs, no further purpose beyond itself: for if punishment has no further aim it cannot be accused of manipulating those on whom it is imposed or against whom it is threatened – of using them as means towards a further end. The other is to show that the purpose of punishment *can* be properly continuous with that of the criminal trial (and with that of moral blame); to justify punishment as a non-manipulative attempt to bring the criminal to see that and why her past conduct was wrong, and thus to bring her to modify her own future conduct for the appropriate kinds of reason.

These possibilities will be explored in the chapters which follow: but I will also have to attend to the suggestion that we cannot and should not hope for a better justification of punishment than that which has been discussed in this chapter; that a proper respect for the citizen's autonomy is expressed as adequately as we can in practice hope to express it in a system of deterrent punishments which aim to prevent crime by giving the potential criminal prudential reason to obey the law.

7

Varieties of Retributivism

He asked a very simple question: 'Why, and by what right, do some people lock up, torment, exile, flog, and kill others, while they are themselves just like those they torment, flog, and kill?' And in answer he got deliberations as to whether human beings had free will or not; whether or not signs of criminality could be detected by measuring the skull; what part heredity played in crime; whether immorality could be inherited; and what madness is, what degeneration is, and what temperament is; how climate, food, ignorance, imitativeness, hypnotism, or passion affect crime; what society is, what its duties are – and so on ..., but there was no answer on the chief point: 'By what right do some people punish others?'

L Tolstoy, *Resurrection*; quoted in E L Pincoffs,
The Rationale of Legal Punishment

I AUTONOMY AND DETERRENCE – DILEMMAS

The last chapter was concerned with the question of whether the consequentialist aim of preventing criminal conduct could generate a justifying account of a system of punishment which aims to inflict suffering on offenders for their offences. I argued that we could generate such an account only if we set certain non-consequentialist constraints on our pursuit of that aim. These constraints may be founded in the requirements of justice; in a concern for individual freedom, and for the rights which that freedom involves; in the Kantian demand that we should respect the autonomy of every citizen, including those who break or are inclined to break the law. A justified system of punishment must provide a cost-effective method of preventing crime which is consistent with these constraints; that method will, I suggested, be deterrence.

Such an account justifies, as a purely consequentialist perspective cannot, a system of punishment, and avoids some of the charges which may be laid against a strictly consequentialist approach to the prevention of crime. It forbids the punishment of the innocent, and the manipulative attitude which simply seeks an economically effective method of modifying criminal conduct; it seeks to prevent crime by giving potential criminals reason to obey the law, and thus treats them as rational agents who must decide for themselves whether to obey the law or not. But in the light of the categorical demand that we should respect the autonomy of the individual, such a justification of punishment is still inadequate. For a system of deterrent punishments offers its citizens irrelevant, and coercive, reasons for obeying the law: it manipulates, not only those whom it punishes, but all those whose obedience it tries to secure by the threat of punishment; its values and purposes are not properly continuous with those of the criminal law and the criminal trial.

Those who think that a Kantian respect for autonomy need not preclude a system of deterrent punishments might offer various replies to this objection.

'We respect a person's autonomy so long as we do not use her *merely* as a means; and a deterrent system of punishment respects this requirement. The point is not just that we still allow as much weight to the criminal's interests as to those of anyone else:[1] such a Utilitarian equality of concern would still permit the punishment of the innocent, or the manipulation of the guilty, if this would bring a great enough benefit. It is rather that the law initially offers the citizen relevant reasons for obedience, and threatens punishment only if those reasons fail to persuade; in threatening punishment it still seeks to guide her conduct by the provision of reasons; and it punishes only those who voluntarily break the law. Kant himself surely allowed that punishment could be used to secure some social benefit: the criminal

must first be found to be deserving of punishment before any consideration is given to the utility of this punishment for himself or for his fellow citizens.[2]

Punishment must be deserved if it is to be justified: but if it is deserved we may use it to secure some social benefit; and in using it thus we do not use the criminal *merely* as a means.'

This reply fails for two reasons. First, the most that Kant can consistently allow is that a punishment which is already sufficiently justified by the criminal's deserts may also bring some social benefit: the prospect of that benefit can play no part in the justification of his punishment, which

---

[1] Compare S I Benn, 'An Approach to the Problems of Punishment'.
[2] I Kant, *The Metaphysical Elements of Justice* 100; see also the *Groundwork of the Metaphysic of Morals* 90–3; and ch. 6(5) above.

must in all cases be imposed on him only on the ground that he has committed a crime.[3]

If we justify punishment as a deterrent, however, its social benefits are essential to its justification. Second, and more crucially, this reply does not meet the objection that in threatening punishment as a deterrent we fail to respect those against whom that threat is made. An offender's punishment is initially justified by his past offence; but a system which threatens punishment against potential offenders, and punishes actual offenders, in order to provide a prudential deterrent against crime fails to accord a proper respect to its citizens as autonomous moral agents.[4]

'Such a complete respect for the autonomy of every moral agent is an admirable moral ideal: but we should not expect to actualise it fully in our legal and penal practices, given the manifest facts of human imperfection.

Often it is rational to be more concerned with the avoidance of the action than with the autonomy of the agent. Better that potential murderers heteronomously refrain from killing their victims than that they authentically act upon their atavistic impulses. Rather than leaving the rule against murder to the rational approbation of each individual will, we add the additional consideration, if any be needed, that if one does murder, one's life will be nasty, solitary or short. In a world of partly rational but not highly moral agents it is the only way of securing compliance and showing everybody that we intend to secure compliance.[5]

The state owes it to its citizens to maintain a system of deterrent punishments as a bulwark against crime; it must protect the citizen against the kinds of coercive interference to which she would otherwise be vulnerable. It must do this, firstly, if it is to claim that she ought to obey the law: in obeying the constraints which the law places on her the citizen makes herself vulnerable to injury at the hands of the lawless; and she cannot be expected or required to do this without some assurance that the state will itself protect her against such injury. And it must do this, secondly, if it is to protect that very autonomy which the Kantian prizes: it must maintain the social conditions in which individual autonomy can be respected and exercised; it must protect the individual against the kinds of interference which would destroy her autonomy or her ability to

---

[3] Kant, *The Metaphysical Elements of Justice* 100.
[4] See ch. 6(5) above.   [5] J R Lucas, 'Or Else' 228.

exercise it. Now if this protection merely took the form of an exhortatory appeal to obey laws which are rationally justified, it would be utterly ineffective. If we are to provide any reasonable protection for the autonomy of all we must be prepared to infringe (fairly modestly) the autonomy of potential criminals by providing them with an additional – admittedly coercive – reason for obeying the law. To insist on the kind of absolute respect for the autonomy of every agent which would preclude the use of punishment as a deterrent would be to ensure the destruction of the social conditions in which alone that autonomy can have any substantial existence.'[6]

This reply would be fully persuasive if we could interpret the Kantian concern for individual autonomy as a consequentialist concern for the preservation and protection of autonomy. We could then weigh the loss of autonomy suffered by those who are threatened with punishment against the increase in autonomy which such a system of punishment ensures for all its citizens. But we cannot do this. If it is, as the Kantian must insist,' categorically wrong to infringe a person's autonomy, no further end can justify such an infringement: for no such end, however valuable, can justify the use of means which are themselves categorically wrong. One who regards the intended killing of the innocent as absolutely wrong must insist that it is wrong even if it is the only way to prevent a larger number of such intended killings, or to preserve a way of life in which innocent life is respected; if the demands of justice are absolute and categorical, we cannot justify an injustice by pleading that it is the only way to prevent some greater injustice, or to preserve a way of life in which justice is likely to be done. It might be 'better that potential murderers heteronomously refrain from killing their victims than that they authentically act upon their atavistic impulses' (or that one innocent is killed than that ten are killed): but the fact that one state of affairs is thus 'better' than another does not mean that we act *rightly* in trying to bring it about, if we can bring it about only by means which are themselves categorically wrong.[7]

Perhaps what this reply claims, however, is not that a system of deterrent punishments is fully consistent with a Kantian respect for individual autonomy, but rather that it is the best we can actually hope for, as imperfect beings in an imperfect world. For can it really

[6] On the state's duty to its citizens, see A C Ewing, *The Morality of Punishment* 50–1; A Wertheimer, 'Punishing the Innocent – Unintentionally'; also J Finnis, *Natural Law and Natural Rights* 262–3.
[7] On these issues see J Casey, 'Actions and Consequences'; R A Duff, 'Intention, Responsibility and Double Effect'; R Gaita, '"Better One than Ten"'; T Nagel, 'War and Massacre'; also J G Murphy, 'Marxism and Retribution'.

be right – is it even possible – to allow such an absolute and categorical status to the demand that we respect the autonomy of every moral agent, that we forswear the use of coercive or manipulative methods for modifying conduct *whatever* the consequences – even if this leads to the destruction of the very social conditions in which that autonomy can be exercised and respected? Should we not rather accept that the Kantian ideal, like other absolutist ideas, is at least in practice and for the present unattainable; that, faced by an irresoluble conflict between our duty to respect autonomy and our duty to preserve the social conditions in which individuals can pursue their goods and exercise their autonomy, we must compromise that ideal to the extent of being willing to use punishment as a deterrent against crime?

This is not to say that we must *abandon* that ideal. It could be fully realised only in a society of more perfect beings, whose relationships could be structured by a complete respect for each other's autonomy: but it need not figure in our present thoughts merely as an object of idle or wishful contemplation. It is an ideal towards which we must still strive, though recognising that it lies far beyond our present grasp. It can find expression in our personal relationships; in our commitment to a system of law which appeals initially to the rational will of the citizen, and to a system of deterrent punishments in preference to other possibly more effective, but more coercive or manipulative, methods of preventing crime. It reminds us of the imperfection of our present nature and present practices, forcing us to admit that we still act wrongly in using punishment as a deterrent. But we cannot, if human social life is to be possible at all, obey it as an absolute constraint on our social practices.

The account of punishment discussed in the last chapter claimed to reconcile a consequentialist concern for crime-prevention with a Kantian respect for autonomy: but this present argument allows that no such complete reconciliation is possible – and thus that a system of deterrent punishments cannot be completely or unqualifiedly justified. We cannot both preserve the social conditions which are necessary for any worthwhile human life and maintain a complete respect for the autonomy of every moral agent. If we *must* preserve those social conditions, we must also recognise the moral wrong which their preservation must involve.[8]

Now if this is indeed our situation – if a society which relied on an

---

[8] On dilemmas of this kind, see Nagel, 'War and Massacre'; see also P Winch, 'The Universalizability of Moral Judgments'.

entirely non-coercive and non-manipulative system of law would simply cease to exist; if we can preserve the possibility of a way of life in which values such as autonomy can play any significant part only by means which are themselves inconsistent with those values – then one who insists that we must, absolutely, respect the autonomy of every moral agent must indeed ask whether she can really accept the implications of this insistence.[9]

Other aspects of the criminal law may present a similar dilemma. Must we, to protect the public and to ensure the conviction of the guilty, allow the pre-trial detention of suspects and defendants; extend the definitions of some offences beyond their proper limits; or refuse to allow defences which should, in strict justice, be allowed?[10] In these and other cases the same argument may be mounted: that a system of law which adhered strictly to the demands of autonomy and justice would be so ineffectual that it would simply ensure its own destruction. The argument could be rebutted if we could deny its factual bases; if we could plausibly claim that a system which treats all its citizens as rational and autonomous agents will actually flourish. But I do not know what evidence could justify such a claim. It is not enough to claim that such a system *would* flourish were it not for the alienating and dehumanising character of our present social structures, institutions and relationships; that a more adequately human society would have no need for coercive or manipulative laws: even if that claim could be maintained, it leaves us with the question of what we are to do *now*. Should we insist on trying to live now as if we were already living in such an ideal society, despite the disastrous consequences of doing so; or should we, recognising our present imperfections, be prepared to compromise our ideals now in the hope that we can thus begin to build Jerusalem? It may be tempting to insist that Jerusalem cannot be built from foundations which deny or betray its most basic values:[11] but can we hope to begin building it without compromising those values?

The width of this particular gap between what is ideally right and what is actually possible depends, however, on the claim that the best or only possible justification for a system of punishment justifies it as a deterrent; and on the admission that a system of deterrent punishments does not fully respect the autonomy of its citizens.

---

[9] Compare R F Holland, 'Absolute Ethics, Mathematics and the Impossibility of Politics'; also R Gaita, Critical Notice of R F Holland, *Against Empiricism*.

[10] See ch. 4(10), ch. 6 above.

[11] Compare A Camus, *The Rebel* ch. 1, *The Just*; also Plato, *Republic* 592b.

That gap might be bridged – or at least narrowed – if we could show that punishment can be adequately justified in non-deterrent terms; but before turning to that possibility we should note a final attempt to defend a system of deterrent punishments.

'We should admittedly respect the autonomy of every rational moral agent: it would be improper and unnecessary to threaten deterrent punishments against such a being. But most of us are in fact and at present only imperfectly rational; we are too often not the autonomous rulers of our souls, but the heteronomous slaves of our irrational appetites. Our autonomy is not, and at present cannot be, fully actual; so it cannot be fully respected. It is not a question of whether potential murderers should heteronomously refrain from killing, or autonomously act upon their "atavistic impulses", since the murderer does not act autonomously. His crime manifests, not that "whole freedom" which is the proper expression of a rational autonomy, but a "wild, lawless freedom" which is the negation of true autonomy;[12] he is the heteronomous victim of his "atavistic impulses". In using punishment to deter him we do not infringe his autonomy: we are protecting him and others from the harmful effects of his heteronomous irrationality. Kant himself can be called in support of this view.

In my role as colegislator making the penal law, I cannot be the same person who, as subject, is punished by the law; for, as a subject who is also a criminal, I cannot have a voice in legislation (the legislator is holy). When, therefore, I enact a penal law against myself as a criminal it is the pure juridical legislative reason (*homo noumenon*) in me that submits myself to the penal law as a person capable of committing a crime, that is, as another person (*homo phainomenon*).[13]

Crime flows from the irrational (phenomenal), not from the rational (noumenal) aspect of my nature: deterrent punishments attempt to mobilise my imperfectly rational nature against my irrational nature. So too we may sometimes coerce or manipulate children who are not yet able to grasp or be guided by the relevant kinds of rational consideration.'

This attempt to show that a system of deterrent punishments is not inconsistent with a complete respect for the autonomy of every fully rational agent need not involve the assumption that 'we' – as would-be philosopher kings – are ourselves fully rational agents

---

[12] See Kant, *The Metaphysical Elements of Justice* 80–1.
[13] Kant, *op. cit.* 105.

who may legitimately manipulate the imperfectly rational beings around us for their own good. None of us is perfectly rational; we may all need to be coerced or manipulated into behaving as we know we should. But we must clarify the meaning and the implications of this claim that we are only imperfectly rational.

The claim cannot be that all criminal impulses are utterly *nonrational* symptoms of mental disorder: for we could not then claim that actual or potential criminals have an obligation to obey the law, and can justly be punished for breaking it. Nor is it enough to claim that, given just laws, criminal inclinations are necessarily *irrational* (though that claim itself is, at best, controversial).[14] A person who is thinking or acting irrationally may still be fully *capable* of rational thought and action; and if he is thus capable a respect for his autonomy requires us to try to modify his conduct only by appealing to relevant reasons. To respect a person's autonomy is to respect his *capacity* for rational thought and action; to try to bring him, by the appropriate kinds of appeal, to exercise that capacity. The claim must rather be that criminal inclinations are symptomatic of the limited nature of our rational capacities. We can to some extent grasp and be guided by relevant rational and moral considerations: so we should operate with a system of criminal law and criminal trials which seeks initially to guide conduct by appealing to relevant reasons. But we are also afflicted by irrational inclinations which impair both our understanding of what is right and our ability to guide our actions in the light of such an understanding: so we must guard against these inclinations by a system of deterrent punishments which addresses our imperfectly rational natures.

The argument thus depends on a general metaphysical account of human nature; and I will have more to say later about the character and implications of such an account.[15] However, I want first to ask whether punishment could have any role in a legal system which treated its citizens as fully rational and autonomous agents. For if it could have a role in such a system, it would not be that of a prudential deterrent; and we may then insist that punishment in an imperfect society of imperfectly rational beings should still have something of the meaning and purpose which it would have in a more perfect society; that even now it should not operate merely as a prudential deterrent. We may blame children for their actions before they are fully able to grasp or be moved by the moral values

---

[14] See A Flew, *Crime or Disease?*; the underlying view that immorality is necessarily irrational is clearly central, in different ways, to both Plato and Kant.
[15] See ch. 8(3), ch. 10(1) below.

which should inform that blame: but our blame should not function merely as a prudential deterrent; it should be part of an attempt to develop and arouse in the child the kind of moral understanding to which it can then appeal.[16] If punishment could be an appropriate response to the wrong-doing of a rational moral agent, then the punishment of an imperfectly rational agent should also partake of the meaning which it would have in the case of a fully rational agent.

If we are to see whether, and how, punishment can be justified in an admittedly imperfect society like our own, we must therefore first ask whether we can provide an *ideal* account of what punishment would be in a better society. If we can explicate such an ideal of punishment, we can then ask how far it could be actualised in a society like our own; and whether, and how, the imperfect character of our social arrangements and of our own natures must force us to compromise this ideal. With punishment, as with other aspects of the criminal law and the criminal process, we must begin with the ideal before we attend to the character and implications of the gap between the ideal and the actual.

2 RETRIBUTIVIST JUSTIFICATION

If we are to show that punishment could manifest a proper respect for individual autonomy, we must show that we have a *right* to inflict suffering on offenders against their express will; and that punishment can be something other than an improperly manipulative attempt to prevent crime. How might we do this?

The obvious alternative to a consequentialist account of punishment as a deterrent is a retributivist account of punishment as something which is deserved for, and justified by, a past offence. I will not try to discuss all the various and diverse views which have claimed or received the label 'retributivist':[17] my main concern is with views which posit retribution as the *justifying purpose* of a system of punishment – as distinct from those which appeal to some notion of retribution to set side-constraints on our pursuit of consequentialist ends, or to explicate the internal logic of a system of punishment which is itself to be consequentially justified. The common feature of the views with which I am concerned is that they find the meaning and justification of punishment in its relation to a past offence, not in some further and contingent benefit which it may bring. We punish a criminal because she has committed a

[16] See p. 56 above.   [17] See J Cottingham, 'Varieties of Retribution'.

crime; and the justification of a system which thus attaches punishments to crimes depends on the propriety of punishment as a response to crime, not on the consequential benefits which such a system will bring. We must bear in mind, however, the familiar consequentialist charge that any such purportedly retributivist justification of punishment amounts in fact either to a refusal to *justify* punishment (as distinct from simply *asserting* its rightness) at all; or to a covertly consequentialist justification in terms of some particular consequential benefit.[18]

Before discussing more familiar kinds of retributivist view, however, we should notice the suggestion that retributive punishment is *logically* required by any system of *law*. A system of law is not just a system of exhortations or requests directed towards the citizen: it is a system of *requirements*, which are *imposed* on her — it claims *power* over her will; and a system which did not punish offenders just because they had broken the law would not be a system of requirements at all — it could not claim such power over the citizen.[19]

This is not the pragmatic argument that a system of law which is to survive as such must in practice be able to coerce into obedience those who will not obey it voluntarily: that portrays punishment as preventive, not as retributive. Nor is it simply the argument that, if we take the law seriously as a system of binding obligations, we cannot consistently just ignore breaches of the law:[20] for our regard for the law could be expressed in a system of formal trials and convictions which condemn offenders, but which do not impose any further kind of punishment. The argument here is that the law's claim to power over the citizen's will can make sense only if that power is asserted against, and imposed on, any citizen who does not accept it voluntarily; and it is asserted and imposed in and through the imposition of punishment. For punishment is essentially a matter of humbling a criminal's will — it is in this sense that punishment must make her *suffer*. She has asserted her own will against the law and its demands; punishment humbles her will in return (in retribution) for that act of self-assertion.[21] Punishment is thus pure retribution: its purpose is simply to humble the wills of those who assert their wills against the law; and that purpose is achieved in and by the very fact of punishment itself.

---

[18] See Benn, 'An Approach to the Problems of Punishment'; T Honderich, *Punishment: The Supposed Justifications* ch. 2.

[19] See H Fingarette, 'Punishment and Suffering'; compare Lucas, 'Or Else'.

[20] See J Charvet, 'Criticism and Punishment'; also ch. 5 above.

[21] Compare Aquinas, *Summa Theologiae* 1a2ae87.a6; discussed by J Finnis, 'The Restoration of Retribution'.

We might object that the law's claim to authority over the citizen need not, as a matter of *logic*, involve such a readiness to impose its power on a recalcitrant citizen; or that it could, as far as logic is concerned, be adequately asserted by a system of trials which subject criminals to the judgment and condemnation of their fellows, without seeking to impose further punitive suffering on them. But the more important point is that, as Fingarette himself insists, this argument does not offer a justification of punishment: it aims rather to shift the justificatory question to a different level – and to show more clearly what it is that needs to be justified. *If* we are to have a system of law as Fingarette defines it, it must include a system of retributive punishments: but why should we have a system of law as thus defined; why should we – how can we justifiably – go beyond a system of formal rules and trials, and attach punitive sanctions to the rules?

Justifying accounts of punishment often allow a derivative or secondary role to notions of retribution: as constraints on our pursuit of the consequentialist aims of punishment; or as part of the internal logic of a system of punishment. But such accounts do not provide, and Fingarette's account does not provide, a *positive* justification for a *system* of punishment in retributivist terms: we must still ask what positive purpose can justify a system of law and punishment whose internal logic is thus retributivist; and we have yet to find an answer which does not appeal to its consequential benefits.

3 RETRIBUTIVISMS – PROBLEMS AND PUZZLES

In pursuit of a retributivist understanding of punishment, we may begin with the 'intuition' which is often thought to underlie such an understanding – that 'the guilty deserve to suffer':[22] for this may suggest that the primary purpose of a system of punishment is to ensure that the guilty do suffer. The justifying aim of punishment would then be identical to its defining purpose – to inflict suffering on offenders for their offences: we need not ask of such a view, as we must ask of a consequentialist view, whether it would require a system of *punishment*.[23]

If this intuition is to justify a system of punishment it must

---

[22] See L H Davis, 'They Deserve to Suffer'. Davis makes it clear that he does not think that this intuition can provide, by itself, a sufficient justification for a system of punishment.

[23] See ch. 6(3) above.

appeal, not to the logical truth that within a system of criminal law and punishment legal guilt makes a person liable to punishment, but to the supposed moral truth that moral wrong-doers deserve to suffer; which may suggest that part of the purpose of a system of criminal law is to ensure that 'the grosser forms of vice' are duly punished.[24] This is not to say that the primary purpose of a system of law is to ensure that every serious kind of immorality is punished: some kinds of crime are wrongs only *because* they are prohibited by the law; the law's primary purpose is still to dissuade its citizens from wrongful or harmful kinds of conduct by forbidding and condemning them; and not all kinds of immorality need be the law's proper concern. (We would, however, need to indicate which kinds of immorality *are* the law's concern: are they simply 'the grosser forms of vice'; or can we identify a relevant category of public, as distinct from private, wrongs?) But the justifying purpose of attaching punishments to the law is now to ensure that wrong-doers receive the suffering which they deserve; and *one* relevant reason for defining a certain type of conduct as criminal could be to ensure that those who engage in it are punished as they deserve.

The thought that the guilty deserve to suffer figures in contexts other than that of legal punishment. If a wrong-doer suffers some natural calamity – especially if it is a consequence of her wrong-doing, or resembles the harm she had done to others – this may be seen, by her or by others, as 'just what she deserves'; as 'poetic justice'; or even as a punishment for what she has done.[25] Or it may be thought 'unfair' that a wicked man's life is, at least in his own terms, successful and happy, while his virtuous neighbour suffers misfortune or deprivation (though we should not forget the alternative Socratic view that it is the wicked man who is truly wretched).[26] Without thinking that the requirements of morality can or should motivate us only if they are backed by some guarantee that the good will in the end flourish and be happy, whilst the wicked will in the end come to grief, we might still feel that in a better world the good would be happy and the wicked would suffer.[27]

[24] See J F Stephen, *Liberty, Equality, Fraternity* 152; and contrast N Walker, *Punishment, Danger and Stigma* 5 – 'Prohibitions should not be included in the criminal law for the sole purpose of ensuring that breaches of them are visited with retributive punishment'.

[25] On the idea of 'natural punishment' see P Winch, 'Ethical Reward and Punishment'; J Teichman, 'Punishment and Remorse'.

[26] See Plato, *Gorgias, Republic, Apology*; S Kierkegaard, *Purity of Heart*; P Winch, 'Can a Good Man be Harmed?'.

[27] Compare I Kant, *Critique of Practical Reason* Part 1 Bk. 2 ch. 2.5, 128–36.

But such an intuition, however natural or deep-rooted it may be, cannot yet justify a system of criminal punishment. A consequentialist might object that an appeal to this intuition amounts either to a refusal to justify punishment at all or to a covertly consequentialist appeal to the damaging consequences of a failure to provide some formal and public satisfaction for our vengeful desires.[28] As it stands, this objection could seem persuasive only if we beg the question by assuming that *all* institutions (or at least all those which inflict suffering) must be justified by their consequential benefits:[29] for even the unargued claim that the guilty deserve to suffer offers a justification for punishment as the imposition on criminals of that suffering which they deserve for their past offences. It is admittedly hard to know what to make of the bare claim that the guilty deserve to suffer – it cries out for further explanation;[30] but we need not suppose in advance that that explanation must be consequentialist.

We must ask, firstly, *why* the guilty deserve to suffer. However, a reply to this question need not refer to consequential benefits which their suffering might bring. It might instead offer an account of the significance of suffering in relation to wrong-doing – of how suffering or the imposition of suffering can be an appropriate result of or response to wrong-doing; and the initial task of a retributivist theory of punishment is to provide such an explanatory account of the relationship between crime and suffering. I will discuss three suggestions: that the imposition of punitive suffering serves to restore a balance which crime disturbs; that it serves to express to the wrong-doer the condemnation which her offence merits; and that it aims to induce in the wrong-doer the pain of guilt and remorse, this being the kind of suffering which she properly deserves, and thus to enable her to expiate her crime.

Even if we can provide a retributivist account of how and why criminals deserve to suffer, however, a retributivist justification of punishment must face a second question: what gives us the right, let alone the duty, to impose this suffering on them? There is, for a non-consequentialist, a logical gap between the claim that wrong-doers deserve to suffer – that it is good that they should suffer – and the claim that it is for us, or for the state, to ensure that they suffer;[31] and a retributivist theory must bridge this gap. For we could think both that the guilty deserve to suffer and that it is not for us to *make*

[28] Compare Honderich, *Punishment: The Supposed Justifications* ch. 2.
[29] Compare Benn, 'An Approach to the Problems of Punishment'.
[30] See N Walker, 'Punishing, Denouncing, or Reducing Crime?' 399–400; Honderich, *Punishment: The Supposed Justifications* 212–15.
[31] See Murphy, 'Marxism and Retribution'; and ch. 7(1) above.

them suffer; that we should do no more than blame them and, perhaps, condemn them through a formal conviction. Any further suffering which they should undergo is, we might say, a matter for them or for God; we have no right to try to impose that suffering on them (because this is not a task which human beings should take upon themselves; or because we lack the moral purity which would make us fit to punish others).[32] The thought that the guilty deserve to suffer could still play its part in our lives and relationships; it could still inform our understanding of and our responses to our own suffering and that of others: but it could not then provide a justification for a system of criminal punishment.

The gap between 'the guilty deserve to suffer' and 'it is right for us to impose that suffering on them' presents a particular problem for a retributivist whose rejection of consequentialist accounts of punishment flows from a concern for the Kantian demand that we should respect each person's autonomy: for though punishment as pure retribution does not involve a manipulative attempt to modify conduct, it surely *coerces* criminals by inflicting suffering on them against their will. How can such coercion be consistent with a respect for their autonomy? The thought that a wrong-doer deserves to suffer might lead us to believe that he should accept suffering which comes to him, as a punishment; or even that he should impose such suffering on himself: but how can it justify an attempt to impose such suffering on him against his will?

Could we argue that the criminal wills her own punishment – and thus that she has a *right* to be punished which is not simply the right to be punished *rather than* be subjected to psychiatric treatment? I will have more to say later about this suggestion, which Kant himself expressed in a very qualified form –

No one suffers punishment because he has willed the punishment, but because he had willed a punishable action. If what happens to someone is also willed by him, it cannot be a punishment. . . . To say, 'I will to be punished if I murder someone', can mean nothing more than, 'I submit myself along with everyone else to those laws which, if there are any criminals among the people, will naturally include penal laws'. In my role as co-legislator making the penal law, I cannot be the same person who, as subject, is punished by the law; for, as a subject who is also a criminal, I cannot have a voice in legislation (the legislator is holy). When, therefore, I enact a penal law against myself as a criminal it is the pure juridical legislative reason (*homo noumenon*) in me that submits myself to the penal law as a

---

[32] See J G Murphy, 'Kant's Theory of Criminal Punishment'; also the quotations from Blackstone and from Tolstoy which head chapters 6 and 7.

person capable of committing a crime, that is, as another person (*homo phainomenon*).[33]

Some initial clarification, however, is appropriate here.

It is clearly not enough to say, for instance, that a criminal wills her own punishment in wilfully breaking a law to which she knows such sanctions are attached: the gunman might say the same of a victim who disobeys his orders. Nor is it enough to add that the state, unlike the gunman, *justifiably* demands obedience to its laws, and thus justifiably threatens punishment against those who disobey: it is the justification of that threat which is at issue.[34] How then can we say that a criminal wills her own punishment – when she makes every effort (short of actually obeying the law) to avoid that punishment?

'In punishing a criminal we are doing just what he himself has willed that we should do. His crime of violence against another's freedom implies a maxim sanctioning such actions; as a rational being – and only as such does his autonomy have value – he must be prepared to will that maxim as a universal law, and thus to will that others should violate his freedom as he violates theirs. In punishing him, the essence of punishment being the hindrance of freedom, we therefore do to him just what he has as a rational being willed that we should do – we respect his autonomy and his will.'[35]

Now there are notorious difficulties in identifying the maxim of a particular action:[36] and thus in determining whether what we do to the criminal in punishing him is the same as what he did to another in committing a crime – whether it is what he has supposedly willed that we should do to him. These are not the familiar problems involved in trying crudely to extract an eye for an eye: for, by offering an abstract account of crime as the hindrance of freedom, this argument can portray punishment as a hindrance of freedom which could match, in its extent, the hindrance which the crime involved.[37] The problems here arise from the need to portray the crime as *wrong* and its punishment as *right*.

The criminal's action is wrong because it coerces another; the maxim of her action must refer to such coercion as what she wills. But how can we claim, in punishing her, that we are both doing

---

[33] Kant, *The Metaphysical Elements of Justice* 105; see ch. 8 below for a discussion of J G Murphy's interpretation of Kant's theory of punishment (in *Kant: The Philosophy of Right* and 'Kant's Theory of Criminal Punishment').

[34] Compare H Morris, 'Persons and Punishment'; and see ch. 6 (5) above.

[35] For this argument, see E L Pincoffs, *The Rationale of Legal Punishment* 8–9.

[36] See O O'Neill, 'Consistency in Action'.

[37] Compare G W F Hegel, *Philosophy of Right* ss.92–100.

what she has willed and coercing her as she coerced another? If she has willed her punishment it does not coerce her; for whether or not '*volenti non fit iniuria*', it is surely true that *volenti non fit vis* – that consent precludes coercion. So if her punishment is to coerce her, against her will, we cannot claim that in punishing her we are doing just what she has willed that we should do.[38]

Furthermore, the criminal's punishment cannot both be right and fall under the same universalised maxim as his crime. We punish him because he has committed a wrong: for his punishment to be justified it must itself be right; but if it is to be equivalent to his crime it must itself be a wrong, and thus cannot be justified.[39] A consequentialist need not face this problem; she can see the punishment as something which is in itself, like the crime which is punished, an evil (as involving the infliction of suffering or the hindrance of freedom), but which is also, unlike the crime, justified by its consequential benefits.[40] This possibility, however, is not available to the retributivist, who must show punishment to be in itself right. For the maxim of the criminal's action must be an immoral one: how then can the fact that he has willed it justify us in willing it too (in punishing him); should we not rather insist on acting on morally tenable maxims? Indeed, if this argument is Kantian, the wrongness of the criminal's action lies in the impossibility of consistently willing its maxim as a universal law. How then can we say that the criminal has, as a rational being, willed the universalised maxim which justifies his punishment (how can a rational being will what cannot be consistently willed); how can we ourselves justifiably act on a maxim which cannot be consistently willed as a universal law?

Kant's own account avoids these problems. The criminal's punishment accords, not with the maxim of his criminal action, but with the laws which he must, as a rational colegislator, will to be binding on himself and on others. *Qua* criminal (*homo phainomenon*) he is coerced and thus punished: but *qua* legislator (*homo noumenon*) he has willed the laws which punish him. But why should a rational being will such laws? Perhaps he would will the laws which prohibit his criminal actions; as a rational being he would will laws prohibiting violations of freedom (his criminal actions are thus at odds with his rational legislative will); but why would he also will the

---

[38] See Kant, *The Metaphysical Elements of Justice* 105 – 'If what happens to someone is also willed by him, it cannot be a punishment'.

[39] See A J Kenny, *Freewill and Responsibility* 72.

[40] Compare J Bentham, *Principles of Morals and Legislation* ch. 13.2 – 'All punishment is mischief, all punishment in itself is evil'.

penal laws which impose punishments on such actions? If we say that he would will such laws because he would see that a system of laws without punishments would be ineffectual, this leads us back towards a consequentialist view of punishment as prevention or deterrence: but what other possibility is there?

Should we say, in Hegelian tones, that the criminal has by his crime coerced the wills of others, denied their freedom, and thus denied freedom itself as a universal value; that his punishment, which coerces *his* will and hinders *his* freedom, is not a negation of freedom and autonomy, but an assertion of their universal value and an annulment of the crime which denied them – and that it thus accords with the universal law by which the criminal himself must as a rational being agree to be bound and protected?[41] But what would this mean?

A consequentialist interpretation might tempt us. In order to preserve freedom, by preventing crime, we may properly hinder the freedom of those who hinder the freedom of others. Similarly, it might be said, though it would be wrong to kill just anyone in order to save a larger number of lives, we may properly kill the non-innocent – those who do or would kill the innocent – in order to save innocent lives. My right not to be killed by others – to have my life respected by them – is conditional on my willingness to respect their lives: if I refuse to respect the lives of others, I lose the right to have my own life respected; and certainly *I* can hardly complain if they then refuse to respect my life. So too my right not to be coerced by others – to have my freedom respected by them – is conditional on my willingness to respect the freedom of others. If I violate the freedom of others by a criminal act, I cannot reasonably complain of injustice if my own freedom is then hindered; if I am prepared to violate the freedom of others, I cannot reasonably complain that the threat that my freedom will be hindered if I hinder theirs is an unfair threat.

This interpretation leads us back towards a view of punishment as a deterrent (a view which Hegel himself firmly rejected);[42] it does not provide the kind of non-consequentialist justification of punishment which a retributivist needs. If the retributivist is to talk of annulment, she must show how punishment can *in itself* annul crime – not merely that it can, consequentially, prevent crime; and we

[41] See Hegel, *Philosophy of Right* ss. 92–100: but see J M E McTaggart, *Studies in Hegelian Cosmology* ch. 5 for an interpretation of Hegel which I discuss later – in ch. 9 below.
[42] Hegel, *Philosophy of Right* (Addition 62) 246; see ch. 6(5) above.

have yet to find a clear meaning for this idea. Furthermore, this consequentialist interpretation denies that the autonomy of *every* moral agent, including the criminal, makes a categorical claim on our respect: just as it is only the innocent who have an absolute right not to be deliberately killed, so too it is only the innocent – those who respect autonomy – who have an absolute right to have their own autonomy respected; punishment has not yet been shown to be consistent with a complete respect for the criminal's autonomy. Nor indeed does such an interpretation show that the criminal wills her own punishment: it claims instead that we may properly ignore or coerce her will.

We have yet to find a clear sense for the idea that punishment is right or good *in itself* as retribution for a past crime; or an adequate justification for the claim that the imposition of retributivist punishments is consistent with a due respect for the criminal's autonomy. Such a justification would need to show either that such punishments are in accordance with the criminal's rational will – *and* that this justifies us in imposing them against her expressed will; or that the imposition of punishment *against* a person's will could still be consistent with, or expressive of, a proper respect for his autonomy. In the following two chapters I will discuss what I take to be the two most promising kinds of attempt to deal with these problems.

One explains the idea that punishment annuls crime by talking of a balance which crime disturbs and which punishment restores; and tries to reconcile punishment with a respect for the criminal's autonomy by talking of the kind of social contract to which rational beings would agree. The other focuses on the idea that punishment enables, or forces, the criminal to expiate or atone for her crime; and portrays punishment not purely as backward-looking retribution, but as a communicative process which seeks to show the criminal the wrongness of her past conduct and to bring her to repentance and reform – a process which thus addresses and respects her as a rational moral agent.

8

Punishment, Fairness and Rights

If the law is to remain just, it is important to guarantee that those who disobey it will not gain an unfair advantage over those who do obey voluntarily. It is important that no man profit from his own criminal wrong-doing, and a certain kind of 'profit' (i.e. not bearing the burden of self-restraint) is intrinsic to criminal wrong-doing. Criminal punishment, then, has as its object the restoration of a proper balance between benefit and obedience. The criminal himself has no complaint, because he has rationally consented to or willed his own punishment. That is, those very rules which he has broken work, when they are obeyed by others, to his own advantage as a citizen. He would have chosen such rules for himself and others in the original position of choice. And, since he derives and voluntarily accepts benefits from their operation, he owes his own obedience as a debt to his fellow-citizens for their sacrifices in maintaining them. If he chooses not to sacrifice by exercising self-restraint and obedience, this is tantamount to his choosing to sacrifice in another way – namely, by paying the prescribed penalty.

J G Murphy, 'Marxism and Retribution', p. 100

I RESTORING THE BALANCE OF BENEFITS AND BURDENS

In this chapter I examine an attractive, but ultimately unpersuasive, attempt to explicate a retributivist justification of punishment: punishment is a just and proper response to a past offence, since it restores that fair balance of benefits and burdens in society which crime disturbs; and it respects the criminal's autonomy, since it accords with his own rational will. This kind of account is given its purest development by Jeffrie Murphy: but others, such as John Finnis and Herbert Morris, have also made use of it.[1]

---

[1] See J G Murphy, 'Three Mistakes about Retributivism', 'Kant's Theory of Criminal Punishment', 'Marxism and Retribution', and 'Cruel and Unusual Punishments'; H Morris, 'Persons and Punishment'; J Finnis, 'The Restoration of Retribution', and *Natural Law and Natural Rights* ch. 10.1; also A von Hirsch, *Doing Justice: The Choice of Punishments* ch.6. My concern in this chapter is primarily with the pure form of the theory, as it is found in Murphy's writings (though my account of the theory will involve construction as well as description): but see n.2 below.

We are offered an account of the meaning and purpose of punishment; of the state's right to punish, and the criminal's right to be punished; and of the moral status of punishment in an unjust and imperfect society.

A *Punishment and Fairness*

In a just society, the law provides a range of benefits for all its citizens, by imposing burdens on all its citizens. The criminal law offers the individual citizen the benefits of peace, security and freedom: it preserves his freedom by protecting him from kinds of injury and interference to which he would otherwise be vulnerable; it provides a secure and peaceful context in which he can pursue his own autonomous projects. It also imposes on him, however, a burden of self-restraint: for the benefits which the law provides can be secured only if citizens restrain themselves from various kinds of interference and violence which they may be tempted to commit against others, in obedience to the law's prohibitions on such conduct. In a just society these benefits and burdens are fairly and universally distributed; the law protects all the citizens, and imposes on them all the burden of self-restraint which makes that protection possible. The citizens may, given their differing dispositions and projects, find the law's burdens more or less burdensome, and its benefits more or less beneficial: but all benefit greatly from the law, since a secure and autonomous life would be impossible without the protection provided by its prohibitions; and all must accept the burden of obeying the law whether they want to or not.

The criminal law thus serves the common good, by prohibiting conduct which is injurious to the interests or the autonomy of others; and the citizens should obey the law because they see its requirements to be thus justified. One who voluntarily breaks the law now gains for herself an unfair advantage: she accepts the benefits which flow from the law-abiding self-restraint of others, but refuses to accept her fair share of the burden of self-restraint which is necessary if those benefits are to be generally available; she accepts the goods but refuses to pay the proper price for them. She gains this advantage not only over the direct victim of her crime, but over every law-abiding citizen: they pay by their self-restraint for the benefits which they and she gain from the law; she shares in those benefits, but refuses to share the burden on which they depend – she is a free-loader who takes unfair advantage of all those who obey the law. Her advantage does not consist in any *consequential* profit which her crime may bring (such as the money she may gain by robbery or tax-evasion): it is *intrinsic* to her crime, and consists in her avoidance of the burden of self-restraint which the law requires of her – and which others accept.

Crime, which gains the criminal this unfair advantage over her fellows, thus of its nature brings about an unfair distribution of the law's benefits and burdens. The justifying purpose of punishment is to ensure that the criminal does not profit by her crime: by hindering her freedom it imposes on her an extra restraint to match the restraint which she refused to impose on herself (a disadvantage which wipes out the unfair advantage she gained over others); it thus restores a fair balance of benefits and burdens among the citizens. And just as the criminal's unfair profit is intrinsic to her crime, so this restoration of a fair balance is intrinsic to her punishment, not a contingent consequence of it. The punishment itself, in imposing an extra burden on the criminal, restores the balance which her crime disturbed.

It is in this sense that punishment 'annuls' a criminal wrong; exacts payment of a 'debt' which the criminal owes to her fellows; and 'restores the balance' which her crime disturbed. Punishment is essentially retributive: its meaning and justification lie in its relation to a past offence, not in any contingent future benefits which it may bring. Such talk of the payment of debts or of the annulment of crime does not, however, imply that punishment is simply a price to be paid for a benefit received, or that punishment can make it as if the crime never happened. Though we are normally as happy if goods are received and paid for as if they are neither received nor paid for, we ought to have neither crimes nor punishments rather than both crimes and punishments. The penal law is not a Price Commission which sets and exacts a fair price for the benefits which citizens receive or take: its 'prices' are punishments for *wrongful* actions which the criminal law prohibits and criminal convictions condemn.

B *The Right to Punish and the Right to be Punished*

The *good* which punishment brings (and which is internal to it) is this: by imposing on criminals a burden proportionate to the burden of self-restraint which they evaded it secures a fairer distribution of benefits and burdens than would exist if crimes were not punished. But does the state have the *right* to impose punishments in order to secure this good? One who takes rights seriously cannot simply suppose that, if one state of affairs is better than another, it follows directly that we act rightly in trying to bring it about: she must ask whether such an attempt is consistent with our rights and with the rights of others – whether we have the right to impose on criminals the punishments which they deserve, and whether in doing so we respect *their* rights. She must ask in particular whether punishment can respect the criminal's autonomy: for though it does not on this account involve an attempt to manipulate conduct, it surely coerces the criminal by imposing on him something which is against his will.

It is not enough to say that the state has a duty to ensure, as far as it can, that the benefits and burdens which it provides or imposes are fairly distributed. A state may, whilst respecting the autonomy of its citizens, *require* them to accept certain burdens for the sake of certain benefits, and submit themselves to balance-restoring punishment if they break the law, so long as 'requiring' amounts to no more than telling them that and why they ought to do this; but this does not yet give it the right to *impose* its punishments on them against their will. Nor is it enough to say that a state which did not punish criminals would soon lose the allegiance of those who were initially willing to obey its laws; or that my obligation to accept the burden of obeying the law is conditional on the state assuring me that I will not suffer unduly, or find myself unfairly disadvantaged, by so doing. Such considerations provide consequentialist reasons for a system of punishment as a means of securing, or a precondition of claiming, the allegiance of the citizens: but they do not show the imposition of punishment to be consistent with a proper respect for the criminal's autonomy.

We could avoid this problem, however, by showing that the criminal has really, despite her apparent dissent, willed her own punishment: for to do to someone what she has willed that you should do is to respect, not to infringe, her autonomy. And we can show that punishment accords with the criminal's *rational* will by appealing to a Rawlsian account of political obligation. Any rational agent, covenanting with others behind a suitable veil of ignorance, would opt for a system of law and punishment which secures and preserves a fair distribution of benefits and burdens by punishing criminals; and in opting for – in willing – such a system she wills her own punishment should she break the law.

The criminal's rational consent to a system of retributive punishments gives the state the right to punish him whilst still respecting his autonomy. Indeed, he now has a *right* to be punished: a right to be punished retributively rather than be subjected to deterrent threats, to preventive detention, or to psychiatric treatment (for retributive punishment respects, as these other modes of treatment do not, his rational will); and a right to be punished rather than be left alone (for he has a right to a system of law and punishment which accords with his rational choice behind the veil of ignorance). His punishment is required by, not merely consistent with, a proper respect for his rational autonomy.

C *Actual and Ideal Punishments*

We have seen how punishment can be justified in a just society whose benefits and burdens are distributed fairly among its citizens; and whose laws thus justifiably claim the obedience of every citizen: in such a society a criminal is justly punished, since she takes unfair advantage of her fellow-citizens. But what can we say of punishment in societies which are, like our own, less than completely just: in which the law itself bears unjustly on some citizens, unfairly denying them rights and protections which it allows to others, or unfairly imposing on them burdens which it does not impose on others; or in which, though the law itself is formally just, other social institutions and structures are such that some citizens are unfairly disadvantaged relative to others?

A system of law must be justified to those who are subject to it, by showing that it secures a fair distribution of benefits and burdens: in an unjust society the law's claim to the citizens' allegiance and obedience is therefore to a greater or lesser degree unjustified. For my obligation to obey the law is an obligation of justice; I owe it to my fellow-citizens to pay by my self-restraint and obedience for the benefits which I receive from their self-restraining obedience to the law. But insofar as I do not receive a fair share of the benefits and burdens in question, I cannot owe this debt of obedience to my fellows; and insofar as my crime is motivated by a need which itself results from my unjustly disadvantaged position, or by a greed which is itself instilled and fostered in me by the very structures of my society, I cannot be accused of *wilfully* seizing an unfair advantage for myself in breaking the law. My punishment is then unjustified: it does not deprive me of a profit which I have *unfairly* gained, or restore a *fair* balance of benefits and burdens; and the state which treats me unfairly cannot claim the right to punish me in the name of fairness.

The fact that this account fails to justify our existing penal practices does not show it to be inadequate: it offers, not a justification of the *status quo*, but an account of what punishment must be – and of what pre-conditions must be satisfied – *if* it is to be justified; an ideal of just punishment against which existing practices are to be measured and, if necessary, condemned as unjust and unjustified. The gap between what, on this account, punishment *ought* to be and what, in our own society, it actually *is* reveals the injustice of our own practices, not the inadequacy of this account; and insofar as the account appeals to values which, besides having an independent claim to our allegiance, supposedly inform our existing institutions, this gap between theory and reality shows those existing institutions to be defective by their own standards.[2]

This account of punishment has many attractions. By portraying punishment as an imposition which wipes out the criminal's unfair profit it explains the relationship between present penal suffering and past criminal wrong-doing, thus giving content to the idea of punishment as retribution which is deserved for a past offence. By portraying punishment as a requirement of justice, and founding the justification of systems of punishment (not merely of particular punishments within a system) on the past voluntary conduct of those who are punished, it avoids the charge that we use those whom we punish as means towards some social benefit. By arguing that the criminal has, as a rational being, willed his own punishment it reconciles punishment with a proper respect for the criminal's autonomy. It is open, however, to serious objections: I will begin with the idea that crime consists in taking an unfair advantage for oneself, and that punishment restores the fair balance of benefits and burdens which crime disturbs.

---

[2] Murphy takes the restoration of a fair balance of benefits and burdens to be *the* proper purpose of punishment (though he allows, in 'Cruel and Unusual Punishments', that once the demands of justice have been satisfied consequentialist aims such as deterrence and rehabilitation may play a part in punishment): but Finnis, for instance (in *Natural Law and Natural Rights*), while taking this to be the defining purpose of a system of *punishment*, emphasises the other purposes which punishment may properly serve – the education of the citizens, the deterrence and rehabilitation of offenders, the reassurance of the law-abiding; and von Hirsch takes desert and deterrence to be individually necessary and jointly sufficient conditions for the justification of punishment. The Kantian/Rawlsian argument that the criminal has, as a rational agent, willed his own punishment is also peculiar to Murphy (neither Finnis nor Morris make any such strong claim, though Morris insists on the criminal's right to be punished, and offers a different reading of the claim that the criminal 'chooses' his punishment); as is the critical contrast between the ideal and the actual (for which Murphy draws on certain Marxist themes) – this contrast, incidentally, serves to meet the objection (see T Honderich, *Punishment: The Supposed Justifications* 33–43, 229–30) that, since benefits and burdens are not in fact fairly distributed, we cannot justify punishment as the restoration of a fair balance of benefits and burdens.

The essence of crime as a legal wrong is, we are told, that the criminal takes unfair advantage of the law-abiding; she refuses that burden of self-restraint which others accept, whilst accepting the benefits of their self-restraint. It is not an objection to such a view that crime may bring no consequential profit to the criminal: for the profit which concerns us here (her freedom from self-restraint) is *internal* to her crime. Nor is it an objection that many crimes are more or less compulsive, and do not involve a *wilful* refusal to accept the burden of self-restraint: for such compulsive crimes do not bring the criminal an unfair profit, and should therefore not be punished. But can we plausibly see *all* crime as consisting essentially in this kind of unfairness?

This picture fits most happily in familiar kinds of 'free-loader' case; cases in which the moral appeal: 'But suppose everyone did that?' has its most obvious force, as an appeal to the demands of fairness. What is wrong with evading one's taxes, or flouting parking regulations, is often not that the particular action directly injures others, but that one takes unfair advantage of the law-abiding. For if these laws are just, they impose fair burdens on all for the sake of fair benefits for all: even if I do not benefit from this particular law, or am required to accept a greater burden than others in this particular context, I benefit from the system as a whole; in breaking the law I take for myself an unfair profit or advantage. We might thus explain the essence of many *mala prohibita*: actions which are wrong only because a law prohibits them; which are prohibited in order to secure some general good; and whose prohibition involves a burden of self-restraint which I ought to accept as a fair price for the benefits which I receive from the system. (Though might we not sometimes rather talk of my duty to assist the common good without thus calculating the benefits I will receive?)[3] But what of central kinds of *mala in se*, such as murder, rape and assault?

A man is convicted of rape. We might expect the judge to address him in these terms: 'You committed a violent and degrading assault on this woman; you showed a callous disregard for her rights and interests; you caused her serious harm; and for this you must be punished'. But it now seems that the judge should not talk in these terms; if she is to capture the criminal wrongness of the rapist's action she should instead say: 'You refused to restrain your violent

---

[3] Compare Murphy, 'Marxism and Retribution' 106 on the role of the 'calculating egoist' in the Rawlsian picture.

and anti-social impulses; you thus took for yourself an unfair advantage over those who do restrain themselves and obey the law; and for *this* you must be punished'. Surely, though, this account of the criminal wrongfulness of rape is perverse: what is wrong with rape is that it attacks another person's interests and integrity, not that it takes unfair advantage of the law-abiding.[4]

To clarify this matter, we should distinguish three questions about rape as a crime: why is rape a moral wrong, independently of any legal prohibition; why should the law prohibit rape; and how should we understand the wrongness of rape as a criminal offence? We have been offered an answer to the third of these questions; and we could draw from it answers to the other two. Morality, like the law, consists essentially of requirements which impose a burden of self-restraint on all for the sake of benefits to all; the purpose of the law is to add weight to the more important of these moral demands, and to ensure that breaches of them are duly punished. Rape is a moral wrong against those who restrain their anti-social impulses, because the rapist takes unfair advantage of them; it should be a criminal offence because the law should prohibit and punish such serious unfairness.

Now we should indeed make rape a crime because of its moral character: but we should not understand its moral character in these terms. What is morally wrong with rape is that it is a grievous assault on its victim's interests and integrity, not that it takes unfair advantage of those who restrain themselves (we do not show a rapist the wrongness of his deed by saying 'But suppose everyone did that?'); and it should be a crime because the law should protect members of the community against such assaults, not because the law should ensure a fair balance of abstract benefits and burdens.

If this is why rape is a moral wrong, and should be a criminal wrong, this is also how we should understand its criminal character; thus questions about the definition and the *mens rea* of rape as a criminal offence ought to concern its character as a moral offence.[5] If instead we understand its criminal character as a matter of taking unfair advantage of the law-abiding, we create an implausible separation between its wrongness as a crime and the moral reasons in virtue of which it should be a crime; between its criminal and its moral character. Nor can we plausibly say that, while the moral

---

[4] This kind of criticism is put forcibly by R Wasserstrom, 'Some Problems in the Definition and Justification of Punishment'; see also G Fletcher, *Rethinking Criminal Law* 417–18; on rape, see R A Duff, 'Recklessness and Rape'.

[5] See Duff, *op. cit.*

character of rape as an assault on its victim is indeed basic to its character as a crime which the law prohibits and a criminal conviction condemns, it merits *punishment* only because the rapist also gains an unfair profit which must be wiped out: for this creates an equally unhappy separation between the meaning of punishment and the meaning of the criminal law and the criminal trial; and it raises a further problem.

Such talk of the criminal's unfair advantage implies that obedience to the law is a burden for us all: but is this true of such *mala in se*? Surely many of us do not find it a *burden* to obey the laws against murder and rape, or need to *restrain* ourselves from such crimes: how then does the murderer or rapist gain an unfair advantage over the rest of us, by evading a burden of self-restraint which we accept? Perhaps this claim assumes a Hobbesian account of human nature. We all have roughly similar pre-social and egoistical desires, which we would ideally like to be able to follow unrestrainedly: but we recognise that we will all benefit if we all agree to restrain our anti-social impulses for the sake of greater peace and security. The law thus imposes a similar burden of self-restraint on us all: even those who do not *feel* constrained by its requirements must have quelled their naturally lawless passions; for we are all naturally inclined to some, if not to all, kinds of anti-social lawlessness.

Such an account, however, is tenable neither as an empirical account of our social and socialised nature, nor as a metaphysical account of a mythical *pre-social* human nature.[6] We must admit that most of us find at least some of the demands of morality burdensome – that they may appear, to imperfect beings like ourselves, as constraints (as *obligations* or *duties*) which we are inclined to resist;[7] and that the possibility, and the fact, of temptation and of an egoistical resistance to the demands of morality is integral to our character as moral agents (as too is the possibility, and the fact, of a genuine and unreluctant allegiance to morality). This provides part of the substance of religious or secularised notions of original sin;[8] and of Platonic or Kantian moral conceptions of our passions and inclinations as an inherently lawless rabble which must be quelled and controlled by reason. But it falls far short of showing that a murderer or rapist rejects a burden of self-restraint which most of us accept, or that the reason why he should accept it is that it is unfair to

[6] See B Williams, *Morality* 21–3; P Winch, 'Human Nature'; also M Midgley, *Beast and Man*; Wasserstrom, 'Some Problems in the Definition and Justification of Punishment'.

[7] Compare I Kant, *Groundwork of the Metaphysic of Morals* 76–8, 101.

[8] Compare I Murdoch, *The Sovereignty of Good*.

·us not to do so; and two further considerations cast further doubt on this picture.

First, we are told that the criminal profits by her crime; and that as a rational agent she wills the law which prohibits such actions: but surely then her true well-being as a rational agent lies in a life lived in accordance with the law; in breaking the law she acts against both her rational will and her own true interests, and thus cannot truly profit by her crime. If she does profit by her crime, how can she be rationally bound to will the law which prohibits it? If she must rationally will that law, must we not then say that her crime – which reflects her irrational nature – cannot truly profit her, since it is inconsistent with and injurious to her rational nature: she is, as Plato thought, to be pitied as one who injures herself, rather than envied as one who profits herself.[9]

Second, what kind of attitude is expressed in the thought that the immoral or criminal agent has gained an unfair profit? That thought is most familiar when we are ourselves tempted by the wrong-doer's actions: we think that someone who has profited by trickery or deceit could do so only because others restrain themselves from such immoral methods – and that we could do as well as him if we did not thus restrain ourselves; we watch a dishonest entrepreneur, or a colleague on the fiddle, or an adulterous spouse, with envious and self-righteously disapproving eyes. Surely, however, we do not think of the murderer or rapist in such terms as these; or, if our condemnation of them does reflect such thoughts, we should surely feel ashamed of ourselves for being thus tempted by what they do. This suggests that the idea that the wicked profit unfairly by their wrong-doing reflects a grudging and less than whole-hearted commitment to the values which they flout – the kind of attitude towards morality which Callicles castigated, rather than that which Socrates urged on us.[10] If this is so – if a more authentic moral concern would preclude such an attitude to the wrong-doer – we cannot found a just system of punishment on the idea that the criminal profits unfairly by her crime. For that idea reflects our own moral inadequacy, rather than any proper moral understanding of the moral character of criminal wrong-doing.

I have argued that we cannot see the essence of *all* crime, or all moral wrong-doing, as the gaining of an unfair advantage over those who restrain themselves in obedience to the requirements of law or mor-

---

[9] The implications of this Platonic view are discussed in chs. 9–10 below.
[10] Plato, *Gorgias*.

ality: thus we cannot portray punishment as an attempt to wipe out an unfair profit which is intrinsic to crime, or argue that this is how and why the guilty 'deserve to suffer'. But still, it may be said, there is more than I have yet allowed to the idea that it is a requirement of fairness that criminals should be punished for their crimes – that it is unfair if they are allowed to break the law with impunity. If we say, outside the context of the law, that it is unfair that the wicked should prosper, the meaning and the focus of our complaint are perhaps unclear – are we blaming God or an anthropomorphised Nature for allowing them to prosper? Though a wrong-doer who holds on to some material profit which she has unfairly gained could be blamed for thus perpetuating the unfairness of her original action, we should not say that a murderer acts *unfairly* if he does not do something to wipe out the 'profit' which was intrinsic to his crime. In the context of the law, however, may we not say that the state has a duty to punish wrong-doers, and acts unfairly if it fails to carry out that duty?

What does this claim amount to? A legal system operates unfairly if its courts punish some offenders, whilst not punishing others who are convicted of relevantly similar offences; or if there are large discrepancies between sentences imposed for similar offences: but it is those who are punished, or punished more severely, who are now treated unfairly, not the law-abiding citizens; and such unfairness occurs *within* an existing penal system, whereas our concern is with the claim that fairness requires the creation of the system itself. It might also be unfair to announce punishments for offences, and then fail to impose them on offenders: but that would be unfair only to those who obey the law from fear of the penalties, not to the whole body of law-abiding citizens; and this is still a matter of the fair administration of an existing penal system, not of fairness as a reason for creating the system in the first place.[11]

If a state which is to impose on its citizens an obligation to obey the law must also commit itself to punishing those who break the law, then it certainly has a duty of fairness to carry out its side of that contract: a law-abiding citizen is treated unfairly if the state, while insisting that he must obey the law, refuses to punish those who do not. What needs to be shown, however, is that the state has a duty of fairness to undertake such a commitment in the first place. A state which, through its laws, prohibits and condemns certain kinds of conduct must perhaps as a matter of consistency be prepared to do *something* about those who break its laws; it cannot simply ignore

[11] Compare Honderich, *Punishment: The Supposed Justifications* 32–3, 42–3.

breaches of the law as if they did not matter: but this argument requires at most that those who break the law should be judged and condemned through a system of criminal trials, not that they must be *punished*.[12] How then can the institution of a system of punishment be a requirement of fairness if, as I have argued, we cannot say that a state which is to impose on its citizens the burdensome obligation of obeying the law for the sake of their mutual good must also, in fairness, impose the burden of punishment on those who refuse to accept that obligation?

Considerations of fairness may of course play a part in justifying a system of preventive or deterrent punishments. If the law is to claim my obedience, we may say, it must in fairness promise to protect me against injury at the hands of the lawless – by threatening and imposing punishments which will deter and prevent criminal conduct: but this does not offer a justification for the kind of *retributive* system of punishment which is in question here. We might by now suspect, however, that the claim that punishment is a requirement of fairness can seem plausible only insofar as it rests on a covert appeal to consequentialist considerations. Thus offenders must be punished, and not merely condemned by a conviction, because only thus can we ensure that the law will be generally obeyed, and reassure those who are initially willing to obey the law that they will not make themselves unduly vulnerable to the lawless by doing so. Consider, for instance, what Morris says about forgiveness as an alternative to punishment.

Forgiveness – with its legal analogue of a pardon – while not the righting of an unfair distribution by making one pay his debt is, nevertheless, a restoring of the equilibrium by forgiving the debt. Forgiveness may be viewed, at least in some types of case, as a gift after the fact, erasing a debt, which had the gift been given before the fact, would not have created a debt. But the practice of pardoning has to proceed sensitively, for it may endanger, in a way the practice of justice does not, the maintenance of an equilibrium of benefits and burdens. If all are indiscriminately pardoned less incentive is provided individuals to restrain their inclinations, thus increasing the incidence of persons taking what they do not deserve.[13]

If forgiveness is a way of *restoring* the equilibrium which crime disturbs (rather than of *accepting* the disequilibrium which crime creates), the reason which Morris offers for punishing, rather than pardoning, most offenders is straightforwardly consequentialist: if we do not punish them, too many people will then break the law.

---

[12] See ch. 5 above.   [13] Morris, 'Persons and Punishment' 43.

Such reasons for a system of punishment whose internal logic is re-tributivist are readily available: punishment provides a prudential deterrent for those who do not respect the law; it reassures those whose allegiance to the law might otherwise be undermined by their fear of the lawless; and it satisfies the reluctantly law-abiding citizen's vengeful desire that criminals should not be allowed to get away with their crimes – a desire which may lack respectable moral content, but which is liable to undermine respect for and obedience to the law if it is not satisfied. But even if the primary reason for pre-venting crime is still to maintain a fair balance of benefits and bur-dens (rather than to protect citizens against the more specific kinds of harm which they might suffer at the hands of the lawless), we are now offered a consequentialist justification for a system of punish-ment which uses the criminal as a means. Thus we have abandoned the claim that punishment can be justified in purely retributivist terms, as a practice which serves, *intrinsically*, to restore a fair balance of benefits and burdens, and claim instead that it serves, consequentially, to ensure that the law is obeyed – and thus that that fair balance is maintained.[14]

We cannot, I have argued, properly portray all crime as the gaining of an unfair advantage over the law-abiding, or punishment as a res-toration of that fair balance of benefits and burdens which crime disturbs; nor can the claim that the state has a duty of fairness to its citizens to punish criminals justify such a retributivist conception of punishment. This must already undermine the further claim that the criminal must, as a rational agent, will such a retributive system of punishment: but that claim itself merits further attention.

3 WILLING ONE'S OWN PUNISHMENT?

We are asked to imagine a group of rational Rawlsian egoists meet-ing behind a veil of ignorance, to choose the principles and insti-tutions which will govern their social life. Such beings, we are told, would opt for a system of retributive punishments which ensure that criminals do not profit by their crimes. This thought-experiment serves two purposes: to provide this account of punish-ment with a rational foundation, thus meeting the charge that it

[14] Compare J Cottingham, 'Varieties of Retribution'; D Harward, 'The Bitter Pill of Punishment'; Wasserstrom, 'Some Problems in the Definition and Justification of Punishment'. Murphy himself does not appeal to such consequentialist consider-ations, relying on the claim that punishment by itself restores a fair balance of benefits and burdens: but compare Finnis, *Natural Law and Natural Rights* ch. 10.1.

rests on an unargued intuition; and to show that the criminal must, as a rational agent, will such a system of punishment – and thus that in punishing her we respect her autonomy. Unfortunately, it can serve neither of these purposes.

There are notorious problems with the Rawlsian project: what characteristics should we ascribe to the imaginary beings in the original position; can we hope to discern what principles they would choose; why should these be the principles which we ourselves should follow?[15] I want to discuss just two questions here: why should we suppose that Rawlsian contractors would opt for a Murphian system of retributive punishments; and how can this supposition render punishment consistent with a respect for the criminal's autonomy?

The first question need not detain us long. A common criticism of Rawls' argument is that he can draw his favoured political principles out of the original position only by covertly building their ingredients into that position itself; that he provides no *independent* rational foundation for those principles. This criticism has particular force against Murphy's use of a Rawlsian scenario: why should Rawlsian beings see crime as a matter of taking unfair advantage of the law-abiding, or prefer a system of balance-restoring retributive punishments to, for instance, a system of deterrent punishments?

> ... the purpose of the criminal law is to uphold basic natural duties, those which forbid us to injure other persons in their life and limb, or to deprive them of their liberty and property, and punishments are to serve this end. They are not simply a scheme of taxes and burdens designed to put a price on certain forms of conduct and in this way to guide men's conduct for mutual advantage. It would be far better if the acts prescribed by penal statutes were never done.[16]

This does not suggest that crime and punishment are to be understood in Murphy's terms, but rather that crime involves various kinds of substantive injury to others; and that Rawlsian contractors, realising that not enough people would obey laws backed only by moral exhortation, would opt for a system of punishment whose primary aim is (subject to the constraints of justice) to deter crime.

Of course, *if* we are rationally required to see crime as Murphy portrays it, and to reject such a system of deterrent punishments as being inconsistent with a proper respect for the citizens' autonomy; we might then say that those in the original position would take the

---

[15] See especially J C Rees' Review of J Rawls, *A Theory of Justice*.
[16] Rawls, *A Theory of Justice* 314–15 (see also 240–3, 575–7).

same view. But our account of what such beings would decide cannot now provide any *independent* foundation for this account of crime and punishment: we can claim that they would opt for such a system of retributive punishments only if we have already shown, without reference to them, that crime and punishment must be understood in this way. The supposed choices of imaginary beings in an original position may provide a dramatic explication of a set of principles: but they must presuppose, and thus cannot serve to demonstrate, that those principles are rationally justified.[17]

An appeal to the deliberations of Rawlsian contractors cannot serve the first purpose which Murphy wants it to serve. But might he not now argue that we can in some other way show such a system of punishment to be the only one which is rationally justified – to be that which we must opt for insofar as we are rational; and that we can therefore still show such a system of punishment to be consistent with, and required by, a proper respect for the criminal's autonomy?

I have grave doubts about the first of these claims, that we can show a particular set of moral or political principles to be rationally inescapable. We can of course argue for our favoured principles, and against those which we reject; we can insist that certain principles deserve the allegiance even of those who are unmoved by them: but we cannot, I think, hope to show that the requirements of a particular morality are requirements of reason itself, which any rational (human) being must accept on pain of being shown to be irrational; or that one who fails to live by these principles – because she holds different moral views, or because she is not sufficiently moved by any moral considerations – is necessarily thinking or acting irrationally.[18] Suppose, however, that we could do this; that, despite the arguments of the last section, we could show that any rational human being would, insofar as she is rational, opt for a system of retributive and balance-restoring punishments: would this be enough to show that in punishing a criminal we are respecting her autonomy – by doing to her what she would will or has willed as a rational agent?

A professional thief is, despite all his efforts, brought to justice and sent to prison. He tries to escape this punishment, insisting that he neither wants nor wills it: but, he is told, he has rationally willed

---

[17] Murphy himself notes this kind of criticism – 'Marxism and Retribution' 106–7; and see Honderich, *Punishment: The Supposed Justifications* 224–7.
[18] See R A Duff, 'Desire, Duty and Moral Absolutes'.

the system of law which imposes this punishment; and we must respect his (real) rational will, rather than the desires which he now expresses. What sense can we make of this?

If we are to justify frustrating a person's present and avowed desires on the grounds that they do not express her real or rational will, we must answer two questions: how do we identify her real or rational will, insofar as it differs from the will which she now avows; and what conditions must be satisfied if we are to claim that, in frustrating her present and avowed desires, we are still respecting her autonomy or treating her as a rational agent.

Jane knows that she tends to get carried away in pubs, and that it is not in her best interests to get drunk: so she asks me not merely to warn her when she has had enough (we know she will ignore such warnings) but to prevent her drinking more than three pints of beer. When I now, despite her protests, forcibly stop her having a fourth pint, can I claim that I am still respecting her autonomy, by acting in accordance with her real and rational will?[19]

I must be able to identify her real will with what she says and wants when she is not in the pub, and show that what she now says and wants does not express a change of mind which I should respect as such. I might do this by showing that the desires which she now expresses must be seen as a temporary aberration: they are at odds with the values and concerns which form the continuing framework of her life; she herself has criticised them as being irrational; and they do not embody an alternative structure of values in the light of which she criticises her own past concerns as irrational. I must presumably also agree that her present desires should be opposed: if a hired killer asks me to help him resist the pangs of conscience which might stop him carrying out his contract, should I not rather urge him to listen to the voice of conscience?

What of the thief, however? He has never explicitly requested or assented to his own punishment; nor, we may suppose, will he ever do so: what does it mean to claim that he 'really' wills or consents to it? Murphy would appeal to 'a public, objective theory of rationality and rational willing':[20] we show that the thief *would*, were he fully rational, will a system of law which prohibits and punishes his thieving; and thus that, as a rational being, he *has* willed such a

---

[19] Compare Murphy's example of the neighbour who, at my request, 'locks up my liquor cabinet to protect me against my tendencies to drink too heavily' ('Marxism and Retribution' 97); his other examples are of preventing the suicide of someone in a state of psychotic depression, and forcing someone to honour a contract (*ibid.* 101, 102).

[20] Murphy 'Marxism and Retribution' 101 (see also 102).

system of law and punishment. But this move from 'would will' to 'has willed' is deeply disturbing: not only because we may be wrong about what a fully rational being would will;[21] but because if we are to ascribe something to a person as *his* will we must surely show that it *does*, not merely that it *would*, express itself in his actual life and conduct. If we admit that the thief has never actually expressed his assent to the laws which punish him; but insist that, since reason requires it, he has rationally willed those laws: we are ascribing to him an abstract, impersonal and metaphysical will which has no connection with his actual, expressed will – and which we can therefore hardly call *his*.[22]

We do sometimes justify what we do to a person by reference not to what he has actually willed, but to what any rational person – and thus he himself, were he rational – would will. If someone is so severely subnormal that he lacks the capacity for rational thought and action, we may detain him and refuse to allow him the freedom to conduct his own life and determine his own actions. When we stop him doing what he now wants to do, or subject him to treatment which he tries to resist, we justify this in part by claiming that any rational person would will that he should be thus coerced were he to fall into such a condition. In claiming this, however, we are not and cannot be claiming that *this* person has rationally willed that he should be thus coerced; or that we are now treating him as a rational agent, and respecting his autonomy. We rather claim that he is not, and thus cannot be treated as, a rational agent; that he has no rational will: for it is only because he has, and can have, no rational will of his own that we can justifiably coerce him as we do, and frustrate his actual will.

Of course, it may be said, this is not the thief's condition: we can find in his actual life an implicit consent to this system of law; and we do not suppose that he is incapable of rational thought and action, or of recognising and accepting the justice of what is done to him. Now we can sometimes ascribe to a person a will which she has never explicitly avowed – we can show that her own actions and responses express or manifest that will: but what can we show that the thief has thus implicitly willed? Perhaps that there should be a system of law which prohibits, and tries to prevent, thefts and other kinds of assault on the person: not merely because he has remained within a system of law which includes such prohibitions (what

---

[21] A fear which Murphy notes, and hopes to meet ('Marxism and Retribution' 101–2).

[22] Compare V Haksar, *Equality, Liberty and Perfectionism* 118–19.

choice did he have?);[23] but because he shows by his own responses to the actions of others that he wishes them to be bound by such a system of law. It is, however, unlikely that his actions or responses will reveal any kind of commitment to the particular theory of punishment which Murphy preaches; and it is also likely that what he wants, as his actions show, is that *others* should obey the law in their treatment of him, while he himself gets away with selectively breaking the law in his treatment of them.

Perhaps such a will is inconsistent: were he fully rational he would will that all, himself included, should obey such laws. Suppose then, for the sake of the argument, that we can convict the thief not only of a failure to will what reason requires him to will, or of a moral failing of partiality, but of a demonstrable inconsistency in his own will; and that he is capable of recognising this inconsistency and of willing – as reason requires – that he as well as others should obey the law and be punished for disobeying it (and he must be thus capable if he is to be responsible, and thus deserving of punishment, for his crimes). We can now show that he would, were he to exercise his own rational capacities, will or assent to the laws which punish him; and we thus provide a little more purchase for the claim that he *has* rationally willed those laws: for we now infer the content of his supposedly rational will not simply from an impersonal account of what any rational being would will, but from an examination of what he himself already wills, and of what that must, if he is to be consistent, commit him to. We might still doubt whether this entitles us to translate our claim about what he *would* will were he to make his will consistent into a claim about what he *does* will as a rational being: but it anyway raises a further difficulty.

When I forcibly stop Jane drinking her fourth pint, an appeal to her previous request that I should do this does not, by itself, suffice to render my present coercion of her consistent with or expressive of a respect for her autonomy. If she is *now* a rational agent, responsible for her own actions, I must treat her as such: I must treat her as someone whose present conduct manifests a wilful and culpable kind of irrationality; as someone who can and should recognise for herself the stupidity of what she is doing, and who could act on that recognition. My response to her must appeal to that capacity for rational thought and action. I can urge her to be sensible; I can offer her what I – and she herself, in calmer moods – regard as good reasons for drinking no more; and I can criticise her failure (her refusal, as I might put it) to recognise the stupidity of what she is

[23] See Murphy, 'Marxism and Retribution' 108.

doing: for these are appropriate ways of trying to persuade a responsible agent to see and to do for herself what she ought to do. But if, when reason fails, I resort to coercive or manipulative measures to stop her drinking, I no longer treat her as an autonomous agent who must determine, and take responsibility for, her own actions: I treat her instead as someone who must be coerced or manipulated for her own good; and her previous request that I should do this shows only that she conspired with me in this surrender and denial of her autonomy.[24]

Must the same not be true of the thief, if we are to treat him as someone who is now a responsible agent? We may try to persuade him to obey the law, by appealing to the relevant reasons which justify its requirements; if he still breaks the law we may condemn and criticise him; we may even try to persuade him that he ought to seek or accept punishment, as a debt which he owes to his fellow-citizens: but we cannot impose that punishment on him, against his present and avowed will, and claim that in doing so we are treating or respecting him as an autonomous agent.

Matters would be different if I could claim that Jane is now, in effect, temporarily disordered; that her first three drinks rendered her *incapable* of rational thought and action. If I stop James killing himself in a state of psychotic depression, in accordance with the will which he expresses or manifests when he is not in this condition, I can claim to be respecting his rational will. For I cannot now appeal to him as someone who is capable of rational thought and action, and who should thus control his own actions, since he now lacks that capacity: I must act on his behalf to secure what he wants as a rational (i.e. rationally capable) agent, since he is unable to do so for himself.

Now it may be tempting to suppose that if Jane's present desires and actions are by her own standards, or by some objective standard of reason, irrational, it must be the case that she is now *unable* to think or act rationally. For, we might say in Platonic or Kantian tones, we act freely and voluntarily only insofar as we follow the dictates of reason (insofar as reason rules in our souls): we cannot *wilfully* fail to exercise our rational capacities, but do so only when we are overcome by our irrational appetites; irrational thought and action must be seen as compulsive or non-voluntary. This kind of view is expressed, for instance, by those who argue that the phenomena of 'weakness of will' can always be explained in terms of hypocrisy, ignorance or incapacity – that it *cannot* be the case that

[24] See ch. 2(3) above.

a person wilfully and voluntarily does what she also sees to be irrational or wrong; and it is opposed by those who think that we clearly do sometimes wilfully and voluntarily do what we see to be irrational or wrong.[25]

There is indeed a tension in our attitudes towards our own and others' irrationalities; between the inclination to see the irrational agent as the helpless victim of irrational appetites or impulses, and the inclination to see him as one who wilfully fails to exercise the rational capacities which he has. This is not the place for a thorough discussion of this problem: we need note here only that *whichever* kind of view we take, Murphy's argument fails.

We are supposing that the thief, in committing his crimes and in resisting his punishment, is at least being irrational: were he thinking and acting as reason requires he would will and obey a system of law which prohibits and punishes the crimes he commits. Now if, by analogy with Jane or with James, we are to claim that in imposing punishment on him against his present and avowed will we still respect him as an autonomous agent – by acting in accordance with his rational will – we must claim that he is now *incapable* of recognising for himself what reason requires of him, or of acting on that recognition: for if he is capable of such rational thought and action we cannot legitimately go beyond trying to persuade him to accept and obey the demands of reason, and condemning him if he fails to do so. If, however, we are to justify punishing him at all we must suppose that he is a responsible agent who can properly be blamed and punished for his voluntary wrong-doing – who wilfully took for himself an unfair profit which his punishment must wipe out: for if he is instead the helpless and compulsive victim of his irrational appetites we cannot claim either that he gained for himself an unfair profit by his crime, or that he can properly be held responsible for it. If Murphy's argument is to justify *imposing punishment* on the thief, it seems that we must be able to show both that he is a rational and responsible agent and that he is not – which is absurd.[26]

[25] See G W Mortimore (ed), *Weakness of Will*; S Khin Zaw, '"Irresistible Impulse" and Moral Responsibility'; D Wiggins, 'Weakness of Will, Commensurability, and the Objects of Deliberation and Desire'.

[26] Murphy himself notes both that 'on Kant's (and also, I think, on Rawls') view, a man is genuinely free or autonomous only in so far as he is rational', and that his retributivist theory presupposes that the criminal is 'an evil person who, of his own free will, intentionally acts against those just rules of society which he knows, as a rational man, benefit everyone including himself' ('Marxism and Retribution' 101, 109): my complaint is that he does not note the radical tension between these two points.

To treat someone as a rational and autonomous agent is to address her and respond to her as someone who is capable of rational thought and action – as someone who can recognise and be moved by good reasons for action. The law itself addresses the citizen in this way: it seeks her assent and obedience to its justified demands. Now I do not myself suppose that the demands even of a just system of law are demands of reason itself; that anyone who refuses to accept and obey them is thereby guilty of irrationality: for I do not suppose that reason speaks with only one voice, or that its voice is always and necessarily the voice of a particular morality. Even if we accept, however, that at least the central rules of a just system of law are such that it would be irrational not to accept and obey them (or not to accept – to will – that those who break the law should be punished), we cannot yet claim that in imposing punishment on a criminal against her express will we are respecting her autonomy by acting in accordance with her rational will. For we cannot readily translate the claim that she *would*, were she thinking and acting as reason requires, will the laws which punish her into the claim that she *has*, as a rational being, willed those laws; and a proper respect for her autonomy will anyway, it seems, allow us to coerce her into conformity with her rational will only if she is incapable of bringing her own conduct into conformity with the demands of reason – in which case she is not a wilful wrong-doer who can be deserving of punishment.

If I coerce someone, forcing her to do what she does not now want to do, the fact that she has herself requested or consented to this coercion does not suffice to render it consistent with, or expressive of, a respect for her autonomy: I must also show that what she has requested or consented to is not itself a denial or in-fringement of her autonomy. If Jane is still a responsible and ration-ally capable agent, then in forcibly stopping her having another drink I infringe her autonomy, despite her previous request. For as a responsible agent she has the right, *and the duty*, to determine her own actions: in stopping her doing this I deny her that right; in asking me to stop her doing this she was seeking to abandon that duty and to surrender her status as an autonomous agent. It is not enough to say that I act not only in accordance with her previously expressed will, but also in order to preserve her own future exist-ence as an autonomous agent; that I stop her doing something which will, if she persists with it, destroy her rational capacities. The cru-cial question is whether what I do to her *now* respects and treats her as a rationally capable and responsible agent; and the answer must be that it does not.

If the thief's case is supposed to be analogous to Jane's, the same point must hold good: if he has rationally willed that he should be punished for breaking the law, and if he is now a responsible and rationally capable agent, it must be up to him to seek and accept that punishment for himself; it is not for us to impose that punishment on him against his present and avowed will.

We must, however, beware of a one-sided diet of examples. Perhaps there are other kinds of case, in which I may coerce someone against his expressed will whilst still respecting his autonomy, and without having to claim that he is now incapable of thinking or acting rationally for himself.

In cases of dire emergency, when there is insufficient time for rational persuasion, I might do to someone else what he would do for himself if only he knew the truth. I push someone out of the way of an onrushing bus, when there is no time to shout a warning; or, knowing that Brian's beer has been poisoned, I dash the glass from his hand as he, laughing off my attempt to warn him, lifts it to his lips. We might say in some such cases that since the context itself does not allow time for the offering and acceptance of reasons for action, I can properly act on the other person's behalf, without infringing his autonomy; or that, though I admittedly infringe his autonomy by using force when rational persuasion fails, the infringement is a minor one, for the sake of his own immediate and obvious good. Neither account, however, can support the claim that in imposing punishment on a criminal against her expressed will we are respecting her autonomy by doing to and for her what she does or would herself want us to do. In her case there is no such immediate threat to her continued existence as an autonomous being, and no such lack of time for the offering of reasons; nor can we claim that the infringement of her autonomy is a minor one – even if we can suppose that she *would* will her own punishment if she only came to accept what reason requires.

Consider another case, however. Susan has borrowed £100 from me, promising to repay it, and giving me permission to use force to extract payment if she refuses to pay when the time comes. She now refuses to pay; I forcibly extract the money from her wallet: can I claim that, in the light of her prior permission, I am now treating or respecting her as a rational agent? If I can, can we not also claim that in exacting by force the debt of punishment which the criminal owes to her fellow-citizens we are respecting her as an autonomous agent? Perhaps the use of such force to exact a debt – to take or re-cover what is rightfully mine from someone who tries to withhold it from me – is consistent with a respect for the other person's auton-omy. I cannot legitimately try to terrorise or manipulate her into paying her debt, since these are improper ways of trying to modify a moral agent's conduct: but in taking from her by force what she ought, but refuses, to give me voluntarily I am not trying to get her to *do* anything; I am responding to her wrongful attempt to deprive me of what is mine.

To portray the matter in these terms is to compare my coercion of Susan to the use of force in defence of one's property or one's life: if this is appropriate (and I am not sure whether it is), it shows that coercion to be consistent with the respect which I owe to Susan as a rational agent. Now her prior consent is not *sufficient* for such a justi-fication of what I do to her in order to extract my money from her; it could not justify an attempt to terrorise or manipulate her into paying her debt, since she cannot give a valid or justifying consent to the use of methods which are themselves wrongful, as a denial of her autonomy. But is it even *necessary* for such a justification of my use of force; or should we rather say that that force is justified or un-justified independently of whether or not she has consented to it?

If I use violence to defend myself against a murderous assault, I may claim that I am still treating and respecting my assailant as a rational and autonomous agent. I am responding appropriately to his voluntary and wrongful action; I am not trying to modify his be-haviour by improper means, but simply preventing him carrying through an attack on which he has illegitimately embarked.[27] I do not see that anything is added to this justification by the claim that he previously consented to my using force against him if he attacked me; or by the claim that as a rational moral agent he would, must or does will the use of force in such circumstances. If my use of force *is* justified, I might say that any rational moral agent would will or consent to it: but to say that my assailant therefore *has* consented to it, as a rational moral agent, is to add nothing more than a mislead-ing rhetorical flourish to an argument which does not depend on it.

Or consider the case of A A Bowman. He was a prisoner-of-war, and thought it his duty to try to escape. He should not, he thought, try to achieve this by bribing a guard; for such an attempt to corrupt a guard would fail to respect or care for him as a moral being: but he could legitimately kill any guard who tried to prevent his escape; for

---

[27] See T Nagel, 'War and Massacre'; G E Anscombe 'War and Murder': I leave aside here the grave problems posed by the morally guiltless assailant.

he would then be responding appropriately and relevantly to the guard's own voluntary conduct, and would still be treating, and respecting, him as an autonomous and responsible moral agent.[28]

I do not pretend that such justifications for the use of force are straightforward or uncontroversial. My point here is simply this: that Murphy's attempt to reconcile coercing someone against her expressed will with a proper respect for her autonomy, by showing that she has herself as a rational agent willed this coercion, must fail for the reasons given in this section; but that he may be wrong to suppose that this is the only way in which such a reconciliation can be brought about. We may be able to show that certain kinds of coercion are appropriate and justified responses to the voluntary conduct of a moral agent without having to claim or show that she has herself willed that we should respond thus. If we could accept that punishment is, as Murphy portrays it, a debt which the criminal owes to his fellow-citizens, we could then go on to ask whether the forcible exaction of a debt can be consistent with a proper respect for the debtor's autonomy, and whether his own consent to this use of force is necessary if it is to be thus justified. I will not pursue this question here, since I have already argued that we cannot plausibly portray punishment in such terms: before we can determine whether the imposition of punishment against a criminal's expressed will can be consistent with a respect for his autonomy, we must provide a more adequate account of the meaning and purpose of punishment.

Before I embark on that task, however, a few further comments on the character and implications of Murphy's account of what can justify punishment are appropriate.

4 IDEALS AND ACTUALITIES

Murphy offers an *ideal* account of the conditions which must be satisfied if a system of punishment is to be adequately justified: these conditions are not, he insists, satisfied in a capitalist society like our own. We cannot suppose that the relevant benefits and burdens are distributed fairly amongst all members of the community; or that every citizen, having voluntarily accepted these benefits, is therefore bound in fairness to accept the matching burdens;[29] or that the

---

[28] See N Kemp Smith's Memorial Introduction to A A Bowman, *Studies in the Philosophy of Religion* xxiii.

[29] Murphy, 'Marxism and Retribution' 108 (surely, however, on the Rawlsian argument, we need only suppose that the citizens would have chosen to accept these benefits in the original position, not that they have in fact chosen to accept them).

'typical criminal' is 'an evil person who, of his own free will, intentionally acts against those just rules of society which he knows, as a rational man, benefit everyone including himself'.[30]

Such considerations – if we accept them – provide various reasons for insisting that punishment cannot be just in a society like our own. Punishment cannot restore a fair balance of benefits and burdens, if no such balance existed in the first place. We cannot say, at least of many criminals, that they have wilfully seized for themselves an unfair advantage by their crimes: we might have to say of some that their crimes are justified, as acts of resistance or self-defence against an unjust and oppressive system; or that their crimes should be excused, since they act not as autonomous agents, but as victims of motives which are forced on them or induced in them by the very society which would then condemn them; or that they have no obligation to accept the burdens imposed on them by the laws of a society which unjustly oppresses them. It might still be true that some criminals, who are not already unfairly disadvantaged, wilfully gain an unfair advantage for themselves by their crimes; and thus that their punishment, whilst not restoring a *fair* balance of benefits and burdens, would at least wipe out that particular unfair advantage: but even this does not give us the right to punish them. For our present system of criminal justice is not well suited to identifying such cases – it would be a matter of luck rather than of good judgment if we actually managed to punish just those criminals who deserve punishment; and we ourselves, who maintain or tolerate a social and legal system which itself perpetrates gross injustices, can hardly claim the right to punish those who act unjustly.

I am concerned here with the implications, rather than the merits, of such criticisms of our existing practices. If they are justified, what then can we do?

If we think that institutions of punishment are necessary and desirable, and if we are morally sensitive enough to want to be sure that we have the moral right to punish before we inflict it, then we had better first make sure that we have restructured society in such a way that criminals genuinely do correspond to the only model that will render punishment permissible – i.e. make sure that they are autonomous and that they do benefit in the requisite sense.[31]

This suggests that punishment could in principle be justified in a more equitable non-capitalist society, in which all benefits and burdens are distributed fairly among citizens who are themselves free

---

[30] *Ibid.* 109 (more generally, 104–9).   [31] *Ibid.* 110.

and autonomous agents. But Murphy also indicates a more radical objection – not only to our existing penal practices but to his own account of just punishment: that his account relies on a theory of rationality (as exemplified by the choices of rational egoists behind a veil of ignorance) which offers as a necessary and universal truth about human nature and human reason what is in fact no more than the reflection of a particular kind of capitalist society.[32] If this objection is sound, then punishment as Murphy portrays it can presumably be justified neither in a capitalist society like our own – since it is then unjust – nor in a more equitable non-capitalist society – since the picture of human nature on which it relies would then be inapplicable. Thus it is not clear that we have yet been offered an account of how a system of punishment could, even ideally and in principle, be justified – rather than an account of how and why punishment could *never* be justified.

Our own system and practice of punishment must in any event stand condemned: it does not and cannot serve the purpose appropriate to a system of punishment. But if we then ask what, if anything, we can justifiably do about crime pending that restructuring of society which will render punishment either justified or unnecessary, no answer is forthcoming – except that we cannot justifiably punish criminals. Unless the whole social structure is so corrupt that anarchy or violent revolution would be preferable to its continued survival the maintenance, together with serious attempts at the reform, of an admittedly unjust legal system might well be, in consequentialist terms, the least of the available evils. This might be the only way to avert human and social disaster; to work towards the necessary transformation of society; or to preserve even the possibility of a just society in the future. But in maintaining such a system of law, and punishing criminals within it, we maintain and perpetuate injustice; and we use those whom we punish as means – as means to the preservation of society – as surely as we do if we punish the innocent or use punishment as a deterrent.

Perhaps there is indeed, given our present situation, nothing we can do which will not involve some more or less serious injustice: but that still leaves us with the question of what we are to do – of how, as citizens or as would-be reformers, we are to respond to our existing legal institutions, or to our own or others' criminal conduct. A theory which discovers such a drastic gap between the ideal towards which we should be striving and the actual in which we live surely owes us some kind of response to this question.

[32] *Ibid.* 103, 106.

I have raised various objections to this version of retributivism: to the idea that crime is a matter of taking unfair advantage of one's fellow-citizens, and that punishment wipes out that unfair advantage; and to the claim that punishment respects the criminal's autonomy, since it accords with her rational will. I want finally to raise two further questions: about the nature of the burden which punishment should impose on the criminal; and about the criminal's own role in his punishment. These questions can be clarified by asking about the likely fate of disordered offenders in a system of balance-restoring punishments.

Such a system will presumably make adequate allowance for those who are mentally disordered when they break the law; if they have not taken wilful and unfair advantage of their fellows, they will not be punished. But what of a criminal who becomes seriously disordered *after* committing an offence? She has reaped the unfair profit which was intrinsic to her crime, and disturbed the fair balance of benefits and burdens: so why should she not now be punished, in order to wipe out that unfair profit and restore that fair balance? Indeed, why should we not say that in punishing her we are treating and respecting her as a rational agent by acting in accordance with her rational will?

I have already discussed, and criticised, two possible arguments against punishing such an offender: that a general principle of humanity forbids us to impose such further suffering on one who is already so seriously harmed by mental disorder; and that the criminal's disorder itself imposes on her a burden sufficient to pay her debt.[33] As to the first, it does not show the punishment of a disordered offender to be inappropriate *as a punishment*: it would still pay the debt which she owes, but it would be cruel to exact that payment from her. As to the second, we must ask whether the courts should aim to preserve a fair balance only of the benefits and burdens which the state itself confers and imposes, or of *all* benefits and burdens. In the former case, mental disorder could not be a substitute for punishment. In the latter case, every offender's punishment would need to depend on the extent to which she is well or ill favoured by fortune; and we should be struck by the oddity of asking whether an offender's disorder is severe enough to serve as a *substitute* for the punishment which she deserves.

We must ask, however, whether the punishment of a seriously disordered offender can impose on him the kind of burden which he deserves. If it is to wipe out his unfair profit it must impose on him a

[33] See ch. 1(1)–(2) above.

burden of restraint which in some way matches the burden of self-restraint he evaded in breaking the law: if he is so disordered that he cannot even perceive his punishment as a burden, perhaps it cannot serve its proper purpose, and is thus inappropriate. Suppose, however, that he can perceive his punishment as a burden; but he cannot, being disordered, understand it *as* a punishment – as a debt which he owes to his fellow-citizens because of his past wrong-doing. I am not sure that, on this account of punishment, there would be anything intrinsically wrong with punishing such a person. He must, 'as a rational agent', have willed that punishment as an appropriate retribution for his past offence: but it does not seem to matter whether he does in fact, as the person he is, see any such connection between what is done to him now and his past offence. What he suffers now need not, as he suffers it, be related to his past wrong-doing; and his actual role as one who is punished – as distinct from his metaphysical role as rational will – is simply that of a passive recipient or victim of his punishment.[34]

If we are to see why the punishment of a seriously disordered offender should be wrong *as* punishment, we must provide a different account of the kind of suffering which punishment is meant to impose on the offender, and of the role which she is meant to play in her punishment. In the next chapter I will explicate an account of punishment which does this: it insists that punishment must aim to induce in the offender a kind of suffering which is, as she suffers it, essentially related to her past wrong-doing, thus relating the purpose of punishment more closely to that of moral blame; and that punishment is a communicative enterprise which seeks the responsive understanding and the participation of the offender, thus rendering punishment more closely continuous with the criminal trial, which seeks the assent and the participation of the defendant.

---

[34] Murphy does insist ('Cruel and Unusual Punishments' 233–4, 242–4) that punishment must not preclude a characteristically human response by the criminal, or prevent him developing his own moral character: but this has more to do with how we ought to treat any rational being (we should not, for instance, torture him, or close off his options for self-development) than with the meaning of punishment itself.

9

Expression, Penance and Reform

And some, we know, when they by wilful act
a single human life have wrongly taken,
pass sentence on themselves, confess the fact,
and, to atone for it, with soul unshaken
kneel at the feet of Justice, and, for faith
broken with all mankind solicit death.

William Wordsworth,
Sonnets upon the Punishment of Death, III

It is not enough that wrong-doers be justly punished.
They must if possible judge and condemn themselves.

P Aynault, *L'Ordre,*
Formalité et Instruction Judiciaire, I.1, ch. 14

I INTRODUCTORY

The criminal law and the criminal trial are, like moral criticism, communicative enterprises which seek the assent and the participation of those whom they address: the law seeks the allegiance of the citizen as a rational moral agent, by appealing to the relevant moral reasons which justify its demands; the trial seeks to engage the defendant in a rational dialogue about the justice of the charge which she faces, and to persuade her – if that charge is proved against her – to accept and make her own the condemnation which her conviction expresses. Laws and trials respect the citizen as an autonomous agent: they aim to guide her conduct by offering her relevant reasons for action. But we have not yet shown that punishment can accord the same respect to the citizen; that its purposes are continuous with those of the criminal law and the criminal trial; or that it too seeks the offender's assent and participation.

A consequentialist account portrays punishment as a manipulative technique for promoting certain further ends: it might (given certain non-consequentialist constraints on our pursuit of those ends) portray punishment as a mode of rational deterrence which has some regard for the citizen as a rational agent; but such a system still manipulates those whose obedience it tries to secure by the threat of punishment, since it imposes on them irrelevant prudential reasons for obedience. The kind of retributivist account which I discussed in the last chapter avoids the charge of manipulation, since it does not portray punishment as an attempt to modify conduct: but its appeal to the criminal's 'rational will' fails to reconcile the imposition of punishment with a respect for his autonomy; and its account of the relationship between crime and punishment (of why punishment is an appropriate response to crime) depends on an unpersuasive picture of the nature of crime.

I turn now to a very different conception of punishment, according to which punishment does express our respect and concern for the criminal as a rational moral agent, and has a justifying purpose which is continuous with those of the criminal trial and of moral blame. This conception is retributivist, in that it makes the relationship between past crime and present punishment central to the meaning and justification of punishment, but it differs from other kinds of retributivist account in ascribing a forward-looking purpose to punishment. This is not, however, a consequentialist purpose (such as that of preventing crime, or bringing the criminal's conduct into external conformity with the law) to which punishment is contingently related as a means: the purpose of punishment, like that of moral blame, is logically rather than contingently related to the 'means' by which it is to be achieved; and the very nature of that purpose requires that it be achieved by bringing offenders to suffer for their offences.

We begin with the familiar idea that punishment has an essentially *expressive* meaning; it aims to communicate something to the criminal. The nature and purpose of this communicative endeavour is then explained by portraying punishment as a kind of *penance* which aims to secure and to express the criminal's repentance of his wrong-doing; and thus as a process of *reform* (or self-reform) through which the criminal can attain or regain a proper concern for the law and his proper place in the community. But to talk thus of punishment as a reformative endeavour is not to suggest that it is a contingently efficient means towards a further and independently identifiable end: for the kind of reform at which punishment aims can be achieved only through the kind of suffering which punishment aims to impose on, or to induce in, the criminal.

Ideas of this kind have been a persistent, if not always prominent, feature of discussions of punishment. They promise to show that punishment must seek the assent and the participation of the person punished; and that it expresses our concern, not merely for some further social benefit or for the restoration of an abstract balance of benefits and burdens, but for the criminal's own good as a rational moral agent and as a member of a moral community.

Two recent writers have made interesting moves in this direction. Lucas, who once argued that we must understand punishment in essentially deterrent terms, now wants to place more emphasis on its retributive, communicative and penitential purposes.[1] Morris, on the other hand, once argued that punishment could restore an abstract and 'rule-established balance of benefits and burdens', but could not restore those 'close relationships defined by feelings and attitudes' which are essential to our personal and social lives, and which wrong-doing disrupts. More recently, however, he has canvassed a 'paternalistic' theory of punishment which makes a concern for the criminal's moral well-being, and for her relationships with her fellows, central to its meaning.[2] My task in what follows is to see what sense we can make of punishment in such terms as these.

2 PUNISHMENT AS EXPRESSIVE

It is often said that punishment has an expressive or communicative purpose: but what is expressed, by whom, and to whom?[3]

Punishment, we may say, expresses condemnation: it denounces and formally disapproves the criminal's act; it disavows that act as one which is not to be tolerated or condoned.[4] This condemnation is expressed by those who officially decree and impose the punishment, which is supposedly imposed on behalf of the whole community: it expresses that condemnation in which all members of the

---

[1] J R Lucas, 'Or Else' (for the earlier account, discussed in ch. 6(3)–(5) above); *Freedom and Grace* p. xii, and *On Justice* ch. 6 for the new account.

[2] H Morris, 'Persons and Punishment' (for the earlier account, discussed in ch. 8 above); 'Guilt and Suffering' (from which the quotations are taken); and 'A Paternalistic Theory of Punishment' for the new account. Compare also R Nozick, *Philosophical Explanations* 4.3; J Hampton, 'The Moral Education Theory of Punishment'.

[3] See A J Skillen, 'How to Say Things with Walls'.

[4] See, among others, J Feinberg, 'The Expressive Function of Punishment'; J F Stephen, *A History of the Criminal Law of England* vol. 2, ch. 17, and *Liberty, Equality, Fraternity* 152; Lucas, *On Justice* ch. 6; Morris, 'A Paternalistic Theory of Punishment'; Lord Denning, quoted in the *Report of the Royal Commission on Capital Punishment* para. 53; H M Hart, 'Criminal Punishment as Public Condemnation'; J Charvet, 'Criticism and Punishment'; A von Hirsch, *Doing Justice: The Choice of Punishments*; W Moberly, *The Ethics of Punishment* chs. 5, 8; N Morris, *The Future of Imprisonment* 78–9. For criticisms, see S I Benn, 'An Approach to the Problems of Punishment'; H L A Hart, *Law, Liberty and Morality* 60–9; Skillen, 'How to Say Things with Walls'; N Walker, 'Punishing, Denouncing, or Reducing Crime', and 'The Ultimate Justification'.

community should share when they contemplate the crime. Though this condemnation is expressed to the criminal himself, punishment may also communicate to the public at large (and especially to potential criminals) a reminder of the wrongness of the criminal's conduct, and to the victims of crime an authoritative disavowal of such conduct.[5] But if we are to avoid the charge that in punishing a criminal we are simply using him as a means to some communicative purpose which is directed at others, its essential expressive aim must be that of communicating to the criminal himself a proper condemnation of his crime.

How can punishment (the infliction of suffering) express such condemnation? The particular kinds of punishment which a penal system imposes may be determined in part by convention: but it is not a matter of convention that we should express condemnation or disapproval to a person by a communicative act which is meant to make her suffer. The infliction of suffering *need* not have such an expressive meaning; and we can express a formal disapproval of someone's criminal wrong-doing simply by the words which constitute a criminal conviction: but the further punitive measures which are then imposed on a criminal can also express condemnation; and since that condemnation is itself meant to pain her, it could not be expressed through measures which are meant to please her.

Why should we think it important to express this condemnation to the criminal? If we care for the law, and regard its requirements as important; if we care about crime, as a breach of the law and a wrong done to others: we may simply need to express this concern – for no *further* purpose, and for no other reason than that to remain silent in the face of crime would be to betray the values which the law expresses, and to which we are committed. We may also hope, however, to bring the criminal to recognise the wrongness of his past conduct, and to modify his future conduct accordingly; and to remind others of the importance of the law's requirements. But this persuasive purpose is not a further end to which expressive punishments are related as an instrumental technique: for such punishments aim not merely to prevent crime, but to bring people to see and to understand the wrongness of such conduct; and it is not merely a matter of contingent efficiency that we can achieve *that* end by communicating to them our condemnation of such conduct.[6]

Our actual motives for condemning the moral or criminal

---

[5] Feinberg, 'The Expressive Function of Punishment'.
[6] See ch. 2(3) above.

wrong-doings of others are no doubt often far less admirable than those suggested here: an envious resentment of those who do what we ourselves are tempted to do; a self-righteous desire to assert our own moral superiority; the satisfaction of finding a scapegoat. But we are talking now of what punishment *ought* to be; of the motives and reasons which would provide a justificatory explanation of punishment. If our actual motives are not such that the punishments which we impose or approve do express a proper condemnation of criminal conduct, we must criticise ourselves for not punishing as we should: but the prevalence of such improper motives does not preclude us from identifying the motives which *would* inform a properly justified system of expressive punishments.

Rewards, like punishments, serve an expressive purpose; and just as the law's formal punishments can be compared with our informal responses to moral wrong-doing, so public and formal rewards can be compared with private expressions of gratitude or admiration. If I want to express my gratitude for someone's help or support, or my admiration for what she has done, I might simply thank or praise her: but I might also, in order to express my feelings more adequately, give her a present, or do her some service. The primary purpose of such expressive actions is not (unless they are corrupt) instrumental: it is to express to her the thanks or admiration which are due to her for what she has done; and though they may also serve and be intended to encourage such conduct, they aim to do so by appealing to the relevant reasons which make that conduct admirable, not by providing an irrelevant prudential reason for repeating it. Expressions of gratitude and admiration, whether verbal or material, are related to the past conduct for which thanks or praise are due, and to the future conduct which they may encourage, as moral blame is related to the past conduct which is blamed and to the future modification of conduct which it may secure: both express an appropriate response to past conduct; both thus also provide relevant reasons for future conduct.

The same is true of public expressions of gratitude and admiration. A community may give public thanks and praise to its benefactors, servants and heroes: these may be simply expressed in some public and formal commendation – a speech or a formal vote of thanks; or they may be given a more tangible form in a symbolic or material reward – a medal, a title, a pension, or exemption from some duty or burden. Such rewards, whether symbolic or material, express the gratitude or admiration which their recipient deserves for what she has done. They may also serve and be intended to encourage such conduct by the person rewarded or by others: but if they are not to be corrupt they must do this by appealing to the relevant reasons which make that conduct deserving of thanks or praise, not by adding to them an irrelevant prudential reason (the prospect of material benefit) for engaging in such conduct.[7]

An account of punishment as a communicative enterprise satisfies the desiderata noted at the start of this chapter. Punishment is now continuous in its meaning and purpose with the criminal trial and the criminal law: it seeks to communicate to the offender that judgment on, and that condemnation of, his conduct which his trial has justified and which his conviction also expresses; to bring him to accept that judgment, to condemn himself, and to modify his future conduct accordingly; and thus to persuade him not merely to *obey* the law, but to *accept* its justified demands and judgments. Punishment, like moral blame, respects and addresses the criminal as a rational moral agent: it seeks his understanding and his assent; it aims to bring him to repent his crime, and to reform himself, by communicating to him the reasons which justify our condemnation of his conduct. A system of criminal law and punishment can now be seen as a unitary enterprise of dialogue and judgment in which law-abiding citizens, defendants and convicted offenders are all called to participate. Our reasons for maintaining such a system of law have to do with the prevention of crime and the good of the community, but we do not simply use citizens or criminals as means to these ends: the law addresses all the citizens as rational moral agents, seeking their assent and their understanding; and punishment is part of that continuing dialogue with the criminal through which the law aims to guide his conduct by appealing to relevant reasons.

Such an account also shows how punishment embodies the condemnatory dimension of the criminal law; it distinguishes a system of punishment from a system of deterrent taxation, and from a licensing system which sets a price on certain activities. Some have suggested, however, that not all the sanctions which the criminal law might impose have, or should have, this kind of expressive meaning. We must distinguish *punishments* properly speaking from mere *penalties* which aim to discourage certain kinds of conduct, but do not condemn them; so we should perhaps narrow the scope of the strictly *criminal* law, and create a new category of administrative or regulatory prescriptions, breaches of which (though they attract

---

[7] On rewards, see Feinberg, 'The Expressive Function of Punishment'; Moberly, *The Ethics of Punishment* ch. 6; P Winch, 'Ethical Reward and Punishment'.

a penalty) will not properly count as *crimes*.[8] But such a distinction between 'punishments' and 'penalties' raises serious problems.

How, firstly, is the distinction to be drawn? Should we say, for instance, that expressive punishments are appropriate to *mala in se*, which are the central and proper concern of the criminal law; while administrative penalties are more appropriate to *mala prohibita*? But many *mala prohibita* should be seen as wrongs, insofar as they involve the breach of laws which protect the interests, safety or convenience of others; insofar as they are either themselves dangerous or troublesome acts, or take unfair advantage of the law-abiding self-restraint of others (and if they do not involve either of these kinds of wrong, why should they be prohibited?): so why should not the relatively modest sanctions which may be attached to them express a relatively restrained condemnation of them as wrongs? More generally, if the law's requirements are justified, there are good and relevant moral reasons for its prescriptions and proscriptions: a citizen who wilfully or negligently breaks the law then acts wrongly, even if that wrong is not a very serious one; and she can properly be condemned by her conviction and by her punishment. Our existing laws might in fact define as guilty some who are innocent of any such genuine wrong – whose conduct should not be condemned: but this is a fault in those laws themselves, and suggests that such people should not be penalised at all, not that they should suffer a penalty rather than a punishment which condemns them.

How, secondly, are such penalties to be understood? They should not be seen simply as taxes, even if this is how some offenders do see them: for they are attached to legal *prohibitions*. But if we instead portray, and justify, them as deterrents; and if we admit, as I have argued, that a system of deterrent sanctions is manipulative: we seem to be saying that the law may use manipulative means to prevent such relatively minor infractions, but may not do so to prevent more serious kinds of crime – which is surely bizarre.[9]

I will not pursue these problems here: my present concern is with the claim that the sanctions which are imposed on conduct which is properly defined as criminal are to be understood and justified as expressive punishments; and there is a familiar and apparently devastating objection to any such claim.

[8] Feinberg ('The Expressive Function of Punishment') and Lucas (*On Justice* ch. 6) both distinguish 'punishments' from 'penalties': see also Walker, 'Punishing, Denouncing or Reducing Crime'; R M Jackson, *Enforcing the Law* ch. 2; and J Feinberg, *Harm to Others* 242.
[9] One who thinks that expressive punishments themselves also serve as deterrents will not see this as a problem; see text at n. 14 below.

Why, we must ask, should we express our condemnation of the criminal's wrong-doing through the kinds of 'hard treatment' (such as imprisonment) which are typically imposed as punishments by legal systems like our own?[10] Hard treatment *can* serve this expressive purpose; and the fact that our actual punishments may not succeed in communicating the appropriate message to those on whom they are imposed might show only that they are inadequate to their proper purpose (and that they properly leave the criminal free to close his mind to them) – not that they cannot in principle serve this purpose. Nor would it be enough, if punishments are to serve this purpose, merely to pretend to impose them.[11] That would hardly impress the offenders towards whom they are primarily directed; and a legal system which is to respect its citizens cannot properly set out to deceive them. But why should we choose this method of expression?

We can imagine a criminal process which ends with the formal verdict of the court – the offender is convicted (and thus condemned) and then released; or a system of purely symbolic punishments which, unlike hard treatment, cause suffering to the offender only insofar as they communicate a condemnation of her conduct.[12] Criminal convictions and symbolic punishments aim to communicate the condemnation which it is, on this account, the central purpose of punishment to communicate: why then should punishment take the form of hard treatment; why is *this* the most appropriate mode of communication?

It may be said that only thus will we *effectively* communicate our condemnation to the criminal; or that formal convictions and purely symbolic punishments do not *adequately* express the appropriate response to her wrong-doing.[13] To which it may be replied that what this actually reveals is the need to relate the expressive purpose of punishment to a consequentialist account of punishment as a means of reducing crime, or to a retributivist account of punishment as the infliction of deserved suffering; that punishment's

---

[10] On 'hard treatment' see Feinberg, 'The Expressive Function of Punishment'.

[11] See Walker, 'Punishing, Denouncing, or Reducing Crime'; 'The Ultimate Justification'.

[12] See ch. 5 above; also I Dilman, *Morality and the Inner Life* 71–2; Feinberg, 'The Expressive Function of Punishment'.

[13] See Lucas, *On Justice* 132–6; Moberly, *The Ethics of Punishment* 140–2.

expressive function can be no more than an aspect of one of these primary functions.

Some who portray punishment as expressive have taken this route. Feinberg, for instance, while insisting that we can understand punishment only if we recognise its expressive function, is equally insistent that we need to justify the use of hard treatment as our preferred mode of expression; and his reference to 'the relation of the expressive function of punishment to its various central purposes' (which he takes to include deterrence, reform and rehabilitation) suggest that the use of hard treatment is to be justified by reference to these 'central purposes'.[14] A consequentialist who wishes to justify punishment in primarily deterrent terms could thus argue that hard treatment serves both to express our condemnation of the criminal's conduct, which might itself dissuade some potential criminals, and to provide a more effective prudential deterrent for those who are insufficiently impressed by mere condemnation. And a retributivist could argue that hard treatment serves both to express our justified condemnation and to exact from the criminal the debt of suffering which he owes to his fellow-citizens.

Indeed, there is surely some tension between the claim that the *primary* purpose of punishment is expressive and the use of hard treatment as the primary method of punishment. For if the primary purpose of punishment is to communicate to the criminal our condemnation of her conduct, the suffering which punishment is meant to cause her must, like that which moral blame aims to induce in a moral wrong-doer, be the pain of recognised guilt. She should understand that, and why, she is being condemned, and make that condemnation her own; she should be pained not merely by the fact that she is condemned, but by the fact that she deserves to be condemned – by her own guilt. The pain which expressive punishments aim to inflict or induce – the pain which wrong-doers deserve to suffer – must be mediated by the criminal's own understanding of the condemnation which they express.[15]

Now purely symbolic punishments fit this picture. We may know that some criminals will in fact be pained by such punishments, if at all, only insofar as they generate further and independently undesirable consequences, such as the loss of job opportunities or the hostility of others; and the prudential incentives for obedience to the law which such further consequences may

[14] Feinberg, 'The Expressive Function of Punishment' 101.
[15] See ch. 2(5) above; Dilman, *Morality and the Inner Life* 71–2; Winch, 'Ethical Reward and Punishment'.

offer opens the way to a manipulative use of symbolic punishments as deterrents. Their essential and proper purpose, however, is not to provide such prudential deterrents to crime, but to bring the criminal to recognise the wrongfulness of her past conduct; to induce the kind of pain which flows from an understanding of the condemnation which they express.

But matters are surely quite different when punishment takes the form of hard treatment: for the suffering which such punishments most obviously and directly cause is independent of their communicative meaning. My understanding of the expressive meaning of my imprisonment (of its character as punishment) will, of course, alter both my understanding of that imprisonment and the nature of the suffering which it causes me: whether I think my punishment just or unjust, I will experience it differently from someone who sees it merely as coercive detention.[16] But imprisonment and the like are painful independently of any expressive meaning which they may have: so is this not liable to distract the offender from their expressive meaning, rather than reinforcing it? And must we not now suspect that the reason for imposing hard treatment on criminals is not to ensure that they suffer the pain of condemnation and remorse, but rather to supplement that pain (in case the criminal does not come to feel it as he should) by some further pain which is to serve as a deterrent or as retribution? If this suspicion is well-founded, however, we can no longer claim that the primary purpose of such punishments is expressive.

Rewards raise a similar problem. If a reward is purely symbolic (a medal or a title, for instance) we can plausibly say that its primary purpose is expressive: it aims to please the recipient by expressing to her our gratitude or admiration; the pleasure which it aims to induce is the pleasure of being justly praised for what one has done; it focuses our and her attention – where it should be focused – on the worth of the action which is rewarded, and offers an appropriate and relevant incentive for performing such actions. Once we give a reward a material content which can be valued or desired independently of its communicative purpose, however, we create the danger that it will be used or received in the wrong spirit, and the suspicion that we replace the purely symbolic by the material in order to provide a bribe – an irrelevant prudential reason for action. (Even symbolic rewards can of course be used or received corruptly, as bribes, if attention is focused on such further benefits as they may bring, or on the pleasure of being praised rather than on the

[16] A point emphasised by Winch in 'Ethical Reward and Punishment'.

justice of the praise; but they are then used or received improperly.) If we offer a financial reward for some noble action, or express our gratitude through some material gift, we may distract attention from the reward's expressive purpose; and we must suspect that our motive is not merely to express our gratitude or admiration – that such rewards are, in intention or in fact, corrupting (we must of course distinguish rewards from repayments; my comments here are not directed against attempts to reimburse a benefactor for such costs as she incurred in helping me).

But yet – this *need* not be the case with a material reward: it *can* be offered and received as nothing other than an expression of gratitude or admiration; my intention in offering it may be simply that this will provide a more persuasive token of my feelings, and that it should be received in just this spirit.[17] So could we not still insist that punishment, even when it takes the form of hard treatment, can and should have a purely or primarily expressive purpose?

We should of course be more worried by the imposition of painful punishments than by the offering of pleasing rewards. We may feel too that in a more perfect world rewards would not take such a material form: perhaps the feeling that rewards should take a material form still reflects a corrupt belief that I should benefit materially from my good deeds (that virtue is not its own reward).[18] But the crucial question now is this. What sense can we make of the claim that hard treatment makes our condemnatory communication more effective, other than that it adds a prudential deterrent which is not provided by formal convictions or by purely symbolic punishments; that it aims not only to bring the criminal to recognise and repent his wrong-doing, but to offer him a prudential deterrent against repeating it? Or what sense can we make of the claim that hard treatment expresses more adequately the condemnation which crime warrants, other than that it also imposes some *further* suffering which the criminal supposedly deserves? For without an adequate answer to this question we cannot justify punishments which involve hard treatment by claiming that their primary or essential purpose is expressive.

The central problem here concerns the relationship between the pain or suffering involved in hard treatment and the kind of pain which expressive punishment is meant to induce in the criminal.

[17] Compare Lucas, *On Justice* 133.
[18] Compare Moberly, *The Ethics of Punishment* 158ff; S Kierkegaard, *Purity of Heart* ch. 4.

Consider, for instance, the suggestion that punishment serves to impose on the criminal the pain of remorse which she ought to impose on herself: we must inflict hard treatment on criminals who are not adequately pained by remorse in order to ensure that they still suffer the pain which they ought to suffer.[19] The trouble with this suggestion is that the pain which the criminal ought to suffer cannot be identified independently, as a contingent effect, of her remorseful recognition of her own wrong-doing; it takes its meaning and its identity from that recognition. But it follows from this that hard treatment *cannot* by itself inflict the pain which the criminal ought to suffer: for the pain which hard treatment inflicts on an unrepentant criminal is unrelated to any such remorseful recognition of guilt.

Or consider the suggestion that punishment serves to express our disapproval 'in a universal currency, capable of being appreciated by any and every man, no matter what his values are'. A criminal who 'is insensitive to the values of society, and is concerned only with his own interests', will not heed the condemnation which a conviction expresses, or 'acknowledge that what he has done was wrong': but by inflicting hard and unwelcome punitive treatment on him we can at least ensure that he will 'be forced to see that [what he has done] was from his point of view a mistake'. Punishment 'translates the disesteem of society into the value system of the recalcitrant individual'.[20] But how can this 'translation' preserve the meaning of that which it purports to translate? If I am dealing with a wrong-doer whose culture conventionally expresses condemnation by hand-clapping, I can communicate my condemnation to her by clapping my hands, thus translating it into a language which she will understand. She, however, receives and understands my clapping as a condemnation; we have yet to show how a punishment which the criminal receives and perceives merely as a coercive and unwelcome hindrance to her own interests can communicate to her the condemnation which we aim to express. Should we not rather say that in this case our condemnation has been translated out of existence?

Could we perhaps say that such punishments aim to bring home to the criminal the nature and implications of his crime? Punishment might be seen, for example, as a forcible exercise in universalising: we bring home to him the injury he has done to others, in fact rather than merely in imagination, by imposing on him what he

[19] See R J Lemos, 'A Defence of Retributivism'.
[20] Lucas, *On Justice* 133–4, 147.

244

will perceive as injurious to himself; by forcibly reminding him how he dislikes having his own interests injured, we try to get him to see more clearly the wrongness of injuring the interests of others. This need not involve a crude application of the Lex Talionis – an attempt to do to him something of the same material kind as that which he did to others: apart from the impracticality and inhumanity of many such attempts, the use of extreme violence or torture, for instance, against one who has treated others in this way would not address him as a moral agent whose *understanding* is to be engaged.[21] What we should impose on him, however, is a hindrance or injury proportionate to that which he inflicted on others.

This rather crude picture of punishment as an attempt to get the criminal to universalise his prescriptions is hardly satisfying: most criminals do not, after all, need to be reminded of what it is like to have their own interests hindered; and such an account implies an abstract conception of crime, as consisting essentially in some hindrance or injury to the interests of others which we can match or represent by a hindrance to the criminal's own interests, which is itself open to objection.[22] But this suggestion, and the two previous ones, point us in the right direction: they lead us to look beyond the simple claim that punishment serves to express condemnation, and to ask more carefully about both the content and the purpose of the communicative enterprise which punishment is meant to be. We need a richer and more subtle account of what punishment is meant to communicate to the criminal (a better understanding of the nature and implications of his crime); of why it should be so important to communicate this (because we hope that this will bring the criminal to repent his crime and thus enable him to restore those relationships which his crime threatened to injure or destroy); and of the part which hard treatment can properly play in this communicative and reformative endeavour (it serves as a penance which the criminal should ideally come to will for himself).

The material for this more adequate account of punishment as an essentially expressive or communicative enterprise has already been provided, in part, in my discussion of moral blame.[23] The central elements of the account can best be clarified by a further discussion of the idea of penance, and of the meaning of a formal system of penances in its familiar context of a religious community.

---

[21] See J G Murphy, 'Cruel and Unusual Punishments' 233–4.
[22] Compare ch. 8(2) above.   [23] See especially ch. 2(5)–(7) above.

I have talked already of penance as a kind of self-imposed punishment: some onerous task or painful deprivation which I undertake or accept because of the wrong which I have done. My penance expresses my recognition, my understanding and my repentance of my wrong-doing to God, whose will I have ignored and whose mercy I now seek; to those whom I have wronged, whose forgiveness I now seek; to the community whose values I have flouted, to which I wish to restore myself. Expressive penance stands to apology and confession as expressive punishment stands to a criminal conviction. In undertaking a penance I both own and disown my sin: I own it as mine – as a wrong which I have done; but I disown it as an act which I now condemn and repent.

But why should I express my repentance in this way, by imposing hard treatment on myself, rather than directly by apology and confession, or by a purely symbolic act? Is it simply, as Lucas suggests, because such a penance provides a persuasive proof of my sincerity – a 'disavowal of the values which the crime manifested, expressed in a way so costly that its sincerity cannot be impugned'?[24] This may be part of the reason: but there is more to a penance than the forceful expression of an already complete repentance.

A penance can assist and strengthen my repentant understanding of what I have done: it forces me to contemplate my sin, and the values I have flouted, rather than being distracted by the other interests and concerns which usually fill my life, and provides a focus and stimulus for my penitent attention. But my attention is not simply focused on my past sin: penance looks to the present, since I must realise that my sin was not merely the aberrant act of a past and separate self, but the manifestation of a vice which is still part of me; and it looks to the future, since it is through my penance that I hope to reform myself and restore my relationships with those from whom my sin has sundered me.

A sincere repentance of my wrong-doing involves a sincere desire to reform myself. I recognise and am distressed by the harm which I have done to others. I see that I have harmed myself, by injuring my relationships with others – by separating myself from God or the Good; from those whom I have directly wronged; from other members of the community whose values I have betrayed; and from myself as someone who truly desires good rather than evil. For I re-

---

[24] Lucas, *On Justice* 133.

alise that my true well-being (and thus the proper object of my desires) lies, not in those material or egoistical goods to which my wrong-doing showed me to be attached, but in a life lived in accordance with the values which I have betrayed, and within a moral community united by shared values and shared concerns for each other. Penance can help to focus my attention on this task of self-reform; it can solicit the assistance and the good will of others in this task, by expressing to them my repentant desire to disavow the wrong which I have done, and my determination to reform and restore myself. I might talk of trying to *purify* myself by a penance which helps to direct my attention away from the selfish and material concerns which led me to sin, towards the Good which I desire; or of *expiating* or *atoning* for my sin by a penance which imposes on me, in painful and material form, a kind of suffering which symbolically represents (and thus expresses my repentance of) the harm I have done to others and to myself.[25]

Penance, as self-imposed suffering which expresses and assists repentance, aims to reconcile the penitent wrong-doer with others and with herself. The particular form which my penance takes can express my understanding of the character of my sin, and of the nature of the Good from which it has separated me. A sin against God may be atoned for in private prayer and meditation; a wrong against another person, or against the community, may be expiated by some task which benefits that person or the community (although we must distinguish penance from restitution, the same task can serve both purposes); I may express my recognition of the way in which I have betrayed or injured my relationships with others by withdrawing into a penitential solitude. A penance will often involve depriving myself of some material or non-moral good (money, comfort, or some ordinary kind of pleasure or enjoyment): this can express my awareness of, and my concern for, the greater importance of the moral good which my wrong-doing implicitly denied; and my recognition that I should not be able to enjoy my ordinary pursuits and pleasures until I have considered and repented my sin.

A penance may be a private act which I conceive and undertake for myself: but it may have a more formal and institutional context, such as that of a church or religious community; and it may in that context be something which is required of me, or even imposed on me, by others. In the simplest kind of case I make my confession to a priest who, in virtue of the authority vested in him by God and by

[25] Compare Dilman, *Morality and the Inner Life* ch. 5; Morris, 'Guilt and Suffering'.

the church, specifies an appropriate penance for me. Both confession and penance are required of me, not merely suggested to me, by the church of which I am a member, and by God to whom I owe obedience and repentance: but there need be no human sanction against failure to perform the penance – no attempt to impose it on me against my will. If I fail to perform it, I might suffer the criticism of my priest or my fellows – but they might instead stay silent, believing it to be a matter between me and God. I might be told that I should not take part in the worship of the church until I have performed the penance – but it might also be left entirely up to me to make my confession, perform my penance, and exclude myself meanwhile from the services in which I should not take part.

But a failure to perform the penance which is appropriate must make a difference to my relationship with God: if my sin has separated me from God; if a penance is the proper way to seek His mercy and restore myself to Him; then a failure to perform the penance must preserve my separation from him. And since the church is a community of believers, bound together by their love of God and by their spiritual relationship to each other in God, my impenitent sinfulness must also injure my relationship with the church and with my fellows in the church: it separates me not just from God but from them. The church may thus naturally (though not inevitably) express such an understanding of the implications of my sin by excluding me from its services, from its holy places, or even from contact and communion with its members. So we find, in the history of the Christian church, detailed rules for such matters: rules requiring confession and penance before communion can be taken, and threatening excommunication against persistent, serious and unrepentant sinners; rules for the 'binding and loosing' of sinners, which specify the periods of exclusion (a physical exclusion from the church which symbolised the sinner's separation from God and from the community of the church) appropriate for different sins, and the penances which must be undertaken or undergone if the sinner was to be restored to communion with God and with the church.[26]

There was a continuing controversy within the Christian church about whether any sin was so serious that it required permanent excommunication; or whether any penitent, however serious his sin, should be offered a way back to communion with God and with the church. But it is clear that the church's response to most, if not

[26] On the history and meaning of penance, see especially J T McNeill, *A History of the Cure of Souls*; K Rahner, *Theological Investigations* vol. 2, 135–74, vol. 10, 125–49.

to all, sins was not simply one of expulsion. The sinner must be excluded (he had by his sin excluded himself) from full participation in the life and worship of the church: but he must be allowed, encouraged and helped to restore himself, through penance, to a full communion with God and with the church; he was still to be treated and cared for as a member of the community.

Excommunication, like penance, is a kind of punishment – it could indeed be seen as part of the penitential process on which a sinner must embark; and the fear of excommunication would provide a powerful incentive to refrain from sin and to undertake penance. But neither excommunication nor penance are penalties which the church *attaches* to sin, either as prudential deterrents or as inflicting some further deserved suffering on the sinner. For such punishments are already implicit in his sin: in excommunicating him the church is recognising, and giving formal effect and expression to, the way in which he has by his sin *separated himself* from God and the church; in requiring a penance of him the church is showing him that this is what he must do to restore himself. Nor are such punishments to be seen merely as prudential deterrents: the potential sinner should indeed fear excommunication and the need to undergo penance – and this fear should dissuade him from sin; but what he should fear is the sin itself, whose nature and implications are represented in his excommunication and penance. He should fear the separation from God and his fellows which his sin itself entails; and it should be that fear (which itself expresses his love of God and his awareness that his own good lies in communion with God and the church) which deters him from sin and makes him welcome his penance as the way back to fellowship with God and man.

Such punishments as these would not, ideally, be coercive. For, ideally, a sinner will voluntarily make her confession, realising the importance of this for her relationship with God and for her own well-being; come to see for herself, with the help of her priest, the nature and implications of her sin; exclude herself from communion until she has undertaken an appropriate penance in the appropriate spirit; undertake that penance, and solicit readmission to the fellowship of the church. Nor does the church coerce her merely by *requiring* her to exclude herself from its services and to undertake a penance: for the satisfaction of these requirements could be left entirely up to her. But sinners will not always thus voluntarily obey the church's rules and requirements; and the church might then begin to *impose* them, by force, on recalcitrant sinners.

It might begin by forcibly excluding from its services an unrepentant sinner who refuses to exclude herself: but this need not be a kind of coercion which fails to respect the sinner's autonomy or her will. So long as the church can justify to the sinner its claim that she has by her sin made herself unfit or ineligible for participation in its services, in forcibly excluding her from those services it is simply defending itself against her unjustified intrusion. Such exclusions are, even if backed up by force, comparable to the loss of trust or friendship which a moral wrong-doer may suffer.

But what if the church goes further than this, and seeks to *impose* a penance on the sinner? The sinner would ideally undertake the penance for herself, because she sees that, and why, it is necessary. Or she might undertake it, not because she already understands and repents her sin, but because she is told that she should undertake it and hopes that, through the penance, she will come to a better understanding and a more genuine repentance of her sin. She still undertakes the penance voluntarily, because she accepts the authority of the church which requires it of her; because she has some understanding both of her sin and of the meaning of the penance; and because, even though she is at the moment disinclined to do penance, she believes that it is necessary if she is to restore herself to the community through a proper understanding and repentance of her sin. Suppose, however, that she refuses to undertake the penance which is prescribed for her; and that she is then forcibly subjected to solitary confinement, to a diet of bread and water, or even to physical beatings: could this be justified as an attempt to force her to undergo the penance which she ought to undertake for herself – and as an attempt which still expresses a proper concern and respect for her as a moral agent?

If such coercive measures are to be justified in these terms, several conditions must be satisfied. First, the sinner must be seen as a member of the church community – a community united by shared beliefs and values, within which her true spiritual well-being is to be found. Second, her sin must be seen to separate her from that community, and thus to be injurious to her: by flouting, and thus implicitly denying, the values which give the community its identity she has broken the bonds which tie her to the community and to God; she has separated herself from her own good. Third, in subjecting her to such coercive treatment (rather than, for instance, simply expelling her from the community) the aim must be not merely to inflict suffering on her, but to bring her, through her suffering, to understand and repent her sin; to accept her penance; and thus to restore herself to full communion with God and her fellows. Fourth, the coercion to which she is subjected must therefore aim to secure her understanding and her assent: if it is to be or become the penance which she needs to undertake, it must be (if not at first, then in the end) mediated by her own understanding and acceptance of its necessity.

This last point is crucial. If a penance is to have its proper meaning, it must be understood and willed as a penance by the sinner herself: if it is initially imposed on her against her express will, it can achieve its proper purpose only if she comes, through her subjection to it, to accept it for herself – to impose it on herself. For an outward penance must express an inward repentance: what is required of the sinner is not merely that she undergo some visible deprivation or suffering, or observe certain external forms, but that she do this in a proper spirit of penitential remorse. The imposition of suffering on an unrepentant or unwilling sinner can be justified in these penitential terms only if it addresses her as a moral agent who can and should come to understand and repent her own sin, and will her own penance: for only then can it become a *penance*.

Now I do not claim that the actual treatment of sinners by the Christian church has always fitted this model. Churches are as prone to abuse their power as any other human institution; and the history of the Christian church is littered with coercive practices which cannot plausibly be justified as genuine and caring attempts to bring sinners to a repentant understanding of their sins. I claim only that we have here an *ideal* model of both voluntary and compulsory penance; a model which can be drawn from the doctrines of the church, and against which the actual practices of the church can be critically measured.

We can, I hope, understand the sense of a penance to which a sinner voluntarily submits himself, as a self-imposed punishment through which he can express his repentance and restore himself to the communion from which his sin separated him. We can also, I hope, see how an imposed penance could bring an initially unrepentant sinner to repentance. If the suffering to which he is subjected is imposed on him in the right way and in the right spirit it can bring home to him, as merely verbal or symbolic condemnation would not, the extent and nature of his sin. He is forced to attend to what he has done, by asking why he is being treated thus: he may thus grasp the communicative content of what is done to him; come to see and accept that he has sinned, and see how this penance can (given its expressive meaning) help to restore him; and come in this way to will his own penance as an appropriate stimulus and vehicle for his repentance.

But even if imposed penance can thus become voluntary penance; even if it can communicate to the sinner a better understanding of his sin, and bring him to repentance: is this enough to justify it? Or must we say that it is still a coercive and unwarranted infringement of his autonomy; that the church, while it may properly excommunicate a sinner and require him to undertake a penance, has no right to *force* that penance on him, or *coerce* him into a repentant understanding of his sin; and that in doing so the church is *using* him as a *means* to his own spiritual well-being? To this it may be replied that the idea of respecting the sinner's autonomy has no place in a doctrine of compulsory penance: a church which is ready to coerce its sinners in this way clearly does not regard them as autonomous agents, but as helpless victims of the flesh and the devil who need to be saved from sin and from themselves. An adequate treatment of these issues would require a fuller account of a church's authority over its members; of its proper interest in their spiritual well-being; and of the conception of sin which might inform its treatment of them. I will not offer such an account here, since my primary concern is with a state's right to impose punishments on its citizens; but two further relevant points may be noted.

First, the church may wish to claim that the imposition of penance on a recalcitrant sinner is still in accordance with her own will (it might thus distinguish, for instance, the coercion of a member of the church from the coercion of someone who is not and never has been a member). This claim could be sustained by showing that she joined the community by a voluntary act of allegiance, such as the taking of vows; or that, though she did not join the community voluntarily (being simply born into it), she still wishes to remain a member of it; or perhaps that, despite her present recalcitrance, she retains a fundamental regard for the authority of the church, for the values which define it, and for her membership of it. For in entering or wishing to remain within the church she explicitly or implicitly accepts its rules, and submits herself to its disciplinary procedures. In imposing penance on her against her presently expressed and sinful will, the church can thus claim to be acting in accordance with her authentic will to remain a member of the community and an obedient servant to God. Indeed, if her enforced penance does bring her to repentance she will herself assent to it, as having been in accordance with her true will. She might then say with Paul, 'the good that I would I do not: but the evil which I would not, that I do',[27] and be thankful that she has been saved from sin.

The imposition of penance on a sinner who does not thus accept the authority or values of the church cannot of course be justified in this way: an appeal to what she 'really' wills cannot depend on what she has avowed (or will avow, since she might remain unrepentant) as her will. The church might appeal instead to the good will which is buried within her soul, and which must be freed from the bonds of sin; and such an appeal may have some content – some connection to her actual life and concerns – insofar as she is or was a genuine member of the community of the church. Now no such appeal to the sinner's (actual or supposed) will is by itself sufficient to render the imposition of penance consistent with a respect for her autonomy: when I stopped Jane drinking, I acted in accordance with her previously expressed will; but I still infringed her autonomy.[28] However, and secondly, we may still be able to show that the imposition of penance is consistent with a respect for her autonomy, insofar as it still addresses her as a rational moral agent.

When penance is imposed on her, she is certainly coerced: she is forced to suffer something painful; and this suffering is meant to force her attention onto what should concern her – her own sin and its implications. But she is not, or need not be, *manipulated*, if the penance to which she is subjected still appeals to her understanding and seeks her acceptance of the relevant reasons which justify the claim that she ought to repent her sin and accept her penance. For her imposed penance then still addresses her as a rational moral agent: it seeks to engage and arouse, but not to manipulate or coerce, her understanding and her judgment; it leaves her free to reject the judgment and the understanding which it seeks to communicate to her. If this is the character of her penance, she is not being used merely as a means; nor is that penance related to the repentant understanding which it seeks to arouse as a contingent means to a further end – it is related to that end as moral blame is related to the repentant recognition of guilt at which it aims.[29]

If the imposition of penance is to be justified in such terms as these, it must be justified as a warranted response to the sinner's own wrong-doing – a response which attempts to bring her to see and to accept for herself the nature of what she has done, and the need to undergo penance because of it. If this response is not to be manipulative, its character and content are clearly crucial: the

[27] *Romans* vii. 19.   [28] See ch. 8(3) above.   [29] See ch. 2(3) above.

infliction, for instance, of extreme physical suffering, or of certain kinds of extreme psychological pressure, must surely count as an attempt to coerce the sinner's will and consent, rather than as an appeal to her understanding.[30] But my point here is simply this: that the demand that we respect the autonomy of others (which includes the demand that we should not manipulate them) may be interpreted, not as forbidding us to impose any kind of coercion on a person against his will, but as forbidding (particularly and especially) the use of coercive measures which aim to coerce or manipulate his will – measures which do not try to justify themselves to him by appealing to his understanding, and by seeking his rational assent.[31]

The sense and implications of this possibility can best be explained in the context of criminal punishment, to which we must now return.

5 PUNISHMENT, PENANCE AND RECONCILIATION

The idea of penance helps us to understand the sense of a voluntary or self-imposed punishment: a criminal who repents her crime (or who is brought by her trial and conviction to repent it) might request punishment, or accept it willingly, as a penance. Now we could imagine a legal system which required and facilitated, but did not enforce, such penances: its courts would convict offenders, specify appropriate penances for them, and provide suitable facilities for those penances; but it would be left up to the offender to submit herself for her penitential punishment. Even in a just system of law, however, it is unlikely that all offenders would submit thus voluntarily to punishment; and the *imposition* of punishment on recalcitrant offenders is a central feature of legal systems like our own: so we must ask whether such coercive punishments can be explained and justified as compulsory penances.

We may begin with the idea of a society, not simply as a collection of discrete and separate individuals (who could have no *common* good or common concerns), but as a *community* whose laws serve and preserve its common good, and of which the criminal is a member. Now a liberal society must accept and encourage a plurality of individual interests and values: but if it is to exist as a community at all its members must (as a matter of logic, not merely of pragmatic necessity) share a regard for certain central values, and a

---

[30] Compare Murphy, 'Cruel and Unusual Punishments' 233.
[31] See also ch. 8(3) above.

concern for each other as members of the community. This is not to say that an analytical or metaphysical inquiry could reveal some unique and univocal set of values which are necessary to the existence of any and every community: but any community must depend on (and is in part defined by) a shared allegiance to *some* core of values; and it is these values which the community's laws must declare and support.[32]

If a community's laws are just, a crime against those laws is injurious to the community. A criminal injures the direct victims of his crime (if there are any); he flouts the duty of care or respect which he owes to them as fellow-members of the community. But he also injures the community itself: he injures its common good by injuring any of its members; he implicitly denies or rejects the values on which the community depends; he damages or destroys his relationships both with those whom he directly injures and with other members of the community, by implicitly denying the values on which those relationships depend.

One who breaks the law in such a community makes himself liable to the criticism and condemnation of his fellows; and this condemnation may be given formal expression through a system of criminal trials and convictions. If his crimes are serious and persistent, the community might even (were this practicable) be justified in expelling him: for, we might say, he has disqualified himself from membership of the community by thus denying the values on which the community itself (and thus his membership of it) depend. But what can justify us in imposing on him a punishment which serves, not as a measure of self-defence against his criminal attack (since it follows his crime); nor simply as an expressive condemnation of his crime (since that is achieved by his conviction); nor as a purely preventive or deterrent measure (since that would deny him the respect which is his due as a rational agent); nor as a penance which he must undergo *if* he wishes to remain in the community (since he is given no choice in the matter); but as a compulsory penance which aims to bring him to repent his crime and thus to reform himself?

What is wrong with expelling a criminal is that it expresses no concern for *him* as a member, albeit a recalcitrant member, of the community; it simply excludes him from the community and its

[32] See D N MacCormick, 'Against Moral Disestablishment'; P Winch, 'Nature and Convention': also J Finnis, *Natural Law and Natural Rights* ch. 6; Morris, 'A Paternalistic Theory of Punishment'; P F Strawson, 'Social Morality and Individual Ideal'; H L A Hart, *The Concept of Law* ch. 9.2.

concerns. What is essential to the justification of punishment as compulsory penance is that, by contrast, it expresses a continuing concern for the criminal as a member of the community: he has injured himself, as well as others, by his crime; and his punishment will, if it is administered and received in the appropriate spirit, help him to repair that injury.

But how can we say that the criminal is injured by his crime – especially if, in terms of the interests and values which he actually avows, and which he may share with his immediate friends and colleagues, he is injured by breaking the law only if and because he is punished for it? The claim that he is injured by his crime follows directly from a certain understanding of the wrongfulness of that crime. When Plato or Kierkegaard argue that a wrong-doer is necessarily harmed by his wrong-doing, their claim is not that his wrongful deeds will produce contingent effects which he himself will, in the end, see to be harmful to him; indeed, the sinner who never realises his wretched state is in the most wretched condition of all. Their claim is rather that what matters above all in a person's life – and what *should* matter to him above all – is his relation to the Good: his well-being is to be *defined* in terms of that relation; one who is separated from the Good suffers by that very separation the worst harm which could befall him, whether he realises it or not.[33]

A more modest and secularised version of the Platonic claim would be this. A person can find well-being only within a community which is, necessarily, structured by certain shared values and concerns, and within the kinds of relationship which such a community makes possible. A criminal who flouts the just laws of her community thereby injures herself: she separates herself from the values on which the community and her own well-being depend; she damages or destroys her relationships with other members of the community, and separates herself from them. She may not in fact be made consciously unhappy by her crime (especially if she avoids punishment); she may attain the ends which she actually pursues, and lead the kind of life she enjoys; and her crime may in fact be consistent with her actual relationships with others (she has no concern for those whom she robs or attacks; her family and friends share her criminal attitudes and goals). But this shows only that she, and those with whom she lives, have turned away from the values which should concern them; that they fail or refuse to see how such criminal pursuits are inconsistent with the existence of a

---

[33] See Plato, *Gorgias* and *Republic*; Kierkegaard, *Purity of Heart*: also Dilman, *Morality and the Inner Life* ch. 4; D Z Phillips and H O Mounce, *Moral Practices* chs. 3–4.

community within which any worthwhile human life is possible; and that their relationships are themselves corrupted by false values. If she would only recognise the moral truth about her criminal attitudes and activities, she would see how they are injurious to her true well-being.[34]

The claim that the criminal is harmed by her crime is thus a moral rather than an empirical claim: it concerns the moral implications of her crime for her life as a member of the community, and the moral foundations of that community and the relationships within it, rather than the contingent effects of her crime on herself or on those around her. Note too that this claim concerns the nature and implications of crime in a genuine community, which is held together by bonds of mutual concern and respect for the shared values which are expressed in its just laws. I will have more to say later about the implications of crime in a society which is not thus a genuine community.

A repentant criminal recognises the implications of her crime, and the harm it has done to others and to herself; and she may hope by her penance to express her remorseful understanding of her crime, and to restore her relationships with the rest of the community. She sees her penance as a benefit to herself; and, just as the harm done to her by her crime is internal to the crime, as a matter of its moral implications, so too is the benefit which her penance brings her internal to its moral character as a penance. She might find that others are in fact self-righteously unforgiving; that despite her genuinely penitential remorse they continue to shun or ostracise her as someone who has disqualified herself from membership of the community: but the fault then lies in them and their response to her penance. She is injured by such a response, but she has still benefited in and by her penance: it has reconciled her to the values which should inform her life and her relationships with others, and has thus restored a proper moral basis for those relationships.

If the imposition of punishment on an unrepentant criminal is to be justified as a compulsory penance, it too must claim to reconcile him to the Good and to other members of the community, and thus to benefit him; and this benefit must likewise be internal to his punishment, at least in the sense that it does not depend (or does not depend entirely) on the actual effect of his punishment on *others*. Even if he is now shunned both by his former criminal colleagues

---

[34] Compare also S Weil, *The Need for Roots*; Morris, 'Guilt and Suffering' and 'A Paternalistic Theory of Punishment'; Finnis, *Natural Law and Natural Rights* 264; A I Melden, *Rights and Persons* 181–4.

and by the self-righteously law-abiding we must be able to say, with Socrates, that it is better for him to have been punished than to have escaped punishment;[35] because he has still been reconciled to the Good. But can this benefit also be independent of his punishment's actual effect on *him*; or does he benefit only if he in fact comes to repent his crime and accept his punishment as a penance?

Hegel's account is instructive here. Punishment serves to annul past crimes –

The sole positive existence which the injury possesses is that it is the particular will of the criminal. Hence to injure this particular will as a will determinately existent is to annul the crime, which otherwise would have been held valid, and to restore the right.[36]

Crime is a form of coercion which denies its victim's freedom and rights; which thus infringes the right as right: this infringement must be annulled by a punishment which coerces the criminal's own will. But punishment is also the criminal's right: it honours and accords with his implicit will as a rational being.

Objectively, [punishment] is the reconciliation of the law with itself; by the annulment of the crime the law is restored and its authority is thereby actualized. Subjectively, it is the reconciliation of the criminal with himself, i.e. with the law known by him as his own and as valid for him and his protection: when this law is executed upon him, he himself finds in this process the satisfaction of justice and nothing save his own act.[37]

Punishment reconciles the criminal with himself – as a rational agent who wills the law: but how does it do this? Are we to say, as Hegel seems to imply, that this reconciliation is *necessarily* intrinsic to the very fact of just punishment: that even if he actually sees his punishment as nothing more than a coercive imposition, it necessarily reconciles him with himself; that even if he is unaware of any 'satisfaction' in his punishment, it is a satisfaction which he must find as a rational agent who wills the law?

Now it is true that the satisfaction which penance brings to the penitent, and the reconciliation which it secures, are internal to the penance itself, not contingent effects of it. But it is also true that that satisfaction and that reconciliation involve the penitent's own understanding: he is satisfied and reconciled because the pain of his penance expresses his painful awareness of the wrong he has done. How then can a punishment which the criminal sees merely as co-

[35] Plato, *Gorgias* 472–3, 476–80.   [36] G W F Hegel, *Philosophy of Right* s. 99.
[37] *Ibid.* s. 220.

ercive, which does not involve his own repentant understanding of his wrong-doing (and which thus cannot be a *penance*),[38] reconcile him with himself, or with the Right? To tell him that, whether he realises it or not, his punishment does thus reconcile and satisfy him implies an objectification of his 'real' or rational will, and a discounting of his actual response to his punishment, which is both problematic in itself and inconsistent with the claim that his punishment respects *him*, the actual criminal, as a rational agent.[39]

Perhaps, therefore, we should follow McTaggart's reading of Hegel. The purpose of punishment, like that of a penance which is imposed on a recalcitrant sinner, is to bring the criminal to understand the nature and implications of her crime; to repent that crime; and *thus*, by willing her own punishment as a penance which can expiate her crime, to reconcile herself with the Right and with her community.[40]

Such a conception of punishment as a communicative and reformative endeavour has a long history. It appears in Plato: both in the more practically oriented discussion of *The Laws*, according to which punishment should serve a reformative as well as a deterrent function –

to bring the criminal and all who witness his punishment in the future to complete renunciation of such criminality, or at least to recover in great part from the dreadful state;[41]

and in the *Gorgias* and *Republic*, in the claim that punishment aims to cure the wrong-doer's soul of its unjust and disordered condition.[42] It is found too in Kierkegaard –

But if he has done wrong, then he must, if he really wills one thing and sincerely wills the Good, desire to be punished, that the punishment may heal him just as medicine heals the sick;[43]

and in Simone Weil –

Punishment is solely a method of procuring pure good for men who do not desire it. The art of punishing is the art of awakening in a criminal, by pain or even death, the desire for pure good.[44]

---

[38] See ch. 9(4) above.   [39] See ch. 8(3) above.

[40] J M E McTaggart, *Studies in Hegelian Cosmology* ch. 5; see also P Bean, *Punishment* 47–53.

[41] Plato, *The Laws* XI, 934.

[42] I will not pursue the problems of Platonic interpretation here: contrast Dilman, *Morality and the Inner Life* ch. 5, with M M Mackenzie, *Plato on Punishment*.

[43] Kierkegaard, *Purity of Heart* 70 (and ch. 5 generally).

[44] S Weil, 'Human Personality' 31; see also *The Need for Roots* 20–1. See also F Dostoevsky, *Crime and Punishment* – discussed by Dilman, *Morality and the Inner Life* ch. 5.

We may find elements of such a view in, for instance, the early Quaker view of imprisonment as the appropriate mode of punishment: prison removes the criminal from his corrupting peers, and provides the opportunity for and the stimulus to a reflective self-examination which will induce repentance and self-reform.[45] One could also cite the importance attached in some societies to the condemned man's acceptance of and participation in his own execution: he was urged to confess his crimes, and to play the penitential part assigned to him in the formal process of execution; for this would express his recognition of the justice of his punishment, and enable him to made his peace with God and with man.[46] The condemned prisoner in classical Athens was expected to drink the fatal hemlock himself: not so that he might by committing suicide avoid the pain or indignity of being executed by others; but so that he might participate in, express his consent to, and will his own punishment.[47]

Punishment is, on this conception, communicative, retributive and reformative. It is communicative in that it seeks to communicate to the criminal a proper understanding of his crime: by imposing on him some material injury which can be seen as injurious even through the eyes of egoistical self-interest, we hope to represent, and to force on his attention, the harm he has done both to others and to himself; by imprisonment, which separates him physically from the rest of the community, we give material and symbolic expression to the spiritual separation created by his crime. It is retributive in that it is a response to his past crime whose meaning lies in the judgment on, and the condemnation of, that crime which it seeks to communicate; and whose aim is to bring the criminal to suffer the pain of remorse which he ought to feel when he considers his crime. And it is reformative in that it aims to bring the criminal, through his understanding of his crime and his punishment, to repent his crime; to accept his punishment as an appropriate vehicle for his repentance; and thus to reform himself – to reconcile himself to the values which his crime denied and to the community to which he belongs.

This is the proper punitive purpose of hard treatment – a purpose which would not be so well served by purely formal convictions or symbolic punishments. It serves in part to make our communicative

---

[45] See Morris, *The Future of Imprisonment* 4–5.
[46] See, for instance, M Foucault, *Discipline and Punish* 38–45; also ch. 1(1) above.
[47] See Plato, *Phaedo*; R F Holland, 'Suicide'; R A Duff, 'Socratic Suicide?'.

endeavour more effective, forcing the criminal's attention onto the implications of his crime; he cannot ignore it as easily as he can ignore or forget a conviction or a purely symbolic punishment. But it should serve too – if it is successful – as a penance which the criminal comes to will for himself: the pain or suffering which begins as a coercive attempt to attract and direct the unrepentant criminal's attention should become the penitential pain which the repentant criminal accepts for himself.

We must be clear about the meaning of this claim that punishment serves a reformative purpose. The claim is not simply that punishments such as imprisonment provide, as a side-effect, the opportunity for some further reformative treatment; but rather that punishment itself, as punishment, should reform the criminal.[48] Nor is the claim that punishment is an *efficient technique* for bringing about some desirable change in the criminal's attitudes and conduct, to be compared with other psychological or physiological techniques for manipulating attitudes and behaviour as an instrumental means towards some independently identifiable further end. The claim that punishment aims at the offender's spiritual reform is quite different from, for instance, the claim that criminals are mentally disordered individuals who need psychiatric treatment; or that the proper purpose of punishment is the efficient modification of the criminal's behavioural patterns.[49]

It is true that some, like Plato and Kierkegaard, talk of punishment as an attempt to *cure* the criminal's soul of its spiritual *disorder*: but talk of a person's soul is not to be confused with talk of her psychological states; and the cure of souls is not to be confused with the cure or treatment of psychiatric disorders. To say that a criminal is spiritually sick or disordered is to offer a moral comment on the values which do, as contrasted with those which should, inform her life and her relationships with others, not an empirical diagnosis of some impairment in her rational capacities.[50] To say that we need to punish her in order to cure her soul is not to say that we need to subject her to some technique which will efficiently modify her attitudes or conduct, and that punishment is in fact the most efficient available technique for this purpose: it is rather to say that she should, for the sake of her moral well-being, come to understand and repent her wrong-doing; and that punishment is the appropriate

---

[48] See A C Ewing, *The Morality of Punishment* 73–4.
[49] See Hampton, 'The Moral Education Theory of Punishment'.
[50] See I Dilman, 'Wittgenstein on the Soul'.

stimulus to, vehicle for, and expression of such a repentant understanding. For punishment, like moral blame, is related logically
rather than merely contingently to the end at which it aims: it aims
at a kind of reform which must involve the criminal's repentant understanding of her past crime; and it is that understanding which
punishment, as a communicative and penitential enterprise, aims to
arouse and express.

This is not to say that punishment (if justly and properly administered) must of logical necessity achieve its purpose – that its end is
in *that* sense internal to it: punishment may in fact fail to bring a
criminal to repent her crime; and it then fails to achieve the end at
which it properly aims. Nor is it to say that there are no technical
questions involved in the administration of punishment: we must
investigate the actual effects on criminals of different kinds and
styles of punishment and ask, among other questions, which of
them will most efficiently serve their communicative and penitential purposes. But it is not a contingent matter that punishment – the
infliction of suffering on an offender for her offence – is the appropriate way of trying to achieve the kind of penitential reform which
is its justifying aim: that aim can, of its nature, be achieved only by
bringing the offender to suffer for what she has done. If someone
suggested, for instance, that we might hope to develop some kind of
drug or psycho-surgical technique which would provide a more efficient and less painful method of securing the kind of reformative
change at which punishment aims, we would not need to question
the empirical plausibility of her suggestion: for the suggestion itself
is incoherent. No such technique could, logically, produce the results at which punishment aims: such techniques do not address the
criminal, as punishment must address her, as a responsible moral
agent who can and should come to understand the moral implications of what she had done; they are not, as punishment must be,
attempts to solicit and arouse her repentant understanding of her
crime; and the acquisition of such an understanding must of its
nature be painful to the criminal.[51]

6 THE RIGHT TO BE PUNISHED

If we understand punishment in these terms, we can see that its purposes are strictly continuous with those of the criminal law and the
criminal trial (and with those of moral blame). It addresses the

[51] Compare J Teichman, 'Punishment and Remorse'; Morris, 'A Paternalistic
Theory of Punishment'.

criminal as a rational moral agent, seeking his understanding and his assent; it aims to bring him not merely to obey the law, but to accept its requirements as being justified: to recognise the wrongness of what he has done, to make his own the condemnation which his conviction expresses, and to guide his future conduct in the light of the relevant moral reasons which the law, his trial and his punishment all offer him for obeying the law. It treats him not merely as a passive victim or subject *on* whom suffering is to be imposed, but as a moral agent *with* whom we are engaged in a communicative process of argument and persuasion – it seeks his participation, not merely his submission: for its aim is that he should come to make the punishment, and the repentant understanding which it expresses, his own.

A sane offender has a *right* to be punished: a right to be punished rather than be subjected to some kind of manipulative or preventive treatment which would not address him as a rational agent; and a right to be punished rather than be ignored or dismissed, since his punishment expresses a proper response to his crime as the wrong-doing of a responsible moral agent, and a proper concern for his moral well-being as a fellow-member of the community. We owe it to him, as well as to those whom he has injured, to condemn his crime and to try to bring him to repentance and reform. But an offender who is now so disordered that she cannot understand or respond appropriately to her punishment is not fit to be punished. If she *cannot* grasp the communicative character of her punishment as a response to her past offence; or come through her punishment to feel the pain of remorse which it is meant to arouse in her; or come to accept her punishment as an appropriate penance for her past offence: her punishment cannot be justified – it cannot properly count – as a punishment, and becomes instead nothing more than mere coercion. For if punishment is to be more than mere coercion, it must be justified *to* the person on whom it is imposed, as a penance which she should come to accept and will for herself.

This means that an offender who is to be fit to be punished, like a defendant who is to be fit to be tried, must be capable not only of grasping the *fact* that what is being done to her is done because she has broken the law, but also of grasping and responding to its *moral* meaning and purpose as a punishment. She must have the capacity and the potential for the kind of penitential redemption which punishment aims to induce: which means that she must already have some concern, which punishment may reawaken and strengthen, for the values which she has flouted; or at least that she has some moral concerns which would enable her to come, through her punishment, to understand and care for the values which the law embodies. If she is, for instance, a psychopath who cannot understand her punishment as anything more than a coercive imposition which is provoked by her refusal to obey our demands on her, we cannot properly punish her. Nor, I think, can we properly punish an offender who is now suffering from amnesia which covers the time of her offence: for if she is cut off by her amnesia from truly recognising and acknowledging that offence as her own, she cannot be brought by her punishment to repent and disown it.[52]

The justifying purpose of a punishment which is imposed on an as yet unrepentant criminal is to bring him to repent his crime, and to accept his punishment as an appropriate penance for his wrongdoing. A punishment may in fact fail to achieve this purpose; and it is indeed essential to the justification of punishment, as an attempt to persuade rather than to coerce the criminal's will and understanding, that it is thus fallible – that it leaves the criminal free to dissent, and to continue to dissent, from the law and from his punishment.[53] Now the fact that his punishment thus fails to achieve its purpose does not show that the criminal is unfit to be punished, as being *incapable* of coming to understand and accept his punishment. Not all unrepentant criminals (nor even all persistent and unrepentant criminals) are disordered psychopaths: we must recognise the existence both of the unrepentantly immoral criminal, who offers no principled defence of his actions but persists in flouting the law's moral demands, and of the principled rebel, who is determined to resist and oppose the values which the law embodies; the mere fact of such unrepentant criminality is not a sufficient criterion of psychopathic disorder.[54] Nor does the fact that his punishment has failed to persuade him to repent show by itself that we were not justified in punishing him. Though we must ask whether that failure might not have been due to some deficiency in the manner or the spirit in which the punishment was imposed on him, rather than to his own obstinacy, the failure of our attempt to persuade him does not by itself show that the attempt was not justified.

Suppose, however, that we are reasonably sure in advance that a

---

[52] See chs. 1, 4(6) above; also Moberly, *The Ethics of Punishment* 133–8. Morris claims ('A Paternalistic Theory of Punishment') that the criminal must already care for the values he has flouted: for reasons discussed in R A Duff, 'Psychopathy and Moral Understanding', I think this requirement is too stringent.

[53] See ch. 10(1) below.

[54] See Duff, *op. cit.*

particular criminal will not be persuaded or brought to repentance by his punishment: must we not then admit that we are not, on this account, justified in punishing him? For if the punishment which is now imposed on him against his unrepentant will is not going to accord in the end, as it should, with his repentant will; if it is not going to become a penance (a *self*-punishment) which he accepts for himself; if the suffering which it inflicts on him is not going to become, as it should, the penitential suffering of one who repents his crime: then surely in punishing him we are simply inflicting pointless suffering on him – or perhaps using him as a means to some other purpose.

It must be admitted that punishment brings no benefit to such a criminal:

> while punishment, which God in his wisdom has connected with every transgression, is a Good, there is no denying that it is such a Good only when it is gratefully received, not when it is simply feared as an evil.[55]

Indeed, it might be said that a punishment which fails to secure the criminal's penitential assent cannot, properly speaking, count as a punishment –

> Punishment only takes place where the hardship is accompanied at some time or another, even after it is over, and in retrospect, by a feeling of justice.[56]

But if a criminal never comes, even in retrospect, to see his punishment as anything other than an evil which is imposed on him, how can it be justified? Plato thought that a criminal who is indeed incurable – whose moral condition is such that we cannot hope to restore him, by punishment, to the Good – should either be killed, since he has no hope of well-being, or be punished simply as an example to others.[57] But we are not, I think, forced to accept this view: we can insist that punishment must be a communicative endeavour to bring the criminal to repentance, without thereby being required to exempt from punishment those whom it will not, we believe, bring to repentance; and without thereby being permitted simply to dispose of such people or to use them as means to our social ends.

So long as we believe that a criminal is a rational and responsible agent, who is thus capable of coming to understand and repent his crime, we have no right to treat him as Plato suggests. To kill him,

[55] Kierkegaard, *Purity of Heart* 81–2.
[56] Weil, *The Need for Roots* 21.
[57] Plato, *Gorgias* 512a, 525c; *The Laws* IX, 862c: see Mackenzie, *Plato on Punishment* ch. 11.

or to use him simply as a terrible example to others, or to refuse to punish him, on the grounds that he is beyond redemption, is to give up any respect or hope for him as a moral agent; and this we may not do. The point here is not that we can never have empirically adequate grounds for believing that punishment will not in fact bring a criminal to repentance: it is rather that we can never have *morally* adequate grounds – nothing could count as morally adequate grounds – for treating a person as being beyond redemption. We owe it to every moral agent to treat him as one who can be brought to reform and redeem himself – to keep trying, however vainly, to reach the good that is in him, and to appeal to his capacity for moral understanding and concern. To talk thus of 'the good that is in him' is not to make some psychological claim to the effect that he 'really' cares for the values which he flouts: it is rather to combine the conceptual claim that every moral agent has the capacity or potential for moral development and reform, with the moral claim that we should never give up hope of bringing him to actualise that potential.

This gives further substance to the idea that every responsible criminal has a right to be punished – though it may not be a right which she is keen to claim: but it may also bring to the boil a number of objections to this account of punishment which must have been simmering during this chapter – objections to which I will attend in the next chapter.

10

The Ideal and the Actual

.. [I]f the state allows its attention to be distracted in the humble task of frightening criminals from crime, by the higher ambition of converting them to virtue, it is likely to fail in both, and so in its fundamental object of diminishing crime.

J M E McTaggart,
Studies in Hegelian Cosmology, ch. V, para.145

But we have lost all idea of what punishment is. We are not aware that its purpose is to procure good for a man. For us it stops short with the infliction of harm. That is why there is one, and only one, thing in modern society more hideous than crime – namely, repressive justice.... All talk of chastisement, punishment, retribution, or punitive justice nowadays always refers solely to the basest kind of revenge.

S Weil, 'Human Personality', 31–2

In the previous chapter I outlined an ideal account of criminal punishment as a communicative enterprise in which we engage with the criminal. Punishment aims to express to her the condemnation which her crime warrants; to communicate to her a more adequate understanding of the nature and implications of her crime – the injury she has done to others and to herself; to persuade her to repent her crime, and to accept her punishment as a penance through which she can strengthen and express her repentant understanding and restore herself to the community from which her crime threatened to separate her: the proper purpose of punishment, on this view, is that it should become self-punishment – a penance which the criminal accepts and wills for herself.

I have tried to show how punishment – the infliction of suffering on a member of the community who has broken its laws – could ideally serve this communicative, reformative and penitential purpose; not that the actual punishments which criminals suffer in our own legal systems do serve this purpose. I have claimed too that this account of punishment (unlike, for instance, an account of punishment as a deterrent) shows its proper purposes to be continuous with those of the criminal law and the criminal trial; and shows that it expresses a proper concern and respect for the criminal as a fellow-member of the community. But even if we accept that punishment *could* ideally serve such a purpose; that it could, if properly administered and properly received within a just and authentic community, serve as a penance which enables criminals to understand, to repent and to expiate their crimes: such an account must face some serious objections.

Some of these objections concern its practical implications and applications. We must ask what kinds of punishment – what principles of sentencing – it would sanction, and whether these are acceptable. We must ask too whether we could in practice hope to institute and administer a system of criminal punishment which would be justified in these terms – and this question will force us to examine the extent and the implications of the gap between this ideal of just and proper punishment and the actual systems of punishment which we have or could in practice hope to have. I will turn to these issues later in this chapter: but we must first attend to a more fundamental objection, which attacks the ideal account of punishment itself rather than its practical applicability.

I OBJECTIONS AND CLARIFICATIONS

'You have noted already that it is the coercive dimension of punishment – the fact that it is imposed on a criminal against her will – that must most obviously concern anyone who takes seriously the demand that we should respect the autonomy of those with whom we deal: but you have not shown how the imposition of a purportedly communicative, reformative, and penitential punishment on an as yet unrepentant criminal can be consistent with, let alone expressive of, a proper respect for her as an autonomous moral agent. Granted that – *if* her punishment achieves its proper purpose – she will come to accept it for herself: is it not still true that, in imposing punishment on her against her present will, we are improperly coercing her; indeed that we are using her as a means to her own spiritual reform? We have in effect abandoned or compromised any attempt at rational persuasion, and instead use force to achieve our ends – to coerce her will into conformity with the law.

Indeed, punishments which aim at the criminal's moral reform actually constitute a more serious threat to his integrity, and a more serious infringement of his autonomy, than those which simply offer him a prudential deterrent. For a system of deterrent punishments aims simply to persuade the criminal to conform his external conduct to the law's demands: it leaves him free to disobey the law, if he is prepared to pay the price, and to maintain an inward and autonomous dissent from the law and its values. Deterrent punishment

> although unwelcome, is limited and external. It affords him and others a reason for not doing wrong, but does not impinge upon the inner citadels of his soul. We may hope that he will see the error of his ways and repent, but we do not insist.[1]

Reformative punishments, on the other hand, try to beat down the criminal's will – to coerce him, by physical pain or psychological pressure, into accepting the law and the values which it embodies.

Furthermore, by what right does the state take this kind of intrusive interest in the moral well-being of its citizens? It is one thing to say that the state should prescribe and enforce those minimal standards of conduct which are necessary for the survival and stability of a society in which individuals will be able to pursue their own autonomous projects: it is quite another to say that the state has either the right or the duty to impose on its citizens some particular conception of the good, or to coerce them into a state of supposed moral well-being. Should we not admit that the spiritual improvement of the offender, and the expiation or atonement of her crime, are matters which "must be left to the just determination of the supreme being",[2] and limit the state to the more modest and appropriate task of enforcing certain minimal standards of conduct?'

These objections can be met – and the meeting of them will also help to clarify some of the crucial aspects of this account of punishment.

They will not be met simply by claiming that in imposing punishment on a criminal we respect him by acting in accordance with his real or rational will; or that he must, as a criminal, be so corrupted by vice that he can no longer be addressed as a rational and autonomous agent – that he is instead a heteronomous victim of sin who must, for his own sake, be *dragged* back towards the Good.[3] We do, it is true, find language of this kind in some accounts of punishment as moral reform. Plato, for instance, argued that no one

---

[1] J R Lucas, 'Or Else' 235 (Lucas is contrasting deterrent punishments with purportedly therapeutic treatment); see also T Honderich, *Punishment: The Supposed Justifications* 90–3.

[2] Sir W Blackstone, *Commentaries on the Laws of England* IV.1; see also N Walker, *Sentencing in a Rational Society* 13.

[3] See ch. 8(3) above.

willingly does evil, since what everyone truly desires is the good: the wicked man commits his crimes from ignorance, in the mistaken belief that they will bring him well-being; in punishing him we try to cure him of his ignorance, and direct him towards what is truly his good – what he truly wants.[4] And Simone Weil says

Men who are so estranged from the good that they seek to spread evil everywhere can only be reintegrated with the good by having harm inflicted upon them. This must be done until the completely innocent part of their soul [that part which 'is on the deepest level and even in the most corrupt of men . . . remains from earliest infancy perfectly intact and totally innocent'] awakens with the surprised cry 'Why am I being hurt?' The innocent part of the criminal's soul must then be fed to make it grow until it becomes able to judge and condemn his past crimes and at last, by the help of grace, to forgive them.[5]

But we should not, I think, read either Plato or Simone Weil as arguing that the criminal is not a responsible agent who should be condemned, as well as pitied, for his crimes; or as claiming, in the way that Murphy claims, that his punishment accords with his real or rational will.

Certainly, on this account of punishment, the criminal is mistaken, and is the victim of his mistake. But his mistake is a moral one: he wills and pursues what is evil rather than what is good, and has a distorted perception of value; his will, his desires, his concerns are misdirected. And it is a 'mistake' for which he is to be blamed, as well as pitied: he has *turned away* from the good; he has *allowed himself* to be seduced into vice; he has *closed his eyes* to what is good – to the interests and needs of others, as well as to his own true good. (This of course presupposes some conception of free will – of sin as a *wilful* falling from grace: but I will not discuss that conception here, save to note that it must, and can, be compatible with the idea of original sin; the idea that we are inherently sinful beings who need help – grace – if we are to be saved.)

We may say that the criminal 'really' wants or wills the good: but we must be clear about the meaning of such a claim, and about its compatibility with the fact that some criminals are whole-heartedly committed to evil ends. If I say of myself, when I have done wrong, that what I did was not what I 'really' wanted or willed; that 'the

---

[4] See especially Plato, *Gorgias*, and the discussion in I Dilman, *Morality and the Inner Life*; I should make clear that in citing such writers as Plato and Simone Weil I am concerned not so much with providing a historically accurate interpretation of what they meant as with the construction of an acceptable account of criminal punishment.

[5] S Weil, 'Human Personality' 31.

good that I would I do not: but the evil which I would not, that I do';[6] I am indeed claiming that I have an actual concern and regard for the good. But in saying that it is what I really want I am not making a factual or empirical claim about the relative strength of my various desires; I am making a moral claim which expresses my recognition of what I *should* desire and value above all, and *condemning* the desires which led me to sin. So too I may say of another who does wrong that this is not what she really wants; and this will have some factual purchase insofar as we can find in her actual life and actions some concern for others or for the good. Even then, however, my claim is not a factual claim about the actual strength of her desires, but a moral claim about what she *should* care for – about what should be deepest and most important in her life; and this claim rests on a moral conception of human life in the light of which I criticise her actual life and concerns.[7]

Even if the wrong-doer is apparently totally and ruthlessly corrupt, I might still say that there is deep within her a perfectly innocent part of her soul, which we must try to reach; and this again is a moral claim about how we should respond to her. We should never see a person, or give up on her, as being beyond redemption: for to see her as a person – as a being with a soul – is to see her as someone who always has the potential for repentance and redemption. This is in part a conceptual claim about what it is to see someone as a person, and about the concept of the soul: but it embodies a profound moral claim about the kind of attitude which we should have towards others – and towards ourselves.[8]

The claim that the criminal really wills the good, and therefore wills his own punishment as a way of restoring him to the good, thus has its place and its meaning within the moral conception of human life and well-being which informs this account of punishment; it helps to explain the claim that punishment expresses a concern for the criminal himself. But surely, it may now be said, this simply reinforces (rather than meets) the objection that in imposing punishment on a criminal we are improperly coercing him: it shows that we are trying to force on him a particular moral conception, which he may not share, of his good.

[6] *Romans* vii. 19.

[7] Thus the claim that the wrong-doer 'really' desires the good may be compared with the claim that law must serve the common good (ch. 3(5) above), or that punishment must be of the guilty (ch. 6(1) above).

[8] Compare I Dilman, 'Wittgenstein on the Soul'; and Wittgenstein's comment that 'my attitude towards him is an attitude towards a soul'. I am not of the *opinion* that he has a soul', *Philosophical Investigations* Part II.iv: on that comment, and the meaning of 'attitude', see P Winch, 'Eine Einstellung zur Seele'.

Now it is easy to see how a purportedly reformative punishment could become an improperly coercive attempt to *beat down* the criminal's will; to coerce him into accepting the attitudes or beliefs which we want him to have, by whatever means may be effective: this indeed is one of the obvious dangers of an attempt to use punishment as a method of moral reform. We should note, however, that if punishment is used in this coercive and manipulative way, it ceases to be a method of moral reform. A process of moral reform must, logically, be mediated by the person's own understanding: its proper aim is that he should come to understand, and therefore to care for and to live by, the appropriate kinds of value; and a process which forces or manipulates his attitudes into conformity with some favoured set of values is not a possible way of achieving *that* end.[9]

But punishment which aims to induce repentance and self-reform need not have such a coercive and manipulative character: it can, and should, be an attempt to arouse and engage – but not to coerce – the criminal's understanding and his will. We try to draw his attention to the nature and implications of his crime; we try to persuade him to recognise and accept the relevant reasons which justify our condemnation of what he has done, and to see and accept his punishment as a penance; and we offer him a particular understanding of his crime and his punishment. But it is up to him to consider, to understand, and to come to accept the message which his punishment thus tries to communicate to him; it is for him to come to repent his crime and accept his punishment; and it is still open to him to refuse to do so. For it is crucial that his punishment, if it is to address him as a rational moral agent, should leave him this freedom to dissent – to remain unpersuaded and unrepentant. We hope and intend that he should come to accept his punishment, and the condemnation which it expresses; but we must leave him free to reject that condemnation, and to regard (and continue to regard) his punishment as nothing more than an unwarranted imposition. We try to reach 'the inner citadels of his soul': but we do not try to break down their gates; we rather try to persuade him to open those gates himself, and leave him free to keep them firmly closed.

This is not to deny or ignore the coercive dimension of punishment: it is imposed on the criminal against her will; she may see it as nothing more than a coercive imposition; the suffering which it causes her may be, as she perceives and receives it, unrelated to any

[9] See ch. 2(2)–(3) above.

repentant recognition of past wrong-doing. But it is to clarify the nature of the coercion which punishment must involve, and to show that punishment can be coercive without being manipulative: we try to make the criminal hear us; but we do not try to force her to believe or accept what we say. Now I could understand someone who claimed that such coercion is still incompatible with a proper respect for the criminal's autonomy and freedom, just as I can understand someone who claims that a proper respect for human life forbids *any* intentional killing, even in defence of oneself or of others: but just as I believe that I may properly kill an assailant to protect my own or others' lives against his wrongful attack, while still respecting and responding to him as an autonomous agent, I also believe that the coercive imposition of punishment on a criminal can be consistent with a respect for her autonomy.[10]

If someone has wronged me or another, I might try to make him hear – though I cannot and should not force him to accept – my criticism: I shout at him; I chase after him as he walks away; I stand in his way as he tries to leave. I force my criticism on his attention, knowing that he will initially perceive it only as an unwelcome and unfriendly intrusion, but hoping and intending that he will come to understand and accept it for what it is. A criminal is forced to attend her trial, in order that she may answer for her wrong-doing, and receive the condemnation which it warrants. She is not forced to answer for her actions, to play any part in her trial, or to accept her conviction – she is free to remain silent, and to reject the verdict and the condemnation which it expresses; but we force her into a position in which she will hear the charges, the trial, and the verdict, in the hope and with the intention that she will respond as she should. The coercion which is necessarily involved in the imposition of punishment is continuous with, though obviously more drastic than, these kinds of coercion; and it can, as they can, be consistent with a respect for the wrong-doer's autonomy. If it is to be thus consistent, punishment must constitute an attempt to pursue the proper aims of a system of law – to persuade the criminal to accept the law's requirements, and her own punishment, by persuading her to accept the relevant reasons which justify those requirements and her punishment; it must address her as a rational agent – it must seek but not try to coerce her consent; and it must be justified to her by reference to what she has herself done – by showing that it expresses a justified condemnation of her wrong-doing, and constitutes a penance which she ought to accept and will for herself.

[10] See ch. 8(3) above.

The constraints set by these conditions on the kinds of punishment which can properly be imposed will be discussed in the next section: but we must first attend more directly to the state's right to punish. For even if we accept that the imposition of punishment can be consistent with a proper respect for the criminal, this does not yet show that the state has the right or the duty to impose such punishments. It may still be objected that in imposing such punishments the state is taking an unwarrantably intrusive interest in the criminal's moral well-being, and is trying to impose on him a particular moral conception of the good. Several points need to be made in reply to this objection.

First, the claim cannot be that the state has no right or duty to impose *any* moral demands on its citizens through the criminal law: for the law must claim to impose obligations which make a moral claim on the citizens' allegiance. The question is not *whether* the state should try to secure the citizens' allegiance and obedience to some set of moral values, but *what* those values should be, and by what methods the state may properly try to secure the citizens' acceptance of them.[11] Should it, in particular, limit itself to declaring the law; to trying suspects and condemning offenders; to imposing purely symbolic punishments, or to requiring but not imposing penitential punishments which involve hard treatment; or may it properly impose such punishments on offenders?

Second, this account of punishment is quite consistent with the view that the criminal law should embody only a restricted and fairly minimal set of moral demands; that it should not aim to promulgate and secure the citizens' allegiance to some complete morality which will guide every aspect of their lives and determine every aspect of their individual or social good. We may say instead that it must, for the most part, be left up to individuals to determine their own values and ends within their own social groups: the proper task of the criminal law is only to identify, and try to secure acceptance of, a more minimal and central set of moral values which are essential to the preservation of the kind of society in which individuals can determine and pursue their own projects and values. This answers the objection that to see criminal punishment as a mode of moral reform is to sanction the extension of the criminal law to cover every kind of immorality:[12] the law's moral and re-

---

[11] See chs. 3, 9(5) above; D N MacCormick, 'Against Moral Disestablishment'.
[12] See A C Ewing, *The Morality of Punishment* 43; compare J Hampton, 'The Moral Education Theory of Punishment' 218–20.

formative ambitions should be limited to securing the citizens' allegiance to this more minimal set of essential values.

One reason for thus limiting the scope of the criminal law is that we must recognise the extent and the importance of moral diversity and disagreement – the extent to which individuals and groups will differ in their conceptions of the good. A state which is to preserve and respect its citizens' autonomy must leave them free to develop and pursue their own conceptions of the good. There will of course be scope for disagreement even about those moral demands which the criminal law must embody: I do not suppose that we could hope to identify a determinate set of moral demands which everyone must or will agree are necessary, in every detail, to the existence and survival of the community. Any set of determinate criminal laws must therefore take particular – and contestable – moral stands; it will try to impose on the citizen moral demands from which he might rationally dissent. But, thirdly, a system of criminal law and punishment does not try to *force* the citizen to accept the moral demands which it embodies. It should tell him that, and why, he *ought* to accept those demands; it will insist on judging his conduct in the light of those demands; it will condemn him if he flouts them, and might impose on him a punishment which aims to persuade him to accept them: but it must, as I have been arguing, leave him free to dissent from them; it must try to persuade, not to coerce, his will.

If we ask, fourthly, why the state should use coercive punishments to assist the proper ends of the criminal law (why it should, if not for reasons of deterrence or prevention, go beyond a system of formal convictions and purely symbolic punishments), the answer must refer to the duty of care and respect which the state owes to all its citizens – both the law-abiding and the criminal. If the requirements of the criminal law are properly justified, as being essential for the survival, the security and the well-being of the community and its members, it must follow that the state (in the name of and along with the members of the community) has a strenuous duty to make every permissible effort to ensure that they are accepted and obeyed. It owes this duty both to citizens who might be the direct or indirect victims of crime – to protect them from the criminal wrong-doings of others; and to those who would perpetrate crimes – to enable them to remain within or restore themselves to the community within which they must live and find their well-being. I have argued that a system of coercive punishments can still be an appropriate way of pursuing the law's justified ends, which still addresses and respects wrong-doers as rational moral agents; and it

275

is the importance of those ends which justifies the use of such drastic measures.

This is not to say that the *consequential* ends of the law are so important that the state may use any means to pursue them which are consistent with the *side-constraints* imposed by the demand that it should respect the citizens' autonomy. For neither the protection of the citizen against injury at the hands of others, nor the protection of the criminal against the harm which he does to himself are further ends to which punishment is related contingently as an instrumental means. This should, by now, be clear enough of the relation between punishment and the moral reform of the offender:[13] but it is also true of the relation between punishment and the protection of others. It might be tempting to say, for instance, that the law's aim in protecting the law-abiding from criminal harm is simply to reduce the incidence of criminal conduct; and that the requirement that it should do this by means of a system of would-be reformative and penitential punishments (rather than, for instance, by a system of deterrent punishments or purely preventive treatment) reflects not the nature of that end but the further moral constraints to which our pursuit of it is subject: but that would be a distortion. It suggests that the law-abiding citizen, and the community as a whole, could be protected by measures which infringed the autonomy of those who were subjected to them; that, for instance, a system of deterrent or purely preventive punishments might efficiently serve the end of protecting the community, and is precluded only because it would conflict with a quite separate moral demand concerned with the autonomy of those who would be subjected to such punishments. But this distorts the law's proper protective purpose.

The law aims to serve the common good – which is the good of a community of rational and autonomous agents: but legal measures which infringe the autonomy of any of the citizens are therefore themselves injurious to the common good; we cannot simply see them as efficient methods of serving that good which fall foul of some independent moral demand. Nor do such measures infringe the autonomy only of some distinct sub-class of actual or potential criminals. A system of deterrent punishments issues its coercive and manipulative threats against every citizen; a system of preventive punishments makes every citizen liable to preventive detention if she breaks the law: all are threatened, all are injured, by such laws. Indeed, one might question the kind of benefit which a citizen gains if he is saved from criminal harm only by measures which infringe

[13] See ch. 9(5) above.

the autonomy of his actual or potential assailants. Socrates thought it better to suffer injustice than to do it, since doing injustice is the worst harm that can befall a person: so might we not also say that it is better to suffer injustice than to have injustice done on one's behalf; that I am injured if I am saved from being wrongfully killed only by the deliberate killing of an innocent?[14]

I do not deny that we may face difficult dilemmas between the demands of efficient crime-prevention and the demands of autonomy, if we realise that the only efficient way to prevent or reduce serious criminal acts would involve improperly coercing or manipulating actual or potential criminals. My point is rather that we misrepresent those dilemmas if we portray them simply as conflicts between the proper ends of a system of criminal law and certain moral side-constraints to which our pursuit of those ends is subject: for those 'side-constraints' must enter into our understanding of the ends themselves. A system of law which seeks to prevent or reduce crime by measures which infringe the autonomy of its citizens is not pursuing its proper ends by morally improper means: it has abandoned its pursuit of its *proper* ends, by compromising its allegiance to the values which those ends embody.

I will have more to say about these dilemmas in section 3. I have tried so far to show that a system of criminal law which aims to serve the common good, and which is to respect the autonomy of its citizens as being an essential part of that good, can still be justified in imposing punishments on criminals, even when those punishments involve hard treatment. If such punishments aim to persuade the criminal to repent her crime, and to accept her punishment as a penance, they can still respect her autonomy; they can be an appropriate way of pursuing the law's proper aims. But I must now turn to consider some of the implications of this view of punishment for sentencing policy and practice.

2 SENTENCING: LEVELS AND KINDS OF PUNISHMENT

I have said very little so far about the kinds of punishment which could serve the communicative, reformative and penitential purpose which I have ascribed to a system of criminal punishment; or about the considerations which should guide courts in sentencing offenders. This is not the place for a detailed discussion of sentencing principles and policy: but I should at least indicate the direction

---

[14] Plato, *Gorgias*; see R Gaita, '"Better One than Ten"'.

in which such a discussion would proceed. We may begin by considering a further objection to this account of punishment.

'If the purpose of punishment is to bring criminals to repentance, this must require a policy of indefinite sentencing and individualised treatment. We cannot know in advance what kind of punishment will bring a criminal to repent: so courts will have to sentence offenders to the indefinite care of rehabilitation centres, which will keep them for whatever length of time, and subject them to whatever kind of treatment, is necessary. But (and quite apart from the fact that such efforts to rehabilitate offenders have – so far – been notably unsuccessful) this would sanction the imposition of disproportionately excessive punishments on offenders who are slow to repent; and it would create inequitable disparities between the sentences served by different offenders for similar offences.'

This is indeed a sound objection to any rehabilitative account of punishment which takes its purpose to be that of bringing offenders' attitudes and conduct into conformity with the law by whatever means may be economically effective:[15] but it is not an objection to the account which I have offered.

Punishment does not, on this account, aim to modify the criminal's attitudes and conduct by whatever means may be effective; nor may we continue punishing a criminal, or impose progressively harsher or more intrusive punishments on him, until he repents. For punishment aims to communicate to a criminal a proper understanding of the nature and implications of his offence, and to persuade him to accept his punishment as an appropriate penance for that offence; and such an aim sets strict limits on the kind and amount of punishment which we may impose. An offender's punishment must be such that it appeals to, but does not coerce, his understanding and his will; and this rules out, as improperly coercive and manipulative, any kind of punishment which (whether by design or in fact) serves to beat, cow or manipulate the offender into submission, instead of communicating to him, and trying to persuade him to accept, the reasons which justify his punishment. It must also be proportionate in its severity to the seriousness of his offence: only then can it communicate to him an adequate understanding of the moral character of his offence, and serve as an appropriate penance for that offence; a principle of proportionality between offence and punishment is thus internal to this account of punishment.

This does not provide us with a measure for determining the absolute level of the punishments which a legal system should

[15] See A von Hirsch, *Doing Justice: The Choice of Punishments* ch. 2.

impose; it provides only a relative principle of proportion: the severity of the punishment, relative to other punishments imposed within the system, must depend on the seriousness of the offence to which it is attached, relative to other offences which the law prohibits and punishes. It is a common objection to retributivist accounts of punishment that they cannot generate an adequately objective criterion for the amount of punishment which is appropriate for a given offence; whereas, it is claimed, a consequentialist account can provide such a criterion. We calculate the benefits and costs of punishments by a common measure – perhaps that of the satisfaction or frustration of desires which are themselves weighted by reference to the strength of the preferences which they express; and we then look for that allocation of punishments which will provide the largest surplus of benefits over costs. Whatever the admitted practical difficulties in carrying through such a calculus, we at least know *what* we are to calculate and weigh; and we can see how such a calculus could in principle be carried through.[16]

I suspect, however, that any attempt to provide an objective and absolute criterion for the proper amount of punishment must fall foul of the same conceptual problem. Whether we are trying, as consequentialists, to weigh the costs of punishment against its benefits or, as retributivists, to weigh the seriousness of an offence against the severity of its punishment, we must render the items which are to be weighed against each other commensurable: but neither consequentialist nor retributivist can offer more than the illusion of commensurability. Consequentialist attempts to establish one unitary standard of value, whether in crudely Benthamite terms of pleasures and pains, or in more sophisticated terms of the satisfaction and frustration of suitably weighted desires, serve only to disguise the diversity of incommensurable values which are involved in practical deliberation.[17] And retributivist attempts to compare the severity of a punishment with the harmfulness or culpability of a crime, or with the extent of the unfair profit which the criminal has gained, or with the extent to which he has coerced others or infringed their rights, can appear to succeed only by relying on a distorted and unduly abstract account of the nature of crime.[18]

If this is right, any determination of absolute levels of punishment must be to some degree arbitrary. Within a society people will hold

[16] See, for instance, Honderich, *Punishment: The Supposed Justifications* 58–60.
[17] See T Nagel, 'The Fragmentation of Value'.
[18] See, for instance, von Hirsch, *Doing Justice: The Choice of Punishments* chs. 8–11; H Gross, 'Culpability and Desert' (criticised by T Honderich, 'Culpability and Mystery'); and ch. 8(2) above.

more or less vigorous and determinate views about the kinds of punishment which are appropriate, or too severe or too lenient, for various kinds of offence; and these will reflect both their judgments about the relative seriousness or severity of various offences or punishments, and their feelings about the proper upper and lower limits of punishment. But there is no independent standard of appropriate punishment to which these feelings are answerable (except insofar as they express beliefs about the kinds of punishment to which no one should be subjected, however serious his crime, on independent grounds of excessive cruelty or inhumanity).

This means that we cannot hope to start from scratch and construct a rational account of the proper levels of punishment which is independent of any particular legal system and the punishments which it actually imposes. For we must ask what kinds and levels of punishment will adequately express and communicate our understanding of the character and seriousness of various offences – and serve as adequate penances for those offences; and any answer to these questions must depend upon the attitudes and expectations which are current in our particular society (attitudes and expectations which will be both reflected in and fostered by the punishments actually imposed by our legal system). We may, for instance, agree in feeling that a sentence of three years' imprisonment would not be adequate for a callous murder: but this is at least in part because we live under a legal system within which such a sentence is relatively light; within which, therefore, it would not serve to express the extent of our revulsion at such a murder, and would not communicate to the murderer an adequate understanding of the nature and seriousness of his offence.

This is not to say that we are simply the prisoners of our existing, socially conditioned feelings. We can hope and try so to modify our attitudes and expectations that less severe kinds and degrees of punishment will adequately serve the communicative and penitential purposes of a system of punishment; there are obvious reasons of humanity for trying to do so; and this account of punishment does not of its nature require that punishments be set at a particularly high or harsh level. My point is only that any such change will need to be gradual, if punishment is not to lose its meaning; and I suspect that, for beings like ourselves, the punishments imposed for at least the more serious kinds of offence will still have to involve hard treatment – some imposition which is painful or unpleasant in itself, and not merely in virtue of what it communicates. For given the extent to which we tend to be taken up by material and selfish concerns, and to be unwilling to confront, let alone to repent, our wrong-doings, a system of purely symbolic punishments would be unlikely to impinge sufficiently on our attention: we need the shock and pain of hard treatment as a stimulus to and vehicle for a properly repentant attention and understanding.

Such comments may seem unacceptably gestural and imprecise: but they will, I hope, indicate a possible and suitable direction for our thought about sentencing; a direction which may be further clarified by a brief consideration of the *kinds* of punishment which could be appropriate.

We must begin, given my comments above, with the kinds of punishment which are or have been imposed by our own system of criminal justice.[19]

This account of punishment does not, of its nature, either sanction or forbid *capital punishment*. An appropriate justification of capital punishment might run as follows. There are some crimes, such as, most obviously, cold-blooded murder and treason, which are in their essence utterly destructive of a community: the murderer who irrevocably destroys another's life for his own profit thereby denies one of the most essential values on which the community depends; and a traitor tries to destroy the community itself, by betraying it to its enemies. Capital punishment – the destruction of the criminal's life – expresses our understanding of the irrevocable character of the wrong which he has done or tried to do; he has rendered his own continued life in the community impossible. But he is not simply killed as one who is unfit for human life; his execution should also serve to reconcile him to the community and to the good. In consenting (as we hope and intend that he will consent) to his execution, he expresses his understanding of the implications of his crime, and his renewed commitment to the community and its values; in and by his death he is reconciled to those with whom he can no longer live.

A less dramatic analogy might help to clarify this. As an academic I belong to a community whose identity (and existence) depends on its allegiance to certain goals and values – to the pursuit of truth and understanding; to the principles of rational inquiry; to the education of students. If I behave in ways which are fundamentally destructive

---

[19] On the matters discussed in the remainder of this section, see especially R Cross and A J Ashworth, *The English Sentencing System*; A J Ashworth, *Sentencing and Penal Policy*; D A Thomas, *Principles of Sentencing* (referred to hereafter as *Cross*, *Ashworth*, and *Thomas* respectively).

of the values on which the community depends (I engage in systematic fraud in my research, or in systematic corruption in my teaching) I may be dismissed – expelled from the community – rather than being disciplined within it; and I may myself recognise, as I come to understand and to repent my wrong-doing, that my dismissal is justified, since I have made my continued participation in the life of the community impossible. In recognising this, and in consenting to my dismissal (or in confessing my own wrong-doing and resigning), I at the same time express my renewed commitment to the values which define the community; and thus, in and by my withdrawal from the community, reconcile myself to it.

Now I think that capital punishment could ideally have this kind of meaning; as could, more obviously, the kind of suicide which amounts to self-execution: but this need not commit us to its reintroduction. Some of the objections to it will concern the gap between the ideal and the actual: we must recognise that, given the way and the spirit in which executions are in fact likely to be administered and received, they are unlikely to have this kind of meaning either for the criminal or for others; and we must be aware of the horror which must attend an execution, and of the grave dangers of error and maladministration.[20] But other objections will focus on the ideal: for we may object that, while a limited community like a university could properly expel a member from its life, no crime should be seen as so irrevocably destructive that it warrants expelling the criminal from human life itself. Every criminal, however terrible his crime, must be given the chance to repent his crime and to restore himself, in life and not just in death, to the community; and while we could understand a person who kills himself by way of execution, it is certainly not for us to impose this on him. My own view is that such arguments should rule out the death penalty: but my point here is simply that the account of punishment which I have offered could be developed in either direction.

Imprisonment has an obvious part to play in a system of communicative and penitential punishments. It expresses, in material form, the way in which the criminal has by her crime excluded herself from the community, but also makes clear that this exclusion need not be permanent or irreparable; it should provide both a stimulus and an occasion for penitential contemplation and self-reform. But we need not therefore be committed to the frequent imposition of

---

[20] For an interesting discussion of these issues, see J G Murphy, 'Cruel and Unusual Punishments'.

lengthy terms of imprisonment. A prison term should be seen as a severe punishment, which physically separates the criminal from her community; it should be reserved for the more serious kinds of crime, which are most destructive of the criminal's relationship with the community and its members. And even a short prison term, if administered and received in the right spirit, can provide a stimulus to and expression for a criminal's repentant understanding: the 'short sharp shock' of a brief imprisonment, or even the 'clang of the prison gate' itself, could ideally serve, not as a prudential deterrent, but as an adequately communicative and penitential punishment.[21] The growing tide of opinion in favour of a general reduction in the length of prison terms, and in the use of imprisonment, owes much of its momentum to a variety of pragmatic and humanitarian considerations: an increased awareness of the actual effects of prison on offenders; a consequent pessimism about its rehabilitative potential; and a belief that shorter prison terms will generally be adequate for purposes of deterrence.[22] But it is a tide in which one who views punishment as a communicative and penitential enterprise can join; and she can also urge serious consideration of such possibilities as weekend detention, as a less severe but still significant form of custodial punishment.[23]

The most familiar alternative to custodial punishment is the *fine*; and it is clear that this too can serve the purposes of communication and penance: a fine inflicts on the offender a material deprivation which can symbolise – and thus direct his attention onto – the harm which he has done; and which could also serve as a penance (if and when he comes to will it for himself) for his crime. Given the role which money plays in our lives, as the focus for so many of our selfish and materialistic desires, a fine seems particularly appropriate as an expressive punishment for a crime which was itself motivated by selfish greed; and as a penance to which an offender can voluntarily submit himself. The amount of an offender's fine, however, should properly be relative to his means: for it is the impact of the fine on the offender himself which serves the purposes of both communication and penance; and that impact depends on his means. We should therefore take the idea of the 'day fine', which is calculated as

---

[21] See *Ashworth* 330–3; *Cross* 81 (on the idea of the 'short sharp shock' for young offenders).

[22] See *Cross* 204–9; *Ashworth* 124–31; also B MacKenna, 'A Plea for Shorter Prison Sentences'.

[23] See *Cross* 62; on current sentencing principles, see *Thomas* chs. 2–4.

a proportion of the offender's income, seriously – whatever its practical difficulties.[24]

We should also attend to other non-custodial punishments, such as *Community Service Orders*.[25] By requiring an offender to engage in some task for the benefit of the community, we can both focus her attention on her crime, as a wrong which injured the community and its members and denied the duty of care and respect which she owes to her fellows; and provide a suitable penance which she can accept for herself. The possibility of this kind of punishment depends of course, to an extent that imprisonment and fines do not, on the offender's own willingness to take part in it:[26] but, given that willingness, it has an obvious appropriateness. So too does restitution or compensation. English law distinguishes compensation sharply from punishment;[27] and it is true that the idea of compensation is quite distinct from that of punishment. If I compensate my victim I am trying directly to repair, even if I cannot annul, the material harm which I caused him, whereas in undergoing punishment I am receiving the condemnation of my community and expressing my repentance to the community. But the same activity – making a financial payment, or providing some material assistance – could serve both purposes; one who causes criminal damage, for instance, could be required to repair the damage which she caused to another's property as a way both of compensating her victim and of undergoing punishment.

Criminal courts also have supposedly non-punitive measures available to them. They may grant an offender an *absolute or conditional discharge*, or *suspend the sentence* imposed on her; or they may put her on *probation*: and such measures are not supposed to be regarded as punishments.[28] This is clearly true of an absolute discharge – though we should bear in mind that the discharged offender has still suffered a conviction which may itself be seen as a kind of punishment.[29] But it is not so obviously true of the other measures, whose effect is to put the offender on notice and, in the case of probation, to offer her some assistance; if she commits a further offence whilst one of these orders is in force she will be liable to

---

[24] See *Ashworth* 288–91; *Cross* 25–6; *Thomas* ch. 9 (on fines and other Financial Orders).

[25] See *Ashworth* 398–407; *Cross* 29–32; *Thomas* 236–9.

[26] See *Cross* 29.

[27] See *Cross* 65–6; *Ashworth* 293–4; *Thomas* 328; and see *Inwood* (1974) 60 Cr.App.R.70.

[28] On these measures see *Cross* 7–22, 55–61; *Ashworth* ch. 10; *Thomas* ch. 5.

[29] See ch. 5 above.

punishment for the original offence as well. For the thought or prospect of that punishment may surely itself play a punitive role: it reminds her of her past offence, and of the need to mend her ways.

Now there is certainly nothing in the account of punishment which I have described which requires us actually to impose punishments on all offenders. Some offences are such, given their character and circumstances, that they warrant nothing more than a formal conviction followed by an absolute discharge, which will adequately communicate to the offender such condemnation as he deserves and impose on him as much penitential suffering as his offence warrants. There will also be cases in which the offender is already so penitent, or has already suffered so much, that further punishment would be inappropriate (I will comment on this possibility shortly). But I am uneasy about such measures as conditional discharges and suspended sentences.

This is not just because such measures seem to serve most obviously as deterrents – as ways of bringing the threat of punishment to bear more sharply on an offender without actually imposing punishment. Certainly if they are used – or received – merely as prudential deterrents they are used or received improperly; and what should ideally deter me from crime is the fear of crime – of doing evil – itself, rather than the fear of punishment. But the fear of punishment can play a legitimate role, if it is or includes the fear of receiving, and *deserving*, the condemnation of my fellows, in dissuading me from crime.[30] It is rather, I think, because what should deter an offender from future offences is the fear of the punishment she would receive for those future offences, not the fear of punishment for an offence which is now past. A court could try to bring home to an offender the nature and implications of her offence by telling her what punishment she *might have* received, and then discharging her; for the very thought of that punishment, without the fact of it, might be enough to jolt her into a suitably penitential recognition of what she has done. But her discharge should be absolute; she should not be left with the prospect of punishment for a past offence hanging over her.

It is true that an offender's conduct *after* his conviction for an offence may cast that offence itself in a new light. This is given explicit recognition in the provisions for deferment of sentence: sentence may be deferred

for the purpose of enabling the court to have regard, in determining his sentence, to his conduct after conviction (including, where appropriate, the

[30] See ch. 2 (5) above.

making by him of reparation for his offence) or to any change in his circumstances.[31]

An offender's response to his offence and his conviction shows something of his relation to that offence and to the law: one who already repents his offence, or seeks to make reparation for it, is in effect doing for himself the work which his punishment would do; and in recognition of that the court may withhold any further punishment. So might we not equally say that one who, after being convicted and warned for an offence, nonetheless continues breaking the law thereby shows *her* attitude and relation to her past offence; she shows that she has not repented or disavowed that offence, and may therefore properly be punished for it? Now I agree that, for reasons to be discussed shortly, a persistent offender may properly be punished more severely than others: but this is something different from reviving a punishment which was provisionally imposed for an earlier offence; and insofar as repeated law-breaking, even after a conviction and the kind of warning which that involves, should make an offender liable to more severe punishment, the punishment should still be attached to the future law-breaking rather than to the earlier offence. I am not suggesting that punishments should be imposed instead of conditional discharges or suspended sentences: rather that more use should be made of absolute discharges – accompanied by warnings about the punishment which might have been imposed for this offence, and which might be imposed for further offences.

Probation deserves some further attention. Insofar as it shares the character of a suspended sentence, it is open to the same objections. But it also offers the offender help in establishing or re-establishing a law-abiding place for himself in the community; and as such it serves a proper role. It can be seen as an institutionalised replacement for the Chinese practice of placing an offender under the care and supervision of his local community. As an ideal, this seems to me admirable: it emphasises the offender's place in the community, and the responsibility which his fellows should have for him, as well as the duty which he owes to them. In practice, however, it is clearly open to serious abuse: it places a great responsibility on both the offender and the community; and it can all too easily become a way of pressurising offenders into conformity – rather than of persuading and helping them to accept their obligations.

[31] *Powers of Criminal Courts Act* 1973 s.1, amended by *Criminal Justice Act* 1982 s.63; see *Ashworth* 407–9; *Cross* 33–4; *Thomas* 380–3: on other ways in which an offender's conduct after his offence can mitigate his punishment, see *Thomas* 217–20.

But probation may also involve imposing special conditions on the offender – concerning where he may live, with whom he may associate, and what he may do. Must we admit that these are purely preventive measures, designed to stop him falling back into criminal ways; and that as such, insofar as they go beyond *advice*, they are objectionable in the same way as, though less drastically than, preventive detention?[32] Or could we say instead that the offender is spared punishment on the condition that he makes some real effort to mend his ways; and that the conditions laid down in his probation order specify what will count or be accepted as evidence that he is making such an effort?

This brief discussion has not been meant to suggest that a system of communicative and penitential punishments would use just the same measures as our existing penal system: my aim has rather been to indicate how some of those measures could play a part in such a system, and thus to clarify its character. If we are to take seriously the idea that punishments should properly serve this communicative and penitential purpose, we need to think carefully and imaginatively about possible alternatives, and ask whether we may not be able to find other forms of punishment which might be more adequate or appropriate to this purpose: two such possibilities may be mentioned here.

First, I have talked already about purely symbolic punishments – public or private symbols which pain the offender only in virtue of what they communicate to her or to others.[33] It may well be true that such punishments would be ineffective: by which I mean, not that they would not in fact prevent crime (for that is not the appropriate criterion of efficacy), but that they would not in fact serve to focus the offender's attention on her offence and thus to stimulate, assist and express her repentant understanding. For such punishments demand much of the offender and, if they are public, of others: the offender must be willing, as I suspect that too few of us would be willing, to accept and respond to her punishment in the right spirit; and others must be able and willing to respond to her in a communal spirit of critical concern, rather than with the mere hostility or contempt which such punishments could all too easily attract. We should at least ask, however, whether we could not hope

---

[32] See ch. 6 above; see also von Hirsch, *Doing Justice: The Choice of Punishments* ch. 14, for a more radical critique of probation.

[33] See ch. 5 above.

to advance ourselves towards a time when a purely symbolic punishment would be adequate for many offences.

Second, it is sometimes suggested that offenders should where possible be confronted by their victims, and required to hear and respond to them.[34] This too could, ideally, serve as an appropriate form of punishment: in facing his victims the offender is made to confront his crime; by seeing what he has done, and by hearing from his victims, he may be brought to a better and more repentant understanding of his crime. The process will be, in intention and (if he is not completely callous) in fact, painful to him. He may initially perceive it simply as something unpleasant which is forced on him: but the hope and the intention must be that he will in this way come to be pained by his crime itself – by his recognition of the wrong he has done;[35] and that this confrontation with his victims may serve as a penance to which he can submit himself, and which would then no doubt include an attempt to apologise or explain himself to his victims. Such punishments would of course be particularly demanding on the criminal's victims: to ask the victim of a brutal rape or assault to face her assailant, or to respond to him in anything other than a spirit of fear, disgust or hatred, is to ask of her more than we can perhaps *require* of anyone. To say that she owes it to the criminal, as a fellow-member of the community, to help him face and repent his crime – though it has some truth as a claim about how victims would *ideally* respond to their assailants – would be insensitively hypocritical unless others in the community, and especially those who make this claim of her, are moved by the same kind of concern for the criminal. Such punishments, like purely symbolic punishments, perhaps belong to the ideal rather than to the practicable: but we should still recognise their ideal role; and recognise too that their impracticality shows as much about the inadequacies of our own responses to crime as it does about the nature of crime.

To talk in these general and schematic terms about the kinds of punishment which might find a role in a system of communicative and penitential punishments is a long way from spelling out the structure or workings of such a system. We would need to provide a far more detailed account of how such punishments are to be related to particular offences: of what kinds and ranges of punishment should be specified for each kind of offence; of the discretion to be allowed to sentencers in sentencing particular offenders; and of the

[34] I was told by Graham Bird of a penal experiment in the United States which involved confronting rapists with their victims.

[35] See ch. 2(5) above.

factors which could properly make a difference to a particular offender's sentence. I will not embark on these questions here:[36] but a few words about some of the factors which could justify a reduction or an increase in sentence may provide some further clarification. Such factors must clearly, on this view of punishment, be concerned solely with the nature and gravity of the offender's offence, and with his own response to it: it is that offence which he must come to understand and repent; and it is as an appropriate response to that offence that his punishment must be justified to him – which suggests that courts should be under a more stringent duty to give reasons for the sentences they impose.[37] I will comment briefly on just two relevant factors here.

First, evidence of genuine contrition and repentance is accepted by courts as grounds for a reduction of sentence.[38] There are practical problems in determining the sincerity of any expressions of contrition when it is known that contrition may secure a reduced sentence; and we clearly cannot, given the present workings of our trial system, take a guilty plea by itself as evidence of genuine contrition:[39] but why should genuine contrition justify a reduction in sentence? An offender who is truly contrite has already done part of the work of punishment for herself: she has recognised and repented her crime, and subjected herself to the pain of remorse; her confession, or her formal plea of 'Guilty' in court, are appropriate expressions of her repentance – as too are such efforts at reparation or restitution as she might make. Her contrition may not show her actual offence to have been any less serious (except if and insofar as it shows that her crime was not the act of one whole-heartedly committed to evil ends): but it may show that she is less in need of punishment, since she is already punishing herself. But contrition, however genuine, will not always render further punishment inappropriate or unjustified: at least in the case of more serious crimes we may say that the contrite offender should still receive, and should indeed accept, a punitive sentence from the court. For repentance is not simply something one does, and is then finished with; the task of coming to understand, to repent, and truly to disown my crime may be a long and arduous one (that is why we need penances – to help us to face up to our crimes, to repent them adequately, and

[36] *Ashworth* is particularly useful on the theoretical questions involved here.
[37] See ch. 4 (5) above; *Cross* 105–6: the only such requirement in English law seems to be that Magistrates' Courts must give reasons for imposing a first prison sentence (*Powers of Criminal Courts Act* 1973 s.20; *Cross* 97).
[38] See *Cross* 193–4; *Thomas* 50–2, 217.
[39] See ch. 4 (10) above; J Baldwin and M McConville, *Negotiated Justice*.

to express our penitence to others). The penitent perpetrator of a serious crime might, if left to herself, find and undertake an appropriate penance: but the court, whose proper task it is to ensure that wrong-doers undergo suitable punishments, may properly specify her penance for her.

Part of the reason for reducing the penitent offender's punishment is that she is already imposing on herself the kind of penitential suffering which punishment aims to induce in her: but she may also undergo such suffering in virtue of the natural consequences of her crime. If my criminal recklessness causes, for instance, the death of someone close to me, or serious injury to myself, it is not absurd to see this as a 'natural punishment' for my wrong-doing:[40] for such suffering may force my attention onto my crime, and bring me to a repentant understanding of it; and I may express that understanding in the way I receive and respond to what I suffer. The fact that I have in this way already suffered for my crime may therefore also justify a reduction in sentence, or even a non-punitive disposal: but we must distinguish such cases from those in which the offender suffers some misfortune which is not thus related to her crime. We may think it right to exempt from punishment a minor offender who has suffered some severe but unconnected misfortune: but such exemptions must depend on a more general humanitarian principle, not on the idea that the offender has already been punished. Thus we should not accept the suggestion that an offender who becomes mentally disordered may be sufficiently punished by her disorder itself;[41] a serious disorder, which impairs the offender's rational capacities, cannot serve the role or the purpose of a punishment (unless, perhaps, it is induced by her own horror at her offence?).

Second, does this account of punishment sanction heavier punishments for persistent offenders?[42] It clearly does not sanction such punishments if their aim is merely prudential deterrence or coercive prevention: but it would allow us to see an offender's persistence as grounds for greater punishment, whilst still insisting that what he is punished for is the offence for which he is now convicted; that offence is itself shown in a new and more serious light if it is shown

---

[40] On 'natural punishment' see P Winch, 'Ethical Reward and Punishment'; J Teichman, 'Punishment and Remorse'; N Walker, *Punishment, Danger and Stigma* 130–1.

[41] See ch. 1(1) – (2) above, and contrast Walker, *op. cit.* 130–1; but see Winch, 'Ethical Reward and Punishment' 224 for the suggestion that there need be no causal link between an offence and a natural disaster which the wrong-doer sees as a punishment for that offence.

[42] See *Ashworth* ch. 5; von Hirsch, *Doing Justice: The Choice of Punishments* ch. 10; for criticism of von Hirsch's arguments, see G Fletcher, *Rethinking Criminal Law* 6.6.2.

to be part of a pattern of persistent criminality – in the same way as it is shown in a less serious light if it is shown to be a momentary abberation by a normally law-abiding citizen. A previously convicted offender who persists in breaking the law shows in his offence itself a more determined and unrepentant criminal intent than one whose present offence is not part of such a pattern. His offence is thus more serious, and his guilt greater: his punishment, if it is to mark and bring him to understand the nature and extent of his guilt, and serve as a suitable penance for his offence, should therefore itself be greater. It is important, however, that his present offence should be part of a genuine pattern of persistent criminality if it is to carry this implication; that it is connected, in time and in character, with the earlier offences in virtue of which he counts as a persistent offender: that is why 'the significance attributed to previous convictions ought to decline with the passage of time'.[43]

I have indicated schematically the kinds of punishment which might figure in a system of communicative and penitential punishments; and some of the factors which would properly be relevant to determining a particular offender's punishment. I have referred to some aspects of current penal policy and practice. But any attempt to discuss how our existing penal institutions and practices could serve the communicative and penitential purpose which is, I have claimed, the proper purpose of a system of criminal punishment; or to explicate the structure and workings of a penal system which would more adequately serve that purpose: is bedevilled by the gap which so manifestly exists between the ideal of a just and proper system of punishment and our own penal institutions and practices. It is to the nature and implications of this gap that we must now turn.

3 THE IDEAL AND THE ACTUAL

I have, it must be clear, offered an *ideal* account of criminal punishment; an account of what punishment ought to be if it is to accord to both law-abiding and criminal citizens the respect and concern which is their due. I have not claimed that our existing penal system is either designed or used to serve that communicative and penitential purpose which a system of punishment should properly be designed to serve: such a claim would clearly be absurd. For though some of the ingredients of this account of punishment have figured

[43] *Ashworth* 225.

in juridical and jurisprudential justifications of punishment; and though it is part of a unitary account of the criminal law and the criminal process which can be related to central features of our existing system of criminal justice: our present penal institutions are obviously administered and modified in the light of a variety of shifting and conflicting purposes – including both consequentialist concerns with the prevention of crime and retributivist desires to inflict suffering on wrong-doers. My claim is rather that a conceptually and morally adequate understanding of the idea of law will show that the criminal law and the criminal process must address and respect the citizen as a rational and autonomous agent; that the same must be true of a system of criminal punishment, if its purposes and values are to accord with those of the criminal law; and that this account of punishment shows, as other accounts cannot, how the imposition of punitive hard treatment on an offender can still accord her that respect which is central to the very idea of law.

Nor do I suggest that our existing penal institutions could be easily adapted or redirected so as to serve the purpose appropriate to a system of punishment; such a suggestion would also be absurd. The extent of the gap between the ideal of punishment which I have outlined and the actuality of existing penal practice must be sufficiently obvious to anyone who is at all familiar with what passes for punishment within our existing legal system: but we should make some aspects of that gap explicit.

First, as to the pre-conditions of justified punishment. If an offender is to deserve the kind of punishment which I have described, she must have offended against the requirements of a system of law which can properly claim her allegiance and obedience – which serves the common good of the community to which she belongs as a permanent or temporary member. The law may be less than perfect: we can still owe it to our fellow-citizens to obey even an imperfect system of law, so long as it can be adequately, even if not perfectly, justified to us in the relevant moral terms. But insofar as the society in which the offender lives does not constitute a genuine community, united by shared values and mutual concern and respect; insofar as the laws which claim to bind her cannot be adequately justified to her: neither her crime nor her punishment can have the meaning which this account ascribes to them. If the social relationships and shared concerns which constitute a community do not exist, or are not reflected in the law, then her crime cannot be destructive of those relationships, and her punishment cannot restore them. And it is surely true that our own society falls far short of constituting such a moral community: we do not, and this includes both law-abiding and criminal citizens, have the kind of concern for each other which the idea of a community requires; and our laws too often cannot be plausibly justified by reference to a genuinely common good.

Second, as to the character of justified punishment. It must be painfully obvious that, quite apart from the deficiencies of our present system of criminal trials,[44] our penal institutions are not well suited to serve the purpose which they ought, ideally, to serve. This is perhaps most obviously true of our prisons: a sentence served in a British prison could not, without callous irony, be described as a way of trying to bring or help the criminal to repent his crime and to redeem himself. Some criminals may indeed find such a meaning in their punishment: they may come, through their punishment, to recognise the wrongfulness of their past conduct, to redeem themselves, and to restore themselves to the community (though they will be lucky if this secures an appropriate response from their law-abiding fellow-citizens). But this has, I suspect, more to do with their own moral character than with the spirit or character of the punishments which are imposed on them: it is, given the actual workings of our penal system, a matter of good luck rather than of good punishment.

Such a radical gap between the ideal and the actual does not, I would insist, show the ideal to be misguided or inadequate; it rather reminds us of the radical imperfection of our existing social and legal structures: but it does force on our attention the question of what we are to do.

It is not enough to say that we should at once begin to reform our social, legal and penal practices so that punishment can be properly justified. That might be a reasonable response if the necessary changes could be rapidly instituted by suitable legislative, judicial and administrative activity: but this is clearly not the case. If the preconditions of justified punishment are to be adequately satisfied, we need to secure deep and far-reaching changes in our social and political relationships, so that our society becomes a genuine community – changes which cannot be simply brought about by political or legislative action. Furthermore, if punishment is to have the character which it ought to have, much will be demanded not only of the criminals who are punished, but of those who administer the punishments, and indeed of every member of the community. For those who administer punishment must be motivated by a genuine

---

[44] See ch. 4 (10) above.

concern for the values which the law embodies, and for the criminal as a moral agent; they must exhibit moral qualities of sensitivity, compassion and understanding:[45] how likely is it that we will be able to staff a penal system with people such as this? And all those in whose name such punishments are imposed must be able and willing, not only to give their own allegiance to the law, but to respond to those who break the law as fellow-members of the community who have flouted its values, but who may be restored to the community by their punishment: how soon, if ever, could we hope to induce such attitudes and concerns in ourselves?

It may seem then that my present position is similar to Murphy's:[46] punishment is not justifiable within our present legal system; it will not be justifiable unless and until we have brought about deep and far-reaching social, political, legal and moral changes in ourselves and our society; and we may indeed find, if and when such changes come about, that there will be no need for punishment – or at least for the kind of punishment which involves hard treatment. For in transforming ourselves into a genuine community we may at the same time largely eliminate the conditions which foster crime, and which make it necessary for punishment to involve hard treatment if it is to serve its proper purpose.

It is true that, whatever the imperfections of our present society, many crimes are still genuine wrongs which can properly be condemned as such. For they still cause unwarranted injury to others; and they are still in themselves destructive, if not of an existing community and its moral bonds, then at least of the possibility of bringing such a community into existence. This, however, does not do much to justify our present penal practices: even if we can claim the right to condemn such criminals, we must recognise that the punishments to which they are subjected do not, and cannot plausibly be expected to, serve their proper communicative and redemptive purpose. Such punishments are almost inevitably perceived and received instead as merely coercive impositions, which are more likely to injure or alienate the criminal than to benefit her by bringing her to repentance; this is true above all of imprisonment – the punishment imposed for the most serious and obviously wrongful offences; and this has as much to do with the the inadequacies of our penal system and of those by whom and on whose behalf punishment is administered as it has to do with the attitudes of criminals.

My position may, however, be more disturbing than Murphy's,

---

[45] See S Weil, *The Need for Roots* 20.　　[46] See ch. 8 (4) above.

for this reason: once we recognise how distant is the ideal of a community in which punishment could be justified, and the dangers which must attend any attempt to strive towards it, we must ask seriously whether it is an ideal towards which we should even aspire. For while I have argued that a system of communicative and redemptive punishments would, ideally, respect and care for the criminal as a moral agent, there is no denying that this ideal is all too easily corrupted. Given the kinds of insensitivity, crassness and self-righteousness to which we are so generally prone, we must suspect that any attempt to use punishment in this way, or for this purpose, would in fact turn out to be more coercively manipulative, and to infringe the criminal's autonomy and integrity far more seriously, than – for instance – a straightforward system of deterrent punishments which is subject to certain simple constraints of justice.[47] Perhaps the ideal is too distant to be a human possibility: for our attempts to attain it might instead destroy it utterly.

I do not know how far such pessimism is justified. Perhaps we could hope that the satisfaction of the pre-conditions of justified punishment – the existence of a genuine community within which the criminal has his place, and from which his crime threatens to exclude him – would also enable punishment to have its proper character; that if we could come to have the concern and respect for each other which would establish us as a community, we would also develop the capacity to impose and receive punishment as it should be imposed and received. This would suggest that, while any direct attempt to transform our penal system into an authentic system of communicative and redemptive punishments would probably be both morally and practically disastrous, a serious attempt to transform ourselves into the kind of community which could justly punish might also make that transformation of our penal system possible.

Whatever our view about the ultimate attainability of this ideal, however, or about the desirability of any attempt to attain it, we must face the question of what we are to do now. Our present penal practices cannot be appropriately justified: they may help to reduce crime by coercing or manipulating actual and potential criminals; but they do not address the criminal as an autonomous moral agent whose consent and repentance we seek. Nor will the kinds of social and moral change which would make punishment justifiable be achieved quickly or easily. What then can we properly do about

[47] See ch. 6 (3)–(5) above.

295

crime, pending the time – if it ever comes – when we can (but may no longer need to) justly and properly punish criminals?

We face here a dilemma which must confront anyone who seeks to apply absolutist and non-consequentialist notions of value and justice to the realm of politics.[48] The categorical demand that we should treat and respect each other as autonomous moral agents forbids us to impose on criminals the kinds of punishment to which they are subjected within our existing legal system; and this means, we should note, that we act unjustly not only if we engage directly in the imposition and administration of punishment, but also if, as citizens, we rely on, or give our explicit or tacit consent to, our existing penal system. Must we then say, and can we really believe, that we must forswear the practice of criminal punishment until such time as punishment can be justly and properly imposed; that we must neither take part in, nor support, nor rely on our present penal institutions? But what if we believe – which is surely plausible – that those institutions do in fact help to prevent or reduce crime; that to forswear punishment would therefore be disastrous for our very survival? The point is not merely that without a system of coercive punishments our lives would be somewhat less comfortable or secure; that is a sacrifice which justice may indeed demand of us – even though we may not be very willing to make it. It is rather that any hope we have of advancing towards the kind of society in which the demands of justice and autonomy could be satisfied may depend on the survival of a society which can be preserved only by measures which themselves flout those demands.[49] Should we then insist that we must *never* compromise those demands, though the heavens fall; or should we be prepared, in an imperfect world, to compromise or sacrifice the categorical demands of justice and autonomy in order to secure, not merely the consequential benefits of moderate peace and security, but the very survival of a society in which those values might one day flourish? What we face, it seems, is not merely a conflict between justice and utility, but a conflict between the categorical and the consequential demands of justice itself: between the demand that we refrain from injustice and the demand that we strive to achieve – or at least to preserve the possibility of – a society in which justice will truly be done.

Many would deny that we face such a dilemma. Some would insist that the values to which I have appealed must, like all values,

---

[48] See ch. 7 (1) above; R F Holland, 'Absolute Ethics, Mathematics and the Impossibility of Politics'; T Nagel, 'War and Massacre'.

[49] Compare J Casey, 'Actions and Consequences'; also ch. 4 (10) above on pre-trial detention.

be interpreted consequentially: the only intelligible demand on us is that we strive to *secure* justice and a proper respect for each person's autonomy; and if our only hope of achieving a society in which justice will be done and autonomy will be respected is to act now in ways which are unjust, and to maintain institutions which are destructive of the autonomy of those who are subjected to them, then this is the price which we must regretfully but justifiably be prepared to pay. To them I would reply that we cannot thus trade off present injustice against future justice, or the autonomy of some against the autonomy of others: the absolute demand that we respect the autonomy of others cannot be adequately translated into the demand that we respect their autonomy unless by infringing it we can increase the extent to which the autonomy of others will be respected – any more than the absolute prohibition on deliberately killing the innocent can be translated without loss into the demand that we should not deliberately kill an innocent unless this is the only way to prevent other innocents being deliberately killed.[50]

Others might claim that there is no real conflict here, since the consequences of forswearing unjust legal practices would not be thus disastrous; that we can without injustice preserve enough of our existing system of law and punishment to avert social disaster. To them I would reply that this shows an unwarranted optimism either about the extent to which our existing legal institutions and practices can be appropriately or adequately justified, or about the likely consequences of abandoning them. To those who might claim, on the other hand, that a society which can be preserved only at the cost of such injustice is not worth preserving, I would say that this evinces either an unwarranted pessimism about the character and possibilities of our present society, or an unwarranted optimism about the likely effects of the kind of anarchistic revolution to which such a claim seems to commit us. And if someone said instead, not that such a society is not *worth* preserving, but that we simply must not preserve it at this cost or by these means, I would either have to remain silent in the face of a moral view which I can neither share nor fully comprehend, or insist that we must also recognise the moral force of the demand that we must preserve it, if we are to avert yet greater moral evils.[51]

[50] See R A Duff, 'Intention, Responsibility and Double Effect'.
[51] Any adequate discussion of this last kind of view will need to grapple with the idea that, *whatever* happens in the world, the Good is 'eternally victorious'; and that the virtuous person *cannot* be harmed, come what may: see especially S Kierkegaard, *Purity of Heart* (especially ch. 6); P Winch, 'Can a Good Man be Harmed?'; also R A Duff, 'Must a Good Man be Invulnerable?'.

Such replies, of course, as they stand constitute assertions rather than arguments: they should serve here to express, rather than justify, my belief that we do face a genuine dilemma; that we find ourselves in a situation in which there is no course of action available to us which is completely justifiable or free from moral wrong. I do not, I confess, have a solution to this dilemma; nor indeed do I think that it is proper to talk of a *solution* – as if the conflicting values could be reconciled without moral loss. I could not myself accept or will the implications of remaining faithful to the absolute demands of justice and autonomy – I would act unjustly to prevent the heavens falling; and I hope that this reflects a moral concern for the consequences of such fidelity, rather than a morally inadequate reluctance to stay true to the values which claim my allegiance. I must then ask myself how far, and in what ways, the absolute demands of justice and autonomy are to be comprised: but I will confine myself here to two final comments.

First, if we do accept that we must still punish criminals, even though their punishments will not be adequately or appropriately justified, what should the purpose(s) of such punishments be? We should, I think, look back to a deterrent system of punishment of the kind discussed in Chapter 6: for this will at least still address criminals and potential criminals as rational agents, offering them *reason* to obey the law. Though such a system of punishment is – I have argued – manipulative, and at odds with the proper aims of a system of criminal law, it would constitute a less seriously damaging infringement of the autonomy of those who are subjected to it than, for instance, a system which aims at the purely preventive detention of actual or potential offenders, or which subjects them to other kinds of manipulative behaviour-modification which do not operate through the giving of reasons.

Second, even if we accept that the ideal of what punishment ought to be cannot – at least for the time being – directly structure our penal practices, this is not to say that it should play no part in our thought and action. Even if it cannot figure as the direct object of our hopes and aspirations, it must still remind us of the radical imperfection not only of our existing legal institutions, but also of our own moral capacities; and such a reminder should induce a salutary humility and restraint in our treatment of, and our attitudes towards, those who break the law. We must be constantly aware of the injustices which we perpetrate, or to which we consent, even if they are necessary; we must strive to reduce, even if we cannot eliminate, the extent to which the law bears unjustly and manipulatively on those who are subject to its demands and to the threat or the fact of its punishments. Furthermore, we must strive so to change ourselves, our social and moral relationships, and our legal and political institutions, that punishment can become what it ought to be – a communicative enterprise which addresses the criminal as a moral agent, and seeks to bring her to repentance and redemption; and we may still hope to allow some scope for communication and redemption even within, for instance, a primarily deterrent system of criminal punishment. For criminal convictions and punishments might still serve to communicate to the offender a justified condemnation of her crime, even if they cannot aim to communicate a richer moral understanding of the nature and implications of her crime; and her punishment might still give her the opportunity to repent her crime, and to treat her punishment as a penance, even if it is not to be imposed on her primarily for this purpose.

I do not pretend that I am happy with the position I have reached. I have offered an account of the values and purposes which should, ideally, inform a system of criminal law and punishment; and an account of what punishment would ideally have to be if it is to accord with those values and purposes, and express the kind of respect and concern which we owe to the criminal as a fellow-member of our community. When I recognise, however, how distant those ideals are, not only from the actual character of our legal institutions, but also from what we can in practice hope to make of those institutions, I find myself driven back towards an account of punishment which I earlier rejected, on the grounds that it rendered punishment improperly manipulative. Others may be less pessimistic than I am about the extent or the implications of the gap between the ideal and the actual: but I believe that it creates very grave problems for anyone who takes seriously the question of whether and how we can justify our existing legal and penal institutions. There are no ready solutions to these problems: but if we are to confront them we must first understand the ideals which generate them; and it is to that task that this book has been primarily directed.

Bibliography

Anscombe G E M. 'Modern Moral Philosophy', (1958), 33 *Philosophy* 1.

Anscombe G E M. 'War and Murder' in R Wasserstrom (ed.), *War and Morality*, p. 42. Wadsworth, 1970.

Aquinas St Thomas. *Summa Theologiae*. Blackfriars, with Eyre & Spottiswoode, 1966.

Aristotle. *Politics*. Trans. H Rackham. Heinemann (Loeb Library), 1932.

Ashworth A J. 'Concepts of Criminal Justice', (1979), *Criminal Law Review* 412.

Ashworth A J. 'Prosecution and Procedure in Criminal Justice', (1979), *Criminal Law Review* 480.

Ashworth A J. *Sentencing and Penal Policy*. Weidenfeld & Nicolson, 1983.

Austin J. *The Province of Jurisprudence Determined*. H L A Hart (ed.). Weidenfeld & Nicolson, 1954.

Baier K. 'Is Punishment Retributive?', (1954/5), 15 *Analysis* 25.

Baldwin J and McConville M. *Negotiated Justice*. Martin Robertson, 1977.

Baldwin J and McConville M. *Courts, Prosecution, and Conviction*. Oxford University Press, 1981.

Bean P. *Punishment*. Martin Robertson, 1981.

Beardsley E. 'A Plea for Deserts', (1969), 6 *American Philosophical Quarterly* 33.

Beardsley E. 'Moral Disapproval and Moral Indignation', (1970/1), 31 *Philosophy & Phenomenological Research* 161.

Beardsmore R W. *Moral Reasoning*. Routledge & Kegan Paul, 1969.

Benn S I. 'An Approach to the Problems of Punishment', (1958), 33 *Philosophy* 325.

Benson J. 'Who is the Autonomous Man?', (1983), 58 *Philosophy* 5.

Bentham J. *An Introduction to the Principles of Morals and Legislation*. Ed. J H Burns and H L A Hart. Athlone Press, 1970.

Bentham J. *Of Laws in General*. H L A Hart (ed.) Athlone Press, 1970.

Black M. 'Saying and Disbelieving', (1952), 13 *Analysis* 25.

Bottoms A E and Brownsword R. 'The Dangerousness Debate after the Floud Report', (1982), 22 *British Journal of Criminology* 229.

Bowman A A. *Studies in the Philosophy of Religion*. Ed. N Kemp Smith. MacMillan, 1938.

Brandt R B. 'Blameworthiness and Obligation' in A I Melden (ed.), *Essays in Moral Philosophy*, p. 3. University of Washington Press, 1958.

Brandt R B. 'Determinism and the Justifiability of Moral Blame' in S Hook (ed.), *Determinism and Freedom in the Age of Modern Science*, p. 149. Collier-MacMillan, 1961.

Campbell T D. 'Discretion and Rights within the Children's Hearing System', (1977), 14 *Philosophical Journal* 1.

Camus A. *The Rebel*. Trans. A Bower. Penguin Books, 1962.

Camus A. *The Just*. Trans. H Jones. Penguin Books, 1970.

Casey J. 'Actions and Consequences' in Casey (ed.), *Morality & Moral Reasoning* p. 155. Methuen, 1971.

Charvet J. 'Criticism and Punishment', (1966), 75 *Mind* 573.

Clark D H. 'Natural Justice: Substance and Shadow', (1975), *Public Law* 27.

Clarkson C M V and Keating H M. *Criminal Law: Text and Materials*. Sweet & Maxwell, 1984.

Cleckley H. *The Mask of Sanity*. 4th edition. C V Mosby, 1964.

Cohen L J. Review of H L A Hart, *The Concept of Law*, (1962), 71 *Mind* 395.

Cohen S. 'Distinctions among Blame Concepts', (1977), 38 *Philosophy & Phenomenological Research* 149.

Cottingham J G. 'Varieties of Retribution', (1979), 29 *Philosophical Quarterly* 238.

Cross R. *Evidence*. 5th edition. Butterworths, 1979.

Cross R and Ashworth A J. *The English Sentencing System*. 3rd edition. Butterworths, 1981.

Davis L H. 'They Deserve to Suffer', (1972), 32 *Analysis* 136.

Devlin P. *The Criminal Prosecution in England*. Oxford University Press, 1960.

Dilman I. 'Wittgenstein on the Soul' in G Vesey (ed.), *Understanding Wittgenstein*, p. 162. MacMillan, 1974.

Dilman I. *Morality and the Inner Life*. MacMillan, 1979.

Donagan A. 'The Right not to Incriminate Oneself' in E F Paul, F D Miller, J Paul (eds.), *Human Rights*, p. 137. Blackwell, 1984.

Dostoyevsky F. *Crime and Punishment*. Trans. C Garnett. J M Dent (Everyman), 1955.

Downie R S. 'Forgiveness' (1965), 15 *Philosophical Quarterly* 128.

Duff R A. 'Must a Good Man be Invulnerable?', (1976), 86 *Ethics* 294.

Duff R A. 'Psychopathy and Moral Understanding', (1977), 14 *American Philosophical Quarterly* 189.

Duff R A. 'Desire, Duty and Moral Absolutes', (1980), 55 *Philosophy* 223.

Duff R A. 'Legal Obligation and the Moral Nature of Law', (1980), *Juridical Review* 61.

Duff R A. 'Intention, Recklessness and Probable Consequences', (1980), *Criminal Law Review* 404.

Duff R A. 'Recklessness and Rape', (1981), 3 *Liverpool Law Review* 49.

Duff R A. 'Intention, Responsibility and Double Effect', (1982), 32 *Philosophical Quarterly* 1.

Duff R A. 'Socratic Suicide?', (1982/3), 83 *Proceedings of the Aristotelian Society* 17.

Duff R A. 'Mental Disorder and Criminal Responsibility' in Duff and Simmonds (eds.), *Philosophy and the Criminal Law*, p. 31.

Duff R A, and Simmonds N E (eds.). *Philosophy and the Criminal Law*. Franz Steiner (ARSP Beiheft 19), 1984.

Dworkin R M. 'Philosophy, Morality, and Law', (1965), 113 *University of Pennsylvania Law Review* 668.

Dworkin R M. *Taking Rights Seriously*. 2nd impression. Duckworth, 1978.

Dworkin R M. 'Hard cases' in Dworkin, *Taking Rights Seriously*, p. 81.

Dworkin R M. 'Principle, Policy, Procedure' in Tapper (ed.), *Crime, Proof, and Punishment*, p. 193.

Eliot G. *Middlemarch*. Penguin Books, 1965.

Eliot G. *Daniel Deronda*. Penguin Books, 1967.

Ewing A C. *The Morality of Punishment*. Kegan Paul, 1929.

Feinberg J. 'The Forms and Limits of Utilitarianism', (1967), 76 *Philosophical Review* 368.

Feinberg J. 'The Expressive Function of Punishment' in Feinberg, *Doing and Deserving*, p. 95. Princeton University Press, 1970.

Feinberg J. *Harm to Others*. Oxford University Press (New York), 1984.

Fingarette H. *On Responsibility*. Basic Books, 1967.

Fingarette H. *The Meaning of Criminal Insanity*. University of California Press, 1972.

Fingarette H. 'Punishment and Suffering', American Philosophical Association, Presidential Address 1977.

Fingarette H, and Hasse A F. *Mental Disabilities and Criminal Responsibility*. University of California Press, 1979.

Finnis J. 'The Restoration of Retribution', (1972), 32 *Analysis* 131.

Finnis J. *Natural Law and Natural Rights*. Oxford University Press, 1980.

Fletcher G. *Rethinking Criminal Law*. Little, Brown, 1978.

Flew A G N. 'The Justification of Punishment', (1954), 29 *Philosophy* 291.

Flew A G N. *Crime or Disease?*. MacMillan, 1973.

Floud J and Young W. *Dangerousness and Criminal Justice*. Heinemann, 1981.

Foot P R. 'Moral Beliefs', (1958/9), 59 *Proceedings of the Aristotelian Society* 83.

Foucault M. *Discipline and Punish: The Birth of the Prison*. Trans. A Sheridan. Allen Lane, 1977.

Franklin R L. *Freewill and Determinism*. Routledge & Kegan Paul, 1968.

Fuller L. *The Morality of Law*. 2nd edition. Yale University Press, 1969.

Gaita R. '"Better One than Ten"' (1982), 5 *Philosophical Investigations* 87.

Gaita R. Critical Notice of R F Holland, *Against Empiricism*, (1983), 6 *Philosophical Investigations* 214.

Gallagher N. 'Utilitarian Blame – Retrospect and Prospects', (1978), 12 *Journal of Value Inquiry* 13.

Galligan D J. 'The Return to Retribution in Penal Theory' in Tapper (ed.), *Crime, Proof, and Punishment*, p. 144. Butterworths, 1981.

Garner J F. *Administrative Law.* 5th edition. Butterworths, 1979.

Gewirth. 'Obligation: Political, Legal, Moral' in J R Pennock and R W Chapman (eds.), *Political and Legal Obligation*, p. 55. Atherton, 1970.

Glazebrook P R (ed.). *Reshaping the Criminal Law.* Stevens, 1978.

Goldman A H. 'The Paradox of Punishment', (1979), 9 *Philosophy & Public Affairs* 42.

Gordon G H. *The Criminal Law of Scotland.* 2nd edition. W Green & Son, 1978.

Greene G. *The Heart of the Matter.* Penguin Books, 1962.

Grey T C. 'Procedural Fairness and Substantive Rights' in Pennock and Chapman (eds.), *Due Process (Nomos XVIII)*, p. 182.

Gross H. *A Theory of Criminal Justice.* Oxford University Press (New York), 1979.

Gross H. 'Culpability and Desert' in Duff and Simmonds (eds.), *Philosophy and the Criminal Law*, p. 59.

Hacker P M S. 'Sanction Theories of Duty' in A W B Simpson (ed.), *Oxford Essays in Jurisprudence*, p. 131. 2nd Series. Oxford University Press, 1973.

Hacker P M S. 'Hart's Philosophy of Law' in Hacker and Raz (eds.), *Law, Morality and Society*, p. 1.

Hacker P M S and Raz J (eds.). *Law, Morality and Society.* Oxford University Press, 1977.

Haksar V. *Equality, Liberty and Perfectionism.* Oxford University Press, 1979.

Hampton C. *Criminal Procedure.* 3rd edition. Sweet & Maxwell, 1982.

Hampton J. 'The Moral Education Theory of Punishment', (1984), 13 *Philosophy & Public Affairs* 208.

Hare R M. *Moral Thinking: Its Levels, Method and Point.* Oxford University Press, 1981.

Harris J. 'The Survival Lottery', (1975), 50 *Philosophy* 81.

Hart H L A. 'Positivism and the Separation of Law and Morals', (1958), 71 *Harvard Law Review* 593.

Hart H L A. *The Concept of Law.* Oxford University Press, 1961.

Hart H L A. *Law, Liberty and Morality.* Random House, 1963.

Hart H L A. Review of L Fuller, *The Morality of Law* (1965), 78 *Harvard Law Review* 1281.

Hart H L A. *Punishment and Responsibility.* Oxford University Press, 1968.

Hart H L A. 'Prolegomenon to the Principles of Punishment' in Hart, *Punishment and Responsibility*, p. 1.

Hart H L A. 'Legal Responsibility and Excuses' in Hart, *Punishment and Responsibility*, p. 28.

Hart H L A. 'Murder and the Principles of Punishment' in Hart, *Punishment and Responsibility*, p. 54.

Hart H L A. 'Legal Duty and Obligation' in Hart, *Essays on Bentham*, p. 127. Oxford University Press, 1982.

Hart H L A. *Essays in Jurisprudence and Philosophy*. Oxford University Press, 1983.

Hart H M. 'Criminal Punishment as Public Condemnation' in R J Gerber and P D McAnany (eds.), *Contemporary Punishment*, p. 12. University of Notre Dame Press, 1972.

Harward D. 'The Bitter Pill of Punishment', (1976), 10 *Journal of Value Inquiry* 199.

Hegel G W F. *Philosophy of Right*. Trans. T M Knox. Oxford University Press, 1942.

Hirsch A von. *Doing Justice: The Choice of Punishments*. Hill & Wang, 1976.

Holland R F. *Against Empiricism*. Blackwell, 1980.

Holland R F. 'Good and Evil in Action' in Holland, *Against Empiricism*, p. 110.

Holland R F. 'Absolute Ethics, Mathematics and the Impossibility of Politics' in Holland, *Against Empiricism*, p. 126.

Holland R F. 'Suicide' in Holland, *Against Empiricism*, p. 143.

Honderich T. *Punishment: The Supposed Justifications*. Revised edition, with postscript. Penguin Books, 1984.

Honderich T. 'On Justifying Protective Punishment', (1982), 22 *British Journal of Criminology* 268.

Honderich T. 'Culpability and Mystery' in Duff and Simmonds (eds.), *Philosophy and the Criminal Law*, p. 71.

Horsburgh H J N. 'Forgiveness' (1974), 4 *Canadian Journal of Philosophy* 269.

Jackson P. *Natural Justice*. 2nd edition. Sweet & Maxwell, 1979.

Jackson R M. *Enforcing the Law*. Revised edition. Penguin Books, 1972.

James W. *The Varieties of Religious Experience*. Collins (Fontana), 1960.

Johnson C D. 'Moral and Legal Obligation' (1975), 72 *Journal of Philosophy* 315.

Kadish M. 'Methodology and Criteria in Due Process Adjudication: A Survey and Criticism', (1957), 66 *Yale Law Journal* 319.

Kant I. *Groundwork of the Metaphysic of Morals*. Trans. H. Paton, as *The Moral Law*. Hutchinson, 1948.

Kant I. *Critique of Practical Reason*. Trans. L W Beck. Bobbs–Merrill, 1956.

Kant I. *The Metaphysical Elements of Justice*. (Part 1 of *The Metaphysic of Morals*). Trans. J Ladd. Bobbs–Merrill, 1965.

Kassmann A. 'On Punishing', (1976/7), 77 *Proceedings of the Aristotelian Society* 221.

Kenny A J P. *Will, Freedom, and Power*. Blackwell, 1975.

Kenny A J P. *Freewill and Responsibility*. Routledge & Kegan Paul, 1978.

Kenny A J P. 'Duress *per Minas* as a Defence to Crime' in M A Stewart (ed.), *Law, Morality and Rights*, p. 345. Reidel, 1983.

Kierkegaard S. *Purity of Heart is to Will One Thing*. Trans. D Steere. Collins (Fontana), 1961.

Kilbrandon Lord. 'Duress *per Minas* as a Defence to Crime' in M A Stewart (ed.), *Law, Morality and Rights*, p. 333. Reidel, 1983.

Kneale W. 'The Responsibility of Criminals' in H B Acton (ed.), *The Philosophy of Punishment*, p. 172. Macmillan, 1969.

Lacey N. 'Dangerousness and Criminal Justice: The Justification of Preventive Detention', (1983), 36 *Current Legal Problems* 31.

Lacey N. 'Punishment, Justice and Consequentialism' in Duff and Simmonds (eds.), *Philosophy and the Criminal Law*, p. 21.

Lemos R J. 'A Defence of Retributivism', (1977), 15 *Southern Journal of Philosophy* 53.

Lewis C S. 'The Humanitarian Theory of Punishment' in R J Gerber and P D McAnany (eds.), *Contemporary Punishment*, p. 194. University of Notre Dame Press, 1972.

Long E L. *A Survey of Christian Ethics*. Oxford University Press, 1967.

Lucas J R. 'Or Else' (1968/9), 69 *Proceedings of the Aristotelian Society* 207. J Rachels (ed.), *Moral Problems*, p. 222. 1st edition. Harper & Row, 1971.

Lucas J R. *Freedom and Grace*. Society for the Propagation of Christian Knowledge, 1976.

Lucas J R. 'The Phenomenon of Law' in Hacker and Raz (eds.), *Law, Morality and Society*, p. 85.

Lucas J R. *On Justice*. Oxford University Press, 1980.

Lyons D. *Forms and Limits of Utilitarianism*. Oxford University Press, 1965.

McCloskey H J. '"Two Concepts of Rules": A Note', (1972), 22 *Philosophical Quarterly* 344.

MacCormick D N. 'Law as Institutional Fact', (1974), 90 *Law Quarterly Review* 102.

MacCormick D N. *Legal Reasoning and Legal Theory*. Oxford University Press, 1978.

MacCormick D N. 'Law, Morality and Positivism', (1981), 1 *Legal Studies* 2.

MacCormick D N. 'Natural Law Reconsidered', (1981), 1 *Oxford Journal of Legal Studies* 99.

MacCormick D N. 'Against Moral Disestablishment' in MacCormick, *Legal Right and Social Democracy*, p. 18. Oxford University Press, 1982.

MacKenna B. 'A Plea for Shorter Prison Sentences' in Glazebrook (ed.), *Reshaping the Criminal Law*, p. 422.

Mackenzie M M. *Plato on Punishment*. University of California Press, 1981.

McNeill J T. *A History of the Cure of Souls*. Student Christian Movement, 1952.

McTaggart J M E. *Studies in Hegelian Cosmology*. Cambridge University Press, 1901.

Maher G. 'Balancing Rights and Interests in the Criminal Process' in Duff and Simmonds (eds.), *Philosophy and the Criminal Law*, p. 99.

Maher G. 'Human Rights and the Criminal Process' in T Campbell, D

Goldberg, S McLean and T Mullen (eds.), *Human Rights: Rhetoric to Reality*. Blackwell, 1985.

Marshall G. 'Due Process in England' in Pennock and Chapman (eds.), *Due Process (Nomos XVIII)*, p. 69.

Martin F M and Murray K. *Children's Hearings*. Scottish Academic Press, 1976.

Melden A I. *Rights and Persons*. Blackwell, 1977.

Menninger K. *The Crime of Punishment*. Viking Press, 1968.

Michelman F I. 'Formal and Associational Aims in Procedural Due Process' in Pennock and Chapman (eds.), *Due Process (Nomos XVIII)*, p. 126.

Midgley M. *Beast and Man*. Harvester Press, 1978.

Midgley M. 'The Objection to Systematic Humbug', (1978), 53 *Philosophy* 147.

Moberly W. *Responsibility*. Oxford University Press, 1951.

Moberly W. *The Ethics of Punishment*. Faber & Faber, 1968.

Moore G E. 'A Reply to my Critics' in P A Schilpp (ed.), *The Philosophy of G E Moore*, p. 542. Open Court, 1942.

Morris H. 'Persons and Punishment', (1968), 52 *The Monist* 475. J G Murphy (ed.), *Punishment and Rehabilitation*, p. 40. Wadsworth, 1973.

Morris H. 'Guilt and Suffering' in Morris, *Guilt and Innocence*, p. 89. University of California Press, 1976.

Morris H. 'A Paternalistic Theory of Punishment', (1981), 18 *American Philosophical Quarterly* 263.

Morris N. *The Future of Imprisonment*. University of Chicago Press, 1974.

Mortimore G W (ed). *Weakness of Will*. MacMillan, 1971.

Murdoch I. *The Sovereignty of Good*. Routledge & Kegan Paul, 1970.

Murphy J G. *Kant: The Philosophy of Right*. MacMillan 1970.

Murphy J G. *Retribution, Justice and Therapy*. Reidel, 1979.

Murphy J G. 'The Killing of the Innocent', (1973), 57 *The Monist* 527. Murphy, *Retribution, Justice and Therapy*, p. 3.

Murphy J G. 'Three Mistakes about Retributivism', (1971), 31 *Analysis* 166. Murphy, *Retribution, Justice and Therapy*, p. 77.

Murphy J G. 'Kant's Theory of Criminal Punishment' in Murphy, *Retribution, Justice and Therapy*, p. 82.

Murphy J G. 'Marxism and Retribution', (1973), 2 *Philosophy & Public Affairs* 217. Murphy, *Retribution, Justice and Therapy*, p. 93.

Murphy J G. 'Cruel and Unusual Punishments' in Murphy, *Retribution, Justice and Therapy*, p. 223.

Nagel T. 'War and Massacre', (1972), 1 *Philosophy & Public Affairs*, 123. Nagel, *Mortal Questions*, p. 53. Cambridge University Press, 1979.

Nagel T. 'The Fragmentation of Value' in Nagel, *Mortal Questions*, p. 128.

Neblett W R. 'Forgiveness and Ideals', (1974), 83 *Mind* 269.

Nino C S. 'A Consensual Theory of Punishment', (1983), 12 *Philosophy & Public Affairs* 289.

Nowell-Smith P H. *Ethics*. Penguin Books, 1961.

Nozick R. *Anarchy, State, and Utopia*. Blackwell, 1974.

Nozick R. *Philosophical Explanations*. Oxford University Press, 1981.

O'Neill O. 'Consistency in Action' in N Potter and M Timmons (eds.), *New Essays on Ethical Universalizability*. Reidel, forthcoming.

Packer H L. *The Limits of the Criminal Sanction*. Oxford University Press, 1969.

Pelikan J. *The Christian Tradition*. Vol. 3. University of Chicago Press, 1978.

Pennock J R and Chapman J W (eds.). *Due Process (Nomos XVIII)*. New York University Press, 1977.

Phillips D Z. 'In Search of the Moral "Must": Mrs Foot's Fugitive Thought', (1977), 27 *Philosophical Quarterly* 140.

Phillips D Z and Mounce H O. *Moral Practices*. Routledge & Kegan Paul, 1969.

Pincoffs E L. *The Rationale of Legal Punishment*. Humanities Press, 1966.

Pincoffs E L. 'Due Process, Fraternity, and a Kantian Injunction' in Pennock and Chapman (eds.), *Due Process (Nomos XVIII)*, p. 172.

Plato. *Republic*. Trans. Lindsay. Dent (Everyman), 1976.

Plato. *Gorgias*. Trans. Helmbold. Bobbs-Merrill, 1952.

Plato. *Apology*, *Phaedo*. Trans. Tredennich, in *The Last Days of Socrates*. 2nd edition. Penguin Books, 1959.

Plato. *The Laws*. Trans. Taylor. Dent (Everyman), 1960.

Poole A R. 'Standing Mute and Fitness to Plead', (1968), *Criminal Law Review* 6.

Quinton A. 'Punishment', (1953/4), 14 *Analysis* 133.

Radzinowicz L, and Hood R. 'The American Volte-Face in Sentencing Thought and Practice' in C F H Tapper (ed.), *Crime, Proof, and Punishment*, p. 127. Butterworths, 1981.

Rahner K. *Theological Investigations*. Darton Longman & Todd, 1963 (vol. 2), 1973 (vol. 10).

Rawls J. 'Two Concepts of Rules', (1955), 64 *Philosophical Review*, 3.

Rawls J. *A Theory of Justice*. Oxford University Press, 1972.

Raz J. *Practical Reason and Norms*. Hutchinson, 1975.

Raz J. *The Authority of Law*. Oxford University Press, 1979.

Raz J. 'Legitimate Authority' in Raz, *The Authority of Law*, p. 3.

Raz J. 'The Identity of Legal Systems' in Raz, *The Authority of Law*, p. 78.

Raz J. 'Legal Validity' in Raz, *The Authority of Law*, p. 146.

Rees J C. Review of J Rawls, *A Theory of Justice*, (1974), *The Human World* 178.

Resnick D. 'Due Process and Procedural Justice' in Pennock and Chapman (eds.), *Due Process (Nomos XVIII)*, p. 206.

Ribot T. *Diseases of Memory*. Kegan Paul, 1882.

Sartorius R. 'Hart's Concept of Law' in R S Summers (ed.), *More Essays in Legal Philosophy*, p. 131. Blackwell, 1971.

Scanlon T M. 'Due Process' in Pennock and Chapman (eds.), *Due Process (Nomos XVIII)*, p. 93.

Schedler G. 'Can Retributivists Support Legal Punishment?', (1980), 63 *The Monist* 185.

Schlick M. 'When is a Man Responsible?' in Schlick, *Problems of Ethics*, p. 143. Prentice Hall, 1939.

Shiner R. 'Hart and Hobbes' (1980), 22 *William & Mary Law Review* 201.

Shiner R. 'Towards a Descriptive Theory of Legal Obligation' in *Proceedings of the 1979 IVR World Congress*, p. 223. Franz Steiner, 1983.

Shiner R. Review of J Raz, *The Authority of Law* in (1983), 33 *University of Toronto Law Journal* 460.

Sidgwick H. *The Methods of Ethics*. 7th edition. MacMillan, 1967.

Siegler F A. 'Hart on Rules of Obligation', (1967), 45 *Australasian Journal of Philosophy* 341.

Skillen A J. 'How to Say Things with Walls', (1980), 55 *Philosophy* 509.

Smart J J C. 'Free-will, Praise and Blame', (1961), 70 *Mind* 291.

Smart J J C. 'An Outline of a System of Utilitarian Ethics' in J J C Smart and B Williams, *Utilitarianism: For and Against*, p. 1. Cambridge University Press, 1973.

Smith J. *Legal Obligation*. Athlone Press, 1976.

Smith J C, and Hogan B. *Criminal Law*. 5th edition. Butterworths, 1983.

Smith S A de. *Judicial Review of Administrative Action*. 4th edition. Stevens, 1980.

Stephen J F. *A History of the Criminal Law of England*. MacMillan, 1883.

Stephen J F. *Liberty, Equality, Fraternity*. Ed. White. Cambridge University Press, 1967.

Strawson P F. 'Social Morality and Individual Ideal', (1961), 36 *Philosophy* 1.

Strawson P F. 'Freedom and Resentment' ((1962), 48 *Proceedings of the British Academy* 187). Strawson, *Freedom and Resentment*, p. 1. Methuen, 1974.

Summers R S. 'Evaluating and Improving Legal Processes: A Plea for "Process Values"', (1974), 60 *Cornell Law Review* 1.

Szasz T. *The Myth of Mental Illness*. Harper & Row, 1961.

Szasz T. *Law, Liberty, and Psychiatry*. MacMillan (New York), 1963.

Tapper C F H (ed.). *Crime, Proof, and Punishment*. Butterworths, 1981.

Teichman J. 'Punishment and Remorse' (1973), 48 *Philosophy* 335.

Thomas D A. *Principles of Sentencing*. 2nd edition. Heinemann, 1979.

Tonry M H, and Morris N. 'Sentencing Reform in America' in Glazebrook (ed.), *Reshaping the Criminal Law*, p. 434.

Tribe L H. *American Constitutional Law*. Foundation Press, 1978.

Trollope A. *The Warden*. Penguin Books, 1982.

Twambley P. 'Mercy and Forgiveness', (1975/6), 36 *Analysis* 84.

Wade H W R. *Administrative Law*. 5th edition. Oxford University Press, 1982.

Waissmann F. 'Notes on Talks with Wittgenstein', (1965), 74 *Philosophical Review* 12.

Walker N. *Crime and Insanity in England.* Vol. I. Edinburgh University Press, 1968.

Walker N. *Sentencing in a Rational Society.* Allen Lane, 1969.

Walker N. 'Punishing, Denouncing or Reducing Crime' in Glazebrook (ed.), *Reshaping the Criminal Law*, p. 391.

Walker N. *Punishment, Danger and Stigma.* Blackwell, 1980.

Walker N. 'The Ultimate Justification' in Tapper (ed.), *Crime, Proof and Punishment*, p. 109.

Walker N. 'Butler v. The CLRC and Others', (1981), *Criminal Law Review* 596.

Walker N, and McCabe S. *Crime and Insanity in England.* Vol. II. Edinburgh University Press, 1973.

Wasserstrom R. 'Some Problems in the Definition and Justification of Punishment' in A I Goldman and J Kim (eds.), *Values and Morals*, p. 299. Reidel, 1978.

Weil S. *The Need for Roots.* Trans. Wills. Routledge & Kegan Paul, 1952.

Weil S. 'Human Personality' in Weil, *Selected Essays*, p. 9. Ed. R Rees. Oxford University Press, 1962.

Wertheimer A. 'Punishing the Innocent – Unintentionally' (1977), 20 *Inquiry* 45.

Whitehead T. *Mental Illness and the Law.* 2nd edition. Blackwell, 1983.

Whitty C W and Zangwill O L (eds.). *Amnesia.* 2nd edition. Butterworths, 1977.

Wiggins D. 'Weakness of Will, Commensurability, and the Objects of Deliberation and Desire', (1978/9), 79 *Proceedings of the Aristotelian Society* 251.

Williams B. 'Morality and the Emotions' in Williams, *Problems of the Self*, p. 207. Cambridge University Press, 1973.

Williams B. *Morality.* Cambridge University Press, 1976.

Williams G. *Criminal Law: The General Part.* 2nd edition. Stevens, 1961.

Williams G. *The Proof of Guilt.* 3rd edition. Stevens, 1963.

Williams G. 'Recklessness Redefined', (1981), *Cambridge Law Journal* 252.

Williams G. *Textbook of Criminal Law.* 2nd edition. Stevens, 1983.

Winch P. *Ethics and Action.* Routledge & Kegan Paul, 1972.

Winch P. 'Nature and Convention' in Winch, *Ethics and Action*, p. 50.

Winch P. 'Human Nature' in Winch, *Ethics and Action*, p. 73.

Winch P. 'Trying' in Winch, *Ethics and Action*, p. 130.

Winch P. 'The Universalizability of Moral Judgments' in Winch, *Ethics and Action*, p. 151.

Winch P. 'Can a Good Man be Harmed?' in Winch, *Ethics and Action*, p. 193.

Winch P. 'Ethical Reward and Punishment' in Winch, *Ethics and Action*, p. 210.

Winch P. 'Eine Einstellung zur Seele', (1980/1), 81 *Proceedings of the Aristotelian Society* 1.

Wittgenstein L. *Tractatus Logico-Philosophicus*. Trans. Pears and McGuinness. Routledge & Kegan Paul, 1963.

Wittgenstein L. *Philosophical Investigations*. Trans. Anscombe. Blackwell, 1963.

Wittgenstein L. 'A Lecture on Ethics', (1965), 74 *Philosophical Review* 3.

Wootton B. *Crime and the Criminal Law*. Stevens, 1963.

Zaw S Khin. '"Irresistible Impulse" and Moral Responsibility' in G Vesey (ed.), *Human Values*, p. 99. Harvester Press, 1978.

REPORTS OF COMMISSIONS AND COMMITTEES

Report of the Committee on Insanity and Crime (*Atkin*)   (Cmnd. 2005; 1923)

Report of the Royal Commission on Capital Punishment (*RCCP*)
(Cmnd. 8932; 1953)

3rd Report of the Criminal Law Revision Committee: Criminal Procedure (Insanity) (*CLRC*)   (Cmnd. 2149; 1963)

Report of the Committee on Mentally Abnormal Offenders (*Butler*)
(Cmnd. 6244; 1975)

2nd Report of the Committee on Criminal Procedure in Scotland (*Thomson*)   (Cmnd. 6218; 1975)

Report of the Committee of Inquiry into the U.K. Prison Services (*May*)
(Cmnd. 7673; 1979)

Report of the Royal Commission on Criminal Procedure (*Philips*)   (Cmd. 8092; 1983)

The Investigation and Prosecution of Criminal Offences in England and Wales: the Law and Procedure (*Philips*)   (Cmnd. 8092–1; 1983)

CASES

Ashdown	(1973) 58 Cr.App.R.399	25
Attorney-General's Guidelines	(1982) 74 Cr.App.R.302	111
Bonaker *v* Evans	(1851) 16 Q.B.162	99
Caldwell	(1982) A.C.341	178
Clarke	(1975) 61 Cr.App.R.320	26
Cox	(1968) 1 All E.R.386	23, 27
D.P.P. *v* Smith	(1961) A.C.290	159
Eaton	(1976) Crim.L.R.390	26
Frith	(1790) 22 St.Tr.307	29
Gardiner	(1967) Crim.L.R.231	28
Gunnell	(1966) 50 Cr.App.R.242	24
Hatt	(1962) Crim.L.R.647	23
Hildersley	(1974) Crim.L.R.197	25
Hodgson	(1967) 52 Cr.App.R.113	25
Inwood	(1974) 60 Cr.App.R.70	284
Local Government Board *v* Arlidge	(1915) A.C.120	114
McBride	(1972) Crim.L.R.322	24
McFarlane	(1975) 60 Cr.App.R.320	27
M'Naghten	(1843) 10 Cl.& F.200	120
Morris	(1961) 2 Q.B.237	24
Officer	(1976) Crim.L.R.698	27
Parker *v* Alder	(1899) 1 Q.B.20	154
Podola	(1959) 3 All E.R.418	30
Pritchard	(1836) 7 Carrington & Payne 303	29
R *v* Thames Magistrates' Court, *ex parte* Polemis	(1974) 1 W.L.R.1371	112
Roberts	(1954) 2 All E.R.340	32
Robertson	(1968) 3 All E.R.557	30
Russell *v* H.M. Advocate	(1946) J.C.37	31
Sang	(1979) 2 All E.R.1222	111
Thornton	(1975) Crim.L.R.51	25
Turner	(1970) 2 Q.B.321	141
Watson	(1976) Crim.L.R.698	27

Index of Names

314

Index of Subjects